# ALEISTER CROWLEY IN ENGLAND

"Aleister Crowley has found the biographer he could have wished for. By staying close to the original sources, Tobias Churton has managed to dive deeply into the emotional life of an unparalleled religious thinker who celebrated life. *Aleister Crowley in England* is like the man himself—profound, witty, imaginative, and joyous."

FRANK VAN LAMOEN, ASSISTANT CURATOR AND RESEARCHER, STEDELIJK MUSEUM, AMSTERDAM

"Tobias Churton's masterful survey of the Beast's declining years battling ill-health and poverty in England, records not only matters Magickal with the author's usual scrupulous attention to accuracy and detail but also reveals other aspects of Crowley's perverse personality, like the luxurious meals he prepared for guests even following bankruptcy, his priapic adventures, seemingly undiminished by chronic asthma, and more. All this is dished up with Churton's customary eloquence and panache, a triumphant addition to the definitive multivolume biography."

PATRICK ROBERTSON O.B.E., HISTORIAN

"Tobias Churton gives the deluxe treatment to Aleister Crowley's often-overlooked final years: As a life of magick, romance, controversy, and intrigue draws to a close, the Beast crystallizes his incredible experiences into his most mature works, does his part for the war effort, reinvents the Tarot, and forges relationships that will carry his legacy well beyond his lifetime. Crowley beguiles and endures to the very end."

RICHARD KACZYNSKI, AUTHOR OF *PERDURABO: THE LIFE OF ALEISTER CROWLEY*

"Resettled in the UK, neither financial problems nor failing health could stop the 'Great Beast' from creating *The Book of Thoth* and a multitude of occult classics. Churton's masterful study of these final decades of Crowley's life is as revealing as it is entertaining."

CARL ABRAHAMSSON, MAGICO-ANTHROPOLOGIST,
FILMMAKER, AND AUTHOR OF *OCCULTURE* AND
*ANTON LAVEY AND THE CHURCH OF SATAN*

"Tobias Churton's excellent series of books exploring the different phases of Aleister Crowley's life and work continues here, revealing much of the deeper details often overlooked in the Beast's later years. Churton has a true gift for finding and correlating the different connections Crowley made with people who were first drawn by his reputation, only to be bewitched by his personal magnetism into staying when they had every reason to shun him."

TOBY CHAPPELL, AUTHOR OF *INFERNAL GEOMETRY*
*AND THE LEFT-HAND PATH*

"With delightful prose and his ever-present understanding of Aleister Crowley's humor and humanity, Tobias Churton expertly separates the man, the myth, and the legend, revealing the clearest picture available of the world's most famous occultist."

TAMRA LUCID, FOUNDING MEMBER OF THE EXPERIMENTAL
ROCK BAND LUCID NATION AND AUTHOR OF
*MAKING THE ORDINARY EXTRAORDINARY*

"*Aleister Crowley in England*, by scholar Tobias Churton, is a very precious and fascinating work, covering the last fifteen years of the Beast in his native England. It throws considerable light on his final period, not well known and as full of crazy events as his early days. A must-have."

PHILIPPE PISSIER, FRENCH TRANSLATOR
OF ALEISTER CROWLEY

# ALEISTER CROWLEY
# IN
# ENGLAND

## THE RETURN OF THE GREAT BEAST

## TOBIAS CHURTON

Inner Traditions
Rochester, Vermont

Inner Traditions
One Park Street
Rochester, Vermont 05767
www.InnerTraditions.com

Text stock is SFI certified

Cataloging-in-Publication Data for this title is available from the Library of Congress

ISBN 978-1-64411-231-1 (print)
ISBN 978-1-64411-232-8 (ebook)

Printed and bound in the United States by Lake Book Manufacturing, Inc.
The text stock is SFI certified. The Sustainable Forestry Initiative® program
promotes sustainable forest management.

10  9  8  7  6  5  4  3  2  1

Text design and layout by Debbie Glogover
This book was typeset in Garamond Premier Pro with Gotham Condensed,
Gill Sans MT Pro, and ITC Legacy Sans Std used as display fonts

To send correspondence to the author of this book, mail a first-class letter to the
author c/o Inner Traditions • Bear & Company, One Park Street, Rochester, VT
05767, and we will forward the communication, or contact the author directly at
**tobiaschurton.com**.

*This book is dedicated to*
*Absent Friends*

# Contents

PART TWO
# WAR

PART THREE
# RETIREMENT

# Acknowledgments

This book would not have been possible without the kind and most generous co-operation of William Breeze, Outer Head of Ordo Templi Orientis, who has provided me with a fabulous array of previously unpublished material to explore without prejudice. His generous assistance with illustrations has also proved invaluable.

I am again indebted to the kindly help afforded me by Assistant Librarian Philip Young and the staff of the Warburg Institute, London University: guardians of the Yorke Collection.

Steve Brachel of 100th Monkey Press deserves special mention, both for assisting with illustrations and for running superb websites dedicated to preserving and extending knowledge of Aleister Crowley through his works and through the enormous body of historical publicity reflecting his activities, or people's fantasies of those activities.

It is a pleasure to be able to thank Keith Richmond of Weiser Antiquarian and Scott Hobbs, director of the Cameron Parsons Foundation, for their positive assistance with illustrations.

—and a special thank you to Jillian Peterson, Registrar and Collections Officer of the Mildura Arts Centre, Victoria, Australia, for her kindness in sending me a copy of William Orpen's portrait of Mrs. Ruby Melvill from the gallery collection

Australia's O.T.O. Grand Master Stephen King not only provided hospitality and a Sydney lecture platform in 2018 but generously shared his research into fellow Australian Mrs. Anne Macky, without whom Crowley's *Magick without Tears* would never have happened.

Thank you, Antony Clayton, for kindly sending me your excellent book *Netherwood: Last Resort of Aleister Crowley* (2012), with its wonderfully researched, humane picture of Crowley's retirement.

Thanks are also due to Sigurd Bune for alerting me to Frieda Harris's friendship with Lesley Blanch and its bearing on Crowley's life in Petersham Road, Richmond, and for the photograph of the Cairo building in which Crowley received *The Book of the Law,* which I'm sure will fascinate many readers. I'm also grateful to Paris's premier translator of works by Crowley, Philippe Pissier, who kindly corrected the original transcription errors made of Crowley's gourmet French and French-inspired dishes; they doubtless taste better correctly described!

Undying gratitude, as ever, is extended to the great publishing team led by Ehud Sperling at Inner Traditions. Thank you, Jon Graham, Jeanie Levitan, Mindy Branstetter, Erica Robinson, Patricia Rydle, Ashley Kolesnik, and everybody else serving in this divine regiment.

# He Never Sold Out

What *is* it about Crowley? I've just googled his name and find 5,370,000 immediate results. Despite great interest, tired myths persist, impervious to four decades of extensive scholarship shattering the old picture. *Old picture?* Popular rag *John Bull* printed the following on March 10, 1923:

> It is over twelve years ago since *John Bull* first exposed the corrupting infamies of that arch-traitor, debauchee, and drug-fiend, Aleister Crowley, whose unspeakable malpractices are said to have driven his former wife and at least one other of his victims mad, while they have already ruined the lives of numerous cultured and refined women and young men, one of whom—a brilliant young writer and University man—has just died under mysterious circumstances at Crowley's so-called "Abbey" of Thelema, in Cefalù, Sicily.

*Old* picture? Now look at an extract from an article in the UK's popular *Mail on Sunday* (February 22, 2020—nearly a century later), about Rolling Stones muse Anita Pallenberg, who died aged seventy-five in June 2017. It centers on Anita's interest in "British occultist Aleister Crowley, the self-styled 'Great Beast 666.'"

> Crowley, who died in 1947, reveled in his infamy as "the wickedest man in the world." His worship involved sadomasochistic sex rituals with men and women, spells which he claimed could raise evil gods, and the use of drugs including opium, cocaine, and heroin.

At one stage he moved to Sicily and set up an "abbey" where he plumbed new depths with a sickening ceremony involving his latest mistress in ritual sex with a goat. Pilloried by most people as mad, Crowley still attracted hippy disciples, with canonization from the likes of The Beatles, who featured him on their *Sgt. Pepper* album cover.

What little difference a century makes—unenlightened by investigation! Innocence is bliss. Indeed, it was during my sunlit (or was it rain-drenched?) days of varsity innocence that I first encountered *The Confessions of Aleister Crowley,* the Beast's "autohagiography"—and yes, *of course* he was joking! Attraction to its author was fourfold: he was intelligent and funny, a romantic poet, a mountaineer and lover of adventure, and an outspoken religious philosopher who confronted existential questions head-on. Not always good, never dull, mostly honest, it was plain he'd suffered obloquy for convictions he couldn't deny. Perceiving physical life in a fatal but not joyless world, he favored zestful life and a spiritual humanity. There was something great in all of this, a greatness greatly obscured—often by himself.

A decade later, opportunity arose to explore Crowley's manuscript legacy. Studying papers entrusted by Gerald Yorke to the Warburg Institute, London, I was struck by the absence of pathology or sinister qualities, the kind one would logically associate with the figure portrayed in the myth. There was no vengeful ogre preying on others' weaknesses, no wild proto-hippy out of his mind on drugs, no cannibalistic murderer permanently indifferent to others' happiness. Nor could I, at any rate, detect psychotic tendencies or proximity to dark forces; weirdness; or repellent, pungent evil. Instead, I found a literate original with curious twists, a mind-broadening writer with a subtle, artistic, and incisive hand, who maintained many friendships with men and women over long years, inviting loyalty, accepting criticism, willing to enlighten all who desired it. He was attractive and entertaining to people not haunted by what he called "the demon Crowley." It is probably also the case, as sometime secretary Israel Regardie proposed in his book *The Eye in the Triangle,* that Crowley's deeper personality was shielded by an armory of neurotic character defenses few could penetrate, or had the pleasure of so doing. And yes, he could on occasion be a self-centered "son of a bitch," as Ninette Fraux, mother of his last surviving child, maintained to her grandson.

His sins seemed primarily to stem from an almost exclusive preoccupation with his mission of personal freedom. He was often at a loss to understand in practice that not everyone shared his mental attitudes, knowledge, energy, or gifts; his impatience with weakness or fear; and his withering disdain for what failed to meet his standards. Exposure of people's weaknesses seldom goes down well—unless one is paying a therapist to perform the service! Materially spoiled in youth, suppressed in early schooling, denied visible parental affection, his attitude to women depended much on what they wanted. He did not believe erotic love meant permanent ties because he saw it seldom did. As susceptible to love as the next romantic, he regarded sexual appetite as one both sexes had the right to indulge without additional responsibility (so long as it conformed to the "true will"), and he generally got tired quickly of people who imposed emotionally, though many women found him understanding and irresistible as lover and companion. When not confronting raw nature apart from mechanical civilization, he felt a need to shock and be noticed, while expecting satisfaction of a prodigious sexual hunger joined to a peculiarly intense, idiosyncratic spirituality.

What happens when someone of such characteristics offers himself as a tool of the gods and chafes at that pressure too?

By 1914 Crowley had spent his fortune. His remaining property was largely mortgaged and later alienated from him while absent in America during World War I. Borrowing money, paying it back when he could, he lived, as an acquaintance observed, "on the involuntary contributions of his friends" or from newspaper and magazine articles, dues paid to his magical Orders, a small trust fund, and sporadic book sales. He tried continually to launch schemes for raising significant sums, almost always with the end in mind of establishing his system "Thelema," and himself with it. He confessed his upbringing made him pathetically incapable of financial discipline (he'd lived by checks on demand); he should have learned, but he could find nothing in him that *cared* for money, not even anxiety generated by his acute need of it. He underwent periods of privation, exposure, and apparent hopelessness that would scare the average person, and which did his health permanent harm, yet never entirely departed from his creed or faith in the "gods" who made what he called "Magick" possible. He never lost interest in art and letters and generated poetry, images, insight, and, on occasion, matchless prose throughout his life. The best from his pen was excellent; the worst, well, who cares?

His personality changed considerably over the years. He undoubtedly mellowed to accommodate more gracefully the limitations of those who entered his peculiar orbit. Curiously, he could also act out opposing characters and mental characteristics.

His religion was essentially a personalized kabbalah with science usurping theism: "God" is what man does not know himself to be. Crowley never in his life sold out, and he was not a charlatan. He believed in his mission, whether right, wrong, irksome, or insane. His mind was happiest in the infinite, with the far-out, but he found plentiful joys down to earth, too. He delighted in pulling the legs of influential people who might otherwise have helped him.

It transpired that Crowley's beef against what he'd been taught was Christianity was not ignoble. He believed from observation that something monstrous had been made out of whatever had existed at the genesis of Christianity's formation, and even in its formative period, superstitious beliefs (such as vicarious blood sacrifice) were transmitted that, turned into monolithic doctrine, created a hell for the spirit of man ("there is no health in us"). Given the effect of late nineteenth-century scholarship on what his parents taught him, he had reason to suspect Jesus's historical existence, or if there was a historical original, to doubt whether what was believed of him subsequently was authentic. Mystical and gnostic interpretation interested, and sometimes inspired, him.

Crowley's understanding was that if, as seems likely, there stood a real figure behind Christianity, he may have been a spiritual master, an inspired God-intoxicated magus or religious genius familiar with ultimate truth, but one whose followers misunderstood or twisted what their supposed avatar saw clearly, blind to the novelty of a historically premature *spiritual freedom*. Crowley consistently quoted from scripture with knowledge of its spiritual meaning. That his parents' exclusive, literalist Protestant religion isolated him from mainstream society and culture hardly endeared him to England's official religion, and when his father, Edward Crowley, died (Crowley was eleven), his stifled feelings of rebellion sought outlet. The feeling one gets from reading his many statements on the subject is that Crowley greatly respected his father—a freelance gentleman-preacher of Plymouth Brethren doctrine—but concluded that his father's reasonable even-temperedness was stymied by Brethren influence. "Plymouthism" for Crowley was Christianity at its logical conclusion: intolerant, unforgiving, throbbing with damnation. Crowley the child wanted to destroy what he believed had removed his father, physically and psychologically. His ire fell on his mother and her brother Tom Bishop as agents of oppression. Significantly, he felt his mother was of a lower class than his father (she was a governess when she married). Crowley believed in aristocracy; that is, rule by "the best," *not,* note, the "old school tie." And the *best* were liberal (generous), chivalrous, commanding, and ruthless only when necessary.

Crowley bet on science. Knowledgeable in mathematics, biology, and chemistry, he enjoyed the company of scientists, conversing with them in their own terms. He desired to extend science's frontiers by extending those of the mind.

Why then did he explore "Magick?" He believed magick was science-to-come; magick was for him the link between matter and spirit. Only Magick gave meaning to his life—a crucial point. He believed science should engage with the spiritual, beyond atomistic opacity, to expand mind and increase intelligence and freedom: there was more *intelligence* to the universe than met the eye. He regarded his life's research as pioneering in this regard. He would be his own working laboratory. The movement in twentieth-century physics toward "sub-atomic" research, where traditional notions of "substance" or "stuff" breaks down into series of paradoxical relationships and relative "points," encouraged his magical vision of a mind-matter continuum, for he saw traditional rationalism breaking down also, with increasing awareness of ulterior dimensions. Mind impacted on "matter," matter on "mind"; *which came first* was a question as elusive at it was unimportant, since unanswerable. Thus he identified flesh with spirit, which, from the long-established religious dualist's point of view, was "Satanic." Crowley considered conventional understanding of a "Satan" a historic error, exacerbated by dogma and the logic of dualism. Rather, *Man* was the fallen angel and heavenly rebel, sunk into the unconsciousness of "matter." Crowley's viewpoint involved a fundamental paradigm shift that still seems counterintuitive, or at any rate discomfiting, to many otherwise modern minds, and mainstream pundits have reacted by dismissing it out of hand, citing Crowley's unenviable, vulgar reputation as sufficient reason to ignore him.

Well, public reputation aside, if Crowley's authentic commitment to science and philosophy had been the complete case, I daresay he would have been rehabilitated along with other Georgian, Victorian, and Edwardian agnostics, pagans, and atheists. He might even have found success in the diplomatic career to which Lord Salisbury's commendation to Trinity College, Cambridge, in 1895, had pointed.

But something happened.

A little-known fact: commentators often remark on Crowley's baroque taste for titles and pseudonyms, his theatrical delight in "playing parts."

*He did not like his name.*

Late in life, he requested friend Gerald Yorke desist from addressing him "Dear Crowley." *Crowley,* he'd always felt, had an *unpoetic* sound: it was not really *him.* Could Gerald at least write "Dear Aleister" to a friend who'd long since exchanged his given Christian names, Edward Alexander, for pen name *Aleister,* mistaking it for the Gaelic equivalent of "Alexander." *Alexander,* Crowley insisted, meant "helper of men."

*Crowley* . . . not really *him.*

Then what *was* really him? Having sought the "helper of men," I wrote *Aleister Crowley: The Biography* (2011). As a drastically edited one-volume affair, it was all right, but finding my original inspiration in Martin Gilbert's *eight*-volume Churchill biography, I had my doubts. However, it wasn't until Australian gallery owner Robert Buratti asked me to contribute an essay to an exhibition catalogue of Crowley's "Nightmare Paintings" in 2012 that a path forward appeared: not a multivolume set, but individual volumes—analogous to Tintin's global adventures! My catalogue essay focused on Crowley's period as a painter. From that seed grew *Aleister Crowley: The Beast in Berlin,* allowing us to join Crowley through a cavalcade of adventures in the streets of late Weimar Berlin. The book worked because the story was largely untold. Aficionados of that book can jump straight from there into this one.

Next, *Aleister Crowley in America* provided in-depth encounter with Crowley's adventures in Mexico and the United States between

He Never Sold Out ⊗ 7

1900 and 1919 and subsequent American legacy. Again, new stories, unpublished writings, and previously unknown characters constituted for many readers a revelation. In 2019 came the biographical, literary, and spiritual adventure, *Aleister Crowley in India,* covering Crowley's engagement with India and Indian thought from 1901 until his death. *That,* I thought, should be sufficient for anyone!

But *no:* another period nagged, calling for deeper treatment and greater comprehension—a difficult one, for sure.

Between 1932 and 1947, Crowley was confined to England: a very difficult time for the country, the world, and him. Often desperate to cross the Atlantic to guide his followers in the United States, he found it impossible for reasons (some dark) we shall discover, and the Beast who had "seen the world" was compelled to make a part-chaotic life, first in Depression-hit England in the 1930s, then under total war when the British Empire and United States of America stood against mad dog Adolf Hitler and unconfined fascist regimes in Japan and Italy, and Crowley did his patriotic best for a country he'd long been accused of betraying in World War I.

Readers unfamiliar with—or who would like to be reminded of—Crowley's life before this story begins may hop to the end of this book, where a chronology summarizes outstanding features of the years 1875 to 1932. Those already familiar with these years may rush headlong into chapter one!

PART ONE

# PRE-WAR 1932-1939

# ONE

# Never Dull Where Crowley Is*

June 22, 1932: "The sun has got his hat on, Hip hip hip Hooray!"—
such was Britain's tune as Crowley reentered a country scored by hunger
marches and food riots. America had the song right: "Brother, can you
spare a dime?"

Back in Berlin, still seething at the Beast's affection for what he
dubbed "street-walker" Bertha Busch, Karl Germer ranted on about
Gerald Yorke. Why hadn't Yorke repaid the money Germer's wife Cora
had lent to get Crowley's books published? Yorke couldn't; his landowning
father, industrialist Vincent Yorke, had tied the money into a trust fund.
Walled off from his cash source, Crowley sympathized with Germer:

> Yorke goes from bad to worse. He will try to put the cash in trust,
> and get off to China in the first week in September.
>
> Letters are quite useless; but if you come here and confronted
> him, and saw his father face to face, you might extract the money
> he owes your wife. Alternatively, send me a *Vollmacht* [Power of
> Attorney] good in England to act for you. It would be fraudulent
> of him to put the money away—and invalid up to two years. But
> prompt and resolute action is imperative.[1]

Blaming Yorke was disingenuous. Yorke did what he could, but it
would never be enough. For Crowley, Yorke's aspiration to the heights
of magick meant never holding back on *anything*. When Crowley sent
Bill (his nickname for Frau Busch) to London in advance, he com-

---

*A pre–World War I proverb in Crowley circles.

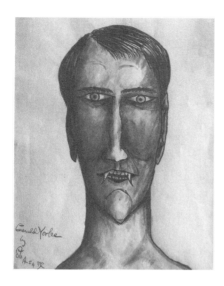

*Fig. 1.1. Gerald Yorke as seen by Aleister Crowley. (Courtesy: Ordo Templi Orientis)*

plained that "the rat Yorke" had lodged her in a "slum." The slum was, in fact, Charlotte Street's fashionable Eiffel Tower restaurant.

Vacating Jermyn Street's Cavendish Hotel on July 6 for a flat at 27 Albemarle Street, Mayfair, Crowley informed Louis Umfreville Wilkinson that he'd appreciate a call any morning before 10. Friendly with him since 1912, Crowley commiserated with Louis over second wife Annie's death: "Dreadfully sorry to hear of your loss. My own first wife [Rose] died in February, but as I had not seen her for over 20 years, Time had spun gossamer over the wound."[2]

A few weeks later, writer-performer Jean Ross (1911–1973) surprised Crowley in Hatchett's coffee house, Mayfair—he'd last seen her

*Fig. 1.2. Louis Umfreville Wilkinson, aka novelist "Louis Marlow" (1881–1966).*

in Berlin when her friend Christopher Isherwood joined Crowley on a jaunt round Kreuzberg's gay bars. Isherwood would twist Jean into the very different "Sally Bowles" in *Goodbye to Berlin,* inspiration for *Cabaret.* Fervently anti-Nazi, Jean would soon join the Communist Party. Meeting another communist sympathizer on August 4, Crowley called on Mrs. Paul Robeson at 19 Buckingham Street, near Charing Cross station, to interest her husband in *Mortadello,* a play he'd sent to film directors G. W. Pabst and Max Reinhardt. Mrs. Robeson complimented *Mortadello* for its elegant verse but regretted that it was this very quality that limited its appeal to modern cinema audiences.

Crowley painted his predicament brightly for Germer's benefit on August 25:

> I am speaking on "The Philosophy of Magick" at a lunch to 600 people on September 15: so hope to do big business. [Christina Foyle, of Foyle's Bookshop, invited Crowley to address her famous literary lunch.]
>
> Yorke is intractable so far. I may have to sue him. Can you send me copies of any letters from or to him showing negligence and mismanagement? E.g. his sending the whole of the pictures when we only wanted 75. . . . As soon as he finds he can't sneak off with our £3000 he'll propose a reasonable settlement, & take credit to himself for his noble conduct. Oh, *very* English!
>
> His cowardice is revolting. If he had only stuck to his guns, we should all be in clover. Even as it is, things are looking up all round.
>
> I do wish you'd write a really nice letter to Mrs. Busch. It is the only point at issue between us. . . . After all, you had nothing but great kindness from her.[3]

Crowley explored every avenue to survive in Britain's capital, save that of closing ranks with the "white-collar wage slave," a slight he unkindly applied to current O.T.O. "heir" Wilfrid T. Smith in Hollywood, clerk for the Southern California Gas Company.

On August 31, Crowley met *Daily Express* gossip columnist Tom Driberg for lunch at the Café Royal, Piccadilly Circus. Driberg (1905–1976) first wrote to Crowley in Tunisia in 1925, when still an undergraduate at Oxford, requesting advice on useful drugs to get him through examinations! Not surprisingly, Driberg left university without a degree, though not before cofounding the university's Communist Party. Actively homosexual, Driberg became a regular lunch partner, noting the Beast's eccentric schemes in his new gossip column, "These Names Make News."*

Crowley's artistic interests brought him to composer Leonard Constant Lambert's studio on September 3. Recently appointed Vic-Wells Ballet's composer and music director, Lambert (1905–1951) introduced Crowley to illustrator Joan Hassall (1906–1988), who four days later showed Crowley his old friend Nina Hamnett's autobiography *Laughing Torso.* "Abominable libels," Crowley declared when Nina's flippant Cefalù narrative mentioned that a baby was said to have disappeared there. Crowley and Leah Hirsig's baby daughter Poupée died tragically at Cefalù in 1920. Having just served a writ on Gerald Yorke for a supposed £40,000 he *would have made* had Yorke *not* been his trustee (September 6), Crowley called on lawyer Isidore Kerman about *Laughing Torso.* Nina's publishers Constable & Co. were notified: an offended Crowley intended to sue.

After a successful speech on September 15 at Foyle's literary luncheon, Crowley spent the next night getting drunk with Laurence and Pam Felkin.†

---

*From 1932, Driberg informed on the Communist Party for Maxwell Knight ("M"), head of new MI5 antisubversive Dept. B5(b). Chapman Pincher (*Their Trade Is Treachery,* March 1981) asserted Driberg, Labor Party chairman before his death in 1976, was from the 1940s double agent for British and Soviet Intelligence. Driberg brought Dennis Wheatley to Maxwell Knight. Fascinated by the occult, Knight met Crowley through Driberg around 1937 (*The Time Has Come: The Memoirs of Dennis Wheatley,* vol. 3, *1919–1977: Drink and Ink,* 131). According to Anthony Masters (*The Man Who Was M,* 1985) Crowley explained the occult to Wheatley and Knight. Richard Spence (*Secret Agent 666,* 2008) asserts Crowley's MI5 file No. 2573 was in 1916—when Major Victor Ferguson at MI5's G branch dealt with subversives—labeled "P.F." (Personal File); by 1933 Crowley's file was a "P.P." (Peace Propaganda): groups anxious to appease Germany or Russia—possibly because of Crowley's informing on Berlin's Soviet COMINTERN representative Louis Gibarti and on Gerald Hamilton, to Col. J. F. C. Carter.

†Son of Dr. Robert William Felkin (1853–1926)—Frater *Finem Respice* ("Have regard to the End"), leader of Golden Dawn breakaway Stella Matutina—stockbroker Robert Laurence Felkin (1891–1957) joined Crowley's A∴A∴ in 1912 and appears in Crowley's diaries as "Christ Child," inspiration for Elgin Eccles in *The Diary of a Drug Fiend.*

Crowley also renewed acquaintance with Euphemia Lamb (1887–1957). Formerly married to medical student Harry Lamb, Euphemia hung out in Bohemian style at the Café Royal before the war after studying at Chelsea's School of Art. Traveling to Paris in 1907, she became Augustus John's model, offering like service to Jacob Epstein and others. Crowley and Euphemia became lovers in 1908 in Montparnasse, playing an "educative" trick on naive Victor Neuburg. Having convinced him Euphemia was in love with him, Crowley took Neuburg to a bordello. Crowley and Euphemia enjoyed the spectacle of Neuburg's suffering over his "infidelity."

Now forty-four, Euphemia lived with Irish painter Edward Grove (they'd marry in 1934).

For a moment, Constable & Co. appeared to cave in over *Laughing Torso,* suggesting an out-of-court settlement, but on the twenty-first, crooked lawyer Edmund O'Connor cornered a habitually sauced Nina Hamnett in a Soho pub and dug up an angle to cripple Crowley's case: a rare copy of Crowley's decadent verses, *White Stains* (1898). Its author doubtless wished the book's printed warning had been observed: "The Editor hopes that Mental Pathologists, for whose eyes alone this treatise is destined, will spare no precaution to prevent it falling into other hands." These lines from the genially entitled "Ballad of Passive Paederasty" give the idea:

> Free women cast a lustful eye
> On my gigantic charms, and seek
> By word and touch with me to lie,
> And vainly proffer cunt and cheek;
> Then, angry, they miscall me weak,
> Till one, divining me aright,
> Points to her buttocks, whispers "Greek!"
> A strong man's love is my delight!
>
> To feel again his love grow grand
> Touched by the langour of my kiss;
> To suck the hot blood from my gland
> Mingled with fierce spunk that doth hiss,
> And boils in sudden spurted bliss;

Ah! God! the long-drawn lusty fight!
Grant me eternity of this!
A strong man's love is my delight!

The case didn't reach court until 1934, but advance tremors disturbed Crowley's peace of mind for months before it.

On September 26, 1932, he moved into rooms at 20 Leicester Square, meeting philosopher C. E. M. Joad (1891–1953) at a party given by a "Mrs. Richards." Joad would become famous in England during the 1940s for appearances on the BBC's *The Brains Trust,* where clever people offered expertise or opinion on pressing questions. In 1932 Joad was distinguished only by interest in parapsychology and expulsion from the socialist Fabian Society in 1925 for sexual misdemeanors. Disenchanted by Labor government, Joad became propaganda director of Sir Oswald Moseley's New Party, resigning on discerning Moseley's fascism. Bitterly opposed to Nazism, Joad favored pacifist causes, something that would have interested Maxwell Knight at MI5.

A curious foretaste of a subject soon to become dear to Crowley's heart came on October 1, 1932, in a letter from Mulk Raj Anand (1905–2004), author of *The Hindu View of a Persian Painting* (1930), living in Hendon. Art collector and publisher Desmond Harmsworth

*Fig. 1.3. Mulk Raj Anand (1905–2004).*

was publishing Anand's new Indian cookbook *Curries and Other Indian Dishes*.* Anand asked Crowley's permission to quote from *Confessions* (Mandrake, 1930): "I have been an admirer of your work for years." Anand's book pioneered the introduction to British housewives of Indian cooking, perhaps inspiring Aleister Crowley, too. Lawrence and Wishart published Anand's social realist book *Untouchable* in 1935, and Anand found success in novels.

Placing *Mortadello* still preoccupied Crowley. His diary records meeting "Hitchcock" upstairs at the Café Royal on October 10, 1932— and again at Pagani's with Driberg for dinner on October 22, then lunch on October 25. It's likely "Hitchcock" was successful English film director Alfred Hitchcock. A report in the *Times* of April 4, 1932, indicated Hitch was devoting the next year to producing, rather than directing films for British International Pictures, and was on the look-out for suitable vehicles for appropriate directors. A link with Pabst or Reinhardt would have interested Hitchcock, especially as he'd experienced the Berlin production system. Thelema devotee Albin Grau had produced Murnau's famous *Nosferatu*. That would have impressed Hitch. Crowley was convinced *Mortadello* chimed in with the German vogue for gaily spun films set in times past about dashing, braided hussars and the like, transporting people from the grime of the times.

Hitchcock only produced one film for B.I.P. (his contract ended in March 1933), *Lord Camber's Ladies,* about an aristocrat who falls for a musical comedy star. It was previewed for the Charing Cross Hospital charity at the Prince Edward Theatre on November 4: a short stroll from the Café Royal.† Hitchcock would have welcomed publicity from Driberg. Is there not a Crowleyan influence on Hitchcock's signature image, as it developed subsequently?

---

*Harmsworth also issued work by Crowley's old friend, Norman Douglas (1868–1952).
†Note a July 31, 1933, letter from Crowley to U.S. devotee Max Schneider. Crowley wanted his "Gnostic Catholic Mass" filmed in Hollywood. While Crowley would play High Priest, the role of Priestess deserved an actress with sex appeal; someone, Crowley wrote, like Benita Hume.[4] Benita Hume (1907–1967) played Janet King in *Lady Camber's Ladies,* alongside Gertrude Lawrence and Gerald du Maurier. Crowley expected Max Schneider to function as Hollywood agent, while Max's wife, Leota, typed up Crowley's scripts.[5]

*Fig. 1.4. Regina Kahl (1891–1945)*
*by Jessie Tarbox Beals (1870–1942).*
*(Courtesy of the Warburg Institute, London,*
*and Ordo Templi Orientis)*

Since May 3, 1932, Wilfrid Smith (Frater 132) lived with singer and voice coach Regina Kahl (1891–1945) in a large house at 1746 Winona Boulevard, Hollywood, with five upstairs bedrooms and a useful attic. Magnetic Regina swiftly took to the role of hostess, attracting dozens to "Crowley Nights," parties for the Equinoxes, Walt Whitman nights, and parties to celebrate the reception of *The Book of the Law*.

Martin Starr's *The Unknown God* reveals that during the summer of 1932, Jane Wolfe entered the attic to work her own ritual based on Crowley's invocation of the "Bornless One" ("Thou who art I before all I am"), soon followed by Regina (who had taken the A∴A∴ probationer oath on February 21, 1931) with her own ritual from Crowley's magical writings, while over the winter, Smith made sterling efforts to fashion temple furniture so the attic could host the Catholic Gnostic Mass

*Fig. 1.5. Georg Liebling in his youth.*

in 1933, public performances of which Crowley encouraged to generate interest. Smith's enthusiastic response bore fruit with the first tryout on Sunday, March 19, 1933, when, with Regina as priestess and Oliver Jacobi as deacon, Smith served as priest to a congregation comprising Max, Leota, and son Roland (who'd moved in in February), Dr. Georg* and Mrs. Alice Liebling, Olita Draper, Jacobi's girlfriend Viola Mae Morgan, John Bamber (a colleague of Smith's at the gas company), Jane Wolfe, and sister Mary K. Wolfe. Theater organist Jack Ross played the organ and took communion.

The attic temple complete, Smith found it just about accommodated thirty, not the hundreds Crowley imagined in his overcooked dreams, pressuring Smith to raise an impossible sum to carry him to Hollywood and celluloid glory. Crowley's imagination was doubtless tickled by the amazing success of Los Angeles–based evangelist Aimee Semple McPherson (1890–1944), who'd attracted huge numbers to the glamour she shed over her "Foursquare Church" established a decade earlier. Smith astutely realized that legally, financially, and socially, the "profess house" activities would be more successful incorporated as a church, with the mass as its raison d'être, than trying to operate a secret society.

---

*So impressed by the ceremony was composer Dr. Georg Liebling (1865–1946)—pupil of Franz Liszt and court pianist to the Duke of Saxe-Coburg-Gotha—that he phoned to congratulate its performers, offering a score to accompany it.[6]

# Potted Sex Appeal

The new year 1933 opened with a little libel action. A flash on the cover of his 1929 novel *Moonchild* seized Crowley's attention when passing Mr. Gray's bookshop at 23 Praed Street, Paddington, on January 7. Its predecessor, *The Diary of a Drug Fiend,* had been "withdrawn," teased the flash, suggesting *Moonchild* was salacious. A chat with lawyer Kerman netted fifty pounds damages on May 10, but ideas for a Berlin travel book and a magic book failed: "All publishers have now turned everything down. I start again Monday." A little desperate, he lunched with "Donegall." Former student of Christchurch, Oxford (like Driberg), Edward Chichester, 6th Marquess of Donegall (1903–1975), penned a column for the *Sunday Dispatch* ("Almost in Confidence") and wrote for the *Sunday Graphic* and *Sunday News* while receiving a salary from the *Daily Sketch.* Donegall assessed Crowley's cosmetic called "IT," supposed to transform its user into a sexual magnet, though he didn't share Driberg's positive view, printed in the *Daily Express*'s "Talk of London" column on January 14:

> I met Mr. Aleister Crowley, the magician.
>
> He is now staying at a fashionable West End hotel; but told me that he is busy preparing a new supply of his *unguentum sabbati—* the ointment with which all good witches anoint themselves before their famous Sabbaths (so unlike the tranquil Sabbaths of Sutherland or Glasgow).
>
> It is a powerful love-charm.

After he spent the last week of January on a "purification" regime, Crowley's weight was down to about thirteen and a half stone, but asthma and stomach pains plagued. Enjoying the Park Lane Hotel's facilities (our present queen learned to skate there that year) Crowley met Marianne, "Baronne de Catona," described generously in his diary on February 13 as "the most marvelous fuckstress alive." A twelfth opus of sex magick with Marianne aimed at curing asthma and bronchitis brought sudden cure the next day, while a second dose of "Amrita" (his sexual elixir derived from the opus) "very actively restored" his sex life. The benefits of this did not go the way of Scarlet Woman Bill Busch, however. She had become "really insane," he complained, threatening blackmail and murder of himself and Gerald Hamilton. Still, Crowley took her to Richmond on March 6 for her birthday, though his appeal that day was reserved for Marianne. "Opus 7" had as its aim "to be irresistible in Sex." Well, Marianne returned to Budapest next day, stimulating Crowley to raise his attractiveness quotient while seeking a suitable marriage partner for Bill so she could stay in England far from Hitler—and him.

"Lord! What a thrill," declared Crowley when he saw Maud Allan for the first time in years on March 11. He'd enjoyed an affair with bisexual Maud, who'd danced away the seven veils in Wilde's *Salome* in a hit theatrical run from 1908 to 1910. She still arrested attention.

Crowley first noted the Notting Hill address of Swedish Count Erik Lewenhaupt (1886–1968) on October 6, 1932, after which he met Erik and second wife, Dora Florence (née Crockett; 1888–1953), regularly. Dora had a studio at Lansdowne House, Berkeley Square, where the nightingale sang. Along with Augustus and Gwen John, Stanley Spencer, Rex Whistler, and Paul Nash, Dora studied under Henry Tonks at the Slade School of Fine Art, specializing in still life and landscapes in vibrant art deco oils.*

Another female artist captivated Crowley's attention that spring. Outstanding poet, publisher, fashion icon, and political activist Nancy

*Erik Audley Emil Lewenhaupt married Azalea Caroline Keyes (1880–1925), granddaughter of California's first chief justice, Serranus Hastings, in San Francisco in 1912. Their son Jan Casimir Eric Emil Lewenhaupt eventually migrated from Sweden to San Francisco in 1949, running a sports business: Anglo-Scandinavian, and finally Ballco Products Inc. Jan became count on father Erik's death in 1968 and died aged 102 in 2018.

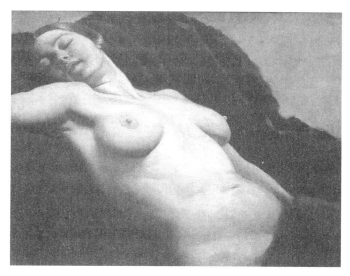

*Fig. 2.1. Dora Crockett,* Nude, *Paris Salon, 1934.*

Cunard (1896–1965) crossed the Beast's path again when he moved into the Astoria Hotel on April 7. They'd met on the Côte d'Azur in 1926, when Nancy's left arm received the "Serpent's Kiss": Crowley's trademark bite from beastly incisors. Many years later, she told Gerald Yorke it was "no trouble at all." Nancy had been involved with black jazz pianist Henry Crowder since 1928. Falling in love during the Venice Ball season, they'd returned to London, to her mother's disgust. Conservative Party doyen Lady Cunard—known to friends as "Emerald"—lamented Nancy's refusal to observe social discretion.

Throughout April 1933 Nancy tirelessly campaigned for the notorious "Scottsboro Boys": nine black youths falsely accused of raping two white girls in Alabama. Crowley signed Nancy's petition: "This case is typical of the hysterical sadism of the American people—the result of Puritanism and the climate." On April 9, the Beast joined a huge demonstration against the "Scottsboro Outrage" in Trafalgar Square. At 8 p.m. it turned, according to Crowley, into an "African Rally": "It would have been a perfect party if the lads had brought their razors! I danced with many whores—all colours." Twenty years later Miss Cunard recounted to Gerald Yorke her gratitude for Crowley's supporting her mixed-race dance events and pro-"Negro" activism.

On April 18 Crowley saw *I Am a Fugitive from a Chain Gang*, with Paul Muni as a wrongly accused convict escaping to Chicago, a theme appealing to Crowley: "I would be one myself if I could get away."

A few days later, Crowley expressed repulsion at events in Germany and Germer's continued attitude toward Bill:

> Still worrying about Frau Busch? I can't waste time recalling the details; you are always a blackguard about women, and *that's* all there is to that. There is only one duty at the moment for you or any other German: to destroy the Mad Dog that made me and all my old pro-German friends tell our old opponents: You were right; we were wrong: the Boche is a foul barbarian at heart; *we can have no dealings but War with them.*[1]

Appointed chancellor on January 30, Adolf Hitler greeted the Reichstag's burning a month later as a divine sign. After he declared the Third Reich on March 15, Dachau concentration camp was opened near Munich five days later. On March 28 Hitler ordered a boycott of Jewish businesses, while marriages between so-called Aryans and Jews were banned on May 5 as a sterilization program began, officially applied to disabled people on July 25.

Germer sent Hitler's horoscope to Crowley. He replied on May 1:

> The horror [horoscope] is good. Saturn in M.C. [midheaven: *medium coeli*] will do the trick.[2]

Saturn in midheaven suggests being burdened by a fateful sense of responsibility, leading to disaster or, with effort, success. A dominant parent's role can be determinative. Without enlightenment, Hitler was his own worst enemy. Crowley dreamed of enlightening him, writing to Germer again on July 2:

> No one in England has any illusion about H[itler]. "Mad Dog" is a complete description. There must be any amount of secret discontent in every class, and this may lead to civil war. If not, if he succeeds in forging a one-pointed weapon, this can only lead to foreign war. There is no other policy in sight, even as a dream! And now he's

definitely antagonized the Pope—*Quem Deus vult perdere* ["Those whom God wishes to destroy, He first sends mad"].[3]

Crowley clarified his stance the following week. He detested "oppression." He liked people who smoked and drank, but if they swore and shouted, Crowley barred them:

What we object to is the attempt to destroy the individual will, the imposition of uniform. . . . [For example,] I quite agree that marriage is a useful institution; but it becomes a vile offence if people are to be bullied into it. . . . But I base most of my objection on Hitler's demoniac foaming-at-the-mouth expression.[4]

Crowley asserted primacy over Hitler in an article derived from discussion on April 24 with New Zealander Ian Coster of the *Sunday Dispatch*. A price of forty pounds for three "autobiographical" articles penned by Coster was agreed a month later. "'The Worst Man in the World' Tells the Astounding Story of his Life" duly appeared on June 18, 1933; "I make Myself Invisible" the following Sunday; and on July 2, "Black Magic Is Not a Myth." Crowley hoped they'd smooth the way to rational understanding when the libel suit came to trial. The first installment got off to a jocular start, hitting the nail on the head:

If there is one subject I detest it is Aleister Crowley. On the other hand, there's no mystery about it. So, if anyone is interested, here goes! . . .

Some well-known journalists have delighted in attacking me in print. James Douglas described me as "a monster of wickedness." Horatio Bottomley branded me as a "dirty degenerate" cannibal—everything he could think of.

Some have been more precise.

In a book I picked up recently the author told a tale of how I murdered cats with terrible ritual in Sicily. . . .

The value of all this nonsense is somewhat discounted by the fact that I am back in England after wandering over most of the world, and go my way without interference. . . .

Legend says that my dossier at Scotland Yard fills a whole room.

There is a story that Lord Byng, when he took over, saw a wing of the building particularly vast and quite unusually guarded.

"What's that?"

"The files about Aleister Crowley."

"Goodness gracious me!"

"Of course, we haven't got the last month's stuff in yet. A bit congested."

"Here, this has got to stop! We can't put up new buildings every few weeks. Close the record!"

Nobody stops to look at me in the street. My appearance is, I suppose, that of a simple country gentleman up in town for a weekend.

All my notoriety arises from the fact that I am a magician.

They say that Satan is my master and that I am his faithful agent. But I am a white magician, not a black one. I belong to a secret order which has representatives all over the world; we are all working for the good of humanity, not for its downfall....

## Magic Today—Science Tomorrow

What is magic today is science tomorrow. The Hindus "worship idols." Yes? But what exactly do they mean by that? As I myself have observed: they get very interesting results from their "worship."

We magicians are men of science who, by the practice of our craft, keep just ahead of popular understanding. The result is that we are misunderstood and blackguarded all our lives.

After we are dead—sometimes centuries after—the world catches up, and discovers that we were benefactors and not villains.

After a mini-bio, Crowley made an interesting swipe at Hitler:

At birth I had three of the distinguishing marks of a Buddah. I was tongue-tied, I had a characteristic membrane, which necessitated an operation, and over the centre of my heart I had four hairs curling from left to right in the exact form of a Swastika.

Before Hitler was, I am.

Having translated Hitler into the past tense and himself into eternity, Crowley explained how at Cambridge his career switched to a sphere beyond time:

I had wanted to be a poet and to attain to the greatest success in the Diplomatic Service, for which the late Lord Salisbury had intended me.

Suddenly all the ordinary ambitions of life seemed empty and worthless. Time crumbles all; I must find durable material for building. I sought desperately for help, for light. I raided every library and bookshop in the University.

One book told me of a secret community of saints in possession of every spiritual grace, of the keys of the treasure of Nature. The members of this church lived their secret life of sanctuary in the world, radiating light and love on all those that came within their scope.

The sublimity of the idea enthralled me; it satisfied my craving for romance and poetry. I determined with my whole heart to make myself worthy to attract the notice of this mysterious brotherhood.

Then one of the first principles of magic was revealed to me. It is sufficient to will with all one's might that which one wills. You who read this—whatever you will you can do. It is only a question of commanding the means.

Having described initiation into the Golden Dawn after his "call" was answered, Crowley delineated the consequences:

I was then a neophyte—a new being born into a new world. I have never gone back to the old world of the gross deceptions and illusions of matter as the senses describe it.

Those who become magicians can travel in the astral plane, visiting distant places while the body still stays at home. They have prepared and proved an elixir of life; they are often seen surrounded with an aura of light.

I have myself tested all these claims and found them true. There is no limit to the possibilities of an attainment.

The day Crowley met Coster he also met an old acquaintance, journalist William Hayter Preston (1891–1964). Intrigued by occultism since adolescence, Preston had pursued his interest alongside freelance journalism, poetry, "freethought," and socialism. According to Jean Overton Fuller—who interviewed Preston for her biography *The*

*Magical Dilemma of Victor Neuburg*— a member of the Secular Society encouraged Preston to find an interesting "modern poet" in the form of Crowley's (then) acolyte Victor B. Neuburg at his dark, book-filled, second-floor rooms in the York Buildings, between the Strand and the Embankment in London's West End. Lunching at Simpson's on the Strand, Neuburg invited Preston to meet Crowley. Some time in 1906, Preston met Crowley, Victor, and Crowley's mother, at Simpson's. Preston recalled Crowley's taking the menu, saying: "You can have boiled toads, Mother, or fried Jesu." Seeing the effect of her son's jibe, Preston was, he informed Jean Fuller many years later, repelled by Crowley's "puerile" rudeness. Further acquaintance led Preston to consider Crowley—at least by the time he met Ms. Fuller in the early Sixties— "vulgar, coarse, overwhelmingly conceited and fake."* Preston took an interest in the O.T.O. but a final bust-up with Crowley in May 1914 ended relations. On that occasion, Crowley was present when Preston, who'd been approached by Neuburg's family, relayed to Neuburg their great anxiety about his relations with Crowley and the latter's obtaining family money through Victor (*Magical Dilemma*, 244). In 1933, as the *Sunday Referee*'s literary editor, Preston made Neuburg the magazine's poetry editor, a position Neuburg generously used to give Dylan Thomas, among numerous talented, aspiring poets, a break in reaching a large audience.

June air stirred Crowley's libido. Anointed with "IT": "all women [come] after me!" he noted. One of them—May Lewis—was removed to Middlesex County Asylum, Hanwell, on July 2 for trying to desecrate a Roman Catholic altar. Next day, Crowley encountered naval officer's widow thirty-four-year-old Pearl Brooksmith, née Pearl Evelyn Driver, beginning a long, bumpy ride as Scarlet Woman while Bill faded from view.

Reports from Hollywood lifted Crowley's spirits. He wrote to Karl Germer on July 2:

> The news from California is good. If I were only there to handle it! They get about 100 people every week to the Gnostic Mass. They ought to strike oil any day.[5]

---

*Jean Overton Fuller, *The Magical Dilemma of Victor Neuburg*, Oxford, Mandrake, 1990, 173–4 (orig. 1965).

Crowley's expectation of transport thither was based on numbers attending Regina's events, not the mass, as he imagined. Smith couldn't afford travel money *and* pay Crowley a $25 monthly donation.

Crowley also presumed Oliver Jacobi undertook fee collection. Appointing Jacobi Grand Treasurer General on July 31 incensed Regina, who found Crowley's approach to finances reminiscent of the tub-thumping fund-appeals characteristic of evangelist Aimee Semple McPherson. Regina insisted she'd seen enough in her country of wildly exaggerated oversell and truth-evaporating hype to wish to associate herself with such hollow propaganda. Imagining Crowley favored candor, or perhaps masochism, she stepped over the mark, playfully threatening to thrash him with a riding crop when he turned up.[6] Affecting disdain, Crowley told Smith that Regina's vulgarities were beneath his notice.[7] Crowley's own overripe facility of language didn't help when embroiled in what were really domestic matters endemic to any household—and *this* one was experimental.

Crowley entered a pattern of writing to regularly unemployed jeweler Max Schneider about Smith's perceived shortcomings, believing Schneider's largely empty assurances of Hollywood connections. Max might feel important, but his actual contribution to the "profess house" frustrated Smith and Regina, tired of his sulking around the house. Smith was self-conscious dealing with Crowley, drafting letters several times lest grammar and spelling rile the O.H.O. Crowley interpreted Smith's reticence as unwillingness to inform and, suspecting Smith, used Max as informant.

By summer 1933, Max's beautiful wife Leota was enjoying a magical role devoted to sexual operations with Smith called "Unto thee, Nuit," despite her anger at Smith's complaints against Max.

While tempers frayed on Winona Boulevard, Crowley visited Pearl Brooksmith at 40 Cumberland Terrace by Regent's Park on July 9. Staggered to learn his name, Pearl gave herself to magical sex six days later, with Crowley penning this touching "epitaph" on July 18:

> Here lies a Pearl of a woman,
> Who lived in open sin.
> One end guzzled semen,
> The other guzzled gin.

He moved in with Pearl and son John next day, launching a summer devoted to eliciting Pearl's mystic gifts amid pink visions, glowing faces, and astral traveling. On September 3 the Beast noted Pearl's "perfect magical phrase: 'I feel the flame of fornication creeping up my body,'" before consecration as Scarlet Woman on the nineteenth.

Crowley still expected imminent manifestation on the West Coast, informing Germer on September 6:

> I am trying to get to California, where the Gnostic Mass is going strong. But they seem unable to get any money, so I ought to go and agitate. Alas, the journey is a snag!—in other ways things are looking up. The real crux is the lawsuit which comes off in October.[8]

The *Empire News* aided Crowley's reputation clearance, printing two of his articles for Sunday reading on the third and tenth of September: "Black 'Masters' Menace" about devil worship in London and "I Have Killed Them!" about vampirism. A few days after the second article, Crowley lunched with *Empire News* crime specialist Bernard O'Donnell; three more articles followed: "The Magician of Loch Ness" (November 12); "They Called Me a Renegade" (December 17, about his World War I disinformation campaign); and "A Ridiculous Accusation" (December 31, 1933, about the sick mentality of black magic).

On October 10, Crowley lodged a huge collection of manuscripts, diaries, and much else with solicitor Isidore Kerman of Forsyte, Kerman & Phillips as a way of settling costs.*

Some years ago, Weiser Antiquarian sold three letters and a rare first edition of *White Stains:* the very copy Kerman read after hearing Hamnett's defense had one.

A letter from Crowley to Kerman dated October 22, 1933, concerned Betty May, whose evidence threatened complications; it was suggested they meet her. Second, a typed letter to Crowley dated November 20, 1933: "I have read this weekend *White Stains,* which you left with me [Kerman] the other day, and I have no hesitation in say-

---

*Bought by Gerald Yorke from Kerman years later for one hundred pounds: the bulk of the Yorke Collection, Warburg Institute, London.

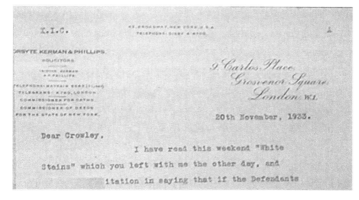

*Fig. 2.2. Letter from Isidore Kerman about* White Stains.
*(Courtesy: Weiser Antiquarian)*

*Fig. 2.3.* White Stains—
*Aleister Crowley's reply.*
*(Courtesy: Weiser*
*Antiquarian)*

ing that if the defendants are in possession of the book your chances of winning this action are negligible. I can see no satisfactory explanation for it, and I shall be glad to see you with regard to the matter." Crowley wrote in his diary that day: "Kerman—up in air over *W*[*hite*] *S*[*tains*]. I insist he call Frank Lewis. We 3 meet at 9.00."*

---

*I cannot trace Frank Lewis (almost certainly a lawyer). A letter to Louis Wilkinson (April 25, 1934) suggests Crowley lodged at Lewis's. Headed "c/o Frank Lewis Esq., 54 Baker Street": "Dear Louis, I am here on *shikar*—we must help the hapless ryot [*sic*]." Shikar is Hindi for "a hunt"; Crowley used it when seeking sex.[9]

Third, Crowley's letter to solicitor Constantine Gallop, written about a year later, signed "Edw[ar]d Alex[ande]r Crowley," where Crowley writes that he "must protest against the view of 'White Stains' which you expressed," referring Gallop to a "statement":

> In 1897 I was an undergraduate at Trinity College Cambridge; also a medical student registered at London University, King's College Hospital. At the instigation of, and with the assistance of, and under the supervision of, my professors, I prepared a medico-legal document designed to confute the thesis of Professor von Krafft-Ebbing (in his book *Psychopathia Sexualis*) that sexual perverts were irresponsible, and should so be held by the law. I made this book in artistic form because that was the only adequate mode of presentation of my thesis. I caused 100 copies only to be printed in Amsterdam. They were distributed from Zermatt, Switzerland, in August 1898 by a Professor of Psychiatry to whom I entrusted the edition. Each copy bears the printed monition that the mental pathologists for whom alone its perusal was intended should use all precautions to prevent any copy falling into other hands. In fact no copy appeared until I was informed by a woman named April Day on March 31, 1933, that Edmund O'Connor had a copy in his safe. This copy (No. 9)—presumably stolen was produced in the High Court in April 1934. . . . Mr. Justice Bennett said from the bench in *Crowley versus Gray* [the Praed Street libel case] that it had never been suggested that I had ever written anything indecent or improper.

*White Stains,* described by Constable's lawyer as "a book of indescribable filth," damaged Crowley's action.

Meanwhile, frustrated at being cold-shouldered by young women frequenting Winona Boulevard, Max Schneider quit with son Roland. Smith wrote to Crowley on December 2:

> Enclose draft for 25 dollars. . . . Max, Roland, and Leonard being no longer with us, the house is a little empty and money matters a little more strained. . . . In the meantime I will do my best to send the 25 dollars a month.[10]

Attempting to avoid legal problems by incorporating a Church of Thelema with himself as sole proprietor, Smith complained to Germer of Crowley's apparent indifference. Germer replied on December 10 that "he [the Master Therion] is at the present too much tied up with his lawsuits."[11] Crowley had informed Germer on November 2 he was "too broke & busy" to attend to letters, adding: "Pearl sends love. All well here so far; but am a bit worried over case."[12]

Moving into the Cumberland Hotel on December 20, Crowley doubted chances for vindication in a British court in 1934—with *White Stains* on his character.

# THREE

# Justice Swift

As London's Big Ben chimed in the New Year 1934, everyone at 1746 Winona Boulevard rose to drink to Crowley's health. Radio communicated a year of reckonings: terror in Russia with Stalin's ruthless purges; Japan's unprovoked invasion of Chinese Manchuria, capped on March 1 when Chinese emperor Puyi became Japan's puppet ruler—the same Puyi Aleister Crowley had shared a ship's dining room with in 1901 sailing to Ceylon from China.

Between severe bouts of asthma and bronchitis, he wiled away spare hours of wintry months with Pearl Brooksmith, leaving smoggy London in late March for the south coast and a breath of sea air. He wrote to Frater 132 on the twenty-first:

> 93
>
> I am now very much better in health. The lawsuit should come off at last about April 10–17. Victory will mean very ample funds; in this case I shall try to come over and visit you for a month or so. . . . I have a long letter from Max Schneider about your troubles. Much of what he says seems reasonable. There seems to have been needless suspicion and mistrust on both sides. *Be men of the world.*
>
> Love to you all.
>
> P.S. Your remittance has duly arrived every month so far; and very thankful I've been for it.
>
> 93   93/93   F∴ly [Fraternally] 666[1]

Crowley co-opted veteran Thelemite Jane Wolfe to bring Schneider and Smith to amity:

> Lord! You were passed to Neophyte God knows how many years ago. In any case Do things! . . . You had better reconcile Smith and Schneider. "Mutual suspicion and mistrust" are needless and most harmful. I think Smith and Vagina [Regina] need social tact and dignity: you could help them in this. Pray for success in Constable lawsuit—April 10–17. . . . Love! &c 666[2]

Crowley versus Constable & Co., publishers of Nina Hamnett's *Laughing Torso,* was heard before a drab King's Bench Division of the Royal Courts of Justice on the Strand between Tuesday, April 10, and Friday the thirteenth (!). Days of cross-examination before a special jury excited the world's press as Therion defended himself against what quickly became a prosecution. Supposedly *his side* highlighting alleged libel, the issue switched to whether Crowley *had* a reputation libel could damage.

*Fig. 3.1. Crowley in top hat arrives at the Royal Courts of Justice, April 1934. (Courtesy: Ordo Templi Orientis)*

## THE TRIAL

Mr. Justice Swift heard the case, with J. P. Eddy and Constantine Gallop appearing for Crowley; Martin O'Connor for Nina Hamnett; and Malcolm Hilbery, K.C. [King's Counsel] and Mr. Lilley representing defendants Constable & Co. and printers Charles Whittingham & Griggs Ltd. The solicitors involved were Messrs. Forsyte, Kerman and Phillips; Messrs. Waterhouse and Co.; Messrs. Edmund O'Connor and Co.; Messrs. Osborn-Jenkyn and Son.

This passage from *Laughing Torso* was quoted as ground for the action:

> Crowley had a temple in Cefalù in Sicily. He was supposed to practice Black Magic there, and one day a baby was said to have disappeared mysteriously. There was also a goat there. This all pointed to black magic, so people said, and the inhabitants of the village were frightened of him.

Defense pleaded justification, and Malcolm Hilbery pleaded very effectively. In legal hierarchical terms King's Counselor Hilbery outranked Crowley's counsel J. P. Eddy, funded to Pearl's best ability.

Eddy's first mistake was to use Hamnett's suggestive anecdotes of Cefalù as a basis for *defending* Crowley, as if Crowley's peccadilloes had to be *understood* by jurors. He *should* have torn Hamnett's account apart, forcing the defendants to defend it. Instead, Eddy set up Crowley's *defense,* fundamentally misconceiving the case dynamics. Despite Crowley's reasonable, often witty answers, the trial resembled a man being pelted by snowballs—some of the snow was sure to stick even were the victim an acrobat. For example, Eddy accounted for Crowley's unconventionality on the grounds he was raised within the Plymouth Brethren (defensive). Crowley studied magic, but he wasn't a black magician (defensive). Eddy then asked Crowley in the witness stand to describe the Cefalù abbey, quickly leading to an admission the abbey had a "chamber of nightmares"—highlighted by Eddy! In fact, the whole trial was based around Cefalù, Crowley's most vilified period. Eddy then asked Crowley to talk about black magic! Eddy referred to Crowley's shaving his head but for a phallic forelock and asked for descriptions of rituals. *Did Crowley sacrifice animals and ask "inmates" to drink their blood?* "No." Obviously, Eddy thought he was preempting Hilbery's attack-to-come, rendering otherwise striking details harmless; but the tactic stimulated doubt in jurors' minds. Crowley *denied* locals were afraid of him but did not *assert* their petition to keep him there.

Hilbery rose and asked if Crowley considered his reputation harmed by accusations of coarse, vulgar conversation. Crowley said it was irrelevant; the issue was whether he practiced black magic. Addressing ordinary people, Hilbery had no trouble firing questions about the titles "Beast 666," and "Master Therion," chosen by Crowley for himself, adding that Crowley was expelled from Italy—*and* from France. Once, by the *fascisti* . . . but *twice?* Crowley defended himself. The first hearing was adjourned, but the stage was set: *Crowley was on trial.*

Reconvened, Hilbery now laid into Crowley's *reputation,* which in normal circumstances a libel can harm—but can you harm a *bad* reputation? Hilbery: "For many years you have been publicly denounced as the worst man in the world?"—*"Only by the lowest kind of newspaper,"* replied Crowley (jurors may have read such newspapers).

Hilbery trashed Crowley as a serious writer, beginning with *White Stains.* "Is that a book of indescribable filth?"—*"This book is a serious study of the progress of a man to the abyss of madness, disease, and murder."* Some defense!

Hilbery quoted selectively from Crowley's poetry: "Have you not built a reputation on books which are indecent?"—*"It has long been laid down that art has nothing to do with morals."* Some defense! "Decency and indecency have nothing to do with it?"—*"I do not think they have. You can find indecency in Shakespeare, Stern, Swift, and every other English writer you try."* Ignoring Crowley's protest that all quotes were out of context, Hilbery read from *Clouds without Water* (1909); "Is it filth?"—*"As you read it, it was magnificent. I congratulate you."*

Hilbery: "Did you say 'Horatio Bottomley branded me as a dirty degenerate cannibal'?"—*"Yes."* Hearing laughter, Swift warned that further mirth would compel him to clear the court.

Hilbery turned to wartime activities in America, of which Crowley had said he was proud. Hilbery: "Was it part of the German propaganda in America?"—*"Yes."* "And written as such?"—*"I endeavoured to have it accepted as such. What I wanted to do was to overbalance the sanity of*

*German propaganda, which was being very well done, by turning it into*
*absolute nonsense. How I got Mr. Carus* [of the *Open Court* magazine]
*to publish that rubbish I cannot think. He must have been in his dotage."*

"That is your explanation, given after the Allied cause is safe and no
longer in danger?"—*"Lots of people knew it at the time."*

Hilbery returned to Cefalù, picking out anything suggestive: a
dagger, an altar, ritual circumambulation, a magic circle, drawings on
the walls . . . Crowley defended himself. Then Mr. Justice Swift raised
the issue: *why,* if his reputation for wickedness, treachery, notoriety,
depravity, bestiality, et cetera was *not* as newspapers described it, and as
Crowley himself had repeated, why did he not take any steps to defend
his character? *"I was 1,500 miles away. I was ill. I was penniless. I wrote*
*to my solicitors and found it was impossible."* Justice Swift: "I didn't ask
you about the state of your health. Did you take any steps to clear your
character?"—*"I wrote to my solicitors, and then it was impossible."* Swift:
"The answer is that you took no steps to clear your character?"—*"Yes."*
This naturally posed the question of *why,* compared to the scope of previous attacks, was he now taking issue with some "gossipy" unmalicious
words of Nina Hamnett's? And if, as Crowley maintained, he'd been
told he'd have needed £10,000 to defend himself against newspapers,
why had he come to court *this time*? Swift: "I imagine you have not
found £10,000 have you?"—*"No."*

Next step was to make Crowley look stupid, a task snidely undertaken by Martin O'Connor (for Nina Hamnett) who picked on
Crowley's claim to have made himself invisible: "Try your magic now
on my learned friend [pointing to Mr. Hilbery], I am sure he will not
object." Crowley would not, of course.

Then came the clincher. The defendants' legal team secured testi-
mony about Cefalù from former model Betty May—now Mrs. Betty
Sedgwick. Despite her having apologized to Crowley after the press in
1923 blew up her account of her husband's death there, she received
money to repeat damning stories. The most damning to an English jury
particularly sensitive about cruelty to animals was the story of Crowley's
cutting a cat's throat and getting Betty's late husband to drink its blood.

Betty's account of abbey life was negative: "improper" paintings,
oppressive discipline, a "pentagram ceremony," a "Scarlet Woman" in
a robe with a jeweled snake. "Did you see any sacrifice at all?"—*"I saw*

*a very big sacrifice, a terrible sacrifice, the sacrifice of a cat in the Temple inside the circle and on the altar."*

And continued: *"Everybody was excited because they were going to have the big sacrifice. Mr. Crowley had a knife with a long handle. It was not very sharp.*

*"The cat was crying piteously in its bag. It was taken out of the bag and my husband had to kill the cat. The knife was blunt and the cat got out of the circle. That was bad for magical work.*

*"They had to start all over again. Finally, they killed the cat, and my young husband had to drink a cup of the cat's blood."*

Eddy now turned in his best contribution. Cross-examining Betty, he undermined her truthfulness: "I suggest you have given evidence which is untrue, and which you know to be untrue?"—*"No."*

"How many times have you been married?"—*"I think four times."*

"How many times have you been divorced?"—*"Three."*

"Before you went to Cefalù, were you a decent citizen or not?"—*"I was, I think. Yes, of course I was."*

"You have written a book called *Tiger Woman*?"—*"Yes."*

"Does it purport to be an autobiography of yourself?"—*"Yes."*

"Is it true?"—*"My whole early life and my latter life is very true, but there is one little thing that is untrue."*

"Are you here because you wanted to make money out of this case and to sell your evidence?"—*"Certainly not to sell my evidence. But I have been subpoenaed to come here."*

Betty agreed she'd written a book called *Tiger Woman: My Story* but said the book's story of her joining a Parisian Apache gang was untrue, as was a statement that she'd herself branded with a red-hot dagger a young English undergraduate suspected of betraying the gang to the police.

The hearing was adjourned, reconvening Friday, April 13. Under Eddy's cross-examination, Betty admitted she'd been paid for stories about Crowley on returning from Sicily, *and* that *somebody else* wrote *Tiger Woman*. Eddy: "I am suggesting that this statement of yours about the sacrifice of a cat and your husband, who, you agree, was a man of refinement, drinking the blood of the cat, is pure fiction?"— *"No, every word of it is true."* Eddy asked if the children at the abbey suffered, as she implied. *"No. I do not think they were well brought up and well looked after. They had to fend for themselves, as it were. They were with the peasants most of the time."* Eddy read from *Tiger Woman:* "They were delightful children, healthy and well fed, and with no appearance of being oppressed by their unconventional surroundings," asking, "Is that true?"—*"I didn't say they were underfed. I didn't approve their upbringing."*

Had the cat story not struck such a chord with the jury, Eddy's demolition of Betty Sedgwick's trustworthiness might have been effective, but it was a Friday; there was haste. Eddy knew Betty was a "bought witness," referring to "expenses" advanced her to come to London revealed in letters from Messrs. Waterhouse and Company (solicitors for the printers and publishers).

Hilbery pounced on the letters' provenance: "Did you ever authorize anyone to extract those letters from your case and give them to Mr. Crowley?"—*"No."* Mr. Justice Swift: "He [Eddy] clearly has no right to have it. Whoever has possession of those letters is in possession, according to this lady's evidence, of stolen property." Swift and Hilbery agreed that the letters stay in Court's custody, implying Crowley obtained them illegally. Swift said witnesses often got expenses; Eddy replied the money at issue was money Mrs. Sedgwick demanded and received.

At this, the hearing went flat. O'Connor brought no further evidence but told the jury all magic was humbug and beyond serious interest, stating: "I hope this action will end for all time the activities of this hypocritical rascal." O'Connor then suggested the jury stop the case. They'd heard enough of Crowley and should return a verdict for the defendants.

Eddy asserted the opposite: "no reasonable jury could do other than find a verdict in favour of Mr. Crowley." Ignoring this, Swift told the jury: "I have been over forty years engaged in the administration of the law in one capacity or another. I thought I knew of every conceivable form of wickedness. I thought everything which was vicious and bad had been produced at some time or another before me. I have learnt in this case that one can always learn something more if one lives long enough. I have never heard such dreadful, horrible, blasphemous, and abominable stuff as that which has been produced by the man who describes himself to you as the greatest living poet."

The jury found for the defendants.

*Fig. 3.2. Crowley defiant, outside the courts.*
*(Courtesy: Ordo Templi Orientis)*

Eddy pleaded stay of execution as he'd been "desirous to point out, before the jury gave their decision, exactly what had to be done before a verdict could be returned at all." Justice Swift replied: "You shall do that at another place when it seems convenient to you to do it. . . . Someday another jury will reinvestigate the matter."

Edward Noel Fitzgerald first contacted Crowley for magical advice the day after Swift's judgment, initiating a lifelong friendship. Seven years later, Crowley opined to Fitzgerald that Swift's abrupt termination of the hearing resulted from what eventually killed him:

> The Late Mr. Justice Swift (who died of drink*—he was habitu-ally drunk on the Bench after lunch—anyone who knows the Law courts, down to the constables on guard, can confirm this) did foam at the mouth about me. But you can say that he referred to me as "the greatest English living poet." He was a bit excited and wanted to get off to golf—it was a Friday p.m. Now, *per contra*. Mr. Justice Bennet, summing up in Crowley v. Grey [Praed St. case], said that no one had ever doubted my high standing, or attacked my liter-ary righteousness. I forget the exact words; but the case, which was fought bitterly, was reported at some length in the *Daily Telegraph*.

---

*Conservative M.P. Sir Rigby Philip Watson Swift (1874–1937) died four days after a heart attack on October 19, 1937.

(I was away, very ill.) Date? 1934, I think; for the life of me I can't place it nearer. It is well worth while to have this looked up, and a cutting or cuttings obtained. "Wickedest man in the World" is only James Douglas and Horatio Bottomley—both had failed to blackmail me. This is a smashing retort; don't forget it! A.C.[3]

While 666 recuperated, 1746 Winona Boulevard prepared for "Crowley Night." Over 150 people heard Crowley's poetry and magical writings while Regina sang to Jack Ross and several voice students' accompaniment. Movie star John Carradine (1906–1988) read Crowley's "O Madonna of the Golden Eyes" and signed the visitor's book with 136 others.

Despite the fun, Crowley was unimpressed when Smith's copy of Church of Thelema incorporation papers omitted the O.T.O., with Smith typifying Max Schneider as anything but "reasonable," though clearly possessed of sufficient erudition to give that impression. While Crowley night was a great success and twenty-seven attended mass the previous Sunday, Schneider denigrated the mass as "amateur theatricals," declaring the expression Crowley's: ruinous publicity, bewailed Smith. Max only paid full dues once, and that was just before leaving, after avoiding chores, depressing everyone by sulking, and claiming people connected to magical powers needed never to worry about money; it always came! Sure, wrote Smith—from younger members! Meanwhile, Smith suffered a $40 pay cut.[4]

On June 22, 1934, the *Nottingham Journal* announced:

> Mr. Aleister Crowley, the author, who appeared in a recent High Court action was arrested on warrant yesterday and charged with receiving five letters the property of Mrs. Sedgwick. Mr. Crowley will appear at Marylebone Police-court today. He was released on bail.

Crowley stood at the Old Bailey on June 22. Bound over on the twenty-fifth with fifty pounds costs to the prosecution (paid by Kerman), Crowley's defense was, he maintained, hampered by a violent attack of asthma entering the witness box. He dropped his appeal in October.

Disoriented throughout the summer, he woke at 5:30 a.m. on August 1 for a walk, "determined to beat it for Morocco—or any place where the frame-up is unknown! Till the hour strikes!!"—the "hour" being that of the country's need. Heading for Chester he heard "Canon Simpson preaching Karl Marx!"—likely an error, for Chester's Canon Hewlett Johnson, "Christian Marxist," had just returned from Russia convinced liberty and welfare were safe under Stalin!

Pearl Brooksmith wrote from 21 Upper Montagu Street on August 12 to thank Smith for a draft—just in time, as costs denuded her savings; and no publisher would touch Crowley for fear of the courts. Therion dearly hoped to be in California, but scarcity and strain prevented it—and added: "What he has done for me I can never repay—and may add that I admire you people on the other side of the water for doing the same and sticking up for him when most of the world are against him."[5] She signed the letter "S[carlet] W[oman]."

On September 17 en route for Southampton, Crowley visited family hometown Alton. Did he ponder his paternal forebears' wealth, enjoyed when Crowley Ales dominated a town whose very name "AL-ton" presaged the New Aeon? From Northlands House nursing home, Westrow Road, Southampton (still functioning), a "feeble" Crowley thanked Smith for five pounds; regular sums were vital. However, Smith should not have used Crowley's title "Rex S.S.," ("Supreme Most Holy King") in his church registration— O.T.O. would do.[6] Despite Pearl's postscript indicating 666 had phlebitis "pretty bad," Smith, frustrated, fulminated: "You really are the limit."[7] Hadn't he *already* sent Crowley *three* unanswered letters about the incorporation? He'd simply followed Crowley's instruction: concentrate on the mass, not the degrees.

Short of shirt and shoes, Smith had his problems. John Bamber (in love with Leota) quit noisily on September 20, followed by Leota. "Deacon" Jacobi found driving 120 miles from San Bernardino a strain. New lodgers might help, and Crowley would probably get his five pounds if they stayed. On December 15, Crowley made light of the "Rex S.S.," issue, thanking Smith for the five pounds that arrived just at the point of utter desperation. Smith shouldn't ever imagine he was neglectful of "you folk," but every time he had a position to communicate, something— good or bad—happened to change the picture.

*Fig. 3.3. The Mapleton Hotel, Coventry Street. A postcard from the 1950s.*

When Crowley was ejected from the Washington Hotel, Curzon Street, on November 9, the Mapleton—a Victorian corner hotel at 39 Coventry Street near Piccadilly Circus—found room. It was nearly Christmas, but where were the wise bearing gifts?

# FOUR

# Unbelievable Terror

While he was living in London on a temporary visa before rejoining wife Cora in the States, late application for an immigration visa compelled Karl Germer's return to Germany. The Gestapo arrested him in Leipzig on February 2, 1935. Handcuffed, Iron Cross–decorated Germer was incarcerated in a Berlin police prison for ten days with the lowest criminals. He endured five hours' cross-questioning on February 11 without charge. Two days later, the Chancellery Clerk signed a *Geheimes Staatspolizeiamt* arrest warrant, committing him to "Konzentrationslager [Concentration Camp] Columbia." *His crime?* "Continued communications with foreign High-grade Freemason Crowley, and for seeking students and distributing his teachings."

*Fig. 4.1. Karl Germer.*
*(Courtesy: Ordo Templi Orientis)*

*Fig. 4.2. Germer's Gestapo arrest warrant. (Courtesy: Ordo Templi Orientis Archives)*

Crammed into a structure built for 130, Berlin's "Columbia Haus" in Tempelhof held some four hundred Jews, communists, social democrats, unwanted rightists, homosexuals, and transvestites arrested after 1934's "Knight of the Long Knives." Under S.S. Commandant Karl Otto Koch's regime, Germer was forbidden to read, denied contact with foreigners, humiliated by Columbia's sadistic guards, and accused of running a passport factory. He suffered over four months of agonizing solitary confinement at Columbia Haus until Cora persuaded Berlin's U.S. consul to intervene. The Nazi authorities responded. "Protective Prisoner 303" was transferred to Esterwegen, one of the worst camps. Esterwegen's dreary lines of huts held 1,200 prisoners on a swamp on the Dutch border. Bullied for "obstinately refusing to tell the truth" about being a Freemason—he wasn't—Germer summarized the experience as one of "unbelievable terror."

Crowley's 1935 diaries have not survived, but surviving correspondence suggests a grim time. Impoverished by the trial, 666 traipsed from hotel to hotel thanks to Pearl and the occasional fiver from Hollywood. He didn't give up, sending the Word of the Equinox to California in

*Fig. 4.3. Esterwegen concentration camp.*

March 1935: "ARMAGEDDON (This is associated with a vision on a plain full of dead men. An adept is on the watch.) The Oracle and the Omen are silent."[1]

Death came in goose steps. Reich Aviation Minister Hermann Göring launched the Luftwaffe on March 11, while Hitler decreed obligatory conscription into Germany's armed forces—condemned by the League of Nations on April 17—the day Crowley was registered bankrupt. Unable to secure credit, Crowley's legal statement insisted that one who'd so enriched the English language might not be expected to excel in accountancy. He added the question: *who was so powerful as to be able to persuade financier and* Sunday Referee *owner Isidore Ostrer to cancel a series of vindicating articles commissioned, Crowley maintained, by Hayter Preston?* (see page 25). The background to this sinister suspicion is perhaps revealed from a completely different point of view in Jean Overton Fuller's *The Magical Dilemma of Victor Neuburg.*

Interviewing Preston in the early sixties, Ms. Fuller says she was curious to know, after all that passed between Crowley, Preston, and Neuburg in May 1914, why Preston had published Crowley's article

"My Wanderings in Search of the Absolute" in the *Sunday Referee* on March 10, 1935? Preston remembered being surprised to receive a telegram from Crowley inviting him to the Old Ship Hotel, Brighton. *Why?* It transpired Crowley wanted to sell an article, and out of softness, Preston accepted it, albeit severely edited at the publisher's behest. According to publisher Mark Goulden (1898–1980), Crowley turned up the Tuesday after publication with a sheaf of what he said were "future installments." Goulden said he had no use for them. Crowley insisted Preston contracted him for a *series*. Preston firmly denied it. Becoming abusive, Crowley was shown the door, shouting, "I'll sue you." He started proceedings for breach of contract, but when it came to court, Goulden recalled to Fuller the judge's words to Crowley: "You have no justification in law or morality." Passing Preston and Goulden, Crowley apparently snarled on his way from court: "You'll regret this." Unmoved by a rather frightened Preston's earlier plea that Goulden desist from court action lest Crowley curse him, Goulden remained content. Preston, though, was depressed for a long time after: a shadow whose weight, Goulden maintained, only left his shoulders when he heard of Crowley's death (*Magical Dilemma*, 244–45). Crowley's bankruptcy apologia in April 1935 insisted a contract was canceled covertly by some mysterious, highly placed person determined to end his career, someone powerful enough even to swing *Sunday Referee* owner Isidore Ostrer (1889–1975) to his will.*

Crowley was down, and Hollywood brought scant comfort: "People are so frightful. Civilization, *sic,* as one contacts it here is an abortion," wrote Smith on May 6, trying to uphold the mass. Addressing communists or pacifists or both, his talks went over their heads: "I would like to see how you would handle some of these sexless pacifist democrats. I don't see any hope until the Word [Armageddon] has in actuality been fulfilled."[2]

Not receiving Smith's letter of May 6, Crowley found the delay incomprehensible: "You might at least have let me know what's gone wrong."[3] *Lack of cash,* Smith explained on May 30, adding: "I know my letters mean little or nothing to you unless there is a monetary enclosure."[4]

---

*See Churton, *Aleister Crowley: The Biography*, 363.

Finally receiving the May 6 depressive letter, Crowley replied to Smith on Old Ship Hotel, Brighton, notepaper:

> Why couldn't you write me when the troubles arose? There *must* be something wrong if you alienate people like Jacobi [unfair: Jacobi couldn't drive the distance]. I get a sort of impression that you interfere too much in the affairs of other people. I feel, too, that Vagina's "personality" would send me screaming to the nearest aerodrome. . . . Bit of the "smug troglodyte" [Smith's phrase] in you too, perhaps?
>
> I've got a cold and a bad temper this morning; so please excuse critical tone of this letter. Don't think I fail to appreciate your real virtues, great loyalty, will-power, courage, and perseverance.[5]

In June, debate moved to Charles Frederick Russell. Repudiating Crowley after Cefalù, Russell had established his own "chain and group" in Chicago: the Choronzon Club or Gnostic Body of God. On June 3 Smith told of mass attenders holding *Russell's* "Word of the Equinox,"[6] while professional astrologer Mary Ellen Green (1884–1936) showed Smith Crowley's *Yi King* paraphrase, plagiarized as Russell's "Book Chameleon." Having quit Russell's club after meeting him, Freemason Rudolf Holm supported Green. Russell's declaration of a period of Five Years' Silence required members (who'd paid $7) to destroy existing papers. Smith reckoned disconcerted newcomers' enthusiasm justified reactivating the O.T.O. degrees.

Examples of Russell's papers were sent on June 14 when Smith announced fifteen would join a revived O.T.O. Annoyed at Schneider's misrepresenting who was paying him, Smith asked Crowley: *If 100 members all paid $15, would Crowley want every cent?*—and were he, Smith, to disapprove, would Crowley make another "Treasurer or what not," "smashing" the organization? "Of course at any time you could announce, *Smith is out and does not represent me.* But I am not so much concerned with Smith as the Organization."[7] Smith hoped "a good crowd" would greet Crowley in the fall.

Such was unlikely, Crowley regretted: "I could not get a visa—at least, I doubt it. It might help me if I were wanted as a witness in a big prosecution of Russell & Co. In any case money is needed over here—and a whole lot of it."[8] Smith should recommend those who'd

paid Russell inform their district attorneys. As to his own approach to
money, it was "quite legitimate" to ask for support for a cause, but no
"magical" reward should be promised. Smith could assure contributors
they'd be repaid "as soon as my triumph over iniquity makes it easy
for me to earn large sums from newspapers and so on." Crowley asked
Smith to contact Dorothy Olsen, though he couldn't believe she'd participated in what he believed was C. S. Jones's theft of rare editions
entrusted to him.*

Crowley considered Smith's imprecations of financial insincerity
again on June 30, writing on Brighton's Hotel Metropole paper:

> There is no good acknowledging me as the Head of absolutely self-
> less Orders like the A∴A∴ and O.T.O. unless you are convinced of
> my absolute integrity. My worrying you has simply been that the lack
> of your usual contribution has meant constant defeat and paralysis,
> whereas if I had income adequate to the circumstances, I should be
> able to make really large sums off my own bat, and send streams of
> fertilizing gold to you and other branches. I want you just now to
> realize that the one essential is to expose the conspiracy against me.
> Do that and I can instantly get $10,000 or $15,000 for the English
> serial rights of my life story *alone*."[9]

Receiving such fantastic stuff, Smith must have felt he was
going mad.

The "conspiracy" apparently related to Crowley's criminal prosecution for allegedly receiving letters stolen from Betty Sedgwick. To demonstrate Russell's deviancy, Smith was encouraged to reprint Crowley's
tract "One Star in Sight" on the proper grade and initiation process of
the A∴A∴—funded by Mary Green. Now was the time to introduce
the O.T.O.'s "Man of Earth Triad": the 0° (Minerval), 1° (Man and
Brother / Woman and Sister), and II° (Magician).

Thanking Smith for five pounds, a letter of August 8 on Savoy
Hotel notepaper suggested the Minerval be performed in California's

---

*Smith thought Olsen was selling books that were in fact lost in a Chicago warehouse—
until 1958, the bulk now held by the Harry Ransom Center, University of Texas at
Austin. Crowley believed Jones a thief to the end.

"fine deserts." A week later, Crowley added a statement to check Russell: initiation could not be bought, only won by "personal endeavor." Russell was "thief, swindler and blackmailer . . . a man of no education."[10] The day Crowley requested the statement's distribution, Germany adopted the swastika as the national flag.

Smith replied on August 22. He'd found a good deserted spot about twenty-five miles round trip from Hollywood. Aiming at twelve Minervals for the equinox, he reckoned his third attempt at the O.T.O. would "go over this time."[11] Despite trouble getting tent, altar, and other paraphernalia for the location, Smith was proud to inform Baphomet that September 21 saw Secretary General Jane Wolfe bring seven candidates at 7 p.m. for the Minerval degree at Playa del Ray. Returning to the Profess House at 10:10 p.m., Sisters Kahl and Wolfe and Brothers Schneider and Jacobi hosted a banquet.

Crowley asked that the Word of the Equinox: LAL (Sanskrit for "red") with the "background of a sandy desert and burnt mountains with corpses and watching adept"[12] be sent to Gerald Yorke c/o Hong Kong and Shanghai Bank, requesting Yorke visit California when returning to Europe in the winter (Crowley and Yorke had supposedly ruptured in 1933 before Yorke went to China for Reuters).

On October 3, the world watched as Mussolini's troops entered Ethiopia. The capital, Addis Ababa, would fall in May 1936, deposing Emperor Haile Selassie, hereditary "Lion of Judah," the oldest Christian monarchy in the world, in the name of a new Roman Empire.

Smith, meanwhile, had spoken with *American Astrology* editor Paul Clancy about publicity for the mass, suggesting Clancy enjoy first copyright of Crowley's recent *Little Essays Toward Truth.* Crowley expected "Wine of the Graal," a prospectus he'd prepared, be used by Smith to secure rights, which would be Smith's to recover loans to Crowley "up to $1000 at least." Crowley reckoned Smith should use Clancy for promotion (with the mass promoted in the prospectus), or, "if you are sure he [Clancy] is straight!" maybe Clancy might publish existing short works "The Three Schools of Magick" or "The Heart of the Master." Expecting problems, Crowley added, "Only remember Dignity!"[13] He wrote again on Waldorf Hotel, Aldwych, paper, on October 30: "If reliable, why not do business with him [Clancy]? Put him in touch with me direct, if you feel so hopeless yourself! Sorry things are so bad. But isn't it a good deal your own fault? You leave such gaps."[14] As it turned out, Clancy published Smith's letter promoting the mass in the November issue, while receiving publishing rights (for a song) to print *Little Essays Toward Truth,* the first of which, "Man," appeared in January 1936, while Smith registered the sixteen lectures in his own name with the Library of Congress (Crowley had said the copyrights were for him).

## A.M.O.R.C. ROUND ONE

Around 1915 Harvey Spencer Lewis founded his part-mail-order "Rosicrucian" initiation system, Ancient and Mystical Order Rosae Crucis.

Crowley met Lewis in 1918 in New York when Lewis stood accused of fraudulent bond sales. Despite Lewis's charter's fanciful origin— allegedly from "Rosicrucians of Toulouse"—and knowing it to be bad form for Rosicrucians to identify themselves as such, Crowley offered to give bail for Lewis out of fraternal amity and hope that Lewis might prove useful. In any event, larceny charges were dropped. On August 28, 1922, Lewis denounced Crowley's "filthy immoral outfit" in a Chicago talk, thinking it safe, as Crowley had been pilloried in print there already (see Richard Kaczynski's, *Panic in Detroit,* 2019). From the audience, C. S. Jones and wife, Ruby, challenged him; Lewis backed down. Meanwhile, Dr. Reuben Swinburne Clymer (1878–1966) had Lewis in his sights for competing with his Quakertown-based Fraternitas Rosae Crucis, Pennsylvania. Clymer's "lineage" came through Edward H. Brown, heir to P. B. Randolph's nineteenth-century quasi-Rosicrucian Brotherhood of Eulis and other Randolphian bodies. Clymer exploited these connections to the full, alienating Brown in the process.

During the summer's campaign against Russell, one Floyd M. Spann asked to inspect Smith's rituals. Posing as ex-Russellite, Spann was Clymer's anti-Lewis rep. Meanwhile, Crowley received Clymer's 128-page pamphlet *Not under the Rosy Cross,* arguing Lewis's sole authority lay in an O.T.O. document derived from "evil black magician" Crowley. Crowley saw an opportunity. If O.T.O. authority was Lewis's fig leaf, Crowley would demonstrate its sufficiency, and Lewis's dependency on it. In August, Crowley addressed a letter to "Very Illustrious Very

Illuminated and Very Dear Bro ∴ [Lewis],"[15] dismissing Clymer as "an ignorant swindler who came to me in New York in 1914–1915 e.v. for support. I kicked him out. As I assume that you know, practically every statement he makes about me is false." Crowley requested Lewis cable his London representative's address, signing the letter, "Yours in the Bonds of the Order, Baphomet X° 33° 90° 97° O.T.O."[16]

Crowley's basis for action lay in Theodor Reuss in 1921 sending Lewis an honorary VII° O.T.O. diploma as a "gage of amity." In Crowley's view, this meant A.M.O.R.C. property came under the O.T.O.'s Head. Crowley wrote again to Lewis on October 22 requesting return of a fraternal favor now that Crowley found *himself* temporarily distressed, to which Lewis replied on November 6, 1935, from the A.M.O.R.C. Temple, San José, beginning: "My dear Mr. Crowley . . ."

Lewis denied interest in Freemasonry as he represented *Rosicrucian* tradition, always separate (i.e., Crowley's references to Memphis and Misraim Rites were irrelevant). He then disputed Crowley's statements that a Rosicrucian Order existed in Europe in 1912; Crowley's activities were distinct from Rosicrucian traditions. Crowley's Rosicrucianism was either his invention or that of another. Reuss was successor to

*Fig. 4.4. Crowley's diploma as National Grand Master General O.T.O. signed by Reuss and Henry Klein, April 1912, indicating his status in the Ancient & Accepted Rite (33°) and in the Antient & Primitive Rites of Memphis and Misraim (90°; 95°).*
*(Courtesy: Ordo Templi Orientis)*

Yarker: "a lovable man, intensely devoted to the landmarks and high ideals of Rosicrucianism," whose "authority derived from and descending through various known and recognized secret chiefs of the Order since the eighteenth century." Crowley's O.T.O. ritual and terminology came from 1911 or 1912, using "Golden Dawn" ritualism distinct from any Rosicrucian rituals "I have seen." The original O.T.O. was Reuss's through Kellner. O.T.O. cofounder Franz Hartmann "was for a time a very secret officer of the Rosicrucian Order. Your claim that Theodor Reuss gave you a charter for the United States is unsupported by all the records. In fact, in 1920 and 1921 Mr. Reuss was bitterly opposed to your activities." Lewis claimed Crowley's organization had nothing to do with Reuss's intentions and had no authority in Europe. Crowley's claim that Reuss wrote to him making him successor stood contradicted by Reuss's correspondence in 1921 "in which he ignores and deplores the organizations which you formed with the rival names or the names that simulated the original O.T.O. and the Rosicrucians." Lewis had since contacted Arnaldo Krumm-Heller who claimed only to be "legate to South America and to Spain," his version adapted for Latin American sensibilities. No Rosicrucian jurisdiction recognized Crowley. Lewis denied that Crowley—a bankrupt—had any power to make Lewis's position unassailable if A.M.O.R.C. helped him and accepted his jurisdiction. "Your suggestion that we have a talk with your representative Mr. Schneider in Los Angeles has been noted. One of our members in that district has already been in touch with him." The letter was signed, H. Spencer Lewis IMPERATOR.

Crowley replied from London on December 2, 1935: "My dear Imperator, It is really very good of you to have answered my letter at such length and with such care. I have never doubted your knowledge of many of the facts in question. But I do not think that any apparent variance between your position and mine is irreconcilable."[17]

As far as Reuss and O.T.O. rituals were concerned, Reuss was almost daily with Crowley from 1912 to 1914, and Reuss approved Crowley's revised rituals. Reuss was "almost invariably present at our ceremonies."

> Reuss was, I think, also a little resentful with the part I had played during the war. It was when he had given up all hope that he wrote (to—not from—Sicily) appointing me O.H.O. to succeed him. The

approach of death naturally restored his equilibrium. . . . I have a letter from the Grand Master of the Order of the Martinists who succeeded Papus, in which letter I am fully recognized, dated March 8th, 1928. The only thing that matters is the ultimate secret of the O.T.O., which is not disclosed below IX°. That secret is important because it confers real powers. I have no evidence of any authority conferred on you except the Reuss Diploma, which is after all a very guarded document, and not in any sense a warrant or charter. Besides, it is revocable. I am sure you will thank me for not referring to the City of Toulouse. What have you then which is definitely Rosicrucian in character? What authority have you apart from the O.T.O.? But if I had no authority whatever, my possession of the ultimate secret would confer it.[18]

In 1910 when Mathers acted against the Equinox, Reuss came and said, "I am the secret chief of the Rosicrucian Order," being one of a dozen or more claimants at the time. Lewis might deny the Scottish or Rites of Memphis and Misraim any factor in the claim, yet "the only document on which you base your claim is devoted to these Rites, as concentrated in the O.T.O. (which is printed in big type across the Diploma) and nothing whatever is said about Rosicrucians. Further my own private seal is at the foot of the document. At the same time I wish to point out that according to my information it has always been strictly forbidden for any Rosicrucian to claim to be one." Crowley added further justification in a direct but still ameliorative tone, making it clear how his reputation was in process of complete vindication as the Betty Sedgwick evidence revealed her having deliberately fooled the judge, of which she proudly boasted.

At the foot of the copy of Crowley's letter to Lewis was a note from a December 2 letter to Max Schneider: "It is perhaps best not to admit having seen the Lewis stuff, as I go for him rather heavily from the last page. Your job is, of course, to get him to put his organization in England at my disposal for the purpose of the vindication, and to guarantee the costs for the best legal assistance."

Crowley's problem was that while from an infra-Order point of view, he had a case, charters only mattered to such "authorities"; property claims based on these meant little in law since anyone could call their organization "Rosicrucian" if they wished, so long as no deliberate fraud was proven. Lewis's sincerity had no legal test. Crowley, for his part, could never prove that before his death Theodor Reuss *had* appointed him O.H.O.; all extant evidence points to Crowley having assumed the position because Reuss denied what Crowley considered highest authority—the Secret Chiefs—and by opposing their will, Reuss abrogated authority to one possessing supernal authority. "They" intended Crowley to lead humankind into the Aeon of Horus, and anybody claiming high spiritual authority had no moral choice but to accept him; they didn't, of course. Crowley would doubtless argue such resistance accounted for the relative decline of opposing Orders today.

While Crowley took the first steps in a long, vain campaign to assume A.M.O.R.C. under his wing in the autumn and winter of 1935, unexpected news lightened his spirits.

American Cora Germer secured an interview between Karl and Berlin's American consul. Consular persistence resulted in Germer's discharge from Esterwegen in August 1935. Hoping the facts of his sufferings could impress the English-speaking world with the realities of life under Nazi rule, Karl, in Leipzig, proposed a 60,000–65,000 word account of his incarceration in English: *Protective Prisoner No. 303*. Camouflaged under assumed name "Dr. Georg Streffer," Germer, risking catastrophe, communicated with Crowley. Cooperating with Dowling-Kimber Secretariat literary agency, Sentinel House, WC1, Crowley wrote as "Michael Dowling" from Sentinel House on September 16, 1935:

> We have approached several people and find that the market is excellent. You would, however, have to come to London, to discuss the matter in a personal interview.—I think there might be an opportunity for you in connection with business, of which I enclose a prospectus.
>
> With kindest regards
> from all, yours very truly,
> Michael Dowling.[19]

Another camouflaged letter winged its way to Leipzig from the same address:

> Yours of Sept. 3 duly to hand. Greatest sympathy.—Poor Lebrun is more seriously ill than you people suppose, we think that the end is only a matter of a few months.—With regard to paragraph 12 of M.K.'s [Martha Küntzel—Sister of the Order, in Leipzig] letter, will you please go to the British Consul and make a sworn statement as to the proceedings at the "Falstaff" Tavern, and ask him to send it to me at this address.* Let me know what fees are payable, and I will transmit them to the Consulate direct.—All here well and writing hopefully.
>
> Signed: Michael Dowling.[20]

Fearing the Gestapo knew he was writing about them, Karl escaped to Antwerp, Belgium. On October 23, 1935, Crowley expressed his relief:

> I have rarely felt such heartfelt joy as this moment when your letter arrived, announcing your escape.—Come to this office [c/o The Dowling-Kimber Secretariat] as soon as you reach London. Mr. D-K is my literary agent, and he is going ahead at once to place your story, which ought to bring you in quite a lot to go on with. Be sure your friends will go all out to fix things up for you.—I say no more now, but rejoice. Will do all in my power. Write me here.[21]

An undated letter got to Karl from 14 Edward Street, W1. Though under a Dowling-Kimber letterhead, Crowley pointed an arrow at it: "These people are washed out—N.G. [No Good]":

> O.K. Saw Gollancz [Victor Gollancz, publisher]—v. [very] favourably impressed by synopsis. Will answer in a day or two. Please send typescript of one chapter—pick an exciting bit! Quick as you can.

---

*Referring to Martha's affidavit describing a meeting at the Falstaff tavern where Betty Sedgwick's payment to give hostile evidence against Crowley was discussed.

And authorize me to negotiate with people on your behalf. I can get better terms. (I am interesting people too in other ways.) If the book is well written, it ought to be a really great success. (If not they can put a man on the job.) I shall see about film rights too. The "Magical Secrets" part offers great dramatic possibilities.

Hope news soon of your arrival. If by any chance I miss you at Liverpool Street [station], phone or call at this address. (GER 2232).

Also arrangements are being made for your comfort, and if you play your cards well—the G∴W∴ accomplished!

Did you see Dr. [Hans Wilhelm] Thost* has been expelled from England?[22]

Crowley wrote an undated letter announcing he'd started reading the manuscript in the morning and found it "very good indeed." It was "better than Lorant [Hungarian Stefant Lorant's account, *I Was Hitler's Prisoner*, published in 1935]—absence of literary frills & technique of presentation improves it. Makes it convincing. And it is very good reading—will start up Ivor Nicholson & Watson [publishers] on Monday morning." Gollancz wouldn't do it.[23]

On November 6, an anxious Crowley wrote again from 14 Edward Street, wishing he could get over to Antwerp for the weekend, but unless it rained doubloons, it wasn't likely. In the meantime, it would help his efforts in arousing interest if Germer sent a "snappy and juicy" synopsis. As Germer attempted to get a Belgian refugee passport to cross to England, Crowley wrote to calm Germer's fears that he might be set upon, or worse (in concentration camps, S.S. murders were disguised as suicides). Crowley made light of such anxieties:

> I don't think there is any danger of openly murderous attacks; and the police will be warned about staging any more suicides as for the two German women in Bloomsbury. Also I'm getting powerful friends.[24]

---

*In November 1935, Thost, who represented Nazi paper *Völkischer Beobachter,* was accused of espionage. Reading Wyndham Lewis's *Hitler* book (1931), Thost corrected Lewis's view that Hitler's *Judenfrage* was a "racial red herring and Hitler was not a threat." Thost insisted the Jewish question was the crux of Hitlerism without which the party would not exist.

A Belgian refugee passport finally secured Germer's crossing to Harwich at the end of November. While a temporary visa was extended from three months, he'd have to leave before the end of 1936.

Meanwhile, Crowley received Smith's complaints over poor relations with Max; Max's girlfriend Virginia was "off her head." Crowley riposted on December 13 that Smith should grasp the psychological situation and make allowances; he'd gathered from Max's letters Virginia was "something of a half-wit." He was also annoyed by Smith's saying it would cost $40 to copyright the *Little Essays Toward Truth;* the sum should have come from Clancy for temporary copyright: "If the copyright is lost, how on earth can you get anyone interested in the book?"[25] Crowley added that he'd keep Smith informed if anything broke over A.M.O.R.C. with Lewis, and that Smith should research the exposures of Swinburne Clymer and of Leon Batchelor, whose addresses, one in Quakertown, the latter in San José, Crowley attached.

# FIVE

# Bar 666

New Year's Day 1936: While Max Schneider handled A.M.O.R.C. negotiations, Crowley sent Smith a copy of Yarker's diploma naming Crowley
National Grand Master 96° Rite of Misraim, recommending Smith note
paragraph six of a "Manifesto" (O.T.O. magazine *Oriflamme*, July 1913)
referring to Crowley's X° covering America, a detail found also in July
1914's *Oriflamme* (p. 19). The "Manifesto" featured in 1919's *Blue
Equinox* (p. 201: "The Authority of the O.H.O. in all English-speaking
countries is delegated by charter to the Most Holy, Most Illustrious,
Most Illuminated, and Most Puissant Baphomet X° Rex Summus
Sanctissimus 33°, 90°, 96°, Past Grand Master of the United States of
America, Grand Master of Ireland, Iona, and All the Britains . . ."). A sup-
portive charter was "not immediately accessible," but had Reuss objected
he "would have done so," as they collaborated almost daily in 1913.[1]
Unbalanced by a stroke in 1921, asserted Crowley, Reuss "carelessly"
issued Lewis's VII° diploma and—ignoring Crowley—C. S. Jones's X°
North American charter of May 5, 1921. Jones accepted Crowley as
O.H.O. in 1925 (before expulsion on October 1, 1934). Believing it
would mollify Lewis into supporting him, Reuss declared Crowley's
O.T.O. link dissolved.

Meanwhile, Crowley was "absolutely sick of the petty squabbles in
your [Smith's] part of the world." Smith should behave like any serious
professional in public life.

Schneider told Crowley Lewis suffered a stroke after a Federal
Trade Commission investigation. Unfortunately the source was "New
Thought" lecturer Rev. Wayne Walker of "The Voice of Healing,"

*Fig. 5.1. Crowley's diploma as Grand Inspector General for the Antient & Primitive Rites appointing him O.T.O. Grand Inspector for "Amerika," signed by Reuss. (Courtesy of the Warburg Institute, London, and Ordo Templi Orientis)*

Huntington Beach, allegedly one of seven priests of an Order of Melchizedek. Performing initiations at Long Beach, Walker had big ideas about saving the world.[2] Crowley recommended Schneider exploit Walker's anti-Lewis stance and get Walker's secretary Irene Love behind a lawsuit to alienate A.M.O.R.C. property. Walker didn't gel with Winona Boulevard's sexual vibe, however, cutting loose for familiar sands.

Writing to Jane Wolfe, Crowley tried to protect Schneider from criticism over girlfriend Virginia:

> Aggravatingly idiotic as your letters always were, their cheerfulness made them welcome. . . . You are to blame. You knew the Cefalù rule of frankness. You ought to have anticipated what Virginia would do, and told Max at the time the facts of the case. Of course, it is also Max's fault for accepting an *ex parte* statement from Virginia. But men are usually loath to question the stories told them by the women they are sleeping with at the moment. In any case these tornadoes in teacups are ridiculous and it is utterly undignified to be mixed up in them, and downright rotten to allow them to side-track the G[reat]. W[ork].
>
> Best of love    93    93/93
> Yours fraternally 666[3]

On February 3, "orgie" with Laurence and Pam Felkin and a "McVicar" led to a party at "Pat's"—perhaps Rudolf Steiner aficionado Patricia

Deirdre Doherty, who'd come up from Cornwall in 1934 to observe hero Crowley in the dock.

Three days later, Crowley recorded his first recipe as gourmet and London Curry Sultan: a salad of onions, green peppers, baked potato, olives, hard-boiled egg, almonds, and lichen with a dressing of oil, salt, vinegar, paprika, mustard, and Tabasco pepper; 666 liked it hot, and many were called to "ordeal by curry" over the next five years.

Tom Driberg lunched with Crowley next day, and when Pearl visited Eastbourne to recuperate from a traumatic hysterectomy on February 10, a "great party" was enjoyed with the Felkins.

Back at the King's Bench division on February 21, Crowley observed a case against painter and former opera singer Countess (from first husband) Lina Monici. Mr. E. N. Noble, K.C., was present: "Pat a v[ery]. good witness. Lina a marvel—captured everyone's sympathy—went on babbling—kept the court in roars—the Judge allowed it!" The previous day at the courts, he'd met someone with Dutch or Belgian name "van der Elst," having oral sex with "her" (?) that evening before visiting Herbert Smith, solicitors. Van der Elst perhaps lived in Addison Road, near the Lewenhaupts, or Crowley may have.

Laurence and Pam dined the following Sunday on Crowley's "Savoury No. 1": "Fried Rye Bread. Smear with Chinese Chili Sauce. Grilled Sardines. Top with Egg fried in olive oil," followed by his first curry four days later: "Pilaw-Rice-almonds, sultanas, onions, saffron, little curry, Lea & Perrins [Worcestershire sauce] Mutton. Parmesan." After dinner it was round to the Felkins for a spelling bee. They discussed van der Elst's "picture-show idea" and the "666 bar idea," the latter a notion to metamorphose from themed bar to curry-specializing "black magic restaurant." The following night Nancy Thomas, possibly Dylan Thomas's elder sister, threw a party.*

Crowley must have felt more comfortable in his rooms to give dinners, for on March 7 the Felkins attended Crowley's spelling bee plus "halawa" curry: an oriental dessert, with fruits, figs, and Carlsbad

---

*Dylan proposed to Caitlin Macnamara in spring 1936 at the Wheatsheaf pub, Rathbone Street; Caitlin had modeled for Crowley's friend, Augustus John, who introduced the couple; perhaps the occasion was Nancy Thomas's party. Crowley was at the Wheatsheaf on July 8.

plums. A few days later, André Pigné (who couldn't find a Masonic opening in France) crossed the Channel, keen to learn the Master Therion's magick; Crowley opened the O.T.O.'s portals on March 12, with Pigné undertaking fourteen lessons for fourteen guineas in Masonry, Qabalah, astrology, geomancy, mantra yoga, and sammasati-dharana. Further lessons, including astral traveling and will-power were given between April and June.

March was jarred by altercations with landlord "Nicholas." Despite legal advice from friend Frank Lewis, Nicholas, raving, smashed Crowley's back door, and after a further unspecified "outrage" Crowley transferred to the Swiss Hotel, 53 Old Compton Street, Soho, to enjoy another oral assignation with van der Elst on March 17, before moving into 59 Great Ormond Street on April 27.

"Slippery Joe" (probably Gerald *Joseph* Yorke) lunched with Crowley at the Café Royal bar on May 5, discussing Thelema as base for the Nazi New Order—coincidentally the theme of Martha Küntzel's letter received next day. Martha remained convinced Hitler was a Thelemite savior! While Belgian fascists won twenty-one seats in the general election on May 24, an article about "forerunner" Madame Blavatsky gripped Crowley's attention—and a diary comment—on June 6:

> She wrote really fine literature—*The Voice of the Silence*. (Also, it is still a bestseller after fifty years.) She had a greater influence on religious thought in Europe than any one since Luther. That is not to be done by fraud. Her tricks and troopers' oaths were her safeguards against going mad—as you would do if you had as many followers and disciples and devotees to pester you as she had . . .

Crowley's gourmet trip gathered pace in early summer. On May 31, "Christ Child" and Pam Felkin were treated to an "aphrodisiac" called Mania-Making: "Kus Kus cooked in butter. Add Zamair paste: cook. Put in Red Macassar Fish. Butter and Sugar in pan. Add honey. Add pistachios. Heat till caramel appears. Pour on to greased pan." Yorke had benefit of a "memorably exotic" lunch "cooked by host himself in a Bloomsbury flat": chili con carne "so hot that it makes strong men weep." Four side dishes were based on "(a) red macassar fish and poppy-seed (b) tamarind-fish (c) Burmese balichow made from rotten prawns (bottled, very Spilsburyesque) (d) Kasoondee-minced mango in spiced oil." June 10 saw "Rice as usual. Omelette Chinese. Poppadam. Prawn Balachow. Poppadam. Zambar of Lobster: Iced."

Meanwhile "worn-out" Pearl caused concern. Her devotion, he noted, was "like that of a penguin to her egg: so exclusive that she is too stupid to defend the position" (May 29). Then on June 14, twenty-year-old Elsie Morris announced Crowley had fathered a child born in January. "Possible," noted Crowley, "but I paid 5/- at the time." Three weeks later, Elsie "raised hell." Crowley tried to reserve his adventures (such as oral sex with lovely Ruby Melvill on twenty-first and twenty-second of June) to his diary, unlike W. T. Smith, who spilled beans too often. A letter about Georgia Haitz, whom Smith had passed on to Schneider, caught Crowley's ire:

> In all these years, the bulk of your activities seems to have been a series of intrigues with quite useless women, trailing behind on the loose. None of them has ever come to anything save Regina. All this is a dispersion of energy and very contrary to silence. You can never get beyond the clique stage of a Movement on these lines, because the interest is purely personal and parochial. You have got to find some point on which to focus general interest, to arouse controversy, to have meetings of indignation and protest all over the country. You have an ideal background. Look at these lunatics Roosevelt, Townsend,* and such! They assert insane principles and sweep the whole country. That is only done by hoisting an impersonal flag, and refusing to be side-tracked by every wandering tart.
>
> This is all my fault. I have never carried out the injunctions about the *Book of the Law* as I should have done. I am now going to concentrate on that. [reproduction with *Comment* enjoined] Copies will be sent to you, and it will be up to you to raise hell.[4]

Crowley had in mind a subscriber's edition of *Liber AL* with supportive writings and the "Comment" he'd never managed, with a pocketed reproduction of the original manuscript, to be published as

---

*Francis Townsend (1867–1960) proposed a tax-increasing "revolving pension plan" in the States, encouraging Roosevelt's social security program in 1935.

*The Equinox of the Gods.* Subscriptions gathered i
on June 17 for twenty-five copies from Michael Hou,
Atlantis Bookshop, Museum Street, founder (1922), for
rarely had a good word, but who remained profitably invol
publishing to the end. On June 22 "California" stumped u
pounds (fifteen pounds to come).

While General Franco and rebel Spanish Foreign Leg
crossed from Morocco to Cadiz, igniting the Spanish Ci
Crowley's London summer was all lunches and dinners with
Melvill, Eve Brachenburg, and Count Lewenhaupt. Poet, no
and pre-war A∴A∴ member Ethel Archer (died 1961) called at G
Ormond Street on July 8. Husband E. J. Wieland ran Crowley's *Equin*.
and book business before the War. Since Ethel's poems adored a fema.
archetype, Crowley dubbed her "Sappho," describing her theme ambigu-
ously in the foreword to her first collection *The Whirlpool* (1911): "the
bell of sterile passion glowing in the heart of the bell of desolation."

Scots poet Charles R. Cammell made his entrée in Crowley's diary
on July 16. His moving account, *Aleister Crowley, the Man, the Mage,
the Poet* appeared in 1951.

Crowley started regular cinema attendance. Bette Davis earned her
first Oscar for *Dangerous* (1935). Crowley's comment: "It was." As for
musical *Give Us This Night*(1936), Crowley added: "But never another."

Loyal disciple James Gilbert Bayley (Frater *Perfectio et Ministerium*,
A∴A∴ probationer March 22, 1910) appeared on July 20, while twenty-
one-year-old Patricia Deirdre Doherty rang repeatedly, probably because

*Fig. 5.2. Charles Richard Cammell
(1890–1968).*

ddle-aged lover ex-Mandrake director Major Robert Thompson
ynne—who shared her interest in Steiner's Anthroposophy and in
rowley—died in an Exeter nursing home on July 17. Crowley met
he future mother of his only (known) son at 4 p.m. five days later. He
revealed her horoscope on the twenty-sixth at a dinner at Ruby's. Ruby
was "mad about Pat." She wasn't alone. In the early hours of the twenty-
first, jealous Pearl kicked Crowley out of bed four times. "Fed up," he
lunched with Zoe Farmer at the Café Royal bar. A colleague of Driberg's
at the *Daily Express,* columnist Zoe would marry successful cinema and
theater owner Sid (later Lord) Bernstein (1899–1993) on November 11,
moving to Coppings, Kent, eyed by many jealous women on both sides
of the Atlantic. Nothing like that for Crowley: on July 24 he had sex
with Eve Brachenburg (whom he'd meet again August 6 at 39 Upper
Marylebone Street at 7:15) and commented, rather wonderfully: "Not
all the filth in London is thick enough to hide me from the Eye of God,
and by that Ray I live."

The gourmet turned his hand to "Vindalu of Bhindi" on July 28:
"Anchovies. Poppadum. Tamarind fish. Zambar of sardines." And
another blast from the past blew in two days later: Crowley's employer
in German propaganda, George Sylvester Viereck joined Germer, Ruby,
and "girl Pat" (Patricia Doherty) for lunch. Crowley noted: "Viereck will
sign affidavit that I had no trouble with authorities in USA. He said
also that after the war he made friends with our N[aval].I[intelligence].
chiefs, who told him that I had been working for them during the
War." As they talked, south Berlin's Olympiapark neared completion.
On August 1, Hitler opened the games as a vast propaganda spectacle to
demonstrate the racing master race. The night before opening, Crowley
joined Pat in *Linga-yoni mudra,* or mystical and magical embrace dedicated to *The Equinox of the Gods* and the New Aeon. Pearl, offtrack,
followed up previous nights' nightmares by attacking "Miss Doherty,
calling her trollop, harlot, whore, and slut in the course of a spate of
venomous abuse."

Perhaps to compensate, Crowley dined Pat at Leoni's Quo Vadis
restaurant in Dean Street, Soho, on August 3, followed by a meeting
with "Edomi" and Guyana-born Abdul Said Ahmed (born ca. 1898),
known as "Rollo," writer of *The Black Art.* Its 1937 successor, *I Rise:
The Life Story of a Negro,* told of immigrant Rollo Ahmed's struggles

in England. MI5 agent Dennis Wheatley learned much from occultist yogi Ahmed, who explained white differed from black magic as a brain considered like a radio could tune to lower, or higher, refined frequencies depending on objective: evil acts required depraved practices; good magic, mortification, and self-sacrifice. Rollo greatly respected Crowley.

Keen for knowledge, Crowley joined Edomi, presumably a musician, at Columbia Records on August 4. Edomi and Rollo were around the next day, and Crowley cooked *"Beau Vindalu:* Prawn Balachow-Zambar of Sardines and Anchovies: top. Iced." Spiritualist and Crowley devotee from Australia Vyvyan Deacon and Ruby lunched the day after on "Iced Vindalu of Bhindi-lowest layer. Madras Chutney. Lamb with red and green Chilis. Usual rice-top layer."

On the tenth, the author of *The Naked Ascetic* (1933) and *The Gateway to Prosperity: Leading to Health, Happiness and Success* (1933), Victor Dane, called on Crowley. Edomi arrived at 11:30 p.m. with Deacon, but Edomi, Crowley sniffed, "behaved disgustingly, making love to Pearl. She, drunk. Slobbered all over him. She means well, but filth is unforgivable." "Filth" to Crowley meant sexual debauches expressing mere physical weakness: to drag the higher into the lower. For him, sex was spiritual exaltation.

The next day, Crowley saw Augustus John, up from Cornwall, while a mock-up of *The Equinox of the Gods* arrived. Crowley paid a guinea for one hundred prospectuses. Correcting proofs from Bristol on August 15, Crowley called Ethel Archer to arrange an appointment with Dr. Martin of the "Lion of Judah." Crowley believed Ethel had some familial relation with Emperor Haile Selassie (1892–1975) who, exiled from Ethiopia in 1935, had settled in Bath. For four years the Lion of Judah received support from the Abyssinia Association. However, their reinstatement objectives crossed government efforts to appease Mussolini. An Indian, Dr. A. W. Martin of the Friends of Abyssinia had become the emperor's adviser upon retiring from the Colonial Service. He embarrassed British officials and vexed the emperor over a dispute accounting for moneys collected in 1936. Crowley's interest is hard to discern. The emperor carried a mystique, evinced in the "Ras (Prince) Tafari" (birth name of Haile Selassie) movement that sprouted in Jamaica, envisioning the Lion in messianic dimensions.

Meanwhile, California's Southern Gas Company discovered

Smith and colleague Oliver Jacobi were members of a group with a nude priestess in its ritual. An "ambassador" confronted Jacobi, who promptly resigned from the Church of Thelema; Smith was demoted. In the meantime, tarot specialist and founder of *Builders of the Adytum* (a Golden Dawn correspondence-course spin-off), Paul Foster Case (1884–1954), signed the visitor's book on several occasions, making no greater impression on Smith than he had on Crowley years before.

Despite unfair criticisms, Smith still believed Crowley "the greatest man in the world," but by November 1936 felt so undermined by Schneider he decided to curtail lodge activity. Crowley advised he maintain the mass with Jane and Regina. While Schneider's comments had warned attendees off, Smith had found some new people, and the church trudged on.

James Cleugh (1891–1969) of the Aquila Press—which had nearly merged with Mandrake in 1930—contacted Crowley on August 20 about the essay on *AL* in the *Equinox* proofs. Cleugh, who would become a longtime friendly acquaintance, showed up for a chili con carne lunch on the twenty-third and again four days later.

Another translator, Anglo-Irish Percival Arland Ussher (1899–1980), entertained Crowley at Ruby's dinner on the twenty-first. Cambridge-educated Ussher published a translation of *The Midnight Court* by Irish Gaelic-language poet, Brian Merriman in 1926. Crowley would speak to Mrs. Ussher on Christmas Day about the "Elixir" (Amrita), noting: "She likes my curries!"

Despite the summer's social whirl, Pearl's frustration peaked on August 23: "When I [Crowley], feeling cold, put on my abbai, she attacked me furiously. People complained about this to agents. Also to her appearing half-naked and screaming." That afternoon, Crowley met Allan Rae at 56 Welbeck Street. Rollo had told Rae that Crowley was a highly evolved personality, and Rae had a room. Evolved personalities were not that common.

Cleugh joined Crowley for lunch on the twenty-seventh, and one "Julie" shared Crowley's supper of, "Oh what a Zambar of Lobster with almost plain rice and a Chinese omelette atop!"

While Crowley sought papermakers and a distributor for the *Equinox,* artist Edward Grove accepted training in astral traveling on September 3 (having a "first-class" vision on the tenth), after which

*Fig. 5.3. Crowley's* Four Red Monks Carrying a
Black Goat over the Snow to Nowhere *(ca. 1929).*
*(Courtesy: Ordo Templi Orientis)*

Crowley played chess with Allan Rae's steward, Leonard Verhoeven. For
kindly bringing tea after 2 a.m., Verhoeven earned not a "Good morrow
fair sir," but "Go and shit yourself." Pearl: a "rumpus" soon erupted over
her temper. Crowley tried calming himself by painting *Rosicrucians in
Tibet,* perhaps like an idiosyncratic earlier work, above (Fig. 5.3).

On September 11 Crowley met Pat's friend, beautiful Greta
Sequeira (1907–1998), with looks like Merle Oberon's and all the class
you'd have expected from 2 Curzon Street, Mayfair. (A two-bedroom
flat in that address is currently priced at £6.5 million.) Perhaps Greta

*Fig. 5.4. Greta Sequeira (1907–1998).*

inspired a trip to the "Turker" at the Imperial Hotel and Crowley's taking his 13 stone, 8 pounds round Hyde Park on "the second really fine day of the year" (September 13).

A couple of days later he inspected the proofs of his "Scientific Solution of the Problem of Government," intended for the *Equinox of the Gods:*

> The third chapter of the Book . . . explains that certain vast "stars" (or aggregates of experience) may be described as Gods. One of these is in charge of the destinies of this planet for periods of 2,000 years. . . .
>
> This "God," Horus . . . rules the present period of 2,000 years, beginning in 1904. Everywhere his government is taking root. Observe for yourselves the decay of the sense of sin, the growth of innocence and irresponsibility, the strange modifications of the reproductive instinct with a tendency to become bi-sexual or epicene, the childlike confidence in progress combined with nightmare fear of catastrophe, against which we are yet half-unwilling to take precautions.
>
> Consider the outcrop of dictatorships, only possible when moral growth is in its earliest stages, and the prevalence of infantile cults like Communism, Fascism, Pacifism, Health Crazes, Occultism in nearly all its forms, religions sentimentalized to the point of practical extinction.
>
> Consider the popularity of the cinema, the wireless, the football pools and guessing competitions, all devices for soothing fractious infants, no seed of purpose in them.
>
> Consider sport, the babyish enthusiasms and rages, which it excites, whole nations disturbed by disputes between boys.
>
> Consider war, the atrocities which occur daily and leave us unmoved and hardly worried.
>
> We are children.

## THE NEXT STEP

The establishment of the Law of Thelema is the only way to preserve individual liberty and to assure the future of the race.

In the words of the famous paradox of Comte de Fénix—the

absolute rule of the state shall be a function of the absolute liberty of each individual will.

Readers may judge the validity of this analysis to when it was written, and to today.

Despite ongoing disputes with Simpkin & Marshall over distribution, Crowley held a *tamasha* (celebration) for advanced copies of *The Equinox of the Gods* on September 22, inviting "Greta Roberts, Sergent, Dolores, Wylie [Tom Wylie of the War Office], Ruby, Reid, Alan Rae, Mike and Mrs. Cammell. Pat, [Edward Noel] Fitz[Gerald; 1908–1958, Frater *Agape,* IX° O.T.O.], and [journalist Bernard] O'D[onnell]."

Two days later, Crowley saw Greta Sequeira with Pat. Greta fancied trying Crowley's Amrita (food of the gods), the health elixir—probably ignorant of its source. Of Portuguese descent, doctor's daughter Greta, like Pat, studied Anthroposophy. Strong in personality, lover of fast cars (she drove a Packard convertible), a flirt with danger—and with Crowley—she didn't succumb to him who inscribed a poetry book: "To Greta, whom I love, but I'd love much more if she were not so elusive." Greta's long blond hair racing with the wind through Hyde Park Crescent intoxicated the poet.

Crowley also wooed Charles Cammell—for support for Thelema. Buoyant as "a child on gossamer" from an Amrita opus the night before, Crowley bounced into a "glorious lunch" with Cammell on September 28, but: "He's timid—'My job! My wife! My child!' (*air connu*='familiar tune')—but will come on." Crowley wrote to Cammell in November:

Dear Cammell, or indeed rather *Cher Maître,*

Pearl Brooksmith has been telling me that you thought it unwise to get after Simpkin Marshall.* I disagree. (a) To avoid publicity is to plead guilty. (b) People will say that I am afraid. (c) The more the affair is ventilated, the clearer it will become that I am the just man

---

*Simpkin-Marshall broke their contract over distributing *Equinox.* Crowley took legal advice.

made perfect. (d) Of my three libel actions I won two; the third was only lost through the rage of that notorious habitual drunkard *le* [Judge] *Jeffreys de nos jours.* On the other hand if we don't do it, the anthology is wet. Any publisher would shriek with mirth at the idea of including my work.

The moral of this is that you should join the Sacred Band which we are organizing to make secret propaganda for the Law of Thelema. If everyone pulls his weight in the boat, we shall flash past the post in a very few months. I can be very useful indeed to the Government; and as soon as I have demonstrated this fact, I shall have an irresistible weight behind me. I am hampered and delayed by present conditions; you can help greatly if you will. I will ask one of the Band to see you about it.

Shelley, Byron, Rossetti, Swinburne, Burton k.t.l. [et cetera] all met this trouble; but I have been honoured by as much abomination as the lot put together. I am asking you to help to win a victory for all time for all of us. PS Your law not my law?? But my law is the Law of Thelema, and affirms your law because it is yours and not A.C.'s. If you reject the Law of Thelema, you deny your own rights to a law of your own, and offer your wrists to the fetters of an alien law.

666.[5]

October opened with two wins at the West London Chess Club, and a lunchtime powwow with Louis Wilkinson at the Café Royal bar (October 5). Wilkinson had received a game letter from Crowley a fortnight earlier: "I wish you would take part in the aristocratic revival. Is the blood of the Umfravilles cold in your veins? Has Wilkinson been unfrocked?"[6] Edward Grove, meanwhile, advanced in magick, invoking the ninth Aire from the Kelley-Dee system: "pronounced name [of *Aire*] wrong!—most impressive thing he'd ever heard in his life. Am seeing his troubles better now." Grove joined Wilkinson and the Beast for a party on October 12. Commencing with a Café Royal dinner, they trooped back to Welbeck Street with Count and Countess Lewenhaupt, Karl Germer, The Girl Pat, C. R. Cammell, Dolores Sileman, George Roberts, Bernard O'Donnell, Pearl, Driberg, Louis Wilkinson Cleugh, Alan Rae, Helen Grant, Fanny Arnson, Julie. Quite a party!

It is likely Crowley's meeting with psychoanalyst Oscar Kollerstrom (1903–1978) of 11 Cavendish Square on October 21 referred to Crowley's persistent belief he could dominate the Theosophical Society. By 1922, four Theosophist Liberal Catholic Church bishops had resigned over homosexuality. That year Sydney police investigated C. W. Leadbeater (died 1934). Chief witnesses were Theosophist couple Mr. and Mrs. Martyn. Mr. Martyn had seen Leadbeater get into bed with a naked pupil and extinguish the light. The pupil was Oscar Kollerstrom. According to Martyn, Leadbeater had told boys in his care to avoid "unpleasant practices," meaning "women."

The day Crowley met Kollerstrom, he went to the Anglo-Austrian Club to see former secretary Israel Regardie and Regardie's friend, recording engineer, soprano, and folk-song collector Ursula Greville (1894–1991). Her former appointment as editor of the *Sackbut* music magazine had displaced composer Peter Warlock.

A diary reference to Crowley's making a record of the first and second "Enochian Calls" on November 18 (thirty-eighth anniversary of his initiation), and the second and third Aethyrs the next day, probably involved Ursula, first female recording engineer and part owner of Syncrophone Co. Crowley had tea with Regardie on the eighteenth, and, judging from Regardie's inscription of his *Golden Dawn* book to Ursula, Regardie was enamored.

On October 27, Crowley's diary records a visit from War Office official Tom Wylie. Friend of Soviet spy Guy Burgess, with access to British military intelligence, Wylie had a reputation for gay parties in his

*Fig. 5.5. Ursula Greville (1894–1991).*

War Office apartment. According to John Costello's *Mask of Treachery: Spies, Lies, Buggery, and Betrayal,* in the spring of 1936, the Church of England's Foreign Relations Council sponsored Guy Burgess, pro-Nazi Captain John Robert Macnamara, J. H. Sharp (Anglican archdeacon for Southern Europe), and Tom Wylie to escort some boys to a Hitler Youth camp in the Rhineland. According to Burgess, the trip was a homosexual debauch. Crowley's connection to Wylie poses unanswered questions.

Allan Rae's patience at Welbeck Street may have been exhausted, for on October 28, Crowley moved into A. E. Richardson's house at 68 Warren Drive in suburban Surbiton. Richardson had been Crowley's pupil for some time.*

On December 13, Richardson, according to Crowley's diary, "wrote guaranteeing rent of 66 [Redcliffe Gardens, Kensington] for 6 months: backing Pearl's £100 loan for Grove &c. He is to have spare room at 66

*Fig. 5.6. 66 Redcliffe Gardens, Kensington, today.*
*(Author's Collection).*

---

*A news item (Nov. 20, 2007) on the LAShTAL site highlighted an auction of Crowleyana sold by A. E. Richardson's son. The son recalls Crowley's visits, including photographs of Crowley in the garden. The son received Crowley's help with Latin, but according to the son, when Richardson's ability to pay declined, they fell out, Crowley putting messages through neighbors' doors about Richardson's "loose morals." The Crowley book collection included works from the 1940s; Richardson's son misdated the Crowley link from 1928 to the early 1930s.

and contribute his share of expenses. I am to educate him in managing the Work."

Leaving a Turkish bath on December 16 at 12 stone, 8 pounds, 8 ounces,* Crowley "came over and entrenched at 66 Redcliffe Gardens SW10." Four days later, Crowley recorded "Richardson's amazing treachery": typically exaggerated language for, presumably, Richardson's letting him down over rent and/or occupancy.

Meanwhile, Germer's temporary visa having expired, he was instructed to leave. He thought of Belgium, but friends told him Nazi agents kidnapped wanted persons from there, and the Nazis wanted Germer because of his book. Hearing Ireland was a "Free State," he went to Dublin, where an engineering firm hired him. Unlike Crowley, Germer prospered. Crowley wrote to him on December 22:†

> I am installed here, but it has been a fantastic nightmare. It really did require magical operations tumbling over each another. . . . Bracewell arrived on Sunday at 1 o'clock to fix everything up with Richardson. He had not come; he had not sent an apology; and that moth-eaten wife of his was playing monkey tricks on the telephone. [Bracewell, Houghton, and Richardson were involved in a publication project] . . . Pearl is here with John [son], but they are going to Eastbourne tomorrow.
>
> I have never met such futile, fumbling foozlers as the Atlantis Bookshop crowd. But "rats and mice and such small deer have been Tom's food for many a year." There are innumerable important pieces of work to be done, and I cannot make a start on any of them.[8]

It wasn't just Crowley. The British Empire was in a pickle, too. On December 11, King Edward VIII, proclaimed king emperor on January 21, abdicated for love of twice-divorced Mrs. Wallis Simpson of

---

*Crowley took "adiposettes" (*Reiss Chemische Werke*) from September, and the diuretic uricedin, often abused by weight watchers. The following month he required an "aertex belt." Had Greta Sequeira made him weight conscious?

†Another undated letter suggested to Germer an alternative option to Dublin: "Those anti-Nazis might pay you a trip to California & fix you a lecture tour. And you might marry a rich Jewess. Do!"[7]

Baltimore. To Crowley's disgust, marital status rendered her unsuitable, and when besotted King Edward refused to relinquish her, the throne passed to his brother, Prince Albert George. Crowley fancied making a few bob with "Bring Back Our King" badges. In his view, George VI's succession was illegitimate; Crowley liked Edward VIII's sense of liberal independence. History has not favored Crowley's preference.

## SIX

# Living in a Turkish Bath

I am giving a series of four lectures on Yoga which I think will cover about half the subject, in which case I shall have to do four more and call them Advanced Yoga. All this is very good, as it keeps me tremendously busy, and not so good as it keeps me penniless.[1]

So wrote Crowley to Germer from 66 Redcliffe Gardens on January 22, 1937. Despite dismal weather, 666 delivered his first "Yoga for Yellowbellies" lecture on February 17 at the Eiffel Tower Hotel & Restaurant, 1 Percy Street, Fitzrovia, informing Germer on the twenty-sixth: "Everything here is bust up again, but the lectures are going better all the time. I am thinking of giving a third series, probably on Magick, in a public hall, and having it properly advertised. . . . I am at present living in a Turkish bath, and I simply do not know what to do about anything. I may be more settled in a week or two."[2] Two days after posting that letter his "Serpent's kiss" tooth broke off in the "Turker." "Alas!" cried Crowley.

Meetings with Edward Grove (who offered to help Pearl with accommodation), Eve Brachenburg, new girlfriend Meg Usher, the "Girl Pat," and Maud Amslie punctuated February—one of the worst London winters Crowley could recall. Poet, journalist, and wine merchant Bruce Blunt "kidnapped" him on February 20 for an alcoholic weekend in Bramdean, Hampshire, and the Cricketer's Arms, near Alresford (still running). Included in J. C. Squire's anthology of *Modern Poets* (1932), Blunt is best remembered for collaborations with Peter Warlock (Philip Arnold Heseltine, 1894–1930). He first met Warlock around 1927

75

when Warlock regularly met composers Constant Lambert and William Walton at Eynsford, Kent. In *Frederick Delius and Peter Warlock: A Friendship Revealed,* Blunt is described as "bon viveur, poet, journalist, and writer on wine, gardening, and the turf."

On March 3, a destitute Crowley moved to the Grosvenor Hotel with Pearl (Richardson having let him down) and gave his third lecture on yoga at the Eiffel Tower. A week later he spent "all night with [Vyvyan] Deacon and Simpson the chef." Vivienne Browning's biography of her father, *An Uncommon Medium* (1993), recalled the late-night drinking sessions that so upset Deacon's Chinese wife, Eunice.

In mid-March, Pearl Brooksmith issued a mimeographed pamphlet to Louis Wilkinson and Karl Germer to attend a guided demonstration of astral traveling:

> Do what thou wilt shall be the whole of the Law. Travelling on the astral plane at 32 Fairhazel Gardens N.W.6. [South Hampstead] Wednesday, March 17, at 8:30 p.m. THE MASTER THERION will give a personal demonstration Admission 2/6. Please tell— and bring your friends. Love is the law, love under will. Pearl Brooksmith.[3]

Crowley's diary for March 17 tells us what occurred:

> Group doing astral travel including Hylton, Pearl, Hugh . . . Eve Brachenburg had good visions. Eileen Curtis couldn't do it, but was shown a gate—BAB!! [Hebrew and Arabic for "gate"]

Moving to a "garret" at 41 Duke Street at 15/- a week (raised to 30/- for what Crowley called the "mock Coronation" of George VI on May 12), Crowley felt he'd hit a new low. . He was back at the Grosvenor on the twenty-fourth. On March 20 he recorded opus forty-five with Adele Lindsay, while a timely seven pounds came from Germer; he could purchase a suit and do business.

Crowley hoped to see Germer at the month's end, but there hangs a tale. Germer's employers wanted him to do business in Belgium. He went to Belgium for a new refugee visa, then to the British passport office in Brussels for a proper visa to Ireland. Sailing to Harwich, he was turned back to Belgium. Attempting to obtain a French visa to regularize his Dublin residence, his Belgian refugee visa prevented it. Returning to Dublin, he was asked after several weeks to leave Ireland— the Irish justice minister telling him that if he could get the *German ambassador* to withdraw his objection to his being in Ireland, a visa was his. Germer contacted *Irish Times* editor Mr. Smylie. Recognizing the fifth column influence, Smylie wished the Dail would too. As is well known, Irish president de Valera favored Hitler. Returning to Brussels, Germer prospered, exporting machinery to England, but visa applications for England were denied. Crowley again tried to place Germer's "Protective Prisoner No. 303," this time (at Germer's suggestion) contacting senior German Conservative People's Party politician Gottfried Reinhold Treviranus (1891–1971). Narrowly escaping S.S. assassins during the Night of the Long Knives in 1934, Treviranus only just reached England to advise Churchill and Anthony Eden about Hitler's character and expansionist plans. Meeting Treviranus on April 14, Crowley was charmed. Treviranus connected him with one Mayer who requested formal authorization to handle the manuscript on April 15. Crowley also wrote to publisher Stanley Unwin. Praising the draft manuscript, Crowley insisted people were sick of so-called professionally well-written stuff (a rewrite had been suggested). Its directness was its strength. He enclosed it to Germer should he want to send it; Germer never did. Germer's manuscript remains unpublished.

On April 25, Blunt took Crowley to the Tichborn Dole, a twelfth-century festival of flour donations, the kind of English tradition that excited Blunt, Warlock, and aficionados of the era's English folk revival.

*Fig. 6.1. Augustus John.*

Crowley met Augustus John off the train at Victoria on the twenty-seventh. As they crossed London to Paddington, Luftwaffe Junker 52 bombers, supporting Franco, descended on the Basque town of Guernica, killing thousands of civilians out for market day. German fighters machine-gunned survivors while incendiary bombs razed the town into a stinking, burning hell.

Crowley wrote to Germer on April 30: he'd struck his worst patch in years. His brain wouldn't work, and all he had left was "courage." In desperation, he designed a crush barrier to deal with overspilling crowds, perhaps thinking of the forthcoming coronation. He drew a design. Its novelty consisted in a plate that, when crowds stepped onto it, kept the barrier upright. He put it to "Blokaert of Reservations Ltd, 45 Pall Mall" ("a nasty bit of work," but Crowley thought he'd found a helpful contact) and suggested Germer's engineering contacts make and market it in the United States and elsewhere. He organized a meeting with Scotland Yard to demonstrate its usefulness to police or troops. Crowley's contact let him down.

He composed a quatorzain, "To Deirdre in Labour," on March 26. Labor ended on May Day with the birth of a son, in Newcastle, or as Crowley noted: *Natus est Filius 666,* sending the boy's horary information to Germer on May 13. The "general picture," 666 wrote, "reminds me of Mustapha Kemal as described in *Gray Wolf . . .* sixpenny Penguin series [a biography he'd just read]. We need one." Kemal "Ataturk" had unified Turkey behind him in a secular state—and that's how Crowley's son by Deirdre Doherty became "Aleister Ataturk [father of the Turks] Crowley," though Deirdre called him Randall Gair. Crowley added to Germer: "Apart from this really wonderful news, things are awful. Unless I can snaffle this Crush Barrier job, I have nowhere to sleep tonight."[4]

On May 22 he resigned himself: "Grove has his wish. I move to 11 Manor Place W2." South of the Thames, Manor Place is in Walworth near St. Mary's church, south of Elephant & Castle. Writing to Germer, he noted of the address, "for the next few days, I fear," adding, "I am living in a very foul slum. The stench is ghastly. There is no food and no hope. Yorke and Grove have their wish. The Asthma has returned."[5]

Still, he managed meetings with Eve Brachenburg, Grove, Pearl,

*Fig. 6.2. 9 Manor Place, Walworth, today,*
*first door on the right.*
*(Author's Collection)*

Edward Noel Fitzgerald, Cammell, Julia (for "cunnilingus"), and a first encounter with Bobby Barfoot on June 25. Clifford Bax (1886–1962), brother of writer and composer Arnold Bax, arranged a dinner for Crowley at the Royal Automobile Club on June 9. Crowley hadn't a clean shirt, couldn't pay his rent, and felt his nerves going; Pearl was at her wit's end—but June 9 marked an important meeting. Bax introduced Crowley to Frieda, Lady Harris (1877–1962), wife of Liberal M.P. Sir Percy Harris, then of 15 North Court, Wood Street, Westminster (they would move to Morton House, Chiswick, at the year's end).

Having met thirty-two-year-old Gabriel Toyne (1905–1963) in May at the Author's Club, the pair enjoyed a "great lunch" on June 18.

*Fig. 6.3. Gabriel Toyne.*

Corpus Christi, Oxford graduate Toyne, poet, actor, Indian linguist, and fencer, left Oxford to stage manage Esmé Percy's company, then turned impresario in Australia, where he and wife Margaret discovered dancer Robert Helpmann, bringing him back to England where Toyne specialized in fight arranging, flashing blades with the stars on major film and theatrical productions. Crowley was thinking of *Mortadello*.

July 1937 saw a gathering to gain subscribers for *The Equinox of the Gods*—possibly at the Atlantis—attended by Cammell, Fitzgerald, Adele Brand, Grove, O'Donnell, Carmela Koenig, Gerald Yorke, Eve Brachenburg, Bobby Barfoot, Professor Henri Chellew, "Chinese Terror" Julia, Edmee, Augustus John, and Mavis de Vere Cole (wife of practical joker Horace de Vere Cole—John's mistress).

On July 5, Crowley's skills brought him victory in one game in four when, as he put it, he "took chess lessons" from Austrian-British chess master and author Ernest Ludwig Klein (1910–1990). He'd play Klein again on September 27 and win the first game. Klein was a Viennese Jew recently migrated to England.

At the month's end, Buchenwald concentration camp was opened.

The LAShTAL Aleister Crowley Society website reported a sale by Adrian Harrington's Rare Books in September 2011 of a letter on Piccadilly Hotel stationery, with stamped Langham Hotel envelope, postmarked July 12, 1937. In it, Crowley admonished a pupil for poor effort: "Adventure is to the adventurous. You ring off before one has time to get 10 yards to the instrument and wail 'no answer.'" "As long as there is all this fear in imagination and feebleness in execution, who is going to trust you with a job on which the fate of millions might depend?" In his P.S., Crowley gave the hapless student another chance: "You have got to see me on Monday. It's up to you to manage it. I shan't try to avoid you, but shan't give you my itinerary. If you succeed, we'll try something bolder at once." Judging from Crowley's diary (September 21), the likely recipient was Edward Grove: "Grove—the man that pranced up to the Temple door, got cold feet at the idea of entering, turned and proclaimed 'There's nobody home.'"

Crowley's attention again turned to A.M.O.R.C., spending several hours on July 26 with occultist, musician, author, music publisher,

Atlantis habitué, and U.K. A.M.O.R.C. publisher Jean Michaud (born Johan Grotendorst, 1884–1961) and alternative health practitioner Professor Henry Chellew at Manor Place. Crowley would meet Michaud for a long talk about Spencer Lewis on August 20 when Michaud let out that Chellew was "a wind-bag."

E. N. Fitzgerald and wife Phyllis cooked Crowley a curry on August 1. Having taken him home, they were given pictures for their kindness. After seeing Pat the next morning, Bruce Blunt drove him— or perhaps him and Pat—to Hampshire, but the car broke down outside Alton. A garage man took them to Blunt's cottage, but a sour-faced Blunt only thawed later, perhaps after Crowley discovered the Castle of Comfort Inn at Medstead near Alton. Some time that day 666 performed an opus with Pat. Purpose: "Let it as it will." He was also performing fairly regular IX° ops with Bobby Barfoot.

Poverty's noose tightened. On Friday, August 6, his "Nuit" ring went the way of the pawnshop, but providence appeared when Crowley received a letter from artist Frieda Harris, written on August 3:

Dear Mr. Crowley,

I am so sorry I have been away since we met—and I fear I must have appeared to be very rude.

Thank you so much for offering to give me a pretense. I shall appreciate it very much.

We have let our flat and I have no abiding city for the moment but it would give me great pleasure if you will lunch with me at the Queens Restaurant Sloane Square on Friday, August 13th, at 1:30 p.m. Will you reply—

c/o Mrs. Blanche
57 Petersham Road
Richmond
Yours sincerely,

Frieda Harris

A "great lunch" was had. Perhaps they discussed Frieda's interest in Steiner's Anthroposophy and Co-Masonry—Steiner had received an O.T.O. charter from Reuss to work part of the Antient & Primitive Rites.

*Fig. 6.4. Photographer Cecil Beaton with a lady identified as Frieda, Lady Harris. (Courtesy of the Warburg Institute, London)*

The subject was probably art—Frieda was experimenting with projective geometry, experiments that bore fruit in her great project with Crowley to come. That evening, Crowley enjoyed a "greater dinner" with Tom Driberg and *Daily Express* features editor John Rayner. Driberg had kindly printed off obituary material on Crowley's old friend, popular science writer J. W. N. Sullivan, who he'd heard had died on August 12.

Disquieting news came with a letter from Martha Küntzel on the twenty-fourth. The Gestapo had taken Norwegian-German Thelemite Friedrich Lekve (1904–1956). Crowley checked the I Ching: "What is the case? [hexagram] 36 *Ming I* Wounded Intelligence. Confirms that the Nazis have got him."*

---

*On September 25, 1937, Crowley learned the Gestapo had raided Lekve: "all books and MSS. Stolen; even my pictures of Sahara destroyed!" Crowley looked to the I Ching for "the future of the Nazi regime" and got hexagram 28, *Ta Kuo:* the weak beam. An undated letter to Germer, around New Year 1937–38 reported the Gestapo had also suppressed Heinrich Tränker's *Collegium Pansophicum.* "Laugh that one off!" wrote Crowley to Germer.

# A.M.O.R.C. AGAIN

On September 9, Fitzgerald arrived early to help Crowley pack for a few days at a bungalow in Camber on the East Sussex coast. While packing, Crowley was amazed to find Yarker's original charter appointing him 90° and 95° of the Antient & Primitive Rites of Memphis and Misraim: predating connection with Reuss or the O.T.O. Dispatching a photostat to Germer to impress new contact Marc Lanval, in Brussels, Crowley "devastated" Michaud with it that evening: "He [Michaud] will think up a plan." He then ran into Pat at the Café Royal: "stupid as usual," but "the boy" was coming on fine.

A pseudonym of Joseph-Paul Swenne (1898–1955), Marc Lanval, naturist sex reformer, author of *An Enquiry into the Intimate Lives of Women* was editor of *Lumière et Liberté* ("Light and Liberty"), official organ of his Belgian League of Heliophile (sun-loving) Propaganda, founded in 1924. Lanval believed the Nazi mentality came from a "homosexual psyche" only countered by full female equality. As "Sar Helios" (stealing a title from Joséphin Péladan) he represented the Belgian Co-Masonic Antient & Primitive Rites involved in Lewis's ("Sar Alden") and others' 1934 assembly of Martinist and Rosicrucian Orders in federation (F.U.D.O.S.I.). The A&P Rites, deemed "spiritual" (i.e., favored by Theosophists), were the sole Masonic Rites admitted. Lewis's rationale was to exclude "false prophets" from misleading seekers (i.e., Crowley and Clymer). Crowley wanted Germer to sound Lanval out and considered a day trip to Brussels (Lanval ran a nudist community in a nearby village). Germer should approach Lanval thus: "He is an honest man, so am I. Lewis is a *fraud*. Lewis plays the Jesus-morality game; M.L. [Lanval] and I are agin it. I have Yarker and Reuss's Charters. What has M.L.?" Germer should "stand prepared to blow Lewis sky high when I give the word—ie: when I have reached USA and started trouble." Crowley wanted to be "Secret Head" of A.M.O.R.C., overseeing proper running, teaching "sense" with value for money.

Crowley's charter discovery perhaps refocused attention on Smith and the California community. An undated letter to Jane Wolfe probably comes from this time. The notepaper indicates the Imperial Hotel, Russell Square, but Crowley drew an arrow to it: "No, I have not come down to this yet! I'm passing by." The rant begins:

Blast *Wilfrid!* [Smith] Why has he not written me a word during the last 7 months? Or sent me any contributions? It has meant the severest privations, and a complete block in the Work at the exact time when a little extra might have turned the wheel altogether. I am really very annoyed. Not answering his letters; acknowledging the Word, is infuriating. In fact, I actually am infuriated. What is the use of any one of you? I had built great hopes upon your efforts, and you did seem to be getting somewhere. And now, what does it all amount to?[6]

Another rant was sent to Smith on September 6:

Dear Lord God, you are all dead from the neck up! Here are all the most important events in the Lewis-Clymer dog-fight, and I learn about them from strangers. What's the good of having a man on the spot? Damn it, you ought to be "on the spot" in the Chicago sense of the phrase. Do get wise to yourself and keep me posted! Shall write again on the 23rd.[7]

Crowley spent the evening of September 14 with Michaud and Chellew, noting in his diary: "Lewis is in full retreat: drops the A [Ancient] off A.M.O.R.C. from his advertisements! *Quelle crapule* [scoundrel]!" Crowley contacted Germer:

—[Spencer Lewis] seems to hope that will clear up all the trouble! So he is on the run. I want to know at once: (1) has Lanval—who is fiercely attacked in the Clymer book—ever had authority from anyone we ever heard of (E.g. Reuss, Papus, de Guaita, Péladan) (2) could he and would he work under and with me, using S.L.'s [Lewis's] dependence on him to take away the Amorc crowd from Lewis and rally them to AL 93? (3) Could M.L. come to London this weekend or next—and talk things over with me? Please hussle this: get him to come if possible. If you want to telephone me, PAD 1580 before 10 A.M. is a safe bet.[8]

On the seventeenth he began a "93 Protocol" for Michaud, beginning: "On this planet all is Trouble and Confusion." The plan was for a secret government of the world, led by Crowley invisibly, uniting world esoteric orders dedicated to freeing humanity.

Two days later he saw Liberal Catholic Church bishop Frederick James at "The Sanctuary," 23 Basil Street, near the back of Harrods. Interested in James's preaching, he'd visited on August 8, finding it shut. Crowley thought the setting good, "aura fair," adding: "Service mediocre. His elocution very poor. Spoke wisely, but without force. He was however very long on receiving the Divoine Loight!" (mimicking a Midlands accent).* He informed Germer on November 1 that "he teaches our stuff correct on nearly all points; differences negligible. I am trying to borrow his Church for lectures on Magick etc."[9]

Frustrated at Germer's not pursuing his strategy, Crowley asked why Germer started things, then withdrew, complaining of head pain? Was there something in Germer's "skull theory"? Had he suffered a traumatic head injury? "I have known you to rage at the suggestion to play a game of chess. There is something in your mind which makes quite trivial thoughts produce really agonizing pain. The same thing happens to me, but the exciting cause is always when I am impotent to do something really important, especially when the trouble is that any one who could and should help won't do so."[10] Could Germer at least get Lanval to tell the truth about Lewis and Co. openly, and "make a statement about how FUDOSI was faked? I want it for private use and not publication."[11] *And where did Lanval get his 96° from? Reuss, Papus?* Little more emerged from Germer on the subject. In late October Crowley went to the *Daily Herald* with an A.M.O.R.C. story, but its female reporter failed to appear.

Crowley met Dr. Anthony Greville-Gascoyne amid polished oak and dark leather at the sedate Author's Club at 1 Whitehall Place on September 24. Acquaintance probably came through Israel Regardie and Ursula Greville. Founder of an East Yorkshire esoteric society, "The Brothers of the Path," alternative psychoanalyst Greville-Gascoyne, like

---

*Crowley's diary, October 13: "Heard Bishop James talk—pure A.C." October 31: "Communicated [took communion] at the Sanctuary. James stated practically all my teaching: even quoted 93 as the Word of the Great Master." He receiving a letter from James on November 1, and they corresponded, meeting on November 6.

Regardie, admired Dion Fortune's Order of the Inner Light. Crowley probably repeated his view that Regardie's recently published Golden Dawn book was a lift from the *Equinox,* with poor drawings.

Crowley spent a quiet Sunday on October 3 editing *The Heart of the Master* (the Master named as "Khaled [eternal] Khan [chief]"), issued by the O.T.O. in 1938 as a rallying call "to fight for Freedom" in the coming cataclysm, foretold in this pocket-apocalypse as a devastating war ("If you want Freedom, you must to fight. If you want to Fight, contact the O.T.O." at a P.O. Box number).

Regular Freemason Louis T. Culling of 816 Broadway, San Diego, had recently contacted Crowley; 666 sent him and Mrs. Diane Culling Thelemic material on October 14. "Louie" Culling met Smith in September, after quitting the Choronzon Club when Russell repudiated *The Book of the Law.* Culling's direct contact with Crowley made him reluctant to play second fiddle for either Schneider or Smith. Owning over 200 acres in the Rainbow Valley near the Palomar Hills, he suggested Crowley (who was expected soon) might enjoy his shack there. Misunderstanding, Schneider told Crowley Culling was deeding his land to Crowley. Excited, Crowley got back to ensure it didn't come under Smith's Church of Thelema umbrella. Twenty acres *was* eventually deeded to the O.T.O. in 1939; the Church of Thelema received forty acres in 1941.

Hearing of Justice Swift's demise on October 19, Crowley commented: "The drunken blackguard Swift dead. (N.B. The sot's swinish injustice gave me the best thing that ever happened: Deirdre and Ataturk!)" Strangely perhaps, the judge's death followed soon after September 30, when Crowley had a peculiar vision of the gold scales of justice statue above the Old Bailey criminal courts: "Saw the Old Bailey surmounted by a gilt statue, holding out the sword of murder and the scales to weigh gold against injustice."

He saw Deirdre for lunch at the Café Royal on October 24, and they dined a week later at Bengali Shah Abdul Majid Qureshi's new Dilkush Delight restaurant in Windmill Street, Soho (*dilkush* means "happy heart"); 666 was also seeing a "colored" girl called Phyllis.

Cash, and the lack of it, was a perennial sore. He informed Germer from Manor Place on November 18 that he'd had no fire for two days, as he lacked a shilling for the meter, and no help arrived from Yorke, who, he said, didn't even try to imitate a "gentleman" any more, becoming cruder and coarser (this probably means Yorke refrained from settling Crowley's charges). Still, 666 worked on "without lust of result." Germer sent him a quid, and Crowley gave it as a "sop" to his landlady, in lieu of rent owed. He needed money to pay for prospectuses and binding for *The Equinox of the Gods,* whose release via the Atlantis simply had to coincide with the winter solstice. Germer advanced the binder's debt.

Crowley busied himself in December at the Atlantis with Mike Houghton, packing and posting prospectuses for *The Equinox of the Gods:* for Crowley a momentous publication destined to coincide with, or even initiate, a war. There were numerous conflicts to choose from. On November 28, Franco warned the Republican government to surrender by December 12 or face an overwhelming offensive, while Japan's invasion of China centered on Nanjing—Beijing having fallen. Germany rattled swords over Austria and the Sudetenland.

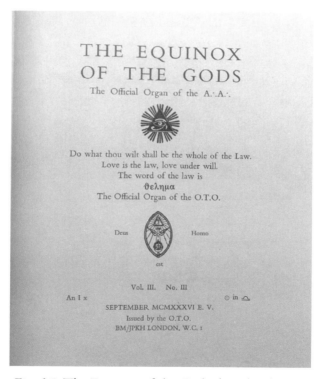

*Fig. 6.5. The Equinox of the Gods (1937) title page. (Courtesy: Ordo Templi Orientis; 100th Monkey Press)*

Crowley talked with photographer V. D. Freedland (or "Syphilis" for short, Crowley quipped), who'd create enduring images of the Beast. Bobby Barfoot performed sex magick for health while Crowley cadged money from any source to keep going, and then came the Big Day, reported by Tom Driberg in "These Names Make News."

Freedland and Yorke, both acting "nobly" according to Crowley, collected five people of the five races (red, yellow, black, brown, white), and took them to one Erskine's room for a party. Deadly dull until hangers-on left, out came the whiskey, and the band trooped to Cleopatra's Needle for the solstice: Wednesday, December 22, 1937, 6:22 a.m. when the "sixty-two year-old magician," as Driberg described Crowley, presented each of the representatives of the world's races with a beautiful copy of *The Equinox of the Gods* and made a Magical Utterance. Crowley informed Driberg that publications of *Liber AL* usually caused a war. *Wasn't that a bit hard on the human race?* asked Driberg. "Ah, if only they'd do what I tell them, it could be avoided." *Somehow,* Driberg concluded, he did not think they would. Foyle's, still sitting on unsold copies of *Magick,* avoided it.

Over Christmas, Crowley suffered with wrenching asthma-bronchitis: "Thick black fog filling lungs with soot, so that I spat black." Perhaps he recalled his positive note of November 21, stimulated by similar winter conditions of the bad old days before smokeless fuel: "Horrible fog. But even fog is evidence of the Sun my father!"

Crowley spent New Year's Eve with one mark of solace amid a generally dead atmosphere: "Rollo Ahmed rang up: the luck-bringing Black Man." Was it only luck he needed?

**SEVEN**

# Seriously on the Path

Rollo Ahmed's call led Crowley to a New Year's Day party at Allan Rae's, where he "explained Aeon-commotions" to photographer Freedland and Laurence Felkin—the commotions being world events interpreted as Aeon of Horus birth pangs. On March 14 Vienna's streets would throb with Austrians joyfully welcoming Hitler after he annexed their country, his birthplace. Yorke gave Crowley lunch at the Escargot on January 5, though Crowley found Yorke disappointing: "Seems to think the G∴W∴ [Great Work] is a jolly lark. He will be enlightened." At the end of the month, 666 wrote to Smith: "Push 93 as the sole way out of the dilemma of Fascism-Communism. Talk of American Liberty. Go after 'em in big plain simple words and ideas."[1] A related thought occurred to him on February 21: "Fascism must always fail because it creates the discontent it is designed to suppress."

After a long break, Smith wrote on January 18. He had three young recruits: Phyllis Pratt, Lew Carroll (Deacon), and Carroll's wife Toni. Toni soon left for another man, to Lew's relief, making way for Paul Seckler, twenty-two, Phyllis's sweetheart. Smith reckoned they'd stick. Regina brought four or five of her drama pupils to read from the *Equinox* on Friday evenings. Heeding Crowley's cry for funds, Smith emptied the O.T.O. coffers ($50), expressing his admiration:

> Your letter is cheery despite everything. You sure have intestinal forti-
> tude, or, in the vernacular, guts. Yes, when a man plays almost a lone
> hand for nearly half a century "In the Reign of a tortured lamb and
> the realm of a sexless Owl" he certainly has got 'em. Love from all.[2]

The Beast had much ado about thespians in 1938, meeting Esmé Percy (1887–1957) on January 31 to discuss *Mortadello*. Remembered as slippery Zoltan Kapasi in Gabriel Pascal's *Pygmalion* (1938), starring Leslie Howard, Percy appeared in some forty movies between 1930 and 1956. Crowley reminded Smith on January 31 that now that "famous English producer" Gabriel Toyne had accepted *Mortadello,* surely Smith could place it as a movie.[3]

On February 2, after "a perfect steak," an "A.1" Clos Vougeot and "excellent brandy after a struggle" at the Adam & Eve in Wells Street, Crowley and Bruce Blunt explored the nearby M. Knoedler & Co. gallery at 15 Old Bond Street where the Toulouse-Lautrec *Paintings & Drawings* exhibition had its final day. A few days later, Crowley dreamt he was running Germany for Hitler with a horse called Sultan.

Lady Harris rang on February 6, encouraging Crowley to phone Esmé Percy before leaving for Casa Prada in Marylebone Road where he again encountered Constant Lambert at 1:30. Casa Prada was the second home and eatery for many musicians; T. S. Eliot frequented it, as did conductor Edward Clark and composer Elizabeth Lutyens, as her memoirs recorded:

> How well I remember many happy evenings there: Constant Lambert's latest clerihew, Parry Jones's stories. . . Dallapiccola reciting Dante . . . and Edward's resounding laugh ringing out.[4]

Crowley returned to dreary Manor Place at 5 p.m. in time for an opus with Bobby—"better than ever"—aimed to "put over 93."

On February 9 a "very blithe and loving" Deirdre and Ataturk joined Crowley and Gerald Yorke for lunch. A couple of days later, Crowley noted caustically: "Never run after a woman. You may possibly catch her." Who was he thinking of—surely not Pat, with whom he shared "lunch of sorts" that day at the Fitzroy Tavern on Charlotte Street, haunt of literary types and bohemians such as George Orwell, Nina Hamnett, Dylan Thomas, Augustus John, and Jacob Epstein. He went to Prada, where, having "feigned not to notice" Constant Lambert, he was miffed when the Felkins "butted in." Then Bobby showed up. The resulting brew was "hellishly boring, humiliating, and expensive." Even the opus with Bobby "to establish 93" was "very poor."

*Fig. 7.1. 57 Petersham Road today.*
*(Author's Collection)*

Thinking he'd got his moment to warm Lambert up at Casa Prada on February 13—the Cammells walked in! But peace there was, for the wicked. A "delightful" lunch was spent with Frieda Harris on the eighteenth in the sunlit window overlooking the Thames at 57 Petersham Road, where Frieda loved to paint. His comment: "She is seriously on the Path." Seeing her again on the twenty-second: "I think she'll find a job for the Masters soon." Right again.

Meanwhile in California, Roy Leffingwell, composer and professional voice announcer, took the probationer's oath on February 24. Crowley felt good about Roy, sensing he'd be stalwart, while—thanks to Roosevelt's WPA educational program—Regina's "Kahl Players," a dramatic troupe Smith reckoned would in time become the "O.T.O. Players," performed Crowley's *Three Wishes*. Several of Regina's students, Smith teased Crowley, had movie contracts, guided by "excellent director" Regina.[5] Crowley had theater on the mind. Frieda sent "two plays" to Gabriel Toyne's wife, stage star Margaret Rawlings (1906–1996; divorced in May), and to theater manager Ashley Dukes (1885–1959).

On March 11 Crowley lunched with Anthony Greville-Gascoyne

who'd distributed 150 copies of *AL* through an A.M.O.R.C. mailing list and whose new *Golden Dawn* magazine favorably reviewed *The Equinox of the Gods*. Ursula Greville's tarot article in June's issue possibly stimulated Crowley to posit the tarot as territory to conjoin with Frieda's artistry.

Shropshire lass Mrs. Sally Pace, thirty-two, of 55 Iverson Road, Kilburn NW6, entered Crowley's life on March 25. Their opus: the "best this year" (Sally was menstruating). Its aim: money (*Aur* = "gold"). Walking up to Kilburn on April 2, he found her again amid Iverson Road's soot-stained, late-Victorian terraces.

Crowley addressed Jane Wolfe on March 26:

> You haven't written to me lately and I miss your letters. They were always so fantastically senseless and irritating that they really did me good. I like to have the news, too, from your angle. But you don't seem to have any! *Mortadello* has been accepted for London, and will I hope be played this year. It makes a great gangster-in-high-life film, and you must be imbecile if you can't sell it. Best of all to you![6]

## HITLER AND GERMANY ACCORDING TO PROTECTIVE PRISONER NO. 303

Probably occasioned by Hitler's having declared himself supremo of all Germany's armed forces, dubbed the *Oberkommando der Wehrmacht*, on February 4—before the *Anschluss Österreichs*—Crowley confided to Germer a prematurely optimistic take on Hitler's fate:

> Dear friend, Adolph has done it this time, we all think. I doubt if he'll last another 6 months; after perhaps some futile military coup, Germany should settle down to a quiet Republic. People are getting tired of extremists everywhere. We have got Musso by the balls, and shall be free to mop up the Japs. Such seems the plan.[7]

Germer's responses to this sunny outlook so impressed Crowley he asked Frieda to show them to Sir Percy Harris as intelligence useful to government, while hoping to ease Germer's path to a visa via the Home Office.[8]

Germer considered the Nazis "Grand Masters of the inferiority complex," given to revenge by atrocity, fired by an "obstinate, possessed fanaticism." Since 1918 the German people had had weakened nerves and by constitution were unable to react to facts and adjust, like the English. Germans still believed they had some great mission to civilization and were not content leaving to other countries what they believed they could do better. As for settling down quietly, there was too much ambition, frustration, and virility still to be released. Sometime in the future the cultural links of senior members of the armed forces made a mutiny or plot against Hitler likely. In the meantime, no one should underestimate German ability to fight proudly to the very last drop of blood, to the last man, even if cornered. *Treue,* meaning "loyalty," faith, German honor would not be surrendered to quiet living, even if sacrifice were *absolutely pointless.* Hitler might ultimately go the way of the suicidal maniac, but before then, his following would be determined to light a fuse of utter destruction and show the world what they could do. Germer said the English did not grasp German character as the French did, who'd had more cause to study it.

Germer believed the Versailles, St. Germain, and Trianon treaties were disastrous follies. Reclaiming lost territories was admirable and necessary. If Germany did not act peremptorily, the Allies would block it. As for Czechoslovakia, before the war, its culture was German, Germer insisted; he knew it well. Three and a half million now lived under Czech rule. History was helping Hitler. England and France were weak; Russia was committing suicide. Why couldn't the French and British understand what was likely? He compared them to King Cnut: don't argue with the forces of Nature. Germer's thoughts were complex. Who could say warrior god Ra Hoor Khuit of *AL* chapter 3 would use methods acceptable to the Archbishop of Canterbury?

Liberal Chief Whip Sir Percy Harris (1876–1952) responded to Germer's analysis on October 13:

My dear Crowley,

I was very interested to read your friend's memorandum written in Brussels. Of course I know there is a lot of truth in what he says and that the Allies blundered badly especially the French in their treatment of Germany in the years immediately after the War. The only

*Fig. 7.2. Sir Percy Harris (1876–1952).*

thing that can be said in their defence is that it is nothing to what would have been if Germany had been victorious. However it is no use "crying over spilt milk." The Germans are now so strong that they are a real menace to the independence of the States that surround them.

It is interesting to note that a man who has suffered from the Natzi [*sic*] Terror views with favour their foreign policy.

Yours sincerely,

Percy A Harris[9]

A meeting was planned with Esmé Percy for March 31. Crowley wrote optimistically to Germer:

I dine with Lady H[arris]. on Thursday to meet a famous actor, Esmé Percy who thinks *Mortadello* "magnificent," and wants to play it. It would help me much if I could appear decently clothed and pay for a drink after dinner, perhaps. So, if you should have a bit of luck. ... If we really come to terms re Mortadello, it means *complete* relief from all financial worry. He's taking it for London would mean a sure sale of film rights for cash. So do what you can![10]

After he met Lady Harris and Esmé Percy at Czardas at 8 p.m., it was so noisy they moved to the Escargot at 48 Greek Street, Soho, talking until midnight: "All O.K. But it looks like a long job." Crowley wrote to Germer on the Sunday: "Thursday dinner went well. Hope to hear some more next week. Meanwhile, Nat Ayer [who wrote "If You Were the Only Girl in the World" for The Bing Boys, 1916] is tackling M.G.M. about it."[11] Co-writer of "Oh, You Beautiful Doll" Nat Ayer (1887–1952) went bankrupt in 1938. Two days after the meeting, Crowley asked if Germer *was* doing the IX° with friend Louise Piazza, could he dedicate it to film rights? Success would reward "the few that have helped me . . . while rich swine like Yorke and Grove stood by and gloated."[12]

Crowley received a ghostly visitation on April 5, when the late Vyvyan Deacon "came in about 7 a.m. Taller, thinner, paler than in life. Dressed in whitish suit of flannels. Seemed to want to speak, but I heard nothing." Two days later he met Frieda at 4:30 at Bentley's Oyster Bar and Grill, 11–15 Swallow Street, St. James's. Telling Germer about the lobster dinner, he said he'd given Frieda a "verbal dose of Concentration Camp," so would Germer *please* send her the first draft whose so-called faults were its virtues. In the meantime, Frieda informed him the Home Office was "run by a dour Scots female and is *non compos mentis*."[13]

Crowley's life had become a whirlwind of appointments, but as he complained to Germer, it was horrible feeling unable to entertain people at his "slum," return invitations, or even obtain dinner dress.

On April 12, he met mental nurse Mrs. Mattie Pickett, widow, living with one son at 139 Alderney Street, a basement flat in Pimlico. Born August 12, 1904, in Galveston, Texas, Mattie Marguerite Maria Razzal was, he informed Germer, "intelligent, romantic, poetical (won $400 for a poem at 14!!!) passionate, pure Thelemite. Has been living for ten years by 'Do what thou wilt' told her by a journalist! So, you see, it does work! A staggerer to have a stranger start to convert me!"[14] He requested from Germer a detailed horary judgment, as Crowley thought she could become "really important." Mattie and Beast performed the IX° on April 22: "The best for years: the perfect mate." Next day he enjoyed a "gorgeous lunch" with Grove's wife, Euphemia, and on Tuesday, April 26, a "good lunch" at Hatchett's Hotel and Tavern at 66–68 Piccadilly with Charles Cammell's wife, Iona. He later took sherry with Gerald Yorke—"not a bad chat"—but it was a very "tigerish day," followed by an evening "snapping at other jungle beasts," while he "couldn't find a good tigress." Having recovered his dress clothes from Whiteley's Furniture Depositories, Laundry and Stables, West Kensington, on the twenty-seventh, he shared an opus with Phyllis Rosamund Hunt aimed at "Gold." Things were looking up, he told Germer: Lady Harris had a good producer interested, and Ashley Dukes might "lend them a theatre," while he hoped to meet London's "best actress" Margaret Rawlings at the Mayfair Hotel the following week.

*Fig. 7.3. Lina Monici,*
Painting of a Woman.

Sunday lunch with painter and former mezzo-soprano at La Scala Countess Lina Monici on May 1 was followed by tea with Pat and Ataturk who were "going on splendidly." After celebrating Ataturk's birthday the next day, Crowley performed an opus with Mattie for "Health, power &c." and continued to be amazed by the Texan nurse: "This is the first truly sympathetic woman I have had for years."

On May 10 he considered via the I Ching how best to handle Frieda: hexagram no. 17, *Sui:* "Following," interpreted as "Carry on as at present," adding wisely, "Don't romance." He then dashed off a complaint to Jane Wolfe at 1746 Winona Boulevard:

> I have read it through frequently [her last letter], and after a couple of bottles of liqueur brandy, I am apt to fancy that I know what it is all about. You keep on referring to people of whom I have never heard as if I had been at school with them. What I think is that you have not got rid of "the lust of result." You should stick to the *Book of the Law,* and leave everything else alone.[15]
>
> You keep on driveling about the "larger work." I don't know what it means—I never did—I never shall—I don't want to! Entirely apart from this, all that I hear of your activities is that you have made the

greatest mischief with regard to the Californian property.* On this note I close.[16]

The next day, May 11, after "her visions" proved "remarkably good," Frieda affiliated to the O.T.O. for ten guineas, choosing her motto as *TzBA* ("Hosts") for the A∴A∴. She wrote to Crowley from Petersham Road on May 12:

Dear Aleister,

Here enclosed cash for the fee for Initiation [one guinea each for first four degrees O.T.O., plus two guineas as Companion, Holy Royal Arch of Enoch, and annual subscription: four guineas]

I am sending you cash as it may be easier for you than cashing cheque Saturday at the Bank. Thank you so much for all the teaching you are giving to me,

Yours very sincerely
Frieda Harris[17]

Frieda took Germer's manuscript to her husband, and Crowley told Germer Sir Percy was so impressed he took it to the Commons to show other members. Within a month, H. G. Wells had a copy.

On May 13 Crowley met Mattie at lunchtime at Pimlico's Shakespeare pub, then taught her the IX° for "Gold," (for a decent house) and paid a house call on prospective pupil John Bland Jameson—actor with money to spend and time to spend it—at 6 Hasker Street's Georgian terrace, Kensington. They shared a good dinner (but no cigars) a week later: "He promises to turn out very well."

May 17: "Tried to phone Euphemia. Grove answered. I was silent. *He:* 'He's afraid to answer.' I said 'Good morning.' He rang off." A lunch with Euphemia next day at Kempinsky's produced an unbelievable explanation of the previous day's exchange: "Grove had no idea that it was I who telephoned!!! Thought it some man who had been pestering Euphemia!"

---

*Crowley referred to the alleged gift of Louis Culling of land in Rainbow Valley; Schneider misunderstood usage of his shack for a deed of property.

On Friday, May 20, Sister Tzaba collected Crowley from Kew, driving to the Bear Hotel, Charnham Street, Hungerford, Wiltshire, for lunch before exploring Avebury stone circle. Crowley's comment: "Pretty good." Having settled on the tarot, Frieda visited the British Museum to investigate past tarot imagery. Together they'd perform a comprehensive blitz on the meaning and exercise of the divinatory cards.

Crowley had had to spend two pounds sub from Germer on a doctor's fee for a painful nasal polypus. It availed little, but following magical sex with Mattie on May 21, Crowley's aggravating condition "miraculously vanished: nose quite free!" The IX° was performed again with Mattie at 1:30 for health and energy: "The best yet. She is a superb artist."

June saw nose-free Crowley regularly meeting J. B. Jameson at the Arts Theatre Club. Exploring fine sex magick with Mattie, his attentions also extended to Maisie Clarke and one Ethel Dolmey: all willing about the flame.

Frieda wrote to Crowley from Morton House, The Mall, Chiswick, on June 7:

> Dear Crowley,
>
> I have been talking to my husband about the Tarot Cards, and he advises me to come to a business understanding with you about our *mutual liability* as you term it.
>
> You say in your receipt for £10—it is an advance on the monies due to me from the proceeds of our joint venture in the production of a Pack of Tarot Cards. . . .[18]

Frieda recognized Crowley's predicament:

> But, as at present things seem a little difficult for you, so will you allow me to give you for your kind help one guinea every time we do work together which should be once a week. Our other meetings being purely social, will not incur further liability. I do hope you will excuse my being so business-like but, as I have told you, I have no money of my own and am responsible to my husband for my expenditure which is really a wise arrangement for me, and I prefer it.[19]

Problems soon arose over Crowley's expectations. Frieda became irate over a misunderstanding, as Crowley insisted it was, when his typist expected Frieda to pay her. Worse was to come. Crowley gave Germer to believe Lady Harris would invest capital once warmed up. Frieda put him right on June 12:

> Dear Crowley,
>
> I am indeed sorry for your difficulties, but you must believe I have not got £150 to give away or invest. I am unable to publish your books, build a temple, pay your liabilities, and am under a genuine promise not to give any guarantee, or raise money by the use of my name, which promise makes it legally impossible for me to do so— and therefore I cannot do any of the things you suggest.
>
>   Perhaps we must stop at once as I cannot use your valuable knowledge. . . .[20]

Another from the same period doubtless banished Crowley's illusions:

> I find you always trying to entangle me in your personal confusions, and I must reiterate that I do not intend to do anything about them, and we must stop this cat-and-mouse pastime, or I shall have to give up the work and my connection with you in it. . . . I am very sorry to write so clearly, but I cannot work when you are making it so difficult, and perhaps you would be wiser to give it up and go to your house in America [Culling's shack in Rainbow Valley].
>                           Yours sincerely,
>                           Frieda Harris[21]

Crowley, however, healed all sores, and a contractual understanding was reached after legal advice. Frieda wrote familiarly as "Jay Chutney" on June 26:

> Dear Sir,
>
> Yours to hand, and in view of your esteemed patronage I venture to enclose the following statement. My legal adviser has couched the

matter in terms from which he refuses to—well let me say in vulgar parlance budge—I trust the same will meet with your honoured approval and in this hope permit me to sign myself,

Yours faithfully,<br>Jay Chutney[22]

Crowley wrote his last letter from Manor Place to Germer on June 30:

Things are now more promising than they have been since 1914. Contract with Lady H[arris]. for Tarot pack settled. She is doing excellent work on them. Would v.d.G. [Brussels occult bookseller van der Graaf] buy the copyright for continental edition? Really a separate pack, printing the names of the cards in French, and my explanatory book translated also? I should want a fairly large advance on royalties. Please start negotiations.[23]

The tarot project would keep Crowley going for six years.

In 1938 artistic director Robert Medley's pro-socialist Artists' International Association hosted a debate between realists and surrealists. Gay surrealist Medley's contact with Crowley probably came via Jameson or Frieda, who wrote a jocular letter to Crowley about a planned dinner:

My dear Lorenzo the Magnificent Heliogabalus and Titian and Rubens and *Perdu Tzaba* combined.

Know then—the meal to bemuse and confuse one Robert Medley, who is but a stripling and of little power, and somewhat like unto me without the all-powerful titled backing, is all too worthy of him for I deem his "preciousness" is of the nature parochial—In fact, think you such a meal befits the bath-dining-room and bed-sitting-room. Still tis a good pull-up for carmen [*sic*] kind of repast, only please begin, oh great one, to materialize my extremely short pocket and ye wines mean £1 in cash . . . the whole meal at £1 a head.[24]

Crowley's diary records the July 1 "meal" when Medley of 5 Adelaide Terrace NW3 sped Crowley southwest to Petersham Road, Richmond:

"He drove furiously: I am alive." They indeed arrived, but the food didn't!

Next day, Crowley met Jameson at the Arts Theatre Club, agreeing to take 6 Hasker Street for 30 shillings a week, including electricity, from July 1 to September 30. Escaping Manor Place required pawning his income to August 1.

Described to Germer as the "Galveston girl," Mattie had returned from holiday on June 27 but was preoccupied with son and mother-in-law. Crowley found he kept "getting off" with girls but stayed true to Mattie nonetheless. A very tired Mattie showed up for an opus on July 4, dedicated to Gold: "she cried off after her third orgasm. We rested, planned, and drank. A marvellous working."

Long before mage Franz Bardon found a following, "Francis Bardon, Esq." from Gilschwitz bei Troppau, Czechoslovakia, requested a price for *Magick* and *Equinox of the Gods*. On July 10 Crowley read that Bardon had found a professor to help translate *Magick*. Crowley asked Germer to send books to Bardon on receipt of three guineas. Contact ceased after Hitler entered the Czech Sudetenland on October 5. Meanwhile, IX° work maintained the Beast. Bursting with health, spirits up, Crowley wrote on July 19 to Louis Wilkinson, whom he'd not met since an evening at El Vino, Piccadilly Place, in January:

Dear Louis,

Where are you? Do come in and see me next time you are in town. Come, indeed, to town on purpose. I'm working very hard with Frieda Harris on a new pack of Tarot cards. It's good fun too. And—I have the best one of U.S.A. over here [Mattie?] No recession! Hope good news of you.

Ever Aleister[25]

Hasker Street agreed with Crowley. He explained to Germer how he obtained it through the IX°:

I like your IX° work. Magical link though should be a piece of actual gold. Gnomes don't like paper money! As long as the cash reached you, it doesn't matter through what channel it came. Gnomes have to look around for ways and means, as we do. May 16 I did one for a

*Fig. 7.4. 6 Hasker Street,
as it is today.
(Author's Collection)*

house, and got this in 3 weeks. Dined here with owner [Jameson] on 19th (I had only met him once before for a few minutes). Got keys June 10. Working now mostly for Amrita. Fit as a fiddle, asthma all gone; arthritic thumb nearly well. Had 6 girls the last 7 days.[26]

Settled in, Crowley was excited to announce "Curry starts!" (July 29). First for ordeal by curry was Frieda: "she enjoyed it thoroughly" and responded generously:

To Mr. Crowley

Supreme Chef

Dear Sir or Madam: As you have not deigned to enclose an account with the celestial curry, I have inquired the price of same at the Indian Restaurant and have deduced from their inferior curries (which average about 5 shillings each dish for 6 persons) I should enclose £1-5 shillings. I fear it may not be sufficient.

Yours faithfully
F. Harris[27]

## CORNWALL—AUGUST 1938

The first day of August reminded Crowley in its quality of the best days with Leah Hirsig in Washington Square, Manhattan, 1918 to 1919. Maisie came to lunch, dinner, and opus, aimed at "Success to Cornwall Expedition." Having asked Maisie to keep house while away, Frieda, having encouraged the holiday idea, provided his return ticket to Penzance.

Greeted at Penzance's Queen's Hotel by an afternoon thunderstorm, Greta Sequeira drove him to a room at Wyn Henderson's famous Lobster Pot restaurant in Mousehole (pronounced "Mowzle"). Meeting Pat and Ataturk next morning (it was overcast), he took afternoon tea with Jameson before seeing him in *As You Like It*. On the sixth, Crowley walked a little inland to meet Pat by the old church at Paul. After two hours' rehearsal of *The Tempest,* Crowley dined with Jameson, then revised his papers for an Amrita consultancy, seeking Jameson's backing.

On August 7, clear skies heralded a "glorious day" designing tarot trumps, lunching with Greta—wooing her on the cliffs—taking photographs at Paul, visiting Morvah's prehistoric standing stones and medieval granite church, all capped by an evening with Jameson at Newlyn's Dolphin pub. The next day: sea bathing and rock scrambling with Ataturk and "Monday" the mongrel.

*Fig. 7.5. Crowley rock scrambling with son Aleister Ataturk and "Monday" the mongrel.*

After visiting Fowey's little port next day, Jameson agreed to an Amrita founder's share for one hundred pounds and a year's magical training. They visited Mousehole's Wharfe Studio on the tenth, inspecting artist Robert Anderson's work: "damned good." By the thirteenth Crowley doubted Jameson's consistency. He didn't take the Great Work seriously enough. Suspecting another dabbler (he was right), Crowley went to Penzance's Union Hotel and caught the 9 p.m. train back to London, where he talked with Edgar K. Bruce, who'd starred with Vivien Leigh and Rex Harrison in *Storm in a Teacup* in 1937.

On the fourteenth he met actress Beatrix Lehmann (1903–1979) of Highgate: ideal, he thought, to play Princess Monica Aretino, "a saint," described in *Mortadello* as "of medium height, very thin and serpentlike, her hair black and crisp; her features like Madonna's. Her eyes are extraordinarily black, keen, and piercing. Her age is twenty. Her hands and feet are very small and white, her complexion like fine porcelain." Sister of literary editor John Lehmann (1907–1987, publisher of Auden, Isherwood, and Graves), Lehmann appeared in Hitchcock's *The Lady Vanishes* in 1938 and played Charley's Mum (opposite Rex Harrison) in Stanley Donen's remarkable movie *Staircase* (1968).

Having sent *The Heart of the Master* to press on August 18, he performed an opus with Maisie Clarke on the nineteenth: "I am now acting quite as a young man—we used four positions, one quite difficult," and again on the twenty-eighth at 1 Gillingham Street, Victoria: a "Superb Operation," and yet another IX° on August 30 for sex energy and health: "A.1."

From mid- to late August, Gerald Yorke was in hospital, so Crowley kept Mrs. Angela Yorke amused: "She is quite unthinkably stupid. Simply not there to any intelligent remark. But very lovely."

August drew to a close with an opus for Gold on the twenty-fourth with one Evelyn Harley ("Thank God for a healthy human bitch!"), and while not pursuing sexual magick he found time for lunch on the twenty-seventh with Louis Fox and James Cleugh and a rare letter from O.T.O.'s Danish Grand Master, Freemason Grunddal Sjallung of Copenhagen.*

---

*Grunddal Sjallung founded the Grand Priory of the Sovereign Order of St. John of Jerusalem in Denmark on June 24, 1946.

September opened with a wrong number: a serendipitous opportunity for meeting Marie Louise Drajici. Having performed an opus with Maisie to get Marie Louise, Marie duly arrived on September 3 at one o'clock: "Marie Louise here. Yes, the bold bad woman, if ever there was one. We drank and caressed for hours: I passed out. Felkins for dinner."

A couple of days later, amid meetings with Maisie, Lesley Blanch, Frieda, Marie Louise, and one "Josie," he dined with Jameson at Victor's: "Marvellous meal: long talk, very satisfactory, mostly about house and proposed temple." Next day: "Annoyed about Maisie, decided to find an even lower whore. Succeeded." "Opus Emmy Butler 141 Lower Marsh SE1. Diffidence caused a snag; Amrita very fine." It went on "for a very long while."

And in the world: September 6 saw Czech President Beneš offer self-government to the Sudetenland (with its largely German population). Rejected by Hitler, Beneš came under Anglo-French pressure to cede it to the Germans. On September 11, Crowley noted: "Grave news on BBC. Will there be immediate war?"

Relaunching gourmet lunches on September 13 with "Sole Derby (Grill it with butter, pepper, Derby sauce). Foie Gras Chambertin '23 Avocado pears. Peaches," he spent an evening pondering how a war could establish Thelema as *the* spiritually revolutionary principle and joined Maisie for an opus: "War to establish 93," spreading the elixir over a dagger to make the "magical link."

Next day's opus with Maisie was likewise directed, and Crowley spent the day consulting about "WAR." Frieda arrived at one for a lunch of "stewed steak steeped in r[ed] and g[reen] chilis covered with bamboo pickle. In casserole: onions on top." Frieda said she'd bring Sir Percy to talk about the crisis. Meanwhile, a letter from Martha Küntzel "raving about the Czechs" got Crowley's goat: "These people are really insane." Freedland phoned in the evening, and 666 "ate and ate and ate" with Louis Fox, before driving "round Whitehall and other places where they sing."

Friday 16 September. *My Almond Chicken*. Steep cold chicken in red and green (or bird's eye) chilis. Add bamboo pickle (in oil), Col. Skinner's Chutney, and lots of almonds. Stew it all up. Oh boy!
Opus Maisie $\Sigma$[sex]-power and appeal.

"Humiliated, disgusted, outraged by the shit Government" for appeasing Hitler, Crowley "broke away to Soho" for an Escargot lunch. After an afternoon nap, he invented Pêche Maisie: "Steep peaches in cream with sugar whipped up with Kirsch and Benedictine. Ice some hours." He had Fox for an "A1" dinner at 8 p.m.

On the thirtieth an opus was performed "to employ the crisis aright to establish 93."

German troops marched into the Sudetenland on October 1. Crowley wrote about "Betrayal" to appeasing Home Secretary Sir Samuel Hoare.

Czechoslovakian president Beneš resigned next day (October 5). Crowley went chasing after Maisie, meeting Peggy Wetton and Josephine Blackley of 256 Newport Dwellings (between Shaftesbury Avenue and Charing Cross Road—largely destroyed by German bombing in April 1941). He managed to put Josephine off the day after to spend a wild evening with Allan Rae and Peggy. On the eighth he and Peggy performed an opus "for a son": an act perhaps of faith in the future from one keen to let off steam, before heading south to Barnes for chess on the tenth.

The thirteenth saw a peculiar opus: "savagely assaulted and raped by Peggy." He was doubtless delirious, as it occurred after a two-day birthday party. Clifford Bax was upset by the déclassé composition of guests. Crowley opined he never thought Bax's social position was so precarious! The day after, Frieda wrote, having just returned from a polite weekend at Bourton on the Water, Gloucestershire:

Dear Aleister

I hope you had a good party. I was sorry not to have been able to be there. I am now in London but I'm going to France with some friends for a week. I am still so tired with headaches. Can't make it out. It must be indigestion and I shall have to inquire into friend Hilton's diet on return.[28]

No indigestion for Gerald Yorke, who enjoyed a splendid lunch on October 22: "Crème Pamplona: mushrooms and onions stewed in milk and cream with curry powder and turmeric, etc., boiled chicken legs in it." In the evening Fitzgerald brought a cold meal that made Peggy sick. She recovered for an opus: *"Bahut achha,"* Hindi for "feeling good."

Crowley wrote to Germer about Hitler:

> Hitler is making slaves to rule slaves. There is no room for any star in his system. His cosmos is based on the false unity of the "State" which is like Daath [false sefira of knowledge on the Tree of Life], not on the Tree at all. He denies individual supremacy of Godhead, and he and his will crash. So shall I, unless I can take the "r" out of crash within a day or two.[29]

Greta Sequeira lunched at Hasker Street on October 26: "Tamarind steak: i.e. stewed in tamarinds, pepper water balls, and some chilis. Not bad: [Louis] Fox liked it a lot." Crowley had the mad idea to stand for Parliament against Sir Samuel Hoare.

In November, new typist Miss Hewitt took dictation on the tarot trumps, while *Little Essays Toward Truth* went to the printer. He talked to John Swain & Son about card reproduction. On the eleventh he met Edgar K. Bruce again with his wife at a dinner with Jameson.

A few days later, Peggy was badly burned in an accident with the Hasker Street stove. Crowley extinguished the fire; Peggy "was utterly heroic and unselfish." Crowley blamed "homicidal" electricians. An opus was performed with Josephine Blackley for Peggy's arm—the elixir smeared on her dressing gown's right arm—and Crowley "retrieved" Peggy from Charing Cross Hospital on the twenty-sixth. In the meantime, Jameson became fractious for no other reason than there was no other reason not to. Finding him increasingly contrary, heavy arguments persisted till 2:30 a.m. on the twenty-fourth. Blaming Crowley for the fire, Jameson was dismissive of poor Peggy, offending Crowley's sense of fair play.

They made up, Jameson attending a great lunch at the month's end with producer Norman Marshall, Esmé Percy, and Frieda on oysters and champagne, with Marshall going off next day with Crowley's *Three Wishes* (a play in three acts). Marshall was that month producing the Stokes brothers' *Oscar Wilde* on Broadway with Robert Morley, opening just before Orson Welles's *War of the Worlds* radio broadcast of October 31, 1938, news of which greatly impressed Crowley.

"We had Norman Marshall here last night," Crowley informed Germer. "He is the man who runs the Gate Theatre; a very nice man; and he thinks we cannot put on *Mortadello* in a small theatre. It demands great space for the crowds and architectural background; but he has gone away with the *Three Wishes,* the idea of which impressed him very much, and as it has been especially written with the idea of a cheap production, it may come across."[30]

"Pat Harvey" joined Crowley for sex magick during December, while the fourth was gilded by lunch with Sir Percy Harris and the ex-mayoress of Bethnal Green, and many hours of cunnilingus with Peggy: "She is really rather a juicy sow." One wonders what he found more enjoyable, but would that be to confuse planes?

Two days later, Louis Wilkinson came for lunch: "Turtle soup. Foie gras en croute. Creole aux fraises. Stilton." Fitzgerald and Pat shared a "great curry" in the evening, after which there was an opus with Hilda Godwin for "$\Sigma$-[sex] power, etc."

Ataturk, Pat, and Frieda lunched at Hasker Street on December 8, followed by "two hours futile hunt in [Hyde] Park until—Friday 9th Opus." This encounter proved fruitful and lasting, for he met Katherine M. Falconer of 83 Blackfriar's Rd. SE1, and their first opus was for health, strength, and sex power. Describing her as "a lady and intelligent," he would regard her as first-rate in all that counted. The sex magick: "A.1. and better."

Pearl paid a call on December 16 as the West End geared up for Christmas. Unfortunately, Pearl couldn't make lunch so he wired Cathrine, who joined Fitzgerald for curried cockles in chicken fat with ginger syrup. Then a knife slipped in Cathrine's hand, cutting Crowley deep in the face above the jawbone, which bled profusely. After Dr. Cosgrove dressed the wound, Cathrine stayed all night to look after him. An opus for "Service of Pan" was performed: "as good as ever, despite loss of blood."

An unusual lunch guest on December 20 was adventurer "James Justice," better known to cinemagoers after the war as "James Robertson Justice" (1907–1975), whose richly oaken tones, oozing with mischievous sap, would grace postwar screens and provide luscious commentary for *Those Magnificent Men in Their Flying Machines* (Ken Annakin, 1965). In 1938, he'd been linguist, journalist, racing driver, hockey coach, and Spanish Civil War volunteer. Then he grew his trademark beard.

Crowley met with Louis Wilkinson at the Majorca restaurant for an "excellent lunch" on December 21. Wilkinson's old Cambridge associate Ronald Storrs (1881–1955), chief diplomatic advisor to the Foreign Secretary (1938–41) failed to show: a shame, as Crowley and he would have had much to discuss. In his *Seven Pillars of Wisdom* (1922), T. E. Lawrence had called Storrs "the most brilliant Englishman in the Near East." In the afternoon, Crowley took a taxi to visit Peggy and in the evening Wilkinson joined Tzaba for dinner: "Bêche-de-Mer Soup, Scrambled eggs, cerises flambées." The day ended with an opus with Cath dedicated to the Great Work.

Crowley reflected in his diary: "Why do women resent being praised for their fucking. What else is there to praise?" Joking, of course.

A praiseworthy Frieda sent 666 a Christmas message: "A Happy Xmas to you and thank you for all the patience and pleasure you have given me this year." Beneath, Frieda drew a sun with a big smile, below which a figure prayed, hands upraised toward the Sun, and the words: "The disciple!"—below which Frieda wrote: "Oh Hell!"

He spent an hour chatting with Frieda on Christmas Day, with bed at 11:00, after a fabulous Xmas dinner, shared, it appears, with Peggy: "Agneau Noël [Christmas Lamb]—Boil Abattis de Poussin (giblets), tamarinds, pepper waterballs, shallots, garlic, lemon peel and juice, mushrooms, carrots. Reduce, strain. Cut lamb into small dice, put in cocotte. Surround with red, green bird's-eye chilis. Cover with liquor from above boiling. Let stand 6 hours. Heat on Bain Marie, and serve with rice or bhindi."

Frieda and Sir Percy invited him to Morton House, Chiswick, on December 27. Two days later a long letter to Jameson probed his character weakness. Crowley cooked a gourmet dish for Louis Fox: "Oysters—Red Caviar—Smoked eel Scrambled eggs Macassar. Faisan à la Crème," topped off by an opus with Cath for "material prosperity." The gourmet struck again next day: "Œufs brouillés Parmesan Champignons à la Crème." Noting with pleasure Peggy was nearly better, he bathed and went early to bed. Waking on New Year's Eve to a gloriously sunny day he dedicated a new dish to Cath: *Fondue*

*Falconer.* Mushrooms cut in small pieces fried in butter; add powdered chilis. Put in parmesan (Chester better) and cook. Pour off butter: add cream and let boil. Pour on Romarin [rosemary] husks (Fried French bread better)." Venturing out to Soho in the evening, he took the telephone number of a man called Donald he met at the Colonial Club.*

---

*Crowley's diary included end of year "Memoranda" with dates of ⊕ with women listed, including Phyllis Hunt, Maisie Clarke, Mattie Pickett, Emmy Butler, Pat Harvey, Hilda Goodwin (or Godwin), Jo Blackley, Ethel Macpherson, Evelyn Harley, Peggy Wetton, Maureen Johnson, Pat Michell, Angela Constadine, Rose Wilson, Marion Bennet, Nan Martin, Gladys?, Barbara Wood, Daphne, Marion Bennet.

# EIGHT

# Khing Kang King

New Year 1939 began with a laugh. Crowley joined Frieda and Louis Wilkinson at the Empire Variety Theatre, High Holborn: home to Britain's top comedians "cheekie chappie" Max Miller and Vic Oliver. Finding Jewish comedian Vic Oliver "very admirable," Crowley asked Germer if he agreed a Jew laughing at himself, his people, and what ordinary people held sacred was "psychic compensation" for years of persecution.[1]

*Fig. 8.1. The Empire Variety Theatre, High Holborn.*
*(Mike Blakemore)*

Frieda accompanied him to Hasker Street for a "great dinner" with Tom Driberg: Volonté Philomène ["strength-loving Will"]—"Noodles in tomato, curry, onions, mushrooms etc. Put them in jelly of turtle fins and warm"—and they talked till 1 a.m. (January 9–10).

On January 21 Max Schneider excited Crowley with news that Louis Culling was deeding Rainbow Valley land to the Order: an investment opportunity to new members, reckoned Crowley.

At the end of a hard January, Crowley was driven to Oxford "through lovely snow-bound hills," to play chess for the Hampstead club. Food at the Clarendon Hotel, 52 Cornmarket Street (now gone) was exceptional, and Oxford, for once, impressed him: "Sauntered through colleges, saw flooded river, very fine, more colleges, great melancholy."

February brought ructions at Hasker Street. Despite pleasant meetings with publisher and translator James Cleugh (discussing the tarot), "fine" work on Atu XIII (Death) by Frieda, a trip to Harrods with Norah Nott, and excellent sex with Cathrine Falconer (for sex appeal), John Bland Jameson burst into "crazy mad" rages. Crowley wondered if a "magical attack" hadn't been launched on the Order, especially when veteran South African member J. T. Windram died unexpectedly. Escaping further mayhem—Peggy and Cathrine fought over him—666 performed an opus with Jo Blackley for "Victory over John" (Jameson). Cathrine returned on the seventh but left again when Peggy insulted her. Bruce Blunt appeared but, disliking Jameson, left. Jameson and Crowley visited the Players Theatre Victorian Music Hall show, possibly to see James Justice, who'd taken up acting there. Next day, Crowley consulted solicitors over his residency contract; Jameson assaulted him on the eleventh.

Frieda begged Crowley not to use law against Jameson and on the fourteenth helped him find another flat—a day capped by dinner at the Shanghai Restaurant and Emporium in Greek Street, Soho, and a Javanese dance show at Sid Bernstein's Phoenix Theatre in Charing Cross Road: "the best show I've seen in years," reflected Crowley.

Though reluctant to surrender Jameson, Crowley left Hasker Street for the Grosvenor Hotel on February 20, sharing a quiet lunch with Jameson and Frieda at the Shanghai the next day so Jameson could meet Gabriel Toyne. Shooting back to Hasker Street, Jameson "violently threw out Peggy into one room in a foul slum," despite her injury preventing her wearing a shoe. Having moved briefly to Gordon Chambers, 20 Jermyn Street, Crowley informed Louis Wilkinson on February 21 of an imminent move to 24 Chester Row SW1, Belgravia.[2]

Jameson's entering a nursing home for emergency surgery suggested malefic forces to Crowley, so after dinner at the White Tower at 1 Percy Street, Fitzrovia, on February 26, Cathrine and 666 performed an opus "to rebuff magical attack."

Crowley took Frieda to some "ghastly bad films" at the London Pavilion cinema, Piccadilly Circus. Tickets came free with ticket No. 93 (Thelema!) bought at a wrestling match some weeks earlier.

*Fig. 8.2. The London Pavilion cinema (right of center), Piccadilly, in 1951.*

After Crowley moved into 24 Chester Row on March 1, an air raid patrol warden called a few days later: Crowley could expect a gas mask. He inspected Frieda's tarot trumps and five of Cups on the seventh: "not quite A.1." Frieda was often irritated by Crowley's exacting design requirements, as this sarcastic note indicates:

> *It seems a pity you* [666] *couldn't think of some more for the Sun* Trump Card—To start with
>    "This is a simple card!" & *then* you say—you want
>    1    a sun—rayed and nebule
>    2    a rose

3  a spectrum

4  12 signs of the zodiac in pictures

5  twins

6  green hill

7  wall

8  pythons' scales

9  druid stones

I don't think it is enough for a large space like 16½ × 10½ [inches][3]

On March 9 Crowley designed the jacket for *Eight Lectures on Yoga.* V. D. Freedland photographed him "extensively" in turbaned guise.

Meanwhile, optimism about California proved premature. Just as Smith had persuaded a radio station to record interview discs for a forty-five-minute feature on the Church of Thelema in February, Anya Sosoyeva—student attendee at Winona Boulevard's New Year party— was murdered by a serial assailant near the City College campus where Regina taught drama, prompting baseless speculation about a local "Purple Cult." You can guess the rest. When the heat died down, an airing was expected for the discs, but when the Hearst press gleaned the church was receiving radio time it cobbled together a love-cult-orgy "exclusive" with salacious girlie photos and "gruesome pictures" (according to Smith).[4] The City College head pleaded that Smith's

*Fig. 8.3. V. D. Freedland image of Crowley for* Eight Lectures on Yoga. *(Courtesy of the Warburg Institute, London, and Ordo Templi Orientis)*

*Fig. 8.4. Disc recording for radio program on the Church of Thelema.*
*(Author's Collection)*

attempt to defend his Church would revive bad publicity for the school. Crowley was only relieved that, for once, murder wasn't pinned on *him*.[5]

Modern druid George Watson MacGregor Reid, founder of the Church of the Universal Bond, visited Crowley at 8:30 p.m. on March 19 for a talk about druids—and Jameson. According to Adam Stout, MacGregor Reid espoused a kind of voluntary communism (analogous to Crowley's "aristocratic communism"). He'd been impressed by MacGregor Mathers (from whom he probably derived his own "MacGregor" moniker). Reid believed Mathers had brought forth gold, regardless of the state of the mine![6]

Crowley's social life received further stimulus in March from a nymphomanic Peggy, a delightful Frieda, "un Lapin" (a man, possibly "Giles" [diary April 1]), Ruby Melvill with Lawrence Evans, sex magick with Maisie Clarke—and on the thirtieth, fellow mystic "Dion Fortune," or as Crowley unkindly described Ms. Violet Firth: "Public Bat No. 1 at The Belfry. Like a hippo with false teeth. Talk—bubbling of tinned tomato soup."

MacGregor Reid phoned on April Fool's Day to tell how Michael "Juste" was "peddling obscene books" to eccentric Lina Monici. Reid then turned up in the afternoon for another couple of hours of "fruitful talk," while Crowley cooked "Ch[ili] [c]on C[arne] plus *Risotto A.C.* plus onions plus mushrooms." Verdict: "Not bad. He [Reid] will tackle J. B. J[ameson]. Michael Juste's spying and treachery fully disclosed."

More cause for female jealousy on April 3, following an opus with Austrian Nellie Butler, née Woolf; Nellie was not the cause: "Peggy blew up thinking Maisie's call was Falconer's." Crowley escaped to see Robert Morley's *Goodness, How Sad!* at the Vaudeville Theatre (turned into Ealing film *Return to Yesterday* in 1940.) Verdict: "the worst play I have seen in my life."

Crowley left us a priceless snippet of dinnertime repartee from April 19:

PEGGY: You think we're fools and crude primitive animals! What are we then?

A.C.: Mind-readers.

A.C. wasn't giving up wonderful Cathrine Falconer for Peggy Wetton. A couple of days later Cathrine posed in the early morning for an "A.1." sketch. I doubt if it was this one (fig. 8.5).

Verdict: "one of the best I ever did." In the evening, he cooked

*Fig. 8.5. Cathrine Falconer, charcoal sketch by A.C. (Courtesy of the Warburg Institute, London, and Ordo Templi Orientis)*

Turbot Porterfield: "Onions, shallots, garlic in butter and Zambar: then mushrooms; then fish *fumet* [stock] and Chablis. Cook turbot steak in this; pour off, reduce, add lemon juice and cream, and serve as sauce."

## RETURN OF THE GOETIC GOURMET

Crowley's *Liber Agape* recommended a good meal beforehand, so an opus with Cathrine on April 22 for Gold was preceded by Turbot (or *filets de sole*) Arles.

The following day Sunday lunch was served to Louis Fox and Gerald Hamilton, Capretto St. George: "Braise kid sliced, in stock. Add onions garlic mushrooms pimentos and Jerusalem artichokes. Add Madeira. Simmer long."

There must have been something about Chester Row that made Crowley want to cook. Perhaps it helped to offset the gathering storm: *cook it while you can*. Greta and one Phoebe came on April 26 for Turbot Avignon: "Poach steaks in fish *fumet* and Chablis; reduce cooking-liquor; add cream and cover with new potatoes and chopped parsley."

By April 30, the chef was well into his stride, calling it a "day of

*Fig. 8.6. 24 Chester Row today. (Author's Collection)*

great social and gastronomical success." Sunday lunch for Ruby Melvill
and Bill Evans consisted of iced curry and chili con carne, while Gerald
Hamilton, Gabriel Toyne, and Louis Wilkinson dined on "*Tournedos
Gabriel* [in Toyne's honor]: Grill veal; set on rounds of fried bread; on
top, poached egg and crossed anchovies; around, mushrooms chopped
and tossed in butter with cayenne and birds' eye chili. (NO eggs: so we
used a mustard and cream sauce.)"

Crowley greeted May Day with Gelée Cherbourg: "Prawns in fish
*fumet* with Shoyu [soy] sauce—a little cayenne—remains of Turbot
Avignon—more cream. Ice." This was probably made for next day's celebration of Ataturk's birthday, to which an assortment came as varied
as Crowley's "Cherbourg Jelly" ingredients: Gerald Hamilton, Ruby
Melvill, Charles and Iona Cammell, Peggy Wetton, James and Marika
Cleugh, James Justice, Louis Wilkinson, Greta Sequeira, Cathrine
Falconer, Pamela Joan Bennett. Chef's verdict: "A great success this
lunch, in some strange way; only explanation seems to be that I wasn't
there: just cooked and let them talk."

The day ended with an opus "in the hand of the lady," Crowley
adding in code that Cath just didn't like sex when menstruating.

Novelist and theater critic for the *Observer* Maurice Richardson
(1907–1978) arrived for lunch on May 4. Richardson was a Communist
Party member, and Crowley was perhaps gleaning information for MI5.

Gerald Yorke arrived for lunch at one o'clock next day for Vindalu
Fernière: "Veal cutlets in rice with apple in Vindalu paste." Crowley
dined Peggy at the White Tower in the evening. He might as well
not have: "She crazier than ever: wants me and C[athrine].F[alconer].
'beaten up' by her pet thugs, and John [Jameson] exorcised by a
priest!!!" Perhaps this revelation affected Crowley's choice of film
when taking Cathrine out on the eighth: an offbeat comedy about
bootlegging, *A Slight Case of Murder* starred Edward G. Robinson
playing his gangster image for laughs. Crowley's verdict: "Excellent
film: one of Edwd. G's best."

One gangster who wasn't pretending was Hitler. Crowley was indignant at Germer's balancing act, defending the Führer's territory claims.
Germer failed to see the true British attitude: "H[itler]'s guarantees
are worthless. . . . This country has made up its mind, as I made up
*my* mind years ago, that the Nazi regime must be destroyed, and we

do not care in the least whether this is, or is not, just. We are seeing red."[7] Having put Germer right, Crowley cooked *Écrevisses Jahannum* for Ruby and Gabriel Toyne's lunch: "Prawns with red bird's eye chilis in Vindalu paste with chili powder and a little honey. Stew in butter." Jahannum is the Islamic "hell."

On May 11 British prime minister Neville Chamberlain warned Hitler that seizing Poland's free port of Danzig meant war. Doubting Britain's will to fight, Hitler signed a "pact of steel" with Mussolini.

In Chester Row, Peggy Wetton's drunkenness caused Crowley to lament on May 15: "Peggy abominable: in cheap *lingerie de cocotte* trying to seduce me!!!!!! Rows and rows and rows. Laurence Felkin to supper. More Peggy on telephone. Gawd! I'm sick of all this." Then he realized how ill Peggy really was: acute gastritis, with threatened ulcer, pleurisy, and near-cirrhosis of the liver. Between meetings with Freedland about publishing Lao Tze's *Khing Kang King* and sex magick with Cath for health, lust, and money, he discussed Peggy's condition with a Dr. Thomas. Light relief came on the eighteenth with Esmé Percy as Count Aristid Karpathy in the movie *Pygmalion,* with Leslie Howard as Professor Higgins, David Tree as Freddy Eynsford-Hill, and Wendy Hiller as Eliza Doolittle: "very good on the whole," thought Crowley. A week later it was Bette Davis, Humphrey Bogart, and Ronald Reagan in *Dark Victory.* Crowley's verdict: "Loathsome, posing, prancing Bette Davis; appalling medical nonsense; and *longueurs-longueurs-longueurs!*" Peggy's ravings resumed, amid cries of vacuous penitence; Crowley found solace in quiet evenings with Cath.

## QINGJING JING

Crowley readers have probably seen photographs of Crowley impersonating Chinese sages. Noted photographer Arnold Genthe (1869–1942) portrayed Crowley as "Master Kwaw Li Ya" (Crowley) in 1915 (see page 120). V. D. Freedland photographed Crowley as Fo Hi (*Fu Xi*), legendary creator of the I Ching, on May 29, 1939, for Crowley's paraphrase of James Legge's translation of the *Qingjing jing* (老君曰:), anglicized as *Khing Kang King.* A *king* is a book, and *qingjing* means "tranquil" or "purity," so taking Legge's title and translation of "The Classic of Purity," Crowley turned it into verse (*Liber XXI*).

*Fig. 8.7. Kwaw Li Ya*
*(by Arnold Genthe, June 1915).*
*(Library of Congress)*

Attributed to Ko Yüan (or Hsüan), Taoist of the Wû dynasty (222–277 CE) in the tradition of Laozi (or Lao Tze or Lao Tzu), meaning "old master," supposed author of the *Daodejing* ("Tao Teh King"), immortal Ko Yüan was legendary for eccentric intemperance. In one tale, shipwrecked, he emerged dry and walked on water! The text begins: "Master Laozi says: The Great Dao has no form; it brings forth and raises heaven and earth. The Great Dao has no feelings; it regulates the sun and the moon. The Great Dao has no name; it raises and nourishes the myriad beings. I do not know its name, so the name I give it is Dao." Or as Crowley put it:

> Lao Kun the Master said:
> Tao is devoid of form—
> yet heaven and earth are brought to birth,
> and nurtured by its norm.
> Tao hath no will to work;
> yet by its way of heaven
> the moon and sun rejoice to run
> among the Starry Seven.
> Tao hath no name; its word
> is growth, and sustenance
> to all; I aim to give it name:
> Tao (heaven prosper chance!)

Crowley equated Taoist creation *ex nihilo* with the kabbalist Ain Soph (absolute Nothing), whence derived the supernal triad (Kether, Binah,

Hokma). All things exist in relation to all things existing in relation, in which exists a formless constant whence motion derives. That is the Tao, union with which brings tranquility of mind, purity of thought: refuge from the storm of life. Crowley's "True Will" finds itself in the Tao.

Crowley and Frieda were working at Morton House, Chiswick, on June 1 when Sir Percy, yawning, entered to inform them: *there'd be no war before August.* The following night, Crowley dreamt of long talks with Hitler; Crowley's subconscious yearned to seize the levers of destiny.

Gerald Hamilton came to lunch on June 4 with companion Alphonse. As homosexual Hamilton carried messages for Sinn Fein, there may have been an intelligence angle to Crowley's interest. On July 29, there was a roundup of suspected IRA members in Britain, nine days after two thousand Nazi guards arrived in Danzig.

Pulp writer of *Witch-Doctors* (1922) Charles Beadle—who'd socialized with Crowley in Paris 1920-29 (and whom he'd met in America during the war)—arrived on the sixth, dining five times chez Crowley before a note of October 23 explained Beadle's purpose: "here to pick my brains re. Montparno [Montparnasse—Crowley's old haunt]"; Beadle wrote novels about Parisian Bohemians.

A letter of June 20 from Wilfrid Smith in Hollywood introduced Crowley to a significant name: Parsons.[8] Rocket-propulsion pioneer John ("Jack") Whiteside Parsons (1914–1952) signed the guest register on

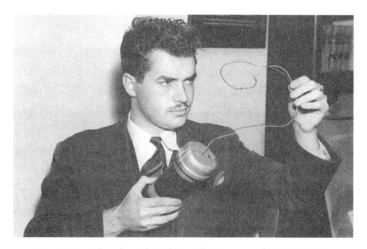

*Fig. 8.8. John (Jack) Whiteside Parsons (1914–1952).*

January 13, 1939, and again on June 17 for a belated celebration of Smith's birthday when Jack joined a group discussing O.T.O. promotion.

Summer beckoned: Frieda took a weakened Crowley to Gloucestershire for a short break on June 28. On reaching picturesque Cotswold village Chipping Campden, however, Crowley's asthma returned.

As her "guest," Frieda gave Crowley three pounds for hotel expenses and took him to Evesham. At Evesham's Crown Hotel, Cicily Mary Crowley (1905–2003), accompanying her parents, observed Frieda and Crowley taking tea. Cicily's memoir describes the family's "black sheep" with an unusual woman of curious red hair, together radiating a strange atmosphere; Cicily kept her head down.*

Having been edified by Evesham's medieval abbey ruins, Crowley saw—from a distance—Forthampton Court, near Tewkesbury: the Yorke patrimony and former residence of Tewkesbury's abbots. Vincent Yorke wouldn't let the Beast in, so Yorke, accompanied by son Anthony, enjoyed a "pleasant evening" with Crowley at the New Inn, Bourton-on-the-Water. Though Crowley was better after the three-day break, asthma soon returned.

Frieda finished the court cards on July 3 and worked on the Swords, while Crowley worked on trump numbers IX and V, accepting a two-month extension of the Chester Row flat lease. He wrote to Louis Wilkinson on July 24:

> Ah me, I fear the cruise is also a dream. Really I'm very depressed. Weather not helpful to soul. . . . As to U.S.A., I wonder would you care to take over the Tarot and do a deal. Heard from [H. L.] Mencken [1880–1956, American writer] last week. Thinks he'll be here in the Fall. [Crowley and Wilkinson knew Mencken in the United States.][9]

He had cause to feel low. Having pawned a ring for two pounds, at least Allan Rae and Jean turned up for a good curry. Two days later he inspected Frieda's Swords and shared a good dinner, but her "Indian dancers [were] rather bogus, even by Indian standards."

---

*The memoir is kept at Winchester's Record Office. Cicily's great-great-great-grandfather Thomas Crowley (1753–1809) was Aleister Crowley's great-grandfather.

He wrote to Wilkinson again on August 2 to say he'd soon be at Petersham Road, Richmond, though nobody was to know. It was Frieda's delicate arrangement, and he didn't want visitors messing it up for him.[10] Crowley hoped Wilkinson might be able to prosecute some A.M.O.R.C. business while in the States, referring to it on August 6:

Spencer Lewis is dead. So there will be no single co-ordinating & directing intelligence to oppose; his family are mere hangers-on, always quarreling over the spoils. So your visit appears timely! I am here, Frieda being in France till Aug 31 or war, whichever comes first.[11]

Despite dull summer weather, he enjoyed a visit from Pat's friend Greta Sequeira, who told him Pat and Ataturk were in Yugoslavia. Downhearted, Crowley worked on trumps VI and XIV; he'd rather have been in America doing some good. Smith wrote from California on August 18. He'd conducted a group Minerval Degree ceremony on August 6 while negotiating with one Wade for a 640-acre tract of Rainbow Valley. If Smith could swing it, he'd get some unemployed people to work the "beautiful valley" into an "ideal retreat." Hopes of cash were dashed: "Just remember Regina and Jane [Wolfe] lose their jobs at the end of the month."[12] Wade succumbed to paranoia, and obstructions became insuperable.

On August 23 Crowley recorded: "Dined with Sir Percy Harris. Educated him." Next day he went to the House of Commons: "Immensely impressed by P[rime].M[inister]—to my utter amazement. After the leaders had said their pieces the show turned into a rag debate at the Union."

On the twenty-ninth he performed an opus for Gold with Ruby Butler; Frieda gave him ten pounds.

On Friday, September 1, Germany attacked Poland.

Next day he went out to find Ruby in Hammersmith, but bumped into nurse Mattie Pickett at the station, now living at 62a Castletown Road, near Talgarth Road, Hammersmith. And at 11 p.m: "one of the best thunderstorms I have enjoyed for many years. It went on for hours."

Sunday, September 3: "Practice air warning 11:30. War declared at noon." Next day he consulted the I Ching: England's chances? *Tui* (Joy). "Excellent."*

Crowley wrote to Karl Germer on September 1:

> The Equinox of the Gods has come indeed; and we must live or die by the Light of the Book of the Law.[13]

---

*Crowley added: "but see Line 5 [hexagram summary]. *Athenia* torpedoed with 246 USA sailors aboard. Probably Montgomery Evans [Montgomery Evans II (1901-1954), wealthy American book collector and friend of Crowley and Arthur Machen (Frater Avallaunius of the Golden Dawn; 1863-1947)]. Moral: Do not *hurry* to safety. My old motto."

PART TWO

# WAR

666

## NINE

# Happy Dust

On September 4, 1939, Neville Chamberlain appointed Churchill First Lord of the Admiralty. A day later, Roosevelt declared U.S. neutrality. By mid-October, the British Expeditionary Force was in France, expecting the French to hold ground; a month later German bombs fell on the Shetland Islands. Signing a nonaggression pact with Germany, the USSR invaded Finland.

Crowley fancied repeating his 1914 to 1917 intentions: countering German propaganda while encouraging the United States to renounce neutrality. He drafted a letter, probably for Sir Percy Harris, on September 4:

> I am looking for a job. I wrote to Carter [Colonel John Fillis Carré Carter, Assistant Chief Commissioner, Metropolitan Police, Special Branch]: no answer yet. I would like to use my connection and A.M.O.R.C. resources (which I could easily pick up given official backing) to get U.S.A in with us again. This would be urgent should Poland crack.
>
> I might also be useful through the sympathetic understanding of the Muslim and Hindu worlds [extremists might foment rebellion in India].
>
> I'll go anywhere and do anything so far as bronchial tubes permit.
>
> Can you give me a letter to somebody of power to use me?[1]

Vulnerable to German invasion, Brussels-based Germer considered *his* usefulness: fluent English, continental contacts, World War I

German intelligence experience. Crowley requested a resumé: "I will see whether I can put it before someone" (possibly Harris), adding *his* solution to Germany's problems: "The best solution—*selon moi* [in my opinion]—is to put back the Hohenzollerns [German royalty], but with liberal constitution such as ours. A[leister]."[2]

Far away in California, W. T. Smith reflected on the paradise of what he hoped to rename "Agapae [*sic*] Valley." Encouraged by landowner Wade—now initiated into the Minerval—that he might yet secure 640 acres of the Rainbow Valley, Smith performed the Gnostic Mass outdoors, dedicating the chosen spot: "Be this Valley and the hills, the earth thereof and the water, the air and the fire, consecrated to the Great Work and the establishment of the Law of Thelema."[3]

On the sixth, Crowley dispatched patriotic poem "England, Stand Fast!" to Western Printing Services, Brick Street, Piccadilly, for a September 23 release, hoping the BBC would back it with rousing music to raise fighting spirit:

> England, stand fast! Stand fast against the foe!
> They struck the first blow: we shall strike the last.
> Peace at the price of Freedom! We say No.
> England, stand fast!
>
> England, one soul of steel, one heart of oak,
> One voice of silver, sound thy trumpet-blast!
> Pass round the watchword through the battle-smoke;
> England, stand fast!
>
> POEM ISSUED BY O.T.O.,
> "ONE PENNY, SEPTEMBER 23, 1939,
> E.V. 10:50 P.M."

"Sir, I have the honour to apply for employment"—Crowley addressed the Naval Intelligence Department, summarizing work for the Allies in the last war: supplying the German Propaganda Kabinett in New York "with false information to wreck their propaganda by inducing them to make psychological blunders: all with the object of inducing the U.S. to enter war on our side." He'd also worked for Colonel Carter: "In 1927 [*sic;* probably a translation error for 1929] I began work for the Special

Branch, this time to work and report on Communist activities, especially in Berlin, where I lived almost continuously for three years."[4]

On September 8 he completed an NID form, naming Sir Percy
Harris, Clifford Bax, Gerald Yorke, and Charles Cammell referees
(Crowley's intelligence contact from World War I, the Hon. Everard
Feilding [b. 1869] had died in 1936). Next day he went to the Swan
Hammersmith to find "the errant Ruby Butler." Her dithering drove
him into the park, where he encountered half-Jamaican Beryl Drayton
and performed an opus "to play my part well in the Great Work." The
elixir was, he wrote, "A.1. Good and copious."

On the eleventh, Director of Naval Intelligence Admiral John
Godfrey, responded:

> The Director of Naval Intelligence presents his compliments and
> would be glad if you could find it convenient to call at the Admiralty
> for an interview. It would be appreciated if you will be good enough
> to communicate with Commander C. J. M. Lang,* Royal Navy,
> Naval Intelligence Division, Admiralty, Telephone: Whitehall 9000,
> Ext. 484, in order to arrange a suitable time.[5]

Crowley considered the interview on the twelfth "as satisfactory
as could be expected." He wrote to Wilkinson on September 15: "Of
course no one can tell what is happening, or is likely to happen; it seems
to me to depend very much on the Soviets, who are likely to take the
chance to smash the Boche; and on Roosevelt if things go badly, we
shall want those blokes in again, and if so, I hope to get sent over there
to exercise my well-known charm."[8]

Three days later, a "silly letter" arrived from Deirdre. Ataturk was
safe "(more or less) in Yugoslavia," mother and son only just escap-

---

*Commander Lang had been NID chief in Hong Kong from 1932 to 1934, a posting
contemporary with the mission of Peter Fleming in China.[6] Peter Fleming's now-famous
brother Ian now worked for Godfrey. Crowley seems to have had a contact other than
Commander Lang in mind, for he wrote on the invitation: "Better ring up Mr. Frost—
Ext. 46 for an interview." According to intelligence writer Phil Tomaselli, extension 484
got you to "the NID section dealing with interrogation of prisoners of war" while extension 46 put you in touch with one W. G. Johns, a senior civil servant. This letter was
found in Crowley's pocketbook when he died.[7]

ing Germany. Patricia had undertaken an epic car journey through Yugoslavia—destination Egypt—to rejoin boyfriend MI6 assassination and sabotage agent James MacAlpine, whom she married. Deirdre's exploits must have made Crowley envious. He wrote to Smith in California: "I am trying to get out to the States, as I think my best usefulness to England at the moment would be to take up my old job. If I can persuade them to appoint me, I may be with you fairly soon. I am still very busy with the Tarot, but it nears completion." Smith's group Minerval initiation, or initiating "in bunches," displeased Baphomet. Initiation should be solitary, such fear being good for the soul.[9]

On October 2, he noted in his diary, "2 A.M. Col. Ellachie or Commdr. Leeds," adding: "Executed [Sir Percy] Harris's mission better than I had ventured to hope." What the mission was, or what Ellachie or Leeds had to do with it, is unknown.

Crowley wrote to the War Office calling for total mobilization into war work. Under Churchill, "TOTAL WAR" became the keynote of government policy, though Crowley was not alone in seeing its necessity.

I have the honour to submit the following propositions for the consideration of H.M. Government. . . . Do what thou wilt shall be the whole of the Law. The nation must be a disciplined organization before the beginning of hostilities, and its existence would be the most potent conceivable factor in their indefinite postponement. I should like to discuss the question of propaganda with your Publicity Experts with a view to issuing a new series of posters based on the Law of Thelema.[10]

A sketch idea for a poster based on a Thelemic principle was included, headed by a drawing of the British Crown with *G*(eorge) and *R*(ex) on either side.

Do what thou wilt shall be the whole of the law . . .
What is your true will?
Probably you do not know yourself.
But—

> It is sure that every man has the root-will to make the
> best of himself . . .
> To do your own true Will—Join the Army![11]

Relief from tension came via an excellent lunch with Greta Sequeira at the mirror-lined Chez Victor French restaurant, 45 Wardour Street, on October 4. Two days later, 666 recorded: "⊕ [opus] Lilian Finch; long cunnilingus for 'U.S.A. job'" "but too quick after long abstinence." On the eighth he sent "England, Stand Fast!" to "Winston," Neville Chamberlain, the BBC—and performed another opus for the U.S.A. job. On October 14, HMS *Royal Oak* was reported sunk by torpedo at home base Scapa Flow, northern Scotland. Crowley "took this very much to heart."

A couple of days later came a cry of poverty—not from Crowley but from Frieda:

> I am in distress about money. Percy has reduced my allowance by half. He has been hit by the taxes and also requires any available cash to finance his personal message. I do not think I shall be able to hold on to my personal flat in Richmond much longer. . . .[12]

Bereft, he wrote to Wilkinson the next day (October 17): "Your silence is sinister."[13] Wilkinson responded with an invitation to the west country. Crowley replied, appropriating Frieda's income problems:

> I *would* dash down to see you; but the war reduced my income to nil, the new taxes have cut that down 30 percent and I am threatened with loss of more than half the balance. Excuse my arithmetic. Yours Aleister.[14]

Getting back to Smith about Rainbow Valley, Crowley requested particulars in estate agents' terms: pictures of film stars' houses "to smarten the prospect." Smith, meanwhile, had offered a room at Winona Boulevard for his visit. "Very kind," replied Crowley, but should he come over, he'd have to be "very independent."[15]

Perhaps he thought insight into California mores might be gained from Aldous Huxley's *After Many a Summer Dies the Swan* about a California millionaire facing death. On a "beastly wet day," Crowley

*Fig. 9.1. Aldous Huxley,*
After Many a Summer Dies the
Swan.

stayed in to read it, concluding: "Clotted Buddhism with a touch of Spinoza and a junk-shop of assorted learning."*

Though repelled by Gerald Hamilton's "egomaniacal" personality, Crowley saw a lot of him. Perhaps Hamilton inspired Crowley's latest aphorism: "People who avoid facing facts are bounded by phantoms."

Crowley noted Ruby Melvill's death on November 4. Society beauty Ruby's biography is obscure. William Orpen (1878–1931) painted her in "fun frills" in 1920. In 1929 she translated the Fortune Press edition of Pierre Louÿs's *Cyprian Masques* with drawings by Beresford Egan— cover artist for Crowley's *Moonchild*.

*Fig. 9.2. Portrait of
Mrs. Ruby Melvill, 1920.
Oil on canvas. Sir William
Orpen (1878–1931).
(Mildura Arts Centre,
Victoria, Australia,
Collection. Senator
R. D. Elliott Bequest,
presented to the City of
Mildura, by Mrs. Hilda
Elliott, 1956)*

---

*Huxley's novel might have inspired Welles's *Citizen Kane* (1941), which also has a main character informed by the excesses of William Randolph Hearst.

Brompton Oratory hosted the funeral on the eighth. The day before, Crowley played at Barnes Chess Club and, oversleeping, awoke ill and missed it, meeting Pearl at Victor's at 5:30—"quite like old times." He once described death as like a clown going through a hoop. Another approach was taken in a letter Germer received on November 7: "The masochistic idea of sacrifice is vile; but readiness to take whatever comes in the course of exercising one's Will is the very Sacrament of Living. *AL* takes care of this . . . the intense relief at being able to go forward. The Gods are on our part—"[16]

Seeking a loft studio far from the war, Frieda bought the old coach house at Rolling Stone Orchard, Chipping Campden, in April 1939. Close to friends of Sir Percy, but distant (she hoped) from his career's social pressures, it seemed ideal for the tarot watercolors, despite Sir Percy's weekend visits in 1940, when he stayed with a Mrs. Heaton on Sheep Street.[17]

On November 7, Frieda complained Crowley's needs unnerved her: "As a matter of fact, you are now receiving from me £104 stipend with £100 for your rent which is more than I have a right to do, but in order to help you to finish this grim work I have reduced my private expenditure and am living as you see."[18] The studio lacked water and elec-

*Fig. 9.3. Rolling Stone Orchard, Chipping Campden, Gloucestershire.*
*(chippingcampdenhistory.org.uk; spring 2017;*
*taken before 1910 by Jesse Taylor, 1865–1938)*

*Fig. 9.4. Tarot design,*
*Frieda Harris, 1939–1940.*
*(Courtesy of the Warburg*
*Institute, London, and*
*Ordo Templi Orientis)*

*Fig. 9.5. Unused tarot*
*design, Frieda Harris,*
*1939–1940. (Courtesy of*
*the Warburg Institute,*
*London, and Ordo Templi*
*Orientis)*

tricity. She was bicycling, not running a car because of rationed petrol prices. Enduring "personal self-sacrifice," she sought suitable frames and hoped to exhibit at the Leicester Galleries, Leicester Square (specialists in modern British art) before the seventy-eight paintings were sold. Sir Percy took pride in her achievement, believing her exceptional paintings would make her name as an artist.

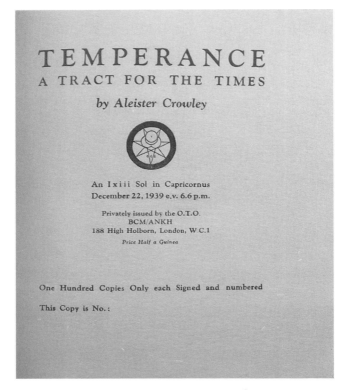

*Fig. 9.6. Temperance, 1939, title page.*
*(Courtesy of Ordo Templi Orientis and 100th Monkey Press)*

Alice Florey came on the thirteenth for a midday curry of beefsteak, chilis, onions, and garlic, with "A. C. Rice": "Best Operation yet with her"—and Bill Busch came to Sunday lunch with Margot Cripps on November 19. Crowley dedicated a new poem to Margot for the solstice collection *Temperance: A Tract for the Times,* which he began preparing on December 7.*

Publishing a moving poem on mortality, and other things, his old poem "Happy Dust," was perhaps prompted by Ruby Melvill's death.

_____

*Published on December 22 as a menu, with gold tassle, the collection extolled pleasure and necessity in drinking, especially in wartime! Crowley told Germer it was vital to get something out with his name on it at equinoxes and solstices; the publications' value would accrue, even if there were losses at first.[19]

One may also read the polyvalent image of "happy dust" as a euphemism for cocaine. The first and final stanzas:

Snow that fallest from heaven, bear me aloft on thy wings
To the domes of the star-girdled Seven, the abode of
    ineffable things,
Quintessence of joy and of strength, that, abolishing
    future and past,
Mak'st the Present an infinite length, my soul all-One
    with the Vast,
The Lone, the Unnameable God, that is ice of His
    measureless cold,
Without being or form or abode, without motion or
    matter, the fold
Where the shepherded Universe sleeps, with nor sense
    nor delusion nor dream,
No spirit that wantons or weeps, no thought in its silence
    supreme.
I sit, and am utterly still; in mine eyes is my fathomless lust
Ablaze to annihilate Will, to crumble my being to dust . . .

What I am, that I am, 'tis enough. I am part of a glorious
    game.
Am I cast for madness or love? I am cast to esteem them
    the same.
Am I only a dream in the sleep of some butterfly? Phantom
    of fright
Conceived, who knows how, or how deep, in the measureless
    womb of the night?
I imagine impossible thought, metaphysical voids that beget
Ideas intangible wrought to things less conceivable yet.
It may be. Little I reck*—but, assume the existence of earth,
Am I born to be hanged by the neck, a curse from the hour of
    my birth?
Am I born to abolish man's guilt? His horrible heritage, awe?

---

*Reck (archaic), "pay heed to"; "what recks it?" = is it important?

Or a seed in his wantonness spilt by a jester? I care not a straw,
For I understand Do what thou wilt; and that is the whole of
   the Law.

Appropriately, he performed ⊕ with Bill for "Health etc."—and the next day, too, with Margot: a threesome of happy dust.

Bill's lease on Crowley's patience was short. Sunday, December 3, was a quiet day "bar irruption by Busch." She was not included in the opus with Margot that day, dedicated to the "Great Work"—the manifestation of the God-Man from darkness.

A letter from Frieda of December 19 was abrupt:

Dear Aleister,

I have a long complaint from Charles Roberts* for introducing you as tenant to his flat [Petersham Road]. Having no money Mr. Roberts demanded £21 for electricity and telephone—he tells me you undertook in writing to pay for these services. I can't help him being down to my limit myself.

Frieda asked Crowley to allow workmen to put the coinbox back on the telephone.

I can give you 3 shillings a week more which will allow you 18 calls. I didn't want to disturb as you're ill.

Yours ever, Priggy Harris,
Lady of the Manor & Universal
provider also Charwoman.[20]

---

*The Richmond Borough Registration District Record of 1939 informs us that lodger Charles C. Roberts (born 1906), a journalist, was chief sub-editor of the "Office of *Edinburgh Scotsman*." Crowley is described as "Author Psychiatrist." We also learn that Lesley Blanch (born 1904; "Chief Features Editor and Writer, *Vogue*"), daughter of house owner Martha M.Blanch (born 1875; described as "Incapacitated"), was registered as Lesley B. Bicknell, having in 1930 married advertising agent Robert A. W. Bicknell (1893–1966); they were divorced in 1941. Crowley also shared the house with Aldo P. Philipson, formerly a teacher in Italy, now "Unoccupied [unemployed] Refugee." This would explain Crowley's diary note of Lesley having problems with "Jewish refugees" (see page 140). The sixth resident was Beatrice A. Woods (born 1908), paid for domestic duties. I am most grateful to Sigurd Bune for this information.

Frieda wrote again on December 22, responding to Crowley's concern about correspondence with Germer being inexplicably delayed:

> Has it occurred to you that the Censor is holding his letters? Both of you are uncertain friends of England! Someone not understanding what either of you are saying may have docketed letters "suspect" and they lurk in a locker to be re-examined.[21]

She then arraigned Crowley over differences in perceiving spiritual beings. Crowley preferred human forms because intelligence was formless and it was natural to clothe ideas thus, in the spirit of "man made in the image of God." Frieda was adamant:

> If I have ever got off this planet it is in a world where there are *no* human figures—I have *never* encountered one. Now I have wanted to very much and believed what you all tell me, but I can't. My gods have no human forms, only curves angles and light movement colour and sound when I draw, the moment I fall on one that is familiar to me I bend the knee and shout Holy! Holy! Holy! They have no moral sense; they are neither good nor bad, only inevitable and therefore right in the true sense and I believe they are gods. Therefore the human form is, to me, only one aspect, and the gods and goddesses could be done just as well in Giraffes, in fact better for me, as the Giraffe's bosom moves. . . .[22]

Crowley regarded her fastidiousness symptomatic of contemporary "soul-sickness" manifesting in artists whose abstraction of "chair" reflected something that could *take no weight,* thereby missing the essential *idea* of "chair." Frieda wouldn't alter her conviction even if Crowley thought she *was* "reflecting the feelings of a degenerate crowd who are either too sex conscious to feel or not sex conscious enough to act." When she'd been lucky enough to push open the door of vision, she saw "only movement, light & form & inexpressible gaiety and I have not made this up to appear clever or mystical." While this mightn't suit "A.C.'s Persian carpet of a mind" it was so.

Still, Crowley was delighted with progress, writing to Wilkinson on December 28: "the Tarot is near completion at last," and enclosed "a very rough draft" of the catalogue for comment. "I have been wondering whether you would not be the right person to edit my book [on tarot], and remember that in these times one gets very anxious about the disappearance of one's accomplices, who are not so easily replaceable as they were when one was twenty."[23] Every friend was as precious as each and every day.

Crowley held Frieda in great respect and affection but was nonetheless staggered when, having suggested she might get inspiration for a female figure from Aubrey Beardsley (whom Crowley met in the late nineties), she replied, on December 29: "Dear Aleister, *Know what you won't do shall be the whole of my Law!* I can bear many things, chilblains included, but I will not draw a lady like Aubrey Beardsley." Thus began a tirade against the artist: "Old Edwardian Indecency drawn by a lineal introvert I call him." Beardsley produced "lifeless ladies which make me vomit." She signed her letter "Jesus Chutney," a favorite *nom de pinceau*.[24] Crowley got back to her in the new year:

> I have often heard artists criticize A.B. [Aubrey Beardsley] They had one thing in common; they could none of them draw . . . he died some years before King Edward came to the throne [reference

*Fig. 9.7. Lesley Blanch.*

to Frieda's "Old Edwardian Indecency"]. I am palsied by your inaccuracy. Period, indeed! His line made an epoch. Your debt to him is evident, and immense. By the way, he is perfect ♎. The culmination of Saturn with Venus in equilibrium almost Chinese is marvellous.[25]

New Year's Eve 1939 saw Frieda's friend Lesley Blanch and "Gubski" for dinner (Lesley's mother Martha Mabel Blanch [1875-1968] owned 57, Petersham Road). Having explored Russia and studied at the Slade School of Fine Art, the remarkable Lesley Blanch (1904–2007) worked as a cover designer until boredom with bland contemporary fashion inspired "Anti-Beige—A Plea for the Scarlet Woman," an article sent to *Harper's* that precipitated her surprise appointment as *Vogue* features editor (1937–1944). Blanch's mildly subversive column covered broad culture, particularly anything Russian. Such should have delighted Crowley, and Russian interest (romantic) explains Gubsky's presence—while Gubsky (1889–1971) may also explain Crowley's latest use of his title "Happy Dust." *Angry Dust* was Nikolai Gubsky's autobiography (1937), and Leonine Crowley was not one to leave it at that.

*Fig. 9.8. Painting of Lesley Blanch and pet dog by Frieda Harris from* The Sketch *("art and actuality" journal; December 6, 1933). I'm grateful to Sigurd Buhne for this.*

# TEN

# What Crowley Does This Year, England Does Next

January 1940 brought a weather gloom barely lifted by lunch at Victor's on January 8 with Driberg and reviewer Maurice Richardson. Lesley Blanch came on the eleventh—she was having "trouble" with Jewish refugees while Margot Cripps had trouble with drink. Perhaps Blanch recommended Russian movie *Prof. Mamlock* (Adolf Minkin, 1938). Crowley took Margot to see the story of a Jewish surgeon who—incredulous about Nazi anti-Semitism—operates on a Nazi leader, only to be machine-gunned. Crowley's verdict: "Not too bad: pretty good propaganda, on the whole. Bad mistake: Mamlock trying to commit suicide."

Generally frustrated, he wrote to close friend Louis Wilkinson:

Yes you are a super-Tartufe [Molière's literary "Hypocrite"]-cum-Uriah-Heep-cum-Britannia. You did not answer my last; you did not come to London in November; you—oh I just can't bear to talk about it. . . . What you say about the "mysteries" is ROT. I want a fresh mind, unprejudiced, to look at a confused mess, and put it into such shape that you can say: Now one can learn. . . .

Your friend, Aleister[1]

The Beast's asthma machine siphon broke on January 29; Cripps was sent to buy another. The driving belt snapped. Bad cash-flow news flowed in from Germer in Brussels on February 1. Informing Germer on the fourth of an opus with Alice to remedy it, Crowley dismissed

Germer's "kingly blood theory," insisting "we all have that blood in some measure; a 'king' is born when the harmony of other strains allow the royal element to dominate the whole character. Great men's sons are rarely worth anything."[2]

On the sixth: "Got rid of Cripps at last—I hope forever." Alice Florey, by contrast, brought "extreme exaltation" as the tarot work reached a climax. Crowley called it "the biggest work of my whole life."[3] A viewing on February 16 left Cammell amazed at the "excellence and uniform achievement" of the cards.

Mid-February brought more snow and freezing ice: "This is the Baltoro Glacier all over again!" quipped the Beast, recalling his 1902 K2 attempt.

Alice must have been away, for on the twenty-third he determined on a sexual shikar. A hunt round London brought first Louisa at 21 Lisle Street, Soho, then Millie at Flat 5, 50 Langham Street, while Compton Chambers no. 9 opened a door on "Diona." He found Ruby Butler at the Hop Poles pub in Hammersmith. Still game, Crowley saw Dora Williams at 42 Rupert Street, off Shaftesbury Avenue, and Mattie Pickett at 62a Castletown Road, W.14. A busy day—and quite a walk!

Bad news from Cairo induced anxiety; Deirdre's life was threatened by septicemia. Relief finally came on April 4: Deirdre and Ataturk were "OK" at 21 Shari el Gameh, Heliopolis. Visiting Frieda in Chipping Campden on February 28 Crowley wrote to Germer about "cruel times," sighing: "Well, life is like it is. Isn't it?" As for the tarot: "Frieda has done a miraculous *Universe*" (Atu XXI), assuring Germer "they are wonderful beyond anything I ever hoped to see."[4]

Back in London, a March 7 opus with Alicia (Alice Florey) for Saturnus's "big prosperity" "went completely crazy," with "very wild biting and scratching" or, as he put it to Germer, "a somewhat frenzied reunion."[5] Next day 666 found "Lilian at 40 Dean Street, Top floor."

Perhaps recourse to strumpets precipitated interest in George Cukor's 1939 comedy *The Women* on March 13, starring Norma Shearer, Joan Crawford, and Rosalind Russell as a bitchy trio. Crowley's verdict: "Pretty good though not (perhaps)—as propaganda against sodomy. Mrs. S. Haines a stupid cow." (Shearer played the naive Haines whose husband was stepping out with "Crystal" Crawford.)

After an evening at the Cammells', Crowley woke to falling snow, spending the afternoon with Alice on a IX° for Germer's income, and success studying the Disks: "Mentally well prepared, held at climax, and often confirmed later. Current sent out forcibly." Maurice Richardson stood him an "excellent lunch" at Victor's on the twenty-first, and two days later came another shikar in Richmond Park, encountering an "amusing" Mary Wilcox. They had a "very good, spontaneous and easy" opus on the twenty-fourth when Crowley cooked *"Suprêmes de Volaille Mary Wilcox.* Toss them [baked skinless chicken breasts.] in butter with a little cooking-liquor of the chicken. Season, add paprika and cream little by little: (or turmeric)."

Perhaps thoughts of the Baltoro Glacier conjured a blast from the distant past when on May 7 Crowley ran into K2 expedition comrade Guy Knowles (1879–1959). Living near Knightsbridge, Croix de Guerre-decorated Knowles had become benefactor to Cambridge's Fitzwilliam Museum. They lunched a month later at Chez Victor and again on June 18 for a "good talk" about the war situation. Perhaps Knowles stimulated Crowley's dream of July 1: "Marvellous dream of Himalayan heights and abysses . . . I am sending a letter, or resending, by affixing stamps of solid gold foil—to Allan Bennett!" (Crowley's old friend and mentor in magic and Buddhism, Allan Bennett, had died in 1923.)

May 10, 1940: Germany's invading Belgium spelled disaster for Saturnus. Arrested by Belgians, transferred to French authority on the fourteenth, Germer was interned in Le Vijean concentration camp. German advance meant transfer to St. Cyprien on the Mediterranean near Spain, infamous for mistreating Spanish Civil War refugees—then to France's worst camp: Gurs, in the Pyrenees. Though primitive conditions shocked Americans into protest, words failed to express the wretchedness endured by bewildered captives, many of whom were Jews willing to fight with France against Germany, but who wound up hating the French as much as their persecutors.

Crowley's ignorance of the situation informed his last telegram to Germer (May 2, 1940):

SERIOUS ASTHMA SPECIAL TREATMENT IMPERATIVE WOULD WELCOME QUICK 50 CROWLEY.[6]

*Fig. 10.1. 30 Clarendon Square, Leamington Spa. (Author's Collection)*

The special treatment was heroin, from family doctor Harold Batty-Shaw of 7 Harley Street.

Frieda informed Crowley on May 19 that Lesley Blanch insisted on having 57 Petersham Road back.* Crowley moved to 15 Richmond Green four days later.

On the twenty-fifth the Beast took the bus to Ealing Broadway and the train to Chipping Campden: "Pleasant day with Frieda. All cards now done; only a few small revisions and the four aces to do over." They drove to Warwickshire on the twenty-seventh to show Frieda Crowley's birthplace: Clarendon Square, Leamington Spa. He proclaimed Thelema from the door of no. 30 before gathering earth and blossoms from the square.

Back in London on the twenty-ninth, so was Cathrine Falconer, whose return signaled an opus on June 1 to "put over 'England, Stand Fast!'" with one "Stuart" of the Ministry of Information: "She [Cathrine]

---

*See Lesley Blanch, *On the Wilder Shores of Love: A Bohemian Life;* edited by Georgia de Chamberet, London, Virago Press, 2015, 160.

is just as perfect technically and with the same prehensile cunt."

Three days later, the bell tolled for Crowley's sex magick when an opus with Ruby Butler was marred by "Weak erection. Too rapid ejaculation. Very feeble concentration: could not formulate purpose," while "Shaw's dope" made him sick. Next day came a letter dated May 10 from Germer, expecting "immediate arrest."

On June 9 Crowley recorded, "Ala Storey goes to N[ew].Y[ork]. on Tuesday." Friendly with Lesley Blanch, Ala Storey (1907–1972) trained at Vienna's Academy of Fine Arts and directed a string of London galleries before running avant-garde St. James's Stafford Gallery in 1938. Renamed the British Art Centre, it assisted the Contemporary Art Society to purchase works for museums now putting them into storage. Storey moved to New York on June 11 to establish the American-British Art Center on West 57th Street. Three days later the Germans entered Paris, and at 12:35 a.m. June 25 the Luftwaffe hit London.

Crowley got out to Chipping Campden on July 2. Objections to his asthma machine at the Noel Arms led to a better room at the King's Arms. "Final approval of all Taro bar [Atu] VIII [Adjustment]." A month later he worried: "Is stipend going to stop?" Money from Frieda arrived on the eighth.

On the eleventh he gave Alice lunch: "Lobster in paprika and cream. A. C. Rice plus onion and garlic. A perfect masterpiece," followed by an opus for "Magical Energy," which worked by "restraint of *bindu*[semen]." A bad night's asthma followed.

Pocked with air raids, July saw the Master Therion's tarot book rejected by publishers Collins, Murray, and Gollancz. London was bombed on the fifteenth and sixteenth; eighteenth (2:00 a.m.); Friday the twenty-third (3:30 a.m.); Saturday the twenty-fourth—two air raids followed by "Raid no 3—bigger and better"; and one on the twenty-fifth at 11:15. On Monday the twenty-sixth, bombers struck at 12:40, then 3:30, more at 9:30: "big, I think," inducing "extreme coughing." The raid raged into Tuesday the twenty-seventh when, after a respite, another occurred from 9:30 to 11:55. Very ill, Crowley witnessed two more raids the next day. Three raids occurred on Friday the thirtieth, with raids on and off all day on the thirty-first. Some relief from asthma attacks came via heroin tablets, ephedrine, and Amytal, but causes were various; he noted on the twenty-first: "vigorous conversation seems to induce attack."

Finally getting a good night's rest on August 2, Crowley fretted over Frieda's stipend. August 4 was spent reading Huxley's *After Many a Summer Dies the Swan* for the fourth or fifth time: "This Buddhist postulate! It is the noble attitude of experience that confutes the unmanly twaddle of these *aus gekochte* [overcooked] writers." Then, more air raids. On the twenty-eighth bombs and retaliatory guns persisted day and night. Too ill to work, Crowley only slept thanks to Luminal, a barbiturate suppressing the central nervous system.

On August 29, Smith sent news from bomb-free Hollywood:

> Frederic Mellinger is now an adherent, a German Jew, and very good within a certain range. He is giving a class on Astrology here every Wednesday. Small attendance however. As was also the case when I had a class on the Kabalah [*sic*] and study of the Book of the Law a few weeks back. I'm going to hold classes again when the hot weather is over. . . . We are inactive in other respects, except for the [Gnostic] Mass. Leffingwell and family flew the coop. Seeds of dissension earlier sown bore fruit, and he has since moved away out to the country. Two people he introduced are faithful, however. . . . I am tired of just telling prospects that do not mature.[7]

Frederic (Friedrich) Mellinger (1890–1970) acted, wrote plays, and directed theater in Berlin before World War I. According to Martin Starr, military service landed him in a French Catholic hospital, where a painting of the Sacred Heart inspired the mystical play *Jacob, der Herr*.[8] Reading it, Elisabeth von Moltke, widow of Theosophist Helmuth von Moltke (chief of German General Staff, 1906–1914), introduced Mellinger to Rudolf Steiner. Attracted to German mystical traditions, he wrote on astrology before quitting Hitler's Germany in 1934 for London. Traveling to Hollywood, Mellinger appeared uncredited in several movies* before hearing of the Gnostic Catholic Mass. Bonding with Smith, admired by Jane, Mellinger was a boon to Winona Boulevard.

Throughout September 1940 the Battle of Britain seared England's blue skies as German troops gathered en masse across the Channel.

---

*Except *Hitler, Beast of Berlin* (1939)—billed as Fred Mellinger.

On September 1, Crowley slept right through a 1:00 to 4:00 raid. Another came at 11:00 and another between two and four o'clock, which he slept through. Cammell and Mabella took him to sherry at Henekey's. On the third, eighteen bombs fell across Richmond Park, very loud and very close. On the seventh, bombing lasted all night. Two days later, Crowley reported: "Air raids heavy over this way. House repeatedly shaken. Afternoon raid severe in Richmond." At 11:50, electricity failed: soon a regular occurrence. On Wednesday the eleventh he slept under the stairway from midnight to 3 a.m., on the sofa 3 to 5:30 a.m., and on the bed 6 to 8:30 a.m.! The next day Charles Cammell and Mabella lunched on Crowley's paprika cream duck and mushrooms: "It really was a miracle. Long nice letter from Frieda. Raid 9:15. Nothing very startling." The next day—Friday the thirteenth—Buckingham Palace was bombed. And the next: seven raids of 10 to 70 minutes pounded London, day and night. It is impossible for us to imagine what this must have felt like. Occasionally, a boon: Cammell was with him one night when a German plane was shot down. Having been struggling for breath, Crowley rushed into the street and danced for joy like a boy, asthma symptoms gone. September 16: "Very much better as to asthma. The air raids have proved an excellent tonic. . . . No business can be done until raids die down."

*Fig. 10.2. After the bombing of London, September 9, 1940.*

*Fig. 10.3. Office workers going to work after London bombing.*

Five days later, he consulted the I Ching: "Shall I get out of London? 45. *Ts'ui* [Gathering Together]." The hexagram appeared next day: "The repetition of *Ts'ui* gave me the answer. I should go to Torquay (my ancestral temple see line 1 of 45) for the winter."* "Ancestral temple" Crowley took as referencing his teenage stay in Torquay with liberal tutor James Archibald Douglas (born 1860), where he discovered normal life outside his parents' religion.

Crowley traveled to Oxford on the twenty-fourth, dining at the Randolph Hotel by the Ashmolean. A taxi driver suggested a room in Marston on the outskirts, but Crowley opted for a nap in the hotel lounge, then headed for Chipping Campden to see Frieda before leaving for Torquay.

His train steamed into an air raid at Bristol—or as Crowley's I Ching reading expressed it: "*Chen* 51!!!"—hexagram for "Shock." He arrived at Torquay's Grand Hotel at 1:16 a.m., September 26, 1940.

---

*Legge's translation: "Žhui, the king will repair to his ancestral temple. It will be advantageous."

## TORQUAY—GREAT MAGICAL RETIREMENT?

Offering good sea air and, he hoped, life, Torquay rose in stone from the port to cliff edges with fine views of the channel. On September 27, while Germany, Italy, and Japan signed a Tripartite Pact, Crowley, misdirected, walked miles up hills and steps around southeast Torquay—without asthma. Hoping for an ideal flat in Middle Warberry Road, he returned to the hotel. A Mrs. Walker phoned to say the flat was his from October to March, while an ex-Café Royal waiter recalled it being said: "What Crowley does this year, England does next."

Feeling guided by the "Masters," he duly paid seven pounds, ten shillings for rooms in Norfolk Lodge, a three-story Georgian house off Middle Warberry Road near Kents Cavern prehistoric caves. On September 29, he wrote to Charles Cammell:

> Cher amie,
>
> Guided by heavenly wisdom I came here. I found myself walking
> 6 miles up hills and long steep flights of steps without discomfort!
> My own Wisdom bade me stay.[9]

When the day came to quit the hotel he couldn't pay. Hotel manager Paul was "most kind" and let him go. Frieda's stipend arrived at 5:30 p.m.

On October 5 a letter came from Gerald Hamilton—odd because someone called "Devey" had approached him about a girl interested in drawing who knew a friend of Crowley. The friend, Hamilton—and the girl, "hunchback" Karin de Beaufort.* They became friends.

He wrote to Smith on the ninth: "This is a lovely place; might be South of France or Northern California. A.1 for G[reat].M[agical]. R[etirement]." He intended to get down to the *Yi King*: "harder job . . . there being nothing much to guide one." He'd lost his rhyming version of the text; could Smith send one? "Please give my love to Jane and

---

*Karin de Beaufort (b. London, October 31, 1906; d. Torquay, 1946; daughter of Arnout Jan de Beaufort (b. Zeist, Netherlands 1872; d. London 1955) and Ella Rythen (b. Stockholm, 1866; d. London, 1958).

Regina and the Bb [brethren] and Ss [sisters]. I should like to hear from you all so much." Crowley hoped the tarot cards would be ready next year at $25 a pack.[10]

That evening* his nerves were "on edge for lack of cunt," and the tone of "clacking" charwoman Mrs. Martin got on his wick.

He finally got his shikar on the twelfth, meeting Hastings barmaid Kitty Long. He bought her dinner and "frigged her."

Over the following weeks he enjoyed conversations with Karen (sometimes "Karin") at "early doors" drinks at the hotel, Crowley's principal social anchorage.

A bad night of asthma on October 11 followed seeing Michael Balcon production *Convoy,* starring Clive Brook and Michael Wilding about the Royal Navy's Atlantic campaign. A cryptic note of that day: "Min. 1 . . . [Ministry?] accepted my suggestion B. *A.* they liked, but said 'technical, can't.'"

> Wednesday, October 16: 9:15 A Jerry [German plane] over—some gunfire. H92 Cl2. [?] . . . Next day walked into Torquay and found an air raid on. One Jerry about 50 miles away, I suppose.

October 20 was a typical Torquay Sunday: "Wrote several long letters 5:30 A.M. to 9:30. Strolled, read papers, and cooked—great success of Roast Lamb and Pommes Lyonnaises. Shikar in wet. Explored Imperial [hotel] and made progress with Clapham barmaid."

In a letter to Louis Wilkinson of October 22 he described himself as a "worrying Minnie at present," concerned at people's reactions to the war effort: "Nobody believes any official propaganda, or newspaper statements, anymore." He sighed: "It's lonely at the top" as Cecil B. de Mille said."[11]

> 26 October Karin here: long talks with masks off, or nearly. Karin's birthday 31st October.

By November 4, Crowley was ill again: "Karin got hold of Dr. Lees at last; he sent his partner Dr. [R. H.] Lodge, *Southover,* Bronshill Rd.;

---

*John Lennon was born that night (October 9, 1940).

I judge, a very able man. At least no nonsense and no waste of time; no attempt to play on the patient's ignorance and fear; no effort to run commercial stunts on the side."

Next day, he was too ill to help himself. "Karin has been an angel, coming every day." Laurence and Pam Felkin visited on the ninth. Karin looked in on the thirteenth and the fourteenth. A Mrs. de Montmorency, of Bramblehurst, Hunsdon Road, entertained him, wife of Hervey Guy Francis Edward de Montmorency, D.S.O., Irish nationalist and Boer War and World War I hero (died 1942).

On October 16 Crowley suffered "the worst attack I ever had, I think." Prescribed morphine sulphate and atropine sulphate, he was seriously ill. Frieda arrived on the nineteenth. Unusually, no diary entries were recorded between the twenty-second and twenty-fourth. Karin came on the twenty-fifth. Two days later a few sunny steps were taken in the garden. On the twenty-ninth he noted: "The moron Bickers* has been telling the world I was dying. Local rag ringing up doctor."

On October 30 he received his I Ching paraphrase from Smith and got on revising it. Bickers brought a Polish soldier, Jankow, to arrange a chess match. Crowley beat him easily on November 1 when Karin brought "a lovely green muffler." On November 2, the doctor declared Crowley cured; the United States was informed. Thinking he was close to death, Frieda believed his recovery a miracle. On the fifth he walked to the highest point of Middle Warberry Road—quite a feat after K2! The next day the grocer stopped his credit, and "utter starvation prospect" was only tempered by a "long delightful chat with Karen."

He informed Wilkinson on December 1 he'd been "damned ill" while "local reporters [had been] lurking behind trees awaiting my decease. However, here I am, and I would I were on my ancestral estates in Rainbow Valley."[12]

A week later, he wrote again to Wilkinson:

I saw an advertisement of one of your London lectures. I wish you were telling the world how to rebuild itself on the basis of the law of Thelema. Perhaps you will when the time comes. All these trou-

---

*Horace A. Sheridan-Bickers (1883–1957), Hollywood scriptwriter and early O.T.O. British Columbia member; temporarily in Devon.

bles have come because quick communication and transport have squeezed the world together, and so destroyed the virtue of the parochial sanctions of traditional customs and religion. Hence a new principle is imperative: one which has no regional or cultural limitations, still less depends on local frauds and fables.

I feel that I shall be back in or near London soon. I weary of the Unburied Dead.

> Oh solitude, where &c.* Love.
> Yours Aleister.[13]

On December 13 (Friday) he received a "really wretched letter from F[rieda].H[arris].—enough to make one despair." His credit broke down. He couldn't rent a "wireless." Creditors from Richmond found his address: "I am what St. Francis of Assisi would call fucked on the financial front."

Crowley wrote to Smith on December 16, worrying about German U-boats around the coast and night bombing.

> The collapse of France was not foreseen, and it has made a lot of difference. . . . Gamelin's [French c-in-c] long inaction sapped the morale of his armies. . . . Don't believe any stories about our being starved out. There is some muddle and delay, but that's the worst of it. Damage by bombs amounts, at a guess, to one square mile in 50,000. It takes about ten tons of High Explosive to kill a baby.

Getting to California only needed funds. They should do some magick "to arrange for passage your end. And you have got to show legally urgent business reasons for my journey. You will have to see a lawyer about this."[14] Dr. R. H. Lodge suggested a trip to the United States might even save his life. Crowley needed a passport and wrote to Frieda about it.

On Friday December 27, he met Sophie Burt (with a daughter-in-law called Joan). Three days later, it was ⊕ for gold. Verdict: "Good, considering all." Perhaps he might make California yet.

---

*From William Cowper: "O solitude, where are the charms/That sages have seen in thy face? Better dwell in the midst of alarms,/Than reign in this horrible place."

# ELEVEN

# Robed as a Warrior

But who are They? [Secret Chiefs]

Since They are "invisible" and "inaccessible," may They not merely be figments invented by a self-styled "Master," not quite sure of himself, to prop his tottering Authority?

Well, the "invisible" and "inaccessible" criticism may equally be levelled at Captain A, and Admiral B, of the Naval Intelligence Department. These "Secret Chiefs" keep in the dark for precisely the same reasons; and these qualities disappear instantaneously the moment *They* want to get hold of you.[1]

January 1, 1941: "Used ceremonial [magick] after so long abstinence. It went very well. P.S. Too well! Started three fire accidents!!!! Message re. My Work for '41 . . . *AL* II:58 (Work in disguise!)?" *AL* II:58:

Yet there are masked ones my servants: it may be that yonder beggar is a King. A King may choose his garment as he will: there is no certain test: but a beggar cannot hide his poverty.

Crowley's using ceremonial rather than sex magick intrigues, as does the message's suggestion of incognito Work.

Mrs. Walker put her lawyer on to Crowley for unpaid rent, so a series of oral-sex opera with randy, foul-mouthed Sophie Burt for "gold" was enacted, as Sophie grew jealous of Karin, and Crowley signed on as air raid warden, only to be fined two pounds on February 13 for blackout infringement! Bad toothache, asthma, invasion threats, and nighttime bombing compounded worries, but faith in the Aeon's progress maintained him, as he confided to Wilkinson on January 27:

> I am very happy about the Law of Thelema. It has always been my idea that you were the ideal man to link the message with the people;* so I felt that I should not worry you about it, but rather let it ripen. We are now, I think, at the time when events will themselves force the issue. The paths leading backwards are all quietly closing; at any moment a word from you might set going an organized advance.
>
> The stored energy is overwhelming; on all sides it flows over in action. All that is lacking is right interpretation of events. With this the weeds of sporadic revolution may whither. Casual upheavals, dealing with symptoms, disappoint. The world needs revolution at the root of life. This is already well at work, but must be brought up into consciousness so that the apparatus of intellect may be applied to it. Write to me. Yours Aleister.[2]

## V

As for intrigue, a P.S. dated Sept. 4 appears at the end of the January 31 diary entry: "Should any one challenge my authorship of 'The V Sign,' I reply in the words of my predecessor in poetry & Magick, Publium Vergilius Maro: *Sic vos non vobis*—If he fail to understand exactly this is an answer, his claim is unlikely to be well-founded. If he does understand, then: Tu it! [thumbs up it!?]"† Crowley's public claim to have originated the *V* for Victory sign came after its inception in June, so why place this "Sept. 4" note here?‡ Perhaps he wanted posterity to see

---

*Probably referring to the "Authorized Popular Commentary" edited by Louis Wilkinson and Hymenaeus Beta—finally published 1996!

†Crowley's quotation from Virgil exists in two forms: *sic vos non vobis melliscatis apes* (Thus you bees make honey not for yourselves) and *sic vos non vobis vallera fertis oves* (Thus you sheep make fleeces not for yourselves; see *Oxford Book of Quotations*, 1941). Bathyllus, a performer, plagiarized Virgil, who answered: "it's there, but not for you" (the false claimant).

‡It is possible the Sept. 4 is an error for Sept. 8. On September 8, 1941, Bernard O'Donnell broke an appointment at Crowley's flat "to write V sign book." "I wrote him a snorter," snarled Crowley. Unfortunately, the dating lacuna leaves the question open: *who was first?*

the sign emerging from his planned thelemic war booklet *Thumbs Up!*

On February 12 he asked himself: *"Thumbs Up!* [planned booklet] being phallic, how can I put it over pictorially or graphically? I can point out the result of 'National Prayer' to the Castrato-deity [i.e., *no balls**]: but I want positive ritual affirmation, like 'Liber Resh,' 'saying will,' and so on." On Valentine's Day he considered alternatives:

Idea of Magical "Union of Men" to beat Nazis. I need (a) symbol to bring victory. (b) a plan (Secret Lodges n[o].g[ood].) (c) a way to put it across. V for Valentine and Victory. V.V.V.V.V. 8°=3□ is rather hot, because of L.V.X. and the Sign of Apophis and Typhon and the Horns of ♑ [Capricorn] The Devil! See Lévi on Vintras. P.S. V is Vau [Hebrew *vav*] a nail: seal in H[itler]'s coffin. But Z=[Hebrew *zain*] a sword much better; and Z is N for Nazi knocked sideways! But Z isn't much of an initial: Zeal about the only relevant word, and to English people the letter itself seems frilly. A א [Hebrew *aleph*] is of course a Swastika![3]

To grasp Crowley's train of thought, first realize he had two symbols in mind: an exoteric one (the *V*) and an esoteric one. The reference to V.V.V.V.V. refers to a Latin acronym for his *Magister Templi* motto (1909): "In my lifetime I have conquered the universe by the force of truth." The note of victory is there.

The *V* in L.V.X. is a Latin *U. Lux* is Latin for "light." L.V.X. in the Golden Dawn referred to the "Light of the Cross," since if the two lines of the *L* and the *V* are extended they form crosses, so L.V.X. is also equated with INRI (written on Jesus's cross), which the Bible interprets as Jesus of Nazareth, King of the Jews, but alchemists understood as *Igne Natura Renovatur Integra:* "The whole of Nature is renewed by Fire."

The sun's burning aspect the Egyptians identified with sun god Seth (Greek form *Typhon;* hence "typhoon"). The Golden Dawn sign

---

*His March 23 diary noted outcomes of "Days of National Prayer": "No. 1 smashed the B.E.F. [British Expeditionary Force retreated from France in May] No. 2 smashed France. . . . No. 3 smashed into Greece, Egypt, and Yugoslavia. No. 4 ought to assure the fall of London." *Thumbs Up!* used them to demonstrate death wish and needless sacrifice of the Aeon of Osiris.

for Typhon involved stretching two arms upward—a *V* sign and middle letter of L.V.X. So the *V* represents also the vigor and force of Seth, killer of Osiris (in the myth). Osiris was symbolized by arms crossing the chest: an *X* or cross, while Isis his bride's weeping gesture was symbolized by the *L*. So L.V.X. meant *L* for birth (Isis), *V* for death (Seth or Typhon), and *X* for rebirth (Osiris), a life-renewing formula.

*V* for Crowley represented the new Aeon made possible by death of Osiris (the old formula). Fulfillment required cleansing the world by spiritual fire (begun, Crowley claimed, in 1904). The new formula would install Horus—crowned and **V**ictorious solar child, revealed at *Al Kahira,* the City of *Victory:* Cairo.

Crowley also sees *V* in the horns of goat Capricorn (♑), an image for Typhon—lusty, bold, wild—also the common idea of the devil, who for Crowley is an image of life force, sex, at nature's core. Sex is not evil, and the devil, as Christians have been taught to fear him, does not exist. The horned one is Pan, Greek for the *All*—Nature. Man's martial instincts, connected to the sex force—and before that, the True Will— would see off the repressive, antilife, antilove force.

Crowley's note, "See Lévi on Vintras" refers to French "Professor of Transcendental Magic" Eliphas Lévi's *Key of the Mysteries,* which Crowley translated ([London: Rider, 1977], 113). It describes meeting a disciple of occultist Eugène Vintras (1807–1875). The visitor spoke of Vintras's "miraculous hosts" bearing symbols in blood. One had the pentagram, magical symbol for man (head and four limbs) but which superstition saw as a symbol of evil when inverted. Crowley's footnote asked how the pentagrams could have been inverted if the hosts were round! Another of Vintras's hosts bore two hermetic serpents whose heads and tails, instead of coming together, turned outward. Above the serpent's head, a fatal *V:* Typhonian fork, character of hell, meaning "Antagonism is eternal"—grist to Crowley's symbolic mill; *V* meant *implacable opposition.*

Crowley then considered Hebrew letters as symbols, toying first with vau ו, hook or pin, extending this to a nail: a nail in Hitler's coffin!—then considered zayin ז, sword. The sword divides, expressing antagonism: the unresolved 2; meaning, no peace with Hitler. English equivalent of zayin is *Z*—and *Z* is an *N*, or Nazi, knocked sideways! Nice idea. Finally, he considered aleph א, an ox. You get the horns and defiance, but its basic form is a swastika, and magick required that symbol's overlord!

The *V*s had it: *V* for Victory.

Crowley's claim to have invented the sign as a war weapon contends with an official version expounded in 1995 HMSO* publication *Persuading the People—Government Publicity in the Second World War* (p. 33) where the *V* campaign is described as "one of the BBC's most enduring contributions to the propaganda war." Apparently, Belgian Liberal politician Victor Auguste de Laveleye (1894–1945), wishing to appeal to French and Flemish-speaking Belgians, realized *V* begins both *Victoire* (French) and *Vrijheid* (Flemish for freedom). Becoming BBC announcer for "Radio Belgique" on January 14, 1941, de Laveleye urged resisters to paint *V* on public buildings. However, confirmation the campaign *actually began* on that date is lacking.

De Laveleye's shortwave broadcasts to occupied Europe were cited in a paper on "broadcasting as a new weapon of war" circulated within the BBC in May 1941. Douglas Ernest Ritchie (1905–1967), assistant news editor since 1939, became assistant director of BBC European Broadcasts in 1941. Broadcasting as "Colonel Britton," he organized the BBC's *V* campaign. However, uncoordinated sabotage allegedly inspired by it upset the Secret Intelligence Service, and an arrangement was struck with Britton advocating softer resistance. Meanwhile, SIS used the BBC to send coded messages to resistance groups.

Only on June 27, 1941, was the famous Morse code *V* (three dots and a dash) followed by Beethoven's Fifth's opening bar broadcast, pounded on drums next day. Sign of the victor, *V*'s effect was magical; was its source?

According to Gerald Yorke, Crowley "told me [Yorke] he [Crowley] suggested the idea to a Col. Britten [*sic*] and that as a result it was officially adopted during the Second World War. No evidence in proof of his claim and statement seems to have survived. This book [Crowley's planned *V*-sign book] would merely have proved that the sign as such was not new."[4] Crowley maintained he'd swung the idea over *surreptitiously,* realizing his authorship would prejudice reception. The person responsi-

---

*Acronym for Her Majesty's Stationery Office (British Government publications).

ble would suffer if "truth" were known: "Of course I am denying strenu-
ously that I ever had anything to do about it, as the bloke who slipped it
over on the idiots of the BBC would get into the most hellish trouble if
it were found out that he knows me. All the same it will help my subtle
intrigues if you pass the word along that I did it! I have something else
in my capacious sleeve which needs to be prepared."[5]

Crowley had several BBC contacts and certainly contacted "Colonel
Britton" with sabotage ideas such as "241" (see chapter 12). One name of
possible significance was chess player Maurice Sutherland, who, according to a letter of Crowley to Edward Noel Fitzgerald, could help Noel
find government work: "Afraid I can't suggest any sort of Government
work. Call on Mr. M. A. Sutherland (Admiralty) Rex House, Regent
St. Say you are a friend of mine, and can he help."[6] Rex House, Lower
Regent Street, had been the short-lived Paris Cinema (closed in 1940);
after 1946, the BBC's "Paris Theatre." Maurice A. Sutherland appears
in Crowley's diaries as "M.A.S." His help was sought over a U.S. visa
(see page 172). A letter to Fitzgerald of March 10, 1941, refers to
Sutherland as "frequent chess visitor to Richmond, I think you met
him"[7] According to an obituary of "Harold Lommer" in *British Chess
News* (December 19, 2019), Sutherland died in 1954.

An example of how secret material got through the BBC emerges
from its History Department (1979 unreleased radio interview).
Interviewee "Alec Sutherland," a Scot, described being recalled from
"secondment to the American Army" to the BBC as a "kind of trouble-
shooter" (Sutherland's phrase) over European Services emanating from
Bush House, the Strand. Problems had arisen when executive memos
(SIS-directed) instructed playing "fill-up" records between bulletins.
One 1941 memo indicated a Polish officer (false name) would bring
and retrieve a disc to be played at a precise time. Unknown to program
assistants, European resistance fighters relied on its encoded message.
Sutherland, probably an SIS plant, revealed in 1979 that assistants' keen
eyes, spotting groove abnormalities, were swapping the "bands" for others of equal length. "And so," according to Sutherland, "they would play
the other band and the wrong bridge would get blown up in Poland.
Now they couldn't be told this—all that could be done was to supervise
them viciously and crack them over the head if they made any kind of
mistake." (Alec Sutherland, 1979).

Crowley wrote to Jane Wolfe at Winona Boulevard on February 12, answering her query about the "Taro" project.

> About the Taro, we ought to have started printing &c this month, but the backer seems to have backed out, for the moment [as Houghton at Atlantis informed him on January 27]. It is very hard to make plans at all, with everybody screaming about invasion. Our whole strategy seems to be directed towards goading the Huns into trying it. My German crowd has been pestering me the last 5 years about *Liber AL* and Hitler. They claim he has got it, or been inspired on the same lines, and is working it out, all wrong of course, but anyhow half of it. Karl, who has no doubt been murdered or worse, urged me in one of his last letters to read Rauschning's *Hitler Speaks*. Yes, it is astonishing how closely his intimate thoughts run on the same rails. . . . The difficulties of communication are great—and your Sanctuary isn't doing much to help things along, is it? . . . Sooner or later we shall break through into younger minds. I've been inclined to think that W. T. S[mith]. somehow puts people off—or is it Regina's manner? Perhaps it is the Masters after all—cooking slowly to get the best effect.[8]

Crowley was unhappy with Sophie Burt: "Except for pseudo-blond tarts, women who are free sexually are usually free socially. Burt can't make the grade; she will not accept the status of friendship; her inferiority galls her day and night." Next day (February 16): "During this long period of semi-sickness, due in part . . . to avoiding the nauseating importunities of Burt, I did a lot of introspection. *Idea:* to find a rational explanation of my life. Is there any possible escape from the official A∴A∴ theory? [Crowley as "Logos of the Aeon"] Answer: NO. But many interesting discoveries enlivened the series of meditations. It is quite certain, in particular, that I have always been insane."

On February 1, unbeknownst to 666, Frater Saturnus was liberated from internment. Wife Cora had procured a nonquota immigration visa—available since September, but the French only allowed access to the U.S. consul in Marseille *four months* after the consul's request that Germer call urgently for the visa. As Germer arranged passage to New York, Crowley met a Major Penny of the Air Ministry, who'd borrowed Dr. Lodge's Christmas gift copy of *Yoga*. Penny was on sick leave—Torquay's Palace Hotel was an RAF officers convalescent establishment.

*Aircraft Engineer & Airships* magazine (June 9, 1927) records an O.B.E. medal bestowed on Major Rupert Ernest Penny, Principal Technical Officer, Air Ministry. Crowley wondered on February 24 if Major Penny's "being in [the] Air Ministry might help my Magical Symbol scheme." He bought Crowley's last available *Yoga*. "He wanted a course of training, if I had been in London. I will suggest a correspondence." The I Ching symbol for Penny was perfect, no. 20, *Kwan*: "Contemplating"—"the very symbol for Yoga!"

On March 1 Crowley consulted the stars to surmise when Russia would enter the war. Stalin suspected a secret deal between Hitler and Britain would leave Russia exposed. While suspicion intensified after Rudolf Hess's flight to Britain in May, Stalin did not foresee an invasion as early as summer 1941. Crowley had few doubts: "The Sickle and Hammer have simply G.O.T. got to come in somehow." Astrological portents "moving up to May 8" were striking, though reason suggested Russia probably would "not [come in] till '42 though so close." The May date is remarkable because evidence suggests Hess's flight to Britain on May 10, 1941, was partly determined astrologically, guidance seeded by anti-Nazi astrologers working for Britain to enhance prospects for Hess's delivery of a British peace deal to Hess's idol, Hitler—leaving Hitler free to demolish the U.S.S.R.

Also on March 1, "X" came to tea for "a long and pleasant talk, mostly by me (hence 'pleasant') about various adventures. Nothing sexual." Meeting again on the third: "She is evidently serious about the Abbey." Looking beyond the war, Crowley contemplated establishing an Abbey of Thelema at Torquay based on "aristocratic communism." "X" was probably Grace M. Horner, introduced by Karen on February 23. Another possible abbey candidate—a "W. Asa of 22 Talbot Road"—showed interest on March 10, agreeing to take tuition on May 6, which he did in a desultory fashion.

On March 14 Crowley heard Germer was: "safe after all. The happiest evening of my life! Even the birth of little Ataturk is not in the same class; for that I expected. This is a stunning joy. Life has again immediate value; the future is all sunrise on transluscent wings." He wrote to Cammell: "Dear Charles, I am drunk with joy. Germer is alive and well. I have to write a dozen letters to U.S.A. to various of my people there, to look after him when he gets there, as he may do any day (he wrote Nov 16 from an internment camp near Pau); all fixed with visas &c; so I must hurry. My health is much better especially since the good news came."[9] Wilkinson was sent the same message on March 16: "I am drunk with joy. Karl Germer is alive and well. Nov 16 he was interned near Pau, and all set to go to the Arsehole [or "Arsenal"] of Democracy. So perhaps we shall all live happily ever after."[10] He told Wilkinson bluntly: "I'm starting an Abbey of Thelema. You had better butt in. Do you know Mallock? Barrister, now/playwright, always rebel." On March 12 an estate agent had driven Crowley to a possible billet on Barton Brow where he met "Mallock, a playwright," who knew Louis Wilkinson well. The Mallocks came from nearby Cockington Court, friends of Agatha Christie (they put on plays before her first marriage). Crowley reckoned Mallock would be good for the abbey: "I hope he may join us. . . . Mallock—the first human voice I have heard for months." He appealed to Wilkinson: "We must collaborate to build the New Order on the planet. Your voice and pen are imperatively needed."

A note was attached to this letter, headed "In Darkest Torquay," relating dialogue with a local:

> Talking of Haw-Haw "That's the fellow in the Tower, isn't it?" *A.C.* "No, it's a man called William Joyce."* "Ah, that's the fellow that wrote the dirty book?" *A.C.* "No, you are thinking of James Joyce, an old blind man and a very distinguished artist; and he <u>never</u> wrote a dirty book." I never thought I should have a good word to say for him! [Joyce died in January in Zurich.]

---

*The interchange appeared slightly differently in Crowley's diary for December 16, 1940: "Talk of German wireless and [Lord] Haw-Haw. When I told the ignorant bastards he was William Joyce, one said 'Isn't that the fellow who wrote the dirty book?' I told him some more." "Lord Haw-Haw" was the nickname for Irish pro-Nazi William Joyce, who broadcast propaganda to Britain from Germany. Joyce had been a British Fascist, known personally to Maxwell Knight when he served as an MI5 undercover agent.

On March 18, Crowley took rooms at Barton Brow for four and a half guineas. Three days later, Wilfrid Smith wrote from Winona Boulevard:

> I think I have at long last a really excellent man, John Parsons. And starting next Tuesday he begins a course of talks with a view to enlarging our scope. He has an excellent mind and much better intellect than myself—and yes, I know that it would not necessarily have to be very good to be better than mine. . . . J.P. is going to be valuable. I feel sure we're going to move ahead despite Max Schneider's continued efforts to discredit me.[11]

A remarkable product of privileged Pasadena, John Whiteside Parsons (1914–1952) was a child when his parents divorced. Mother Ruth Virginia, née Whiteside, doted on her gifted, good-looking son, who reckoned an Oedipus complex impelled interest in witchcraft coupled to a disdain for Christian morals.[12] Poor writing skills suggest dyslexia, but intelligence was plentiful, rockets being his passion. In 1935 he became an unpaid research fellow in the Aeronautical Laboratory of the California Institute of Technology (Caltech), from which emerged the Jet Propulsion Laboratory: basis of the U.S. jet industry and postwar space program. His brilliance was rewarded with a Caltech salary in 1939. Lacking typical graduate culture, Parsons attempted to draw a line between his magical interest and the security-bounded world of jet and fuel research. An original scientific mind was a boon to Thelema: everything Smith didn't have, Parsons appeared to. There were problems, however.

In April 1935 Jack married Helen (born Mary Helen Cowley), whose father had died prematurely in 1920. Her mother Olga remarried Burton Ashley Northrup, who moved the family from Chicago to Southern California and fathered two daughters with Olga: Sara (also called Betty) and Nancy. According to Martin Starr's *The Unknown God* (2003), Northrup was crooked and sexually abused Sara; Helen resisted, and Northrup was imprisoned for fraud in 1928. Helen dropped out of high school to work for her family, attending night-school classes in business law at Pasadena Junior College. Helen's aunts were very religious, but evangelism made no impression; she wanted something else. As a young chemist at the Hercules Power Company, Jack wooed Helen through 1934, inspiring her with dreams of their belonging to the stars.

Married, Helen soon found "Handsome Jack" unfaithful, and at some point, half-sister Sara began an affair with Jack. Jack had his own moral order—he cheerfully informed Helen of his adventures—and Helen didn't want to lose him through nagging. They stayed together because, through it all, Jack made life fun, though unfulfilling emotionally; he didn't want children.

Jack's friends, homosexual John Baxter and lesbian sister Frances, who fancied Helen, introduced the couple to Winona Boulevard. The profess house was a draw for gays, through Regina's theatrical friends.[13] Jack and Helen Parsons were initiated on February 15, 1941, as Smith informed Crowley,* believing the profess house was at last on a roll.

This was all distant from Crowley's world. Ensconced on April 5 at Barton Brow, Barton Cross, Torquay, with "broad views over land and sea," he wrote to Wilkinson: "The Abbey of Thelema is now a Fact in Nature—such as it is." It was "A New Order on Earth."[14] There would be no accounting; honor and chivalry counted. Poverty he defined as money withdrawn; there was enough for all. If someone went into Torquay, they could buy provisions. Private property would be respected. If anyone stole, others could pillage the thief, till the thief saw the benefit. They would help one another realize their true wills. He called it "aristocratic communism" and invited Wilkinson to participate.

On April 11 he wrote to Frieda suggesting legal action against Mrs. Walker, whose bill for Warberry Road, Crowley maintained, was ludicrous.

> Thought you might like a spare copy of "Temperance" for Easter; so enclose one. Would you please give the "Songs for Italy" to Percy? I *do* have lapses into human frailty. I am ashamed all right; but I can't help feeling that I could be so much more useful to mankind if I were gently levered into my proper place as a poet. *And* prophet.

---

*Crowley didn't receive Smith's letter until April 10.

Crowley's *Songs for Italy* poems (1923) dealt with the danger of Mussolini. Crowley thought it only fair that someone who saw in Mussolini in 1923 what the country now saw in 1941 (Britain was fighting Italians in Libya and Somaliland) "should have a little credit and consideration. It is shaking hands with thieves and treacherous murderers that leads to trouble. (Yes, I *do* hate the political game!) Besides, the vision and forethought which I had in '23 might still be useful to the world in this catastrophe."[15] British troops had evacuated Benghazi, Libya, on April 3 as Rommel's Afrika Korps advanced in support of the Italians.

On April 15 Crowley heard Max Schneider needed a job now that his eyes were too weak to make jewelry, while Roy Leffingwell and his wife were slightly injured from a car crash. Leffingwell promised to deed Crowley ground for a temple.

In the early hours of the twenty-first, several houses in Lower and Middle Warberry Roads were destroyed by bombing, including the chief air raid warden's, in which two of his children were killed. Four others died, and eight were injured in Middle Warberry Road—Crowley's departure had been timely, for him at least. The Imperial Hotel was also damaged. Crowley rightly reckoned the Luftwaffe's main target was Plymouth. Among Plymouth's many dead was Louis Wilkinson's ex-wife Frances Gregg, mother of son Oliver, who would help Crowley in years to come. Author of *The Mystic Leeway,* Frances had been Ezra Pound's friend and lover to Hilda Doolittle and John Cowper Powys before marrying Powys's friend Louis Wilkinson. A few days later, Crowley spoke to an officer from Plymouth who said little was left standing, with casualties running into four figures.

Hearing Germer was safe in New York on May 3, Crowley appointed him official U.S. Legate for the O.T.O. and Rites of Memphis and Misraim. On the West Coast, meanwhile, Smith followed Crowley's instructions, indicating to L.A.'s Department of Justice, Immigration and Naturalization Service that "great poet and writer on Philosophy and Religion, Edward A. Crowley (Aleister Crowley)" was "desirous of coming to America." The Church of Thelema, based on his teachings, provided sponsors. From the paperwork we learn Smith was fifty-six, had been in the States twenty years, was paid by the gas company $160 a month as bookkeeper, and had $200 in the bank.[16]

On May 9, Frieda confirmed Nicholson & Venn Galleries of

46 High Street, Oxford, would hold a tarot exhibition on June 7. Seeing the catalogue on May 13, however, Crowley entered a "black rage." To him it appeared an abomination of bad grammar, stupid explanations, general confusion, and obfuscation. Having himself produced a clear catalogue approved by Louis Wilkinson, Frieda could use *his* version or "count me out altogether." Frieda "blew in" on the fourteenth for a long talk and "A.1. dinner" at the Imperial. Conclusion: "She won!" Crowley was nothing if not flexible.

Between the ninth and fourteenth, extraordinary events occurred.

## RUDOLF HESS

On May 9 Aleister Crowley had an extraordinary vision:

> Above earth vast dull sphere-crust. Hard to pierce. Within, rich cream formed by dancing figures. Then immense crimson-and-cream robed Man-Angels; they seemed to be directing the war. Many [May?] land! And sea-scapes, vast scale, utmost beauty. I was concentrating badly, and could not make much of it. But they wanted me among them robed as a warrior.[17]

On May 9, as Hitler's deputy Rudolf Hess dressed for his fateful flight from Augsburg, and Luftwaffe bombers warmed up for the biggest attack of the Blitz, German submarine *U-110* fell into Royal Navy hands. The submarine's value was as nothing compared to what it secreted. At precisely the time Crowley experienced his vision of vast, beauteous seascapes shaped by will of spiritual giants, Britain captured the latest German cryptography machine: Enigma. Its possession gave Britain and her Allies immense power.

Curious portents were not unique to Crowley. Before 6 a.m. on the morning of May 10, John Colville, Winston Churchill's private secretary, lay half-awake in his Whitehall air-raid shelter. Waking moments *before* a bomb fell nearby, thoughts turned to a novel he'd read in early 1940 by Ian Fleming's brother Peter. *The Flying Visit* described a forced landing in Britain by Adolf Hitler.

Shortly after 11 a.m., Colville entered the Foreign Office to take a call from the Duke of Hamilton in Scotland. Someone very important, someone whose identity he would only disclose to the prime minister in person, had parachuted there. Hamilton was ordered to fly straight to R.A.F. Northolt to tell Churchill.

Colville later wrote in *Footprints in Time:*

> I make no pretense to psychic powers; but I think it strange that Peter Fleming's story, which I had read many months before and had long since forgotten, should have come flooding into my half-conscious brain that Sunday morning.[18]

Hitler's deputy Hess had fallen from the skies intending to contact what he believed would be pro-peace sympathizers connected to the Duke of Hamilton. Captured, Hess was brought first to the Tower of London, then a series of camps for interrogation.

Four days after Hess's landing, Crowley wrote the following letter to the Naval Intelligence Department:

> Barton Brow, Barton Cross, Torquay.
>
> Sir,
>
> If it is true that Herr Hess is much influenced by astrology and Magick, my services might be of use to the Department, in case he should not be willing to do what you wish.
> Col. J. F. C. Carter Scotland Yard House SW1
> Thomas N. Driberg Daily Express
> Karl J. Germer 1007 Lexington Ave. New York City
> Could testify to my status and reputation in these matters.
> > I have the honour to be, Sir,
> > Your obedient servant,
> > Aleister Crowley[19]

The original letter has an embossed O.T.O. letterhead and the copy in the Warburg Institute has been photographed (see page 166). Gerald Yorke wrote comments on it. The words *AC to Ian Fleming* have been crossed out. Yorke wrote: "As a result of this letter Ian Fleming wanted A.C. to interview Hess in Scotland but it never came off. There was an exchange of letters on the subject."

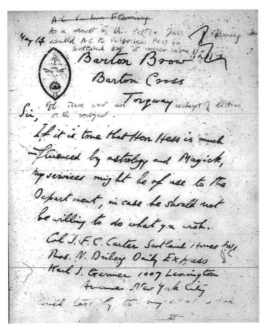

*Fig. 11.1. Crowley's letter regarding Hess. (Courtesy of the Warburg Institute, London, and Ordo Templi Orientis)*

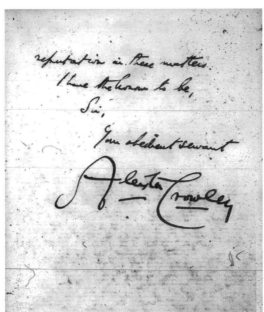

*Fig. 11.2. Second page of Crowley's letter regarding Hess. (Courtesy of the Warburg Institute, London, and Ordo Templi Orientis)*

Yorke contacted Ian Fleming's wartime colleague at the N.I.D., spy writer Donald McCormick (a.k.a. Richard Deacon). Beneath the following note by Yorke, Yorke included McCormick's jocular reply in the manuscript folder: "Extract from the letter from Donald McCormick to G.J.Y.":

Oddly enough, Ian Fleming, under whom I worked in the Foreign Department of the *Sunday Times* for many years, had a vague theory about this. The trouble with Ian was that one could never be quite sure when he was being serious, or when he was joking; he loved an air of mystery. He wanted Crowley to interview Hess when the Nazi leader landed in Britain; it never came off and the very idea must have horrified the Admiralty! But there was an exchange of letters on the subject.

If the idea of a Crowley interrogation of Hess was Fleming's idea, then Fleming may have encouraged Crowley to write the letter. The official reply to Crowley's offer appears to be the following, sent to Crowley on May 17, 1941, from the "Intelligence Division, Naval Staff, Admiralty, S.W.1.":

The Director of Naval Intelligence presents his compliments to Mr. Aleister Crowley and regrets he is unable to avail himself of his offer.[20]

That D.N.I. Admiral John Godfrey was professionally interested in astrological influence on Nazi leadership is evinced in wartime MI5 chief Guy Liddell's diary (April 10, 1941):

DNI [Director of Naval Intelligence] is employing Louis de Wohl to read horoscopes of the most important Admirals in the navy and those of Hitler, Mussolini, Darlan, and Portal. Merritt of NID is his intermediary. It is believed that DNI himself is a strong believer in astrology. On the other hand it may be that since Hitler works on these lines and de Wohl is acquainted with the workings of Hitler's astrologer [*illegible*] hopes to work out the most propitious [time] for Hitler to act. The whole business seems to me to be highly misleading and dangerous.[21]

Declassified British intelligence associates Swiss astrologer Louis de Wohl with an aborted MI5 plan to draw out the implications of a letter sent to Hamilton by Hess's mentor, diplomat Albrecht Haushofer (1903–1945). Evidence supporting the idea that Hess's coming to Britain was engineered by a secret service operation first emerged in 1992 in the *Sunday Telegraph* (January 5) after Ministry of Defense folder DEFE 1/134, dealing with censorship of Hess's mail, was released. A letter sent to the Duke of Hamilton from Hess's friend Haushofer (shot for treason in 1945 after implication in Stauffenberg's bomb plot) was opened by a postal censorship clerk on November 2, 1940. *Why* Hamilton had been contacted interested Captain Knight's anti-fifth-columnist operations at MI5 B5(b). The Duke of Hamilton was head of R.A.F. coastal command for the corridor through which Hess would fly in May 1941. Was Hamilton a suspect, and if so, could he be used to net further security risks? MI5 wanted to co-opt Hamilton, but Hamilton only agreed to go to Lisbon to meet Haushofer given sufficient guarantees. According to Liddell's diary, the matter was left there.

Speculation that Ian Fleming was a key figure behind Hess's flight first emerged in Anthony Masters's biography of Maxwell Knight (*The Man Who Was M*). According to Masters, Commander Ian Fleming seized on the intelligence to concoct an outlandish plan whereby the recently busted "Link" of leading British pro-German peace sympathizers (led by Admiral Barry Domvile) could assume sufficient virtual form to motivate Haushofer into persuading Hess to launch a last-ditch peace mission, trapping Hess and potential contacts. The alleged plot involved encouraging Hess—through doctored Haushofer correspondence—that a faction existed powerful enough to pressure Churchill into negotiating with Hitler.

Godfrey wrote he was "unable" to employ Crowley's offer. Uncertainty persists as to why the Hess affair did not yield propaganda capital. James Douglas Hamilton's *The Truth about Rudolf Hess* offers Foreign Office man Con O'Neil's memorandum of June 23, 1941: "the indiluted truth of the Hess case does not make good propaganda." The public were not to imagine a negotiated settlement was possible. Amid intense enemy bombing, the will, already subject to demoralizing rumor, might crack. The barbed olive branch Hess appeared to offer had to disappear.

From extant evidence it appears that though Fleming and Knight probably consulted Crowley at some time, when it came to direct employment, Crowley presented problems. Some insight into Crowley's position as voluntary asset comes from a previously unpublished copy of a memorandum sent to the War Office, gathered up with undated draft proposals for mass mobilization and propaganda on Thelemic lines probably from late 1941 or 1942:

> I ask that my application should receive special consideration as I have never asked for acknowledgement or reward for such service as I have been able to render, except the honour of being permitted to serve my country.
>
> In the last war, unable to obtain employment in any of the Services, I temporarily sacrificed my friends, my reputation, and my fortune by pretending to be a "rebel Irishman" and so making the German propaganda grotesque and odious to the American people. I entrusted my secret only to Commodore (now Admiral) Guy Gaunt and my friend the Hon. Everard Feilding. I was fortunate enough to do serious damage to the enemy, as they confessed by throwing my friends in Germany into concentration camps.
>
> Having been publicly attacked on my return, this business was thoroughly investigated by Col. J. F. C. Carter (he was then head of the "Special Branch") and my conduct was vindicated and applauded.
>
> When the present war broke out, I at once offered my services to the N[aval] I[ntelligence] D[epartment] and gave as my principal claim to employment the fact of what I had done in the previous war to bring America in on our side. (see copy of letter enclosed). They refused my application but I suppose this was on account of my age. Notwithstanding, I have been able to give the Department a few items of information for which I was thanked.
>
> As to what I have done entirely on my own account, let the documents herein enclosed speak for themselves. *Thumbs Up!* "La Gauloise". . . .[22]

On the back of a carbon copy of the Thelemic poster propaganda outlines and proposal "to form a flexible body of initiates to place at the service of government as required" addressed to the War Office, Crowley added:

Dear Wyllie [sic; possibly a pun],

This is the idea of D.C.'s old pal. I enclose it as additional material for the new draft.

Yrs. A.C.[23]

"Wyllie" was gay War Office official Tom Wylie, whom we may recall attending Crowley's *Equinox of the Gods* party on September 22, 1936, and his visiting Crowley a month later. Tom Wylie worked for MI5 with a flat in the War Office famous for gay parties (see chapter 5). It would help to know who or to what title "D.C." referred to.

It's possible the timing of Hess's mission was deliberately coincident with some of Germany's deadliest bombing of the war (over 1,400 people killed in London on May 10); Hess's peace offer came with threats. On May 12 Crowley wrote to Fitzgerald: "Raids over here almost every night; this house is constantly shaken. This on the main airway to Plymouth and S[outh].Wales."[24] On May 15, feeling the intensity, he recommended girlfriend Alice Florey leave London at the weekend for Staines.

I am convinced that the Huns will try to wipe out London altogether: if not this weekend, next, or when the moon is right for them—or clouds. Would it be possible to construct a heavily armoured plane with nothing but a search-light, to point out the game?

Four days later he found Torquay "deliberately machine-gunned and bombed," with two houses smashed just opposite the Imperial Hotel. In London, Fleet Street and the Strand were hit.

Amid the carnage, it must have been an odd kind of relief to turn his mind to affairs in peaceful California. He wrote to Smith on May 15: "Fra: Saturnus may visit you. . . . He knows me, and world affairs; you had better act just as he wishes."[25] Smith—probably not in reply—wrote to Baphomet on May 19: "We have had several letters from Germer since he got to New York. . . . Leffingwell and family—6 altogether—are back in the fold after having been away from us for a time. 2 more prospects for June want to be married. Have you a ceremony or should I make one from your writings?" This is what Smith had done for Jane's mother, whom she wanted buried in the Church of Thelema.[26] The day Smith wrote, Crowley received a rent ultimatum from the agent. An allegedly hysterical Mrs. Middleton arrived on the twenty-sixth; she wanted him out the house next day at the latest. Crowley dubbed it "the Middleton Raid" and called the police.

On May 27, amid the ruins of his Abbey dream, he contemplated his next move, only to receive a love letter from Pamela Felkin: "—quite maddening. Just 40 years too late." The next day he packed, with nowhere to stay. On the thirtieth he declared in his diary: "Burnt my boats, magically, by deciding to discard anything not wanted for Rainbow Valley in the Palomar Mountains." What an optimist! He decamped to boarding houses Suncrest and Rockmount before Laurence Felkin offered a room briefly at his place, The Lawn, Ray Mead Road, Maidenhead, Berkshire—closer to the prospective Oxford show on the seventh. Frieda's show, however, was canceled.* The gallery was "hostile" to Crowley, as he discovered when he went to investigate on the eleventh.

After Crowley quit Torquay on June 4, he spent a hot and sticky June in Maidenhead, moving from the Felkins' to the Thames Hotel, then to a dingy room at 14 Lassall Gardens. Occasionally he canoed from Boulter Lock, reminiscing about writing *AHA!* in a canoe under Cookham Weir in 1909 and long-gone adventures on the Hudson and Lake Pasquaney in the States: "gliding, deliciously lazy, through the mesh of the Veil of Isis my mother, my sister, and my ever-virgin bride." Maidenhead was also significant in Crowley's psychohistory for it was at the Bear Hotel, Maidenhead, in his last term at Cambridge in 1898 that he had ended his first intimate, homosexual friendship, telling older Cambridge graduate Herbert Charles Pollitt—the man he once said "made me a poet"—that he was devoting himself to religion, in which life Pollitt had no place: an act he always regretted, for Pollitt he truly loved.

On June 23, Crowley bussed it to London for the day, lunching at Demos, a favorite Greek restaurant in Shaftesbury Avenue. Also at

*Instead, Frieda arranged an impromptu show in a large room at Oxford's Randolph Hotel but didn't inform Crowley.

Demos was a consular official from the Foreign Office about to experience the day's second memorable surprise. Startled—and relieved—by news that Germany had invaded Russia, Robert Cecil's second surprise was finding a large man in an old knickerbocker suit on an adjacent table embroiled in a chess puzzle. Reaching for a carafe of water, Cecil spilt some on Crowley's table. Conversation ensued about chess—Cambridge, too, probably, Cecil being an undergraduate contemporary of Philby and Maclean (he would write traitor Donald Maclean's biography, *A Divided Life*).

In unpublished memoir, *The Will and the Way,* Cecil maintained meeting Crowley was purely accidental, claiming only a promotion fifteen months later made secret information accessible—a claim best seen in the context of a diary note of April 8, 1940, by Churchill's private secretary John Colville: "Lunched at the Travellers with Robert Cecil, who gave me very secret figures intended to show that the Ministry of Supply is being mismanaged and our ammunition output utterly neglected." A footnote on Cecil adds: "Intelligent and well-informed member of the Diplomatic Service, expert on German affairs."[27]

Crowley returned to London next day, meeting Torquay pupil Asa and taking him to Victor's with Alice Florey. Alice and Maurice Sutherland joined Crowley at Demos. Crowley then secured credit from Apex Printing to place *Thumbs Up!* Sutherland subscribed to "No. 7" of *Thumbs Up!* and 666 borrowed one pound, nine shillings. "M. A. S[utherland] to see U.S.A. Embassy re. my passport—visa etc. Luck stayed with me to the last; the tweeds arrived, & I got a taxi!" Iona Cammell's tweed samples would precipitate the end of Crowley's relations with her and husband Charles, while identity and ration card muddles compounded in the great heat, leaving Crowley quoting the Sibyl's prophecy to Aeneas: *Bella, horrida bella, Et Thybrim multo spumantem sanguine cerno:* "Wars, horrid wars, I view—a field of blood, And Tiber rolling with purple flood."

Asa ("really charming man; very straight") visited Maidenhead, as did Alice, as Crowley finalized *Thumbs Up!*—including its curse "so that I can blast anyone at short notice"—and Mrs. Sullivan wanted him out of her property! How did he find leisure to correct *Thumbs Up!* proofs for Apex and think about the world's future? But he did, writing on June 30:

Modern conditions have made "the nation" an impossible political unit. Federation does not save it; and besides, is totally impracticable. The "individual" remains; this has the merit of being philosophically justifiable, and, in practice, would require planet-wide control. To introduce it needs absolute ruthlessness and supreme wisdom: this makes it inconceivable as propaganda. But it can be the secret formula of the real rulers, who must be "few and secret." See *AL* I:10 and elsewhere.

Having received *Levant and Other Poems* by Robert Cecil (1941) Crowley lunched with its author at Demos on July 1: "Really—the man I have been seeking," noted Crowley in an exultant mood that fueled a "wild evening" at Skindle's Thames-side restaurant in Maidenhead, where he presold several copies of *Thumbs Up!* Mrs. Sullivan told Crowley she lived in constant panic, turning his light off; Crowley made a "row," and she turned it on again. Alice mediated with Sullivan next day.

On the fourth, Cecil failed to show for lunch at Victor's. Crowley wired an S.O.S. to Frieda, whose five pounds helped mollify Sullivan temporarily after the "harridan" served notice again. Four days later, in frightful heat, Crowley was at Victor's with Greta, Sutherland, and Alice. A late afternoon thunderstorm brought relief, but not from debt; Whiteley's wanted payment for storage. Then he found an "excellent service flat" at 10 Hanover Square at three and a half guineas deposit; he took it from July 12, still aiming for the United States, which plan, he noted, needed "intense work at this end."

He spent the last few days in Maidenhead reading Oscar Wilde (thinking of Pollitt?) and canoeing, offering solace from the heat, and giving him "a feeling of gentle power with perfect freedom, especially from the burden of Time."

"Evacuation" from Maidenhead went "according to plan" and at 10:40 a.m., July 12, he arrived at 10 Hanover Square, Mayfair (barely recognizable today from its bustling wartime appearance). The next day, the heat broke: a lightning bolt struck Piccadilly Circus less than sixty yards from Crowley, tearing up twenty square feet of wood blocks as the thunderstorm raged.

Three days later, he saw Driberg at Victor's at 12:45, followed by Robert Cecil at 1:30. "This lunch went off very well: I brought out my last Clos de Conte [cigar]." The next day he played chess with Sutherland: two draws, one loss, three wins, and the influential Curwen Press returned *Thumbs Up!*, claiming pressure of government work.

Crowley wrote to Wilkinson on the seventeenth: "Frieda was knocked silly by the Oxford Tragedy; I've told her to rest properly." As for himself, he was "somewhat cribbed, cabined, and confined, but very cushy, comfortable, and cosy in a service flat where they apologize 'I'm afraid there's very little for breakfast this morning <u>except</u> eggs and bacon' and bring three whacking great rashers; Honey to follow. Well now, let me know as soon as you are in London; or when to expect you."[28] He saw Greta that day at the Sanctuary, who gave him eleven shillings for No. 27 of *Thumbs Up!* On the eighteenth Michaud—who'd chucked A.M.O.R.C.—also paid for *Thumbs Up!* while Crowley showed Cecil some chess strategies.

On July 22, Gerald Hamilton was arrested on the No. 18 bus, for antigovernment, pro-peace machinations. Crowley's comment: *"What an imbecile this brilliantly clever wretch is!"* He had lunch next day with "Tom" (probably Driberg—or Wylie?). On the twenty-fourth, Crowley visited the U.S. consulate about the visa. The consul was busy; Crowley couldn't wait and enjoyed a "very pleasant evening" with Cecil: "He is thawing." Cecil's consular contacts were probably helpful, for on the twenty-fifth "very charming" U.S. Vice Consul John Ordway saw Crowley and advised a quota visa. Crowley consulted the "quota girl."

On the twenty-seventh the Cammell issue came to a head. Alice told him about "Iona's muddles" and tried to clear them up. Playing chess with Sutherland, Crowley sold him some tweed samples for two pounds, five shillings. Charles Cammell sent an "annoyed" letter the next day with Iona's bill. Crowley's diary comment: "Ha Ha." Crowley was selling the samples to keep himself going, and Iona expected money.

On July 30, Cecil paid two pounds, nine shillings for a copy of *Magick,* and Crowley's mind was back on the *V* project. Because it was registered now in the public mind, journalists Donegall and Bernard O'Donnell were contacted.

Louis said Steele told him that Joyce [Lord Haw Haw] broadcast suggestion that I should do Black Masses for religious revival in Russia!

Next day: "Can't get O'Donnell, Tom [Driberg], or Donegall re my V stunt. Got O'D[onnell] later." On August 2 he admitted authorship of the *V* sign to Jean Michaud. Meanwhile, he found himself in the "Iona Mess," dubbed the "Moss Murder" (relating to tweed) in a letter to Iona on the fourth.

A bright shaft penetrated the miasma on August 1 when two copies of "England, Stand Fast!" were accepted by the Masons Arms's landlord. Crowley wrote to Gerald Hamilton about the poem and the *V* sign:

All the real people like it. But no newspaper will print it. Their filthy trade has corrupted them wholly. They really [*illegible;* think?] that the "man in the street" likes the pansy poetastry of W. H. Auden & Co. But my time is coming! It is sure to leak out sooner or later that I invented the "V" campaign. I have been wondering whether you had spotted it. Of course, I never expected it to take the form it has actually done—it was out of my hands after the first strike, and the BBC themselves don't know—at least I hope not, or there will be trouble for somebody![29]

Like the "noisome beast" that stalks Jerusalem's ruins in Ezekiel 14:21, Crowley, on Sunday, August 3, inspected the devastation around Limehouse. Clement Attlee's cosmopolitan constituency, with its legendary Chinatown, was all but destroyed, the majority of surviving Chinese having left since the big attacks in May. Returning to Hanover Square he phoned O'Donnell; O'Donnell had guessed about the *V* sign. Sutherland arrived and "discussed the V-sign &c." Crowley consulted the I Ching whether he should produce a book about it with photos and establish its history. The next day he wrote to Wilkinson:

I also want to see you about my little V-stunt. I am told that Haw-Haw has found out and attacked me again. The possible consequences of the disclosure are formidable. It might (1) kill the whole campaign; or (2) get me into very serious trouble; or (3) upset the godly in the U.S.A.; or (4) God alone knows! It would do more harm than good for me to disclaim it—the obvious simple get-out. The evidence of the photographs [in the *Equinox*] is quite impossible to rebut or explain away. They have been accessible to all—one of them (the most incriminating of course) was published in 1909. They could say, I suppose, that they (the BBC & co.) didn't know, that I had pulled their legs as I'm well known to be fond of doing, and so on. But then they would have to abandon the whole plan; at the very best there is bound to be fantastic confusion. Do come and counsel your unhappy bungler![30]

On August 5 he met "Everett" of small-time printers John Swain and Son Ltd. about the *V* sign. As Swain subcontracted lithographic artists, "Everett" was probably Ethel Fanny Everett, born in London and educated at Royal Academy Schools. She'd designed posters since 1914 and had a contract with Swain.

Sutherland visited on the sixth: "A delightful evening: much talk of V campaign ([David] Low [political cartoonist] attacked it, by the way, in a cartoon tonight) and interesting chess." Crowley tried to raise Driberg's interest in the *V* project next day at 12:30 at the Dog and Duck, Bateman Street, Soho, but Driberg was in "one of his stickiest moods. These journalists cannot understand how, through their polluting trade, they are out of touch with the real people of the country."

On the tenth Crowley had a long Sunday lie-in, dreaming of a tremendous show full of anti-Christian fights. At one Christian meeting he changed the words of a hymn, and a woman vomited hysterically; he saw enough for a long novel! He'd been reading Rupert Gleadow's *Magic and Divination.* Hauling himself from bed he headed for the Fitzroy, where Alice informed him Nina Hamnett had told her John Bland Jameson wanted to see him. Crowley's view was that only a spell in the army could clear the chaos from Jameson's wayward mind. Alice had benefit of cunnilingus in the evening, and Sutherland arrived at 8 p.m., objecting to Crowley's use of the Catalan chess system.

On August 11, Crowley signed off *Thumbs Up! A pentagram—a pantacle to win the war by Aleister Crowley The Beast 666. In hoc signo Vinces. 1941,* and Crowley wrote to Edward Noel Fitzgerald, reserving his copy:

After "Thumbs Up!" comes "The V Sign," Thanks to "Lord Haw-Haw," it is now quite generally known that I invented this campaign.

He has pointed out, quite justly, that I have persuaded some hundreds of millions of people to worship the Devil![31]

August 12 was the thirty-eighth anniversary of what Crowley called "my idiot first marriage, which helped me towards El Kahira." El Qahira was "City of Victory," Cairo, where Rose led him to his destiny. Alice arrived, and Crowley was "horrid" to her: "I just can't stand personal contacts"—an interesting admission. Journalist Donegall was granted a view of the tarot, considering it "A.1." They talked of the *V* sign and what Donegall saw as Crowley's (presumably impersonal) job as "Magus for [the] West."

A long, sad letter came on the fourteenth from Charles Cammell:

P.S. Considering the friendly relations that have existed between us for so long, and the interest I have always taken in your literary work, I am completely at a loss to understand your present attitude.[32]

On the eighteenth Crowley sent a "mad letter to Cammell"—and effectively ended relations; Cammell never understood why.

On Friday, August 15, writer Eileen Bigland telephoned and "cheerfully agreed to tackle the V sign." Eileen Bigland (born 1898) specialized in travel books to faraway places, with political and social themes (she was sympathetic to communist activities in the East; see her autobiography *Awakening to Danger*, 1946). Her precise role in the project is unclear. Anyway, she came for tea with Pearl, Alice, and Paula, which delighted the Beast, and again for lunch on the seventeenth, when they worked on "The V sign" all afternoon.

The next day, he had dinner at the Café Royal and a drink with Great War artist, C. R. W. Nevinson. Crowley received a letter from Nevinson on November 17: "CRW Nevinson wrote in answer to the 'superb letter' that I wrote him on his father's death. Such encouragements not only rejoice me on my pilgrimage, but restore my faith and fortify my will."

On August 20, an advance copy of *Thumbs Up!* arrived, offering readers more than a glimpse of Crowley's spiritually phallic patriotism. Opposite an old photograph of Crowley making two horns on either side of his head with phallic thumbs up, was a synthesis of positive signs: above a bold black *V* sign was Crowley's esoteric sigil, enclosed

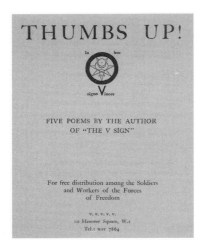

*Fig. 11.3.* Thumbs Up! *title page. (Courtesy of Ordo Templi Orientis and the 100th Monkey Press)*

in a circle. Around the twin signs are the words Emperor Constantine applied to the Christian cross, *In hoc signo vinces:* "In this sign shalt thou conquer." *No,* implies Crowley: *this* sign! The victors of the War would be the free man and free woman, guided by the True Will or "Secret Self," revived by free-flowing sexual and spiritual energy, bathing the planet in a morally cleansing light and refreshing innocence expressed in love, energy, unbridled scientific curiosity.

Crowley's *V* campaign signified a plan for a new planetary order, based on the sovereignty of the individual's True Will and unity of nature and spirit, signaling an end to tyrannies—political, social, and religious—establishing a rational, cosmic, individualistic but freely co-operative existence. The war, properly interpreted, would mark a historic turning point from which attempts to return to the previous order would prove futile, regardless of how violently such reactions might be pursued. Crowley foresaw the downfall of any system in the way of the true will. To imagine Crowley content with a legacy of witchcraft, new ageism, or reputation as "founder of modern occultism" misses the mark.

Searching for a *V*-sign publisher, Crowley talked long on August 21 with Reginald Ashley Caton (1897–1971). Timothy d'Arch Smith described Caton as grim and unlovable, which might explain Crowley's thinking the talk was too long.[33] Nevertheless, Caton's Fortune Press did publish over six hundred books, including Robert Cecil's *Levant and other Poems* (1941). Having begun with gay erotica in 1924, Caton was prosecuted in 1934 for obscene libel. He published Dylan Thomas's early work (*18 Poems*), as well as Philip Larkin's first novel *Jill* (1946). During the war, paper was scarce, but seedy Caton hoarded stocks and capitalized on the disappearance of much magazine poetry publishing. Crowley paid fifteen shillings for a copy of *The Diary of a Drug Fiend* the next day and took it to Caton, then collected copies of *Thumbs Up!* and sent them off. First recipient: Gerald Yorke. Cecil came to the flat at 8 p.m. for chess and pleasant talk, "but we get nowhere in particular."

"Yorke delightful throughout." This uncharacteristic note on Gerald Yorke appeared after Yorke joined him on a trip to Cambridge on August 27. Crowley "proclaimed the Law from [the] High Altar, Trinity Chapel" and dropped into tobacconists "Colin Lunn" (new owner A. J. Littlechild remembered him). Littlechild brought out two pipes Crowley left there in 1906! Familiar to undergraduate Crowley, Lunn advertised in the *Equinox* before the Great War.

Crowley cabled Germer urgently on thirtieth:

ILLNESS COMPLICATING SITUATION STOP INSTANT REINFORCEMENT NECESSARY AVOID IMMEDIATE FATAL ISSUE STOP JOURNEY PROSPECT APPEARS CULMINATING FAVOURABLY LOVE CROWLEY[34]

Eileen Bigland kept breaking appointments in September, and Asa sent a moaning letter eliciting a stiff riposte. Lunch with Wilkinson at Bentley's Grill in Mayfair (Swallow Street) on the second suggested his old friend was as broke "as any of us." So Crowley went to the pawnshop to scrape a fiver. At least chess with Sutherland cost nothing. Caton rang on the fourth to say Eileen Bigland had missed an appointment. By contrast Leffingwell and Schneider were both excited about his viewing the Rainbow Valley ranch. *If only!* In the meantime Crowley took his financial complaints to poor Frater 132. *Why couldn't Smith set aside fixed percentages of O.T.O. monies?* "I trust that Fra: Saturnus will stand no more of your amiable dishonesty." As for Smith's request for an O.T.O. wedding ritual, Crowley's response was a leg pull:

There is at present no rite of marriage. Obviously, both parties should be trained experts, and their first performance approved by

the assembled Church. Then a brief reminder of the Duties and
Privileges relevant, and a special benediction. This could be put into
the Mass, and they should officiate at the next Mass, performing the
Lance and Grail section actually instead of symbolically. That seems
the sort of thing. But we may have to wait until the next war if we
are keen on universal applause.[35]

On September 6, Alice suggested Crowley send *Thumbs Up!* to
General de Gaulle. Crowley thought he'd better write a French song for
Free France (he'd heard French patriots singing raucously at the "French
Pub" in Soho's Dean Street). Crowley woke at quarter to midnight and
began "Vive la France!"—finished as "La Gauloise" at 2 a.m. the next
morning. Here follows a verse and chorus from the English language
version of Crowley's rousing song:

**"La Gauloise"**
***(Song of the Free French)***

Men of courage, undefeated,
Men of honour, Rise!
Betrayed, bruised, dragged to the ground,
Bah! the first wound of war!
Beyond, the dawn of glory!
Shine, Victorious Sun!
Chorus—
Everything before us, Banner advance!
High, firm, strong! Vive la France!

In the late afternoon he entertained Cecil Court bookseller Harold
Mortlake, along with Michel Saint-Denis, "doyen du Théâtre Français,"
whose name appears next to the acronym B.B.C.*

---

*Michel Saint-Denis (1897–1971): influential French actor, theater director, and drama
theorist. Invited to London in 1935, he founded the London Theatre Studio with
George Devine and Marius Goring, working with Alec Guinness, Peter Ustinov, Michael
Redgrave, John Gielgud, and Laurence Olivier. He directed the B.B.C.'s French program
(*Radio Diffusion Française*) under the name Jacques Duchesne. The encounter perhaps
provided a first excursion for Crowley's lyric, sent as a card to Charles de Gaulle.

Ten days later, he cabled Karl Germer in New York: "INFORM EVERYBODY ALEISTER INVENTED V-SIGN FOR VICTORY CROWLEY ADDRESS 10 H[ANOVER] SQ."

Disappointment on September 8 at Bernard O'Donnell's failure to show up to write the *V*-sign book was offset the next day when Germer sent nearly twenty pounds for fifty *Thumbs Up!* Nine days later, Smith composed a letter:

> We have had several social affairs here lately. Jane and Regina worked like hell to pull them off. A good few hundred people have heard your name in the last 2 months, and they managed to send Germer 100 dollars out of their efforts.[36]

Longtime A∴A∴ member (since 1910) James Gilbert Bayley (1885–1978) bought the last piece of tweed on the fifteenth: "What a good man he is!" Sharing drinks with Robert Cecil on September 24, Cecil promised help "later"—possibly with the visa or in placing Crowley's Thelemic War schemes.

After seeing Cecil again on October 3, Crowley felt assured Cecil would "see through" the passport matter and get the Beast out on the range. A "delightful talk" with Frieda was followed by a dinner invitation with Lesley Blanch *Au petit coin de France,* whose "French" cooking disgusted the Beast *qui savait ses oignons.* Three days later Karen de Beaufort arrived from Torquay; they went to the Ebury Court Hotel for a drink and met again on the fourteenth. Crowley meanwhile showed his *War aims of 93* to Cecil at the Masons' Arms at 6:30 on October 10. Pleasant, the talk was "all too short," though Cecil "highly approved" the *War aims* (soon to emerge as *Liber OZ*)—as did Harold Mortlake and Captain Gerald Yorke, posted at the time defending East Anglian air bases.

Before he left for Moreton in the Marsh—and Frieda's country tarot exhibition—on October 15, the Foreign Office sent Crowley four exit permit forms. Glorious weather added to the "intoxication" of seeing all Frieda's paintings exhibited. Frieda was not so pleased, irritated by philistine reactions repeated by unsophisticated visitors.

Crowley had again written to the N.I.D. on September 29, offering specialist services. However . . .

17 October 1941, Naval Staff [?], Admiralty, S.W.1.

The Director of Naval Intelligence has to thank Mr. E. A. Crowley for his further offer of services, but regrets there is no vacancy in this division for which he could be considered.[37]

Crowley was ill in bed at the month's end. He'd poisoned the front of his thigh with an injection before cleaning the skin, creating an abscess. He wrote to Wilkinson on October 30, his mind teeming with desire to formulate, or encapsulate, the rights of "Man" according to Thelema:

The Herrenvolk theory is sound; but the Masters are not a tribe. Those who dare, will, know and can—the old formula [from Éliphas Lévi]; I must stick it into the cards somehow!—are the lords of the Earth / This doctrine is very prominent in *Liber AL;** it constantly recurs.[38]

Bedridden for over a fortnight, he wrote to Fitzgerald keen for contact: "Next publication *OZ* (*Liber LXXVII*) a manifesto of 'Thelemic war aims.' It has a 'The Devil' (Atu XV) from the tarot on one side; so it goes out as instead-of-a-Xmas-card. Several people are sending it to their friends. I think one can produce them at sixpence."[39]

*Oz* is Hebrew for "goat"; its gematria: 77. On November 12 Frieda begged him not to publish it. Readers may guess why. . . .

Frieda and all Judeo-Christian civilization could object that it contradicts the fifth commandment, but what was Britain being restructured to achieve if it was not total war against those who would "thwart these rights"? The day before writing to Wilkinson about *Liber OZ,* Crowley noted in his diary, "Another crazy letter from F.H. [Frieda Harris] begging me not to publish *OZ*. Sent out Anti-Xmas cards!"

Freida reasonably considered its last line taken out of context might be used to sanction murder. Crowley was amused and aghast. Every British soldier, airman, and sailor was involved in actively killing those who strove to thwart these rights! They should not feel guilty about it. Crowley went straight to the heart of the pacifist dilemma. Was Britain

---

*Liber AL* II:18: "the lords of the earth are our kinsfolk."

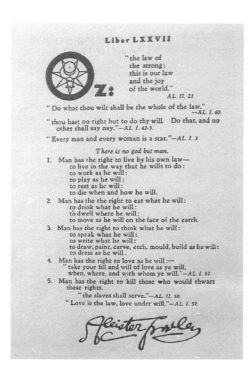

*Fig. 11.4.* Liber OZ *(LXXVII)*
*on a wartime postcard.*
*(Courtesy of Ordo Templi*
*Orientis and the 100th*
*Monkey Press)*

only defending women and children? No, it was violently attacking her enemies with everything it could muster—and was right to do so. He found the notion of young men being sacrificed in a "good cause" hideous, immediately evoking World War I's carnage and waste. If there'd been more emphasis on striking killer blows to the enemy at minimal human cost in 1914 to 1918 rather than simultaneously celebrating and lamenting sacrifice of the flower of England, the war might have been over sooner, with surplus energy to crush the demented spirit of German state militarism once and for all.

No, the line stayed: "I have been trained and taught by history; the sturdy, rugged nature is the only kind that makes revolutions." "If you're not dogged, you'll be dogged!" Fifteenth: "Oh I thank *all* the gods: I am alive!"

Of course, it must be observed that these are rights of "man," not *men* (i.e., the context is universality, progress for the spiritual being that is "man"—under the Thelemic law, "Do what thou wilt"); one has no right to remove the same right from another that guarantees one's own right to live. Our law encapsulates this principle in the right of self-defense combined with absolute prohibition of murder. A Quaker pacifist might say God's will insists victims "turn the other cheek," something impossible if decapitated. Context is all.*

Fitzgerald wrote to Crowley from his current location in "the Black Country," (industrial region west of Birmingham) and received a surprising reply (November 30):

> I remember Brum [local name for Birmingham] as it was 60 years ago!! Even then it knocked me down. "inspissated gloom." And yet . . . ? Incredible but true. My most romantic and significant honeymoon began there; Midnight Dec. 31–Jan.1, 1897–8.[40]

The date marks the night Herbert "Jerome" Pollitt, entered Crowley's room at the grand old Queen's Hotel, Stephenson Street, Birmingham, and seduced him for the first time.

On December 7, 1941, without provocation, Japanese aircraft bombed the U.S. naval base at Pearl Harbor, Hawaii. Roosevelt reversed American neutrality, declaring war on those who would, we may say, "thwart these rights." Two days later, Crowley, on a train to Chipping Campden from Paddington to see Frieda, suffered a bad attack in stomach and chest: "241 [Asthma] again and coughing phlegm." He carried on, writing to Wilkinson from 10 Hanover Square a week later:

> I think it excellent that Japan has come in. It cleared F.D.R.'s [Roosevelt's] feet instantly. Also, I hope that it may bring about the dawn of common sense—in time!—we must not only disarm but disintegrate these types of mind [Japanese and German state-worshipping totalitarianism]. We must restore society to fundamental values.[41]

---

*Diary, September 20, 1943: "The Criminal Law according to Thelema. All offences are reduced to one: to deprive another of his right (e.g. to live, to own goods, to sleep—as by making undue noise—and so on). Therefore, the 'offender' denies his own right to similar protection; and he is treated accordingly. He can be reinstated on his purging the offence."

Mixed news from Smith—sent on December 20:

We had to discontinue the parties which, with some donations, enabled us to forward to New York for you 200 dollars, because of the hard work involved and the amount of the returns therefrom. Reckon keep up 50 dollars a month.[42]

On Christmas Day, Crowley was delighted when Robert Cecil brought the "finest wine" (Pommard '34), but critical of Cecil's approach to initiation: "He wants initiation IF and WHEN &c (*air connu* ["the familiar tune"—like Jameson]). BUT." Crowley wrote to Cecil about the "Oath of the Beginning."

In America, on December 26, flashing the Victory *V* sign, Winston Churchill addressed a joint session of Congress in Washington. Reading the speech's last paragraph convinced Crowley Churchill asserted a New Aeon theory:

Prodigious hammer-strokes have been needed to bring us together today.

If you will allow me to use other language, I will say that *he must indeed have a blind soul who cannot see that some great purpose and design is being worked out here below of which we have the honor to be the faithful servants.* It is not given to us to peer into the mysteries of the future. Still, I avow my hope and faith, sure and inviolate, that in the days to come the British and American peoples will, for their own safety and for the good of all, walk together in majesty, in justice, and in peace. [my italics]

The magick was working . . . and Crowley dispatched his anti-Christmas cards: "the law of the strong: this is our law and the joy of the world" (*AL* II:22).

*V*

# TWELVE

# In the Hour of Battle

*I hope one day to be able to leave the English hypocrites to their own beastliness, and live in my own world. Until I am wanted; in the hour of battle.*

ALEISTER CROWLEY, *THE WORLD'S TRAGEDY*
(PRIVATELY PRINTED, PARIS 1910)

New Year's Day 1942 was a bad day for Crowley's asthma. Needle-supplier Heppell's was short and morphine slow to relieve. By January 9, diarrhea, indigestion, and constipation were so intense he told Germer should "treatment" (heroin) cease, another bad attack would "finish the job." He also confided his impression that Smith and Regina's personalities constituted "cause of their long failure" but was pleased Roy Leffingwell was setting to music his "Hymn to the American People on the Anniversary of their Independence" as a patriotic rouser, and Germer had best arrange a U.S. *Thumbs Up!* to fulfill Crowley's "Magical Strategy," then added: "By the way, four quite independent people have just told me that I am very like Winston: personally to some extent, more in ways of speech and thought. I think he is the only man for us; but we fear for him as not feeling strong enough to get rid of the deadwood."[1] Before turning savage poetic attention to the "deadwood"—particularly in Britain's Foreign Office—Crowley examined F.O. boy Robert Cecil's magical diary, not without a trace of envy: "'Crime does not pay'??? He [Cecil] lives at Claridges [Mayfair's luxury hotel]. Air of settled prosperity plus ambassadorial dignity."

Crowley held grudges—perhaps the most repellent of several sour personality traits. Falling out with the Cammells probably colored his view of "spiritualist" journal *Light,* with its articles on psychic, mystical, and occult research, denigrated to Fitzgerald as "a dull imbecility of fraud." Charles Cammell edited it:* "I'm too disgusted to dig him out. A case of 'If the light that is in you be darkness, how great is that darkness.'"[2]

Addressing Wilkinson from Hanover Square—"why did they drop the *g*?" Crowley quipped—we learn that the "qabalah" of *Liber 77* ("Book of the Goat") is 70 + 7, for the Hebrew *ayin* + *tzaddi* make the word *oz* (pronounced "ez"), meaning goat or strength: "Look out for a Revolution at the Autumnal Equinox," warned Crowley.[3] Victory at El Alamein in the autumn (October 30, 1942) marked a turnabout in Britain's military fortunes.

Crowley awoke from a dream on January 10: "War had broken down everything: long, many incidents. I had to rebuild—Tedious." Next day he cooked up a devilish plan ("241") "chiefly to ease the V-fatigue," composing a letter to "Col. Britton" at the BBC.

Crowley felt Britain's chance of victory was being stifled, and at 7 p.m. on January 12 experienced a "tremendous impulse" to fire a furious poem about "our inbred fucked-out families who are strangling us." "Fucked out" also gives the acronym for the Foreign Office; the poem pulls no punches:

### "Landed" Gentry[†]
*By the Author of the* V *Sign*
Our inbred F.O. families
Produce their pullulating legions:

---

*See *Light* 61, no. 3149 (May 22, 1941), 165; Cammell's "Power of the Word" on the potency of prayer observes, "The power of the word is the core of the ritual of all Magic." Crowley's influence?

†"Edition of 1942, Burke—& Hare"—a skit on *Burke's Peerage* and *Landed Gentry* index of the upper classes. Irishmen Burke and Hare were notorious killers and body stealers. Note also the reference to "Blimps"; 1942 was the year Powell and Pressburger produced the controversial movie *The Life and Death of Col. Blimp,* based on cartoonist David Low's blimpish general, out of his depth and times: a movie now hailed but which Churchill wanted suppressed.

Red-tape worms in bled-White Hall tease
    England's anaemic nether regions.
Bridge, polo, cricket, pansy piety,
    Tart-and-great lady so-society,
    Dumb devotees of Dividends—
    Ah! "who will save us from our friends,"
    Our inbred F.O. families?

Bald ovoid soft-boiled addled Blimps,
Brass-hatted hero Humpty-Dumpties,
Cathedral choughs and Palace pimps,
    Burst-big-drum battling Rumty-Tumpties,
U-boats and tanks and Messerschmidts
    Are dam-bad-form-Sir to the wits
    That stop with Agincourt and Ramillies!
God bless our inbred F.O. families!

The Bolshie is a godless cad;
    What we want is devout servility;
    Maybe the Junker is the lad
    "To leave us still our old nobility."
Maybe—I trust we shall not live
    To see the black alternative—
To see the men of England rise
    And strangle in their Old-School Ties
    Our inbred F.O. families

Pontiffs in high places,
Ravens of rapacity,
Vultures of voracity,
Sparrows of salacity,
Parrots of loquacity
    With intestinal statis,
How you hate sagacity,
    Audacity,
    Vivacity,
    How you fear pugnacity,

Baffle pertinacity,

You Imps of Incapacity![4]

Crowley finished "'Landed' Gentry" "after a fashion" on January 30—dedicating it to Gerald Yorke!

Neither the poem nor a letter from Dion Fortune (Violet Firth) soothed the anger boiling within. His fellow occultist received *Thumbs Up!* while its author contemplated isolating a pacifist pestilence. A break in the clouds, he noted excitedly on January 13: "Karl Meyer [*sic*] and Mr. Rotha discuss producing Tarot as a film!"*

Lunching at Oddenino's, Piccadilly, on the sixteenth, Crowley presented his "Plan 241" to Robert Cecil, who promised to convey it to Col. Britton personally. According to *Army Talks* magazine (vol. 4, no. 18, September 16, 1945), the *V* campaign began on June 6, 1941—three years before D-Day, its "originator" was Douglas Ritchie aka "Colonel Britton," whose identity was only revealed after V.E. ("Victory in Europe") Day (May 8, 1945): "the resonant, calm, assuring voice of Britain itself, talking to the tens of millions who were largely numb and dumb, sweating it out under the German heel."

Cecil's *The Will and the Way* describes Crowley's plan "as black as black can be"; 241 being Greek Cabala for *ACΘMA* ("Asthma"), Crowley willed it upon the tubes of Germany's war effort. Plan 241 combined dropping leaflets with BBC radio messages urging people rendered murderous or suicidal from despair to kill two "Huns" before ending their life, leaving the card "241" (two for one) on the bodies of German soldiers. Crowley's talent for morbid psychology predicted more psychotic outbursts among depressed or deluded servicemen, triggering a rash of insane fears multiplying beyond control. Further propaganda could then manipulate panic.

---

*Screenwriter of *The Cabinet of Dr. Caligari* Carl Mayer escaped Nazi rule in '33 to meet documentary filmmaker Paul Rotha. Mayer was trying in 1942 for a documentary about London but couldn't find sufficient backing (perhaps the project included Crowley's tarot work). He was diagnosed with cancer, and poor treatment hastened Mayer's premature death in 1944. Rotha went on to head B.B.C. documentaries after the war. Perhaps "Mayer" was Treviranus's contact (see page 77).

A draft of Crowley's letter addressed "Dear Colonel Brittain [*sic*]" survives: "This plan, written in words of one syllable, might be broadcast in German and all languages of the occupied countries as part of the V-campaign." Having (to his own satisfaction) stimulated the *V* campaign in the first place, he wished to deepen its effects. Cecil passed Plan 241 to the Political Warfare Executive, who rejected it; somebody noted that the pun on "241" was incomprehensible to persons without English. On February 1 Crowley noticed a *Sunday Express* story: "2 HUN OFFICERS SHOT BY [A] SOLDIER."

Troubled by Winona Boulevard, Crowley composed a "horribly difficult" letter to Smith on January 24. Beginning "My dear Wilfrid," Crowley strained to bring to Smith's consciousness how psychological limitations (attributed by Crowley to egoism, class, and education) stunted progress: "Your ideas are all right; your steady devotion to the Work is an invaluable asset; and this must no longer be wasted, or even turned into antagonism and contempt by these defects of manner and presentation."[5] To which Smith cabled in reply:

WORRIES ENDED. UNDERSTAND. WRITING WILFRID SMITH.

Crowley cautioned Germer on January 24: "we don't want a row." Replacing Smith was not desirable, "but we've got to put things right." He also explained the exit permit issue, with an ironic twist on government motive: "P.S. The Government sees clearly that my personal presence here is essential to speedy victory. I have told nobody here about this, and I advise you to tell nobody there. I think that the practical difficulties are so great that they make it a rule to refuse permits unless the urgency is evident to *them;* so I shall renew my efforts when I can muster stronger grounds."[6]

Readers may recall Crowley's note about gallery manager Ala Storey going to New York in June 1940 (see page 144). Hearing she'd established the British Art Center, Crowley saw an opportunity for the tarot project, cabling Germer on January 28:

NIGHT LETTER TELEGRAM RECEIVED STOP ALA STORY [*SIC*] AMERICAN BRITISH ART CENTER EXPECT YOU CALL

THERE OFFER COOPERATE TAROT STOP PERIQUE* PLEASE[7]

## WINSTON PLUS CIGAR

Back at Oddenino's on January 21, "one Paget," next to Crowley, opined how he resembled Winston. Crowley's reaction: "Soon began to believe it!" A week later he was arranging a "Winston Churchill" photograph: "Everett said soft hat and big cigar would make likeness notable."

The Beast's life was filled with coincidences. Posing in Churchillian mode, wrapped under scarf and Homburg smoking a huge cigar was Crowley's way of assuming form of the "god" of the moment—*Winston: spine of victory.* Image necessitated the right cigar. After conveying the latest on 241 over lunch at Demos, Robert Cecil left Crowley on a freezing Friday afternoon (January 30) by Watkins Bookshop in Cecil Court. Crowley crossed Charing Cross Road into Leicester Square. At 2:55 p.m. he saw cigars in the window of Galata. The tobacconist was shut, with a sign: BACK AT 3.

*Fig. 12.1. Crowley as Churchill.*
*(Courtesy of the Warburg Institute, London,*
*and Ordo Templi Orientis)*

---

*Perique, along with Latakia, was his favorite tobacco; hard to get in London.

I felt ill: wind was cold; rain started. Yet I waited. About 3:10 a woman came, also locked out. About 3:15 she thought she could find the boss, and went off, asking me to wait. He rushed down and opened. He was Zitelli,* a Turk; Churchill's own Cigar Merchant!!! So I got the actual thing I was looking for in the most fraternal spirit.[8]

Back home after a "great dinner" with Frieda, he read his completed "'Landed' Gentry" to "laughter and cheers," then his epic poem about Russia, "The City of God" (first published in the *English Review* in 1914): "A. C. broke down and wept like a child!"

On the Sunday following, J. G. Bayley turned up at Hanover Square at 11:30 a.m. to photograph Crowley as "North Sea Pilot." Crowley appeared in a wet sou'wester smoking a massive meerschaum (perhaps one saved by Colin Lunn's tobacconist the previous autumn), looking up and optimistic: a tribute to navy and merchant seamen risking all bringing supplies to Britain.

*Fig. 12.2. A.C. as "North Sea Pilot" (J. G. Bayley). (Courtesy of the Warburg Institute, London, and Ordo Templi Orientis)*

---

*Mr. J. Zitelli, Turkish proprietor of the Galata Cigarette Company, Havana cigar and cigarette merchants, opened a store in Carlton Street, near Piccadilly Circus circa 1900. Churchill began patronizing Zitelli for Romeo y Julieta and Patriarcas cigars in July 1936. In August 1941 a *News Chronicle* reporter wangled information from Zitelli about Mr. Churchill's supply, printing the story that Zitelli had sent him six hundred before a holiday, which Churchill returned, saying he was not a hoarder; he bought his cigars in bundles of twenty-five. The article ended with a quote from Zitelli: "No one who can select a fine cigar with the unerring instinct of Winston Churchill can possibly be anything but a very great gentleman." When Zitelli wrote apologizing for his unconscious part in the scoop, Churchill's private secretary Mrs. K. Hill phoned Zitelli to say the prime minister thanked him for his letter and he was "not to worry about the matter" (Stephen McGinty, *Churchill's Cigar: A Lifelong Love Affair through War and Peace,* 55–56).

He gave Bayley "lunch, drinks, &c." Looking at the contacts next day over tea with Alice, he decided three were good as rough ideas. A cable from Germer, meanwhile, informed him that new U.S. regulations exempted British-born applicants from the usual visa procedure. Crowley wrote to the U.S. consul for the new regulations visa on the third and to Germer two days later: "I got your cable about the visa and have written. But the snag is the Exit [permit from Britain]. It happens that pull is required. I think your best line is *Thumbs Up!* [demonstrating Crowley's patriotic stance.]"⁹

Germer arranged *Thumbs Up!*'s publication in the States, when visiting California later in 1942. The *V* campaign spread to America, and a typed note on the rare U.S. version of *Thumbs Up!* indicates its significance:

> This American reprint of Aleister Crowley's "THUMBS UP!" was made possible by the generosity and enthusiasm of a few of his many friends on this side of the Atlantic, as a contribution to the V for Victory campaign.
>
> To follow the example of the English edition, a limited number of copies have been made available "for Free Distribution among the Soldiers and Workers of the Forces of Freedom." Contributions to the printing of a much larger edition may be sent to:
>
> V
> P.O. Box 2411
> HOLLYWOOD, CALIF.

February 1942 was marred by poor relations with Frieda, whom Crowley thought hysterical, a cacophony of tantrums "raging against truth," remarking on the ninth: "The pettiness of the intrigues to keep me out of everything is not only despicable but nauseating." Tired, he wrote to Louis Wilkinson on February 6:

> Frieda has been here for the last six weeks, which is delightful, but hellish for her, with her family vampires draining her of every ounce of energy, and her horde of Bloomsbury-minded parasites, satellites, and sycophants constantly poisoning her mind. She has no defence because

she hates reality; she will not understand that truth and only truth can make one free. It goes hard with escapists when they approach the Grand Climacteric. . . . Do write me how it goes with you: far better, hie thee hither on thy coal-black charger. Damn it, I'm utterly worn out with hearing other people's burdens. My ass still baulks: if I can pull off a pending deal, I shall take an honest-to-God rest cure.[10]

Above the pettinesses of life, Crowley made an interesting memorandum: "Note on the Magical Link and Immediate Intuition: How we know things. I think there is some quality in all phenomena, so essential and all-pervading that we are unconscious of it, which *contains* the Neschamic faculty and that of interaction. Oh how badly I am putting it!" Immanence of higher Mind (*Nous*) is a staple Hermetic axiom. Life is often a case of relearning things we know (cf., quantum anomalies).

## "DEFEATIST ACTIVITIES OF REALLY SERIOUS GROUPS"

On February 4 over lunch, Alice showed 666 an article by Hugh Cudlipp of the *Sunday Pictorial* about Major General J. F. C. Fuller, inventor of Blitzkrieg and Panzer-type strategies, and Crowley's former collaborator in the A∴A∴ and *Equinox* till quitting in 1911. Since the early 1930s, Fuller (whose wife, mother, and maternal grandfather were German) favored Oswald Moseley's fascist networks, committed to the idea that fighting Hitler rather than the U.S.S.R. was suicidal.

*Fig. 12.3. Major-General John Frederick Charles Fuller, C.B., C.B.E., D.S.O. (1878–1966).*

According to Jonathan Pile, from 1939 to 1940 Fuller joined an "Information and Policy" group that met at St. Ermins Hotel, Caxton Street, along with Richard Liversedge (possibly an error for Robert Liversidge), Lady Domvile (wife of Admiral Barrie Domvile—interned 1940 to 1943—of the busted "Link" group that liaised with Nazis to keep Britain from fighting Germany), and Domvile-contact Norman Hay.[11] Crowley knew Gerald Hamilton also opposed Britain's warring with Hitler, on communist and pacifist lines, serving time accordingly. Crowley cultivated Hamilton for information on "defeatist" groups.

On February 6, Hamilton informed Crowley by phone he'd bring a "Mrs. Cunninghame" to Hanover Square the following late afternoon. Crowley's comment: "She knows well and has influence with J. F. C. F[uller]. She will negotiate with him." Now, this might have entailed Crowley's wishing Fuller back in the Thelemic fold, as being preferable to British fascism (i.e., saving Fuller's soul), but given other contacts of Hamilton's, it's as likely Crowley was spying in his own subtle way (he knew how to keep a secret, despite his self-advertisement aspect).

Crowley gave lunch for Bruce Blunt at the Piccadilly Brasserie on February 10. A cryptic note for the twelfth tells us, "Cecil to visit 53 plus 26." Judging from a later entry, these were likely "qabalah" for initials of secret government departments or persons. Frustrated with progress in this direction, he wrote to Germer on February 14: "P.S. I'm quite well enough to work for England, and my brain never worked better. Why the devil don't they use me? Bad war news plays hell with my nerves."[12]

Meanwhile, he sent out "'Landed' Gentry" to numerous M.P.s and friends, hoping Sir Percy would read it in the House of Commons or contact William Gallagher, the House's sole communist M.P. Crowley kept close to Gerald Hamilton, a man on the verge of arrest under "18B" internment legislation for speaking to a German minister in Dublin. As in Berlin from 1931 to 1932, Crowley had to give Hamilton the impression of fellow-traveler sympathies. He could then spill the beans:

February 17, 1942, To the Director of Naval Intelligence, Admiralty, SW1:

Sir,

I have the honour to report that I am now in a position to discover the details and progress of the defeatist activities of seriously important groups.[13]

Written on the day he had a "useful talk" with Cecil, Cecil's advice appeared in code: an inverted triangle (water) followed by the sign for Virgo, after which: "IV better than 64." The 64 is gematria for "N.I.D." Hebrew equivalents (*nun, yod, daleth*). Cecil was saying perhaps that either MI4 or MI5 was more receptive to Crowley than N.I.D. (MI4 dealt with aerial reconnaissance).

Meanwhile, snow came thick and heavy; pleurisy plagued the mage. Despite the condition, he entertained Hamilton on February 25. Hamilton brought "Liversedge." This was likely someone who, according to Jonathan Pile's *Churchill's Secret Enemy*, participated with Fuller in the Information and Policy group (1939–1940) that strove for a deal with Hitler. Pile perhaps mistranscribed his "Richard Liversedge" for Robert Liversidge (1904–1994), real name Jacob Perisweig, Jewish businessman whose business entailed meeting fascist-sympathizing intelligence personnel such as Norman Thwaites.

In 1939 Liversidge obtained an intelligence position in Bomber Command, but MI5 found him implicated in a bribery scheme to release internees. Interned in 1940, he was released on December 31, 1941, after a high-level legal battle. Crowley's noting "Liversedge's" being Jewish, despite the pseudonym, rather confirms he was MI5's suspect with pro-fascist contacts. Crowley did not like "Liversedge," dismissing him as "low-class."

By contrast, Smith wrote his promised letter on February 27, addressing Crowley as "Dear Father," before explaining how an operation for "hemeroids" (*sic*) had eased years of debilitation and afforded time to think: "I have just gone through a revolution inside and out," he wrote. "I am going to quit the office and damn the consequences. Be patient for a few months, give me a hand and if nothing happens, well hell."[14]

Crowley replied sometime in March: "I was rejoiced exceedingly to get your letter. Whom the Lord loveth he chasteneth; and scourgeth every son whom he receiveth. I have certainly not spoiled you by sparing the rod." Crowley called Smith an idiot for having treated himself all the years rather than seeing to his condition properly, but then it was understandable with (the long list of negative epithets from) C. S. Jones bringing him down. His early "education" behooved him to be "restrained, quiet, dignified. You lack tact; so do I, but I can take a special line—which you can't—to counterbalance this failing. I have great hope of Helen [Parsons]'s influence. On what Jane tells me, she is ideal for you, should train you to give the right impression." Crowley asked for photos of all the recent people in the lodge. "Don't use words unless you can spell them right," "Father" counseled. "The important thing is *to be yourself,* and not to strut about with a false nose and a tin tiara."[15]

Crowley responded on March 4 to Germer's failure to secure Ala Storey's interest in the tarot. "I'm not surprised at your experience with Ala Storey: *all* Frieda's friends are like that, when they're not plain share-pushers or other low type of crook! She did not visit Bloomsbury unscathed."[16] Crowley wrote again on the ninth and said he'd deal with Ala Storey separately.

Crowley wrote to Wilkinson on March 5: "I'm getting L.G. ["'Landed' Gentry"] printed, waistcoat pocket size," and wailed, "I'm up to the Brahmarandra Cakkra* in arrears of letters."[17]

The next day Crowley received a surprise visit from Lord Tredegar: "Evan Morgan came in!! With Christabel," that is, Lady Aberconway (1890–1974), wife of Henry McLaren, 2nd Baron Aberconway, "and a lovely goil!" Crowley would visit wizard aristocrat Tredegar later in the war. Lord Aberconway was, up to the war declaration anyhow, an active appeaser of Hitler.

Crowley's interest in observing "defeatist" groups is perhaps implied in a letter to Germer of March 9 regarding U.S. immigration requirements: "Say that I am most eager to contribute to war effort, and unhappy that Exit Permit and Visa difficulties hamper me from doing so. Remember: snag No. 1 is Exit Permit. If Bank of E[ngland]. *would support my application,* the rest would be easy."[18]

The following afternoon (March 10), "Liversedge" (for whom Crowley had obtained rare Latakia tobacco in a "deal" involving Hamilton and

---

*That is, the *cakkra,* or chakra, at the crown of the head where, in Vedantic jnana yoga, the spirit of Brahman enters the subtle system. See Churton, *Aleister Crowley in India* (2019).

*Fig. 12.4. Van Raalte's Tobacconists, Piccadilly Circus.*

Van Raalte's Tobacconists, Piccadilly Circus, on January 28) brought with him "Col. Thwaites," described tellingly in Crowley's diary as "an Octavian-Fascist"—a reference to Octavian Goga of the Rumanian fascist national Agrarian Party. Lt. Col. Norman Thwaites, M.C., C.B.E., served as No. 2 in British military intelligence in New York when Crowley was in America, running the innocuously named "Passport Control Office."[19] Thwaites had chaired the fascist front "January Club" discussion group founded by fascist Moseley in 1934.[20]

On March 16, Crowley met again artist Lina Monici: "shabby, much thinner, but looking very well."

Two days later, Hamilton brought Sir Frederick O'Connor to Hanover Square: "most able and intelligent, knows lots of places I know, even the Yalung [Glacier]!! A day of overwork, notably a précis on India for O'C[onnor]."

Irish diplomat Lt. Col. Sir William Frederick Travers O'Connor, C.V.O. (1870–1943), had fought in the British Army—participating in Sir Francis Younghusband's 1904 Tibet invasion—with great experience of Asian cartography, travel, and Indian and Tibetan culture.[21] Crowley met him again on March 26 at a "Fork Luncheon" at 16 Gordon Square WC1 with some "Japs," Sir Francis Younghusband, Lady Swaythling, Mr. Ritchie (former secretary, China Institute), and Monsignor Barton Brown. Barton Brown was watched by MI5, being Hamilton's fellow

*Fig. 12.5. Lady Swaythling.*

exponent of peace terms to the enemy's benefit. Hamilton and Barton Brown would commiserate with Barry Domvile after the latter's release from detention on July 29, 1943.

Crowley's very different intentions are visible in a March 19 letter to Max Schneider about how to attract young people to Thelema. What youth wanted was action, blood—not to be asked to sit in asana and calm their emotions! "What you must do is to inflame them with the romance of the Order and its Work, with the Marvel-story of the 'Cairo Working' as told in the *Equinox of the Gods,* instill the idea of the new Aeon, the coming of the Crowned and Conquering Child, the birth of Freedom as outlined in *Liber OZ,* the plan of the Master Therion to bring about the revolution by the 4 wars started 9 months after the 4 publications of *Liber AL,* and the need for each one of them to go forth and smite and Establish the Law."[22] Of course, 666 was right on the nail. His fascinating phrase the "Marvel-story" makes prescient reference to the power of Marvel Comics (founded 1939), fount of the action-hero marrow of today's youth-oriented Hollywood with testosterone-stuffed gods such as "Captain America" (1941). He clearly had Jack Parsons in his mind's eye.

The next day, after a "most amusing" lunchtime talk, with Cecil offering to write to T. S. Eliot at Faber & Faber about publishing Crowley's tarot, Crowley read a letter from Captain O. L. Gordon of HMS *Exeter,* thanking him for No. 17 of *Thumbs Up!,* accepting it on behalf of the ship. "I could cry," gushed a very moved Crowley. HMS *Exeter* had taken the savage brunt of the Battle of the River Plate in December 1939, stimulating Crowley's "Toast" for *Thumbs Up!* dedicated to "Those Brave Men" and "to all Their Comrades."

... TOAST

**(Battle of the River Plate)**
Sinking merchant-men is fun;
Chivalry is senseless,
Prove your honour as a Hun,
Murder the defenceless!

*Chorus:*
Horse and bridle, whip and spur!
Give the Hun the Willies!
Gentlemen! Exeter, Ajax
and Achilles!*

Noble Nordic deeds we've done,
(Baby-killing German!)
Bomb them every mother's son,
Jewish-English vermin!
(*Chorus*)

Cruiser sighted—time to run!
Well! there's one way surer;
Scuttle quick and say we won,†
Trusting to the Führer!
(*Chorus*)

Crowley was thinking about reorganizing the O.T.O., wisely addressing long-standing disciple Jane Wolfe on the issue on March 20: "I quite appreciate the other side of Smith, much more than he can possibly believe, since I am usually nagging or denigrating him. . . . I have no doubt at all that Smith's qualities outweigh his defects 85 to 15; but our problem is like Katisha's. People came hundreds of miles to see her left heel" (a reference to *The Mikado;* actually it was Katisha's right heel and left elbow).

Crowley suggested Jane imagine being a person uplifted and

---

*In the naval action off Uruguay, cruisers *Ajax* and *Achilles* also attacked Germany's battleship *Graf Spee*—destroyer of unarmed Atlantic merchant ships.
†The *Graf Spee*'s Captain Langsdorff scuttled his ship when the British blocked his exit from Montevideo.

impressed by *Liber OZ* or *Eight Lectures on Yoga,* then making an effort, "keyed-up to expect"—only to arrive at *Smith.* What's the first impression? "A cheeky Cockney, destitute of atmosphere, lacking presence and personality, who doesn't know quite what to do with his hands." The person would be put off by Smith's "sordid middle-class amateur theatrical effect. You'd have to know him a long while to like and respect him." Crowley wanted real leadership qualities: "the trout must believe that what he sees is what he has been looking for." Crowley knew his own limitations:

> Now, you don't have to remind me that I'm the world's worst flop. I can't suffer fools gladly: I tell the truth: I frighten people out of their lives. Generally speaking, I can't bear people at all, unless there's something I can learn from them. But I am all right for externals; I can be seen (and even photographed) or heard without exciting repugnance. And I can hold my own in any company.
>
> Monsignor Barton Brown came to see me last week; he was very much impressed by my knowledge and understanding of theology, and the inner workings of papal policy. (He is one of the pope's private chaplains, and the kingpin of Romish intelligence intrigue over here. Regards Hinsley [Arthur Hinsley, Catholic cardinal, archbishop of Westminster] as a nasty (and negligible) nuisance).* Sir Frederick O'Connor came to tea yesterday, and was amazed to find I knew as much about the Himalayan valleys as he did, and had plenty of height, and intimacy with Mahayana Buddhism, to set against his years in Nepal and Tibet. But there you are! With the big shots I am at home, all right but that only makes them nervous! As Lord Tyrell [British ambassador to France] said in Paris: "he is the most able and most dangerous man in Europe."
>
> I cannot find any solid virtue in Regina. In U.S.A. some flamboyance is expected, even required. . . . [Crowley thought Helen Parsons a better bet.] But is she her own mistress? Does she really understand the Law, and feel that the only thing worthwhile doing is to get it accepted anywhere as the basis of the "New Order?" Does she *believe*

---

*Intelligence on Barton Brown at National Archives, Kew; Code 6 file 1896: "Activities of George Bernard Morgan and Monsignor Barton Brown."

*Fig. 12.6. Jane Wolfe by the beach, Cefalù. (Jane Wolfe Papers; Courtesy of Ordo Templi Orientis)*

in Magick, in the Masters, in the Plan of the New Aeon? I wrote to Max on strategy [see page 199], based on your paragraph about his failure to "hold students." Love to all of you! But especially, to my dear old pal in the Tent on the Beach [a reference to Jane's magical retirement at Cefalù]. Yours Aleister[23]

On March 21 Hamilton brought along someone Crowley noted as "John x (Lady Tredegar No *n*)." Crowley asked this John* "to suggest Temple to his lordship," his lordship being Eton and Christchurch Oxford educated Evan Morgan, 2nd Viscount Tredegar (1893–1949). Lord Tredegar assisted MI8 (Signals Intelligence; in 1942 under MI6). Crowley would be invited to Evan's "Magic Room" at Tredegar House, Monmouthshire, so perhaps Crowley considered a joint enterprise.

Meanwhile, Crowley devised a plan for Cecil to help with the tarot (it would backfire) and informed Wilkinson he couldn't find a printer who would touch "'Landed' Gentry."

---

*Neither of Evan's marriages bore issue, so "John" could have been Evan's cousin Frederick Charles John Morgan (1908–1962), son of uncle and heir Frederick. However, an entry for March 22 notes "Ham[ilton] and John Stripe for tea." Perhaps "John" was Evan's boyfriend.

*Fig. 12.7. Evan Morgan,
Lord Tredegar
(1877–1955).*

Crowley had a shock on March 31 when he met Cathrine: "ALAS Met Cathrine!! Ill-dressed, old, dirty, skin discoloured, smile and perky speech quite gone." She was living at Room 64, Elm House, Raleigh Hall, Swinnerton, Staffordshire—an ordnance war-work hostel (now a fairly remote Territorial Army headquarters).

Another shock was a booklet on *Liber 77* sent by Jane. He told her she lived in the world's no.1 place for slick photography, yet "the whole booklet would disgrace a hot dog stall. . . . and you did the most accurate and exquisite [painting] work on the *Chambre des Cauchemars* [at the Villa Santa Barbara, Cefalù]. How then do you let such vile production get past you?" It was "horrible" . . . "breaks my heart."[24] On April 1 he wrote again to Jane about *Liber OZ* (77). She should drop the illustration of the goat (!) and get the "best printer in L.A." They couldn't even read a cable, referring to "Archie's fraternity"! "No wonder you were puzzled," wrote Crowley, "I cabled 'Collecting ARCHI_V_ES fraternity' to explain why I need extra funds badly. Especially if I am coming over, I can't leave MSS., stock, all sorts of valuable books and papers, scattered in various warehouses to eat up strange charges. . . ."

He changed subject: "Jack Parsons sounds promising. ♄ in Asc[endant] with trine of Mercury ☿ exact with Mars ♂ is admirable, especially with Gemini ♊ rising. Intelligence, sobriety, driving power, all sorts of good things. Venus fire moon ♀ should make him good looking and popular." There were "dangerous" aspects also: "beware pride, exuberance, and accidents. Jupiter is hardly dignified, too; and Saturn is bad in Cancer ♋; so we'll hope for the best."[25] He suggested raising money by sending one hundred dollars for a specially printed card, "The Devil" or "Love" or "Art" (for the movies). "Like people raising money for [a] Spitfire." He had high hopes of the effect of the cards on Hollywood producers.

Crowley reiterated his approval of Jack Parsons in a letter to Germer on April 4:

> Jack Parsons seems pretty good stuff. Saturn rising in Cancer is weak, but the trine of Mars conjunct Mercury should help him a lot. Yet people with Mars conjunct Mercury are often quarrelsome and difficult to work with; and Saturn is rather neat square Sun. Still, a remarkable horoscope . . . he seems to be taking the lead already: Jane talks of Smith "helping him in an advisory capacity."[26]

Monday, April 13, found Cecil "jabbering, mostly about poetry." Responding to Cecil's offer about approaching T. S. Eliot at Fabers, Crowley had "looked over" Eliot's *The Waste Land:* "nauseated and ineffably contemptuous." The tarot publication plan was never mentioned. Crowley's thoughts on modern poetry crystallized: "NOTE: 'Modern' 'school' of 'poetry'; the much beslavered 'observation' is all sniffing sexual privies. They never get away from it; and they see only the sordid dirty side of it."

A Detective Sergeant Cornish called on April 15, possibly about Crowley's luggage, suspected stolen from Hanover Square. They had a long talk. Four days later he finished a draft for an anti-Nippon song ("Axe the Axis!"): "too tough, I fear, for the Women's Clubs"*—and he wrote a lovely letter of self-justification for book-collector and Atlantis habitué Ben Stubbins: "The Masters work in a manner altogether beyond our apprehension; they see the Universe from a totally different standpoint and dispose of powers at whose nature we can only guess. We, by contrast, are like savages looking at telephones. Obviously this

---

*Revised and copied June 7, 1942.

is the fantastic imagination of a light-hearted youngster: but that is just what I am.

"Look at the spiritual gaiety of my poems written in the last six months! Is that to be expected from a man whose whole career must appear to the world as a pitiful, even a grotesque failure? And a sick man at that! They seem more like the work of a boy in his teens, ablaze with physical energy, confident and happy in the glory of first love returned in full measure. This is what initiation does to you!" Crowley opined, as regards *Liber AL* that what in it seemed unbearable in 1904 was now commonplace. He put it to Stubbins: *what role in the Great Work would he perform?*[27]

He elucidated further on *Liber AL* in another letter to Stubbins of April 22: "The Law of Thelema is the only basis possible for the new social system which the War has made instantly imperative." He recommended his essay, "The Scientific Solution of the Problem of Government," and "as a special personal gift, please accept a copy of 'Songs for Italy.' These are very rare and valuable, of great historical interest as they prove that I knew in 1923 what it took Winston Churchill till 1941 to find out!" He hoped Stubbins might form a syndicate to publish the tarot: "the vindication of my life's work for the last 44 years; and will be the Compass and Power of the good ship Magick for the next 2000 years." Crowley gave Stubbins a host of insights in a series of letters that summer, including a prophecy against a burgeoning consumer society, making goods that no one needs, insisting: "It's the individual, not the State that survives."[28]

As so very often, Crowley found a comfortable billet snatched from under his feet. He tried to explain to Germer what happened at the end of April: "At Xmas or thereabouts the manageress of No. 10 Hanover went on the drink and started elaborate swindles; arrested, tried, bound over. But the bosses were worse, adding blackmail . . . to the rest. And my only two good big suitcases have been lost or stolen. . . . Well, it meant two moves inside a week. This broke me." He moved into a flat at Arlington Chambers, 5 Dover Street W1 on May Day, and everything was "lovely" until "the owner manager developed homicidal mania; dashed upstairs in the middle of the night, in pajamas, and attacked a party two rooms away from mine. I thought this excessive, even in wartime. A C.I.D. [Criminal Investigation Dept.] man

(I had asked police to find my luggage) recommended this place. Pretty queer too, but I think I can stick it."[29]

He didn't inform Germer he was kicked out by "Topping" after the maid refused to clean the filthy W.C. (Crowley maintained the flush was faulty), and so, thanks to Detective Sergeant Wilson (who'd found a lost box of Crowley's books), he moved to suite 105, Hamilton House, 140 Piccadilly, on May 6 with no telephone or bell in the room.

Two days earlier he'd played chess with Maurice Sutherland, who was "at his most boring and boorish. No wonder he has failed at the Admiralty, with the manners of a mule." He wrote to Wilkinson on the eighth, trusting his old friend would restore him, as always.

A striking anecdote of Crowley at Hamilton House comes from a June 23 letter from Wilkinson's fourth wife Joan Lamburn, widow of Llewelyn Powys (died 1939), to American suffragist and writer Alyse Gregory (1884–1967). Joan was dining with Louis at the Café Royal when he asked if she'd like to see Crowley, living nearby.

> . . . so we went along to this big house in Piccadilly where he had a furnished flat. It's really a brothel. Louis is so innocent he had seen & understood nothing on his previous visit, but the moment we entered the cheaply furnished hall with its dusty palm tree in the middle & its Lloyd Loom chairs & insolent looking porter in gold braid I knew where I was. . . . The porter took us upstairs to the first floor, opened a door & walked in, calling out, "Crowley? Are you there, Crowley? Mr. Wilkinson *and a friend* to see yer!" & then said to Louis "Go on in, Sir." We went into a sort of ante-chamber with a filthy uncurtained window looking on to Piccadilly, a few stuffed chairs & sofa & a table on a bare wood floor. It was growing dusk. Crowley emerged from a bedroom where he had been muttering. He seemed rather taken aback but assured Louis we hadn't disturbed him and that there was no one in the bedroom. He was dressed in flannel pyjamas & Bedouin-like yellow silk robe from which his hands came out looking like hen's claws. He sat by the window and talked in a wheezy high-pitched voice in a tone of complaint. . . . In the fading light there was a touching dignity in the dumpy little figure by the window. He has told someone, or he has been told, that he resembles Churchill, but I thought he seemed more like Queen Victoria—an

ageing, pettish, harassed queen robbed of her happiness. . . . We only stayed about 50 minutes & as we went through the hall again the porter said, "You've been very *quick*, sir!" A whore of the first water was coming up the steps—aged about 55. Perhaps it was the manageress coming back from a walk in the Park. . . .[30]

## CAMBRIDGE SPY

Collin Brooks (1893–1959) of the Society of Individualists, editor of *Truth* magazine, and an old friend of Wilkinson, invited Crowley to dinner with a "nice letter." Brooks had been aide to Lord Rothermere (died 1940), owner of the *Daily Mail* and *Sunday Dispatch,* which Brooks had edited. Declassified MI5 documents (2005) demonstrate Rothermere's pro-Hitler orientation in 1938. Rothermere even wrote congratulating Hitler on annexing Czechoslovakia. Brooks knew Rothermere's fascist views well. His published journals show Brooks found the B.U.F. [British Union of Fascists] extreme, though nonetheless considered Rothermere did a service in trying to keep Britain out of war with Germany. Crowley would note on May 17 that *Truth* (Brooks) called explorer Sir Richard Burton the "spiritual twin of [adventurer Edward John] Trelawney [1792–1881, friend of Byron and Shelley], Havelock Ellis and myself, omits the 'Aleister.' A finely subtle compliment: first time, too! *Eppur si muove!*"*

The timing of Brooks's invitation might suggest ulterior motives. Soviet spy Guy Burgess cultivated Collin Brooks in 1942 and 1943. Exposing selected political and social scandals since 1936, *Truth* magazine was controlled by senior intelligence figure, anti-Churchill and pro-fascist appeaser Joseph Ball (1885–1961). For the Russians, interested in Rothermere's German links, Brooks was "an important Burgess target." Crowley would lunch with Brooks and Burgess on July 9.[31]

Crowley told Wilkinson on May 13 he was sending de Gaulle "La Gauloise" in the hope of a paper publishing it and getting a tune written. A flattering reply arrived from de Gaulle on May 21, which I here translate from the French:

---

*"And yet it does move," attributed to Galileo when interrogated about the Earth's moving around the sun.

De Gaulle 4 Carlton Gardens SW1 20 May '42.

French National Committee for Foreign Affairs (*Comité Nat[iona]l Française Affaires Étrangères*).

Monsieur, General de Gaulle has asked me to thank you for your letter of 12 May. We've read your song with lively interest. We're touched by the beautiful feelings you have expressed in so charming a fashion. Sincerely and respectfully . . .

Crowley spent the evening of May 26 with Collin Brooks drinking at Maison Basque: "Both bloody drunk—let's hope for the best!" Crowley inscribed for Brooks a precious copy of his *Collected Works* first given to Crowley's late friend, financial journalist Raymond Radclyffe of the *English Review*. He had asked Brooks on the twenty-third to promote "La Gauloise."

On the thirtieth, Crowley went to see Bette Davis and Ann Sheridan in *The Man Who Came to Dinner* (1942). Verdict: "Great fun."

As Japanese forces penetrated the Pacific, California felt the heat, but a great U.S. naval victory off Midway Island on June 7 reassured a nervous population. General Douglas MacArthur suggested New Guinea and New Britain as Japan's next targets after a Japanese submarine shelled Sydney Harbor, while Crowley wrote to Jane Wolfe at 1746 Winona Boulevard on the eighth: "I am terrifically overworked trying to get odds and ends collected from all parts of the earth so as to enable me to migrate to sunnier climes."[32] A letter to Smith displayed a different tone. Smith couldn't be a X° (O.T.O. Head in the U.S.) as he was Acting Deputy Grand Master, nor could he claim IX° because he lacked the relevant papers, which Crowley would send, as he had to Schneider. Furthermore:

You don't seem to have the knowledge, the tact or the presence necessary. Nor have you any original work to your credit. We want Aldous Huxley. Show him where his theories fail him, and how *AL* can solve all his problems. He wouldn't treat you like an equal at all; one sharp snub, and Good-bye Smith! *No?* All right Have a shot![33]

Outwardly, things looked good for "Agapae Lodge." On June 9, core members entered new premises, quitting forever what they called "Grim Gables." Spotted by Jack and Helen Parsons in January, 1003 South Orange Grove Avenue's sixteen-room, five-bedroom structure in its own grounds on Pasadena's "Millionaire's Row," lined with palms, was built for the president of Caltech's board of trustees, Arthur H. Fleming; Einstein was Fleming's guest there. It had been empty since 1940, and remedial repairs were required, on which basis Jack negotiated a two-year lease for $100 a month.[34]

Entry was solemn. At 11 a.m. Jane stepped inside with a signed portrait of Crowley, followed by Smith with the sacred lance and *Liber AL*. Regina bore a copy of the *Stele of Revealing* painted by Smith's previous wife Kath, and Helen clutched a model Ark for O.T.O. ceremonial. Mellinger's horary chart looked propitious.

Crowley was gearing up for Jane to do the "dirty work" over Smith. Come September, and tipped into reaction by Jane's ill-judged letter about Smith's cramping Jack's style and ambition, the allegedly "lower middle middle class" Smith was heading for trouble—though Crowley was *wrong* about Smith's class. As Martin Starr has made clear, Wilfrid's father was *upper* middle-class solicitor Oswald Cox, M.B.E. (1868–1957), though "Smith" issued from Oswald's indiscretion with housemaid Minnie Wenham when she was sixteen. The child received Grandmother Cox's maiden name.

Crowley began the salvoes over Smith's use of language: "Dearly beloved brethren" did not sit well with Baphomet. "Doesn't Smith know that this is a stock phrase, ridiculing the *soi-disant* Elmer Gantry type of hedge-row parson?" Smith's "Manifesto" issued as a Thelemic war cry and demand for members to conform to discipline was dismissed as arrogant: "No wonder your contacts always came to nothing. As *you* know, not every one can wear a robe." In the photographs of the mass sent to Crowley back in the 1930s, it was glaringly obvious to him at least that Smith looked somewhat out of place in a ceremonial robe.

He has no "presence," no personal dignity. But I had hope that your experience of stage & screen would have somehow put this right; in any case, there was nothing else I could do. All this is a terrible pity, because Smith is such a good man in so many ways, and the faults are of the kind that in the real world don't amount to a plugged nickel. But they just kill the external side stone dead. The glib shows of a Spencer Lewis get by. He too, by the way, looked grotesque in a robe. . . . Why "Saladin," in the name of Allah? Why take the pseudonym of [William] Stewart Ross [1844–1906; Scottish writer who used pseudonym "Saladin"]?

Now don't you get the idea that I undervalue Smith. But his good qualities are swamped by his unfortunate appearance and manner. . . . Well, do your best to straighten it all out![35]

A strange surprise hit Crowley on June 12. He saw "Doris Gomez" at Fortnum & Mason. Their last encounter involved performing the IX° and cocaine hunting in New York in 1915! Doris was now fifty-seven and *sans maquillage* "looked healthy & hearty! Most encouraging." She was now Mrs. Malcolm Campbell of 2 The Close, Salisbury.

On June 20, Crowley doubted Cecil's progress in magick, describing him as "very Godlike: *without parts or passions*"—but meeting at the Piccadilly Brasserie a week later left a different impression: Cecil was "very near to seeing the Light." In fact, according to Cecil's memoir, he had, on the evening of June 24 (St. John's Day), gone out to a wood near his home in Chislehurst, Kent, to perform the adoration to Ra expected of one taking the oath of the probationer in the A∴A∴. What Crowley may not have known about Cecil was that in his wish to undertake the whole tarot "show" (noted by Crowley on May 19 with regard to his book) he was involved with the London exhibition of Frieda Harris's seventy-eight tarot paintings, even writing the catalogue introduction, ignoring Crowley's original contribution. Signs of Frieda's discomfort were evident when Crowley informed Stubbins she was "more lunatick and sore vexed than ever. It is really rather heartbreaking,"[36] but he was utterly flabbergasted when on July 1 Frieda opened what he called a "secret show" of the tarot at the Berkeley Galleries. "Amazing treachery," he called it on July 8; he'd been neither invited nor informed, so anxious was Frieda that his reputation not prejudice her great moment—but what of *his?* Crowley visited the Berkeley Galleries on the fourteenth: "She had put Ace of Swords in window!!!!" To Crowley, *that* suggested antagonism. Frieda claimed all credit, reserving none for Crowley, or the Order.

A fairly startling diary entry for July 9: "Collin Brooks *Bolivar* 6–7 with Guy Burgess (once brought by [Christopher] Isherwood) and Peter Pollock a dream in rose amber. Pleasant talk: he thought standard puff very helpful! Said it was worth £500." The "standard puff" was probably a proposal for Brooks; "£500" hardly seems right for "La Gauloise," perhaps he was trying to interest him in the tarot book. The occasion might confirm Burgess's clandestine interest in Brooks, or in Crowley. Steel heir Peter Pollock (1919–2001) was Guy Burgess's boyfriend; they'd met in 1938 and remained lovers for years. Burgess got Pollock— who had a passion for the arts and artists—to spy on foreigners for MI5.[37] Burgess was one of Maxwell Knight's recruits from right-wing political organizations; in his case, the Anglo-German Fellowship.

Two days later, Crowley had a "nice lunch" with Cecil, who told him the "passport man" was "ignorant of 1914 to 1918 facts." Crowley's Home Office file record containing reference to pro-German propaganda in America in World War I was prime objection. Crowley probably suggested they contact Carter, but substantiating Crowley's version was likely another stumbling block, as somebody or some persons considered Crowley's reputation earned; besides, he had no service record, and there may have been an objection from J. Edgar Hoover, whose F.B.I. would raid Germer's New York apartment after hearsay reports he considered Germans a superior race; Hoover's agents had investigated Crowley inconclusively in 1918–1919 (see Churton, *Aleister Crowley in America*).

On the thirteenth Crowley heard Germer's second wife Cora had died in New York. He still owed her money, and they'd traversed many a run-in in Berlin 1930 to 1932 (see Churton, *Aleister Crowley, The Beast in Berlin*). Crowley made no comment but encouraged Germer to marry again soon.

On Bastille Day (July 14), 1,000 copies of "La Gauloise" were distributed around London. He'd met B.B.C. editors Kenneth McAlpine and one Sullivan about promoting it but was informed promotion required a "tune." The next day he bought nine pounds' worth of cigars from Zitelli, possibly for the sixteenth, when he hosted a dinner for Brooks. He was very tired on the night, and dinner was "not much of a success." On the eighteenth he received a letter from Jack Parsons, rising star of 1003 South Orange Grove, though Crowley reckoned the number more redolent of the 1003 conquests of Don Juan!

On Saturday, July 18, he caught a "slow, dirty crammed train" with no first-class or corridor from Paddington back to 1941 haunt Maidenhead for an "A1" party with an Arthur Hornsby, a Dr. de Moor, Pam ("gorgeous") and Laurence Felkin at Skindles restaurant by the Thames. Dinner at Lady Waldie-Griffith's on the twenty-first was the best he'd eaten "since the war!" But her incessant voice was a "continuous suppressed scream." He was "stabbed in the back" when an interview with Philip Johnston of the *Star* (ostensibly about "La Gauloise") conducted just before leaving London appeared on the twentieth repeating the story that he'd worked for the Germans for money in World War I. It was sarcastically headlined "HE HATES GERMANS NOW." Crowley rightly called it "malicious garbling and misrepresentation" and considered suing. Frieda was equally indignant and raved. On the twenty-second he planned to go to Kerman's to dictate a libel writ but was ill and called it off. Instead he put his energies into writing to Helen Parsons with ideas for attracting good publicity to the lodge, while considering getting Roy Leffingwell to set "Hymn to Pan" to music—quite a task!

On July 27 he ran into Louis Wilkinson at lunch with Lady Denny. "Her uncle, Sir Edward, was one of my father's greatest friends. Haven't thought of him since '86—56 years ago!"* The next day he met a young Peter Brook of Magdalen College, Oxford, busily staging *Dr. Faustus* at London's Torch Theatre. Leopold Bick, who played Mephistopheles, visited a day later and "talked very well about Magick, his aims and so on. In fact, we almost fraternized. He stayed an hour, and I was sorry to have to get rid of him!"

An air raid alert sounded at 3:40 on July 31. It began only after the "All-clear": very heavy over south London, with searchlights, gunfire, and rockets.

August 1 brought news from Brooks that Frieda was again showing her paintings without telling 666, this time for three weeks at the Royal Watercolour Painters Society in Conduit Street. Surprised by Crowley's appearance on the fourth, Frieda said she'd just written to tell him—"I don't think," quipped Crowley, who found the presenta-

---

*Sir Edward Denny (1796–1889), Anglo-Irish baronet, M.P. (Tralee), and Plymouth Brethren hymn writer, celebrated for not increasing tenants' low rents.

tion impressive. He thought she must be crazy, soft-soaping him with her "if only you'd keep quiet" routine, then lying to the public while telling her friends she did it all for A.C.'s "sweet sake." "I don't want to put forward my name; but I do hate fraud and falsehood." At the same time, he received an "Open Letter" from an "Order of Hidden Masters." This was Michael Juste (Houghton) and colleagues. Reading like an accusation, their Open Letter begged Mr. Aleister Crowley to correct the untrue proposition circulating in London that Lady Harris was solely responsible for the seventy-eight tarot paintings, while anyone who knew, knew she knew practically nothing about the tarot's occult symbolism but what was mimicked from Crowley, true author of the essence of the works. A casual remark to "Hidden Master!!" Juste saw Juste blow into a stammering rage with bluster and threats. Truly amazed at the reaction, Crowley said he'd be a little "hidden master" himself next week, seeking cover from such pomposity.

Sir Francis Younghusband's death saddened Crowley on the second, their having met in the spring: "I feel chilly and grown old." "Mostly bored and feeling feeble." Readers will have noticed a serious decline in sexual activity (to zero), along with increased bronchial problems and heroin intake (up to a grain a time and rising).

He wrote to Ben Stubbins on August 6: "Dear Brother Ben, Your grand loyal letter cheered and encouraged me more than I can say." He explained where Frieda had gone wrong. "I am very fond of F. H. and hoped to make her a real artist; and I cannot even avert the wrath of the insulted God [Hermes]!"[38]

Hurt he was, but returned to the exhibition on the twelfth, taking "overbearing malignant coarse cow Deborah [Hogg]" to meet a nervous Frieda for what turned out a "terrific day," meeting B.B.C. man Royston Morley at the Antelope in Belgravia and opening a welcome letter from seventeen-year-old Peter Brook. Crowley visited Peter's rehearsals at the Torch Theatre on the fifteenth at midday: "My appreciation of his intelligence grows every time I see him." Crowley guided *Faustus* on stage effects and conjuring skills.

Bruce Blunt appeared paralytic drunk on the fifteenth, sleeping the night in a chair. Crowley eased him up next morning and took him to the Antelope, lending him a pound. On the seventeenth, Peter Brook came in the afternoon, and Crowley felt "more and more fed up with every damned thing on earth," noting that had his father lived, he'd have been 107 that day.

Smith wrote on August 18: "This was a tough move. I have worked like hell, so have Helen and Regina. Without them we would not have been here anyway. Of course, others have helped, but damn it all, so few seem to have any spirit to put into mundane things. It is so much easier to sit on one's arse and talk philosophy. . . ." Crowley received a letter from Roy Leffingwell on August 19. Roy's connection with movie star Tyrone Power "might help." Meanwhile, on the twenty-second, Crowley consulted Kerman about legal action against Frieda, looking through their letters and finding "very valuable admissions."[39]

As he informed Germer, Crowley spent late August at the Ascot home of Brigadier General Rudolph Trower Hogg, C.M.G., C.I.E. (1877–1955) and Deborah Hogg, perhaps his daughter. Appointed brigade commander of the newly formed R.A.F. in 1918, he retired in 1919 after a distinguished career in the Indian Army, serving at Galilpoli in World War I. "I am staying with General Hogg at his Ascot Place for the longest rest and quiet I can manage. French and Gaselee compliment me on my French [in 'La Gauloise']."[40]

Returning to London on August 28, Zatelli told Crowley that Foreign Office librarian Sir Stephen Gaselee (1882–1943) spoke very highly of his work. Crowley noted Gaselee's address; Sir Stephen bought a copy of *Fun of the Fair* on December 17. When Gaselee died in 1943 Crowley expressed genuine sorrow.

*Fig. 12.8. Brigadier General Rudolph Trower Hogg (1877–1955).*

Robert Cecil's boat came in on September 1. He was appointed assistant private secretary to Sir Alexander Cadogan, permanent secretary (head) of the Foreign Office. Cadogan's private office linked MI5, S.I.S. [Secret Intelligence Service], and S.O.E. [Special Operations Executive]. Cecil had entered the secret war effort's inner sanctum. For a man with a consular background the promotion was almost fantastic (a year later he'd become a private secretary to Sir Stewart Menzies, head of S.I.S.). Cecil related that had he been able to tell Crowley, the mage would probably have claimed it as vindication of the probationer oath, but Cecil was, he says, bound by another: the Official Secrets Act.

On September 2, Crowley sent Wilkinson a copy of his reply to the Order of Hidden Masters' Open Letter: "I am glad you approved my answer to Order. H[idden].M[asters]. No, he is not a disciple. He may be Atlantis Bookshop, who hate and fear me, and are annoyed with Frieda."[41] Five days later, he received a long letter, "making my mouth water," from Roy Leffingwell. It held the tune to "La Gauloise." Now would the B.B.C. listen?

Returning to Ascot on the eleventh, the general and Saffron were on holiday, and Deborah nagged less than usual, for most of the time. He was back in London on August 25 after harrowing scenes—if we take the diary drama at face value!

One of the first things he'd have picked up in Hamilton House was an invitation of September 18, 1942, from "N[ick]. Carter" from 12 Buckingham Palace Road:* "It is some months now since your last visit, and therefore I write to invite you here for another chat at a time to suit your convenience."[42] Former MI5 Section G intelligence officer, later Assistant Commissioner "A" of the Metropolitan Police (1938–1940), Col. John F. C. Carter, C.B.E. (1882–1944), was code named "Nick" after fictional detective "Nick Carter."

Hamilton turned up on September 26 "still vomiting bile against England." Relief came next day with a trip to *Dr. Faustus* rehearsals. He thought of making Helen up as a "particularly ugly grinning devil convulsed with laughter at F[aust]'s bemused rhapsodies." He

---

*Carter's address is curious; 12 Buckingham Palace Road was also R. A. Caton's Fortune Press address; he was publisher of Cecil's poetry. Other business included pornography and property; he interviewed paying poets in the cellar—suggesting the seediness of Len Deighton's *The Ipcress File*.

contributed other ideas, too, pity he wasn't directing perhaps! Crowley lunched with Brook two days later at the Piccadilly Brasserie. Next day he was amazed to receive a stipend from Frieda with "no warning it would stop."

*Dr. Faustus* dress rehearsal on September 30 had "God-awful" elements, according to Crowley, including Helen's stilted walk, but on October 1, the opening was "A1 all things considered." He thought of the whistling cabbage: "The marvelous thing is that the animal should be able to do it at all." This, he corrected himself, wasn't fair. It held the audience.

Bayley and girlfriend Tub came to tea and play; they went out. When Crowley stopped to do the "Evening Adoration" (Ra in its setting), they "sauntered on," pretending they didn't know him. "What a herd!" He went to see Acts I and III again on the third, much improved since the first night. The previous day, after having written to Wilkinson eulogizing the "London Production of Marlowe by a boy of 17," adding that he hoped soon to "escape to U.S.A. or Glory,"[43] he heard from the Passport Office: Not "at the present time." On the fifth he informed Germer—who'd married for the third time on September 23—"the Passport office still considers my presence on the spot an essential condition of Victory."[44]

Determined to advance "La Gauloise" he decided to get de Gaulle, Donegall, and Yvonne Arnaud to contact the B.B.C.

Anxiously waiting for a call from Peter Brook, Crowley had "dealings with 132 [Smith]" on October 4:

> Your letters, for many years, seem to have sought to give the impression that you are being bundled about all the time, mostly with "chores," so that you cannot concentrate on the Great Work. Poor ill-used, wronged, misunderstood dogsbody! You seem to think this is an excuse. It is not; it is a confession. . . . And now I hear that you are sitting on Jack's tail to prevent him getting off the ground. That simply won't do . . . I should hate it if the hair by which the sword hangs over your head were to snap . . . take this friendly admonishment . . . Baphomet OHO [Outer Head of the Order: official notification].[45]

Brook arrived at 12:30 next day for "two hours' very intense magical talk." Crowley conveyed his interest to Shakespeare scholar Louis Wilkinson: "I am very keen on Peter Brook; am trying to get him to do *The Tempest* rather than *Coriolanus,* as Prospero is Shakespeare's magical refutation of *Dr. Faustus.* I am serious about this: think he came out of his retirement ad hoc. If P.B. will, I might go to Oxford for a week or so to coach him. Will let you know any move." On the thirteenth he informed Wilkinson he was going to try for Oxford "for a few days at least."[46] A week later he was all set for Oxford's Randolph Hotel. His mind was certainly focused on *performance.* On October 7 he enjoyed Barbara Stanwyk in *The Gay Sisters* (1942; directed by Irving Rapper): "damned good characterization, and A1 acting."

Cathrine was back in London, at Greencoat Place SW1, on the thirteenth. She wrote to her old lover, who was making a will, leaving everything to O.T.O. Treasurer Germer, who informed Crowley on October 14 he'd married Sascha Ernestine André Elly Aszkanasy, a Jewish lady, as Crowley recommended. Sascha didn't share Cora Germer's aversion to 666. Exchanging kind letters, she sent cigars, chocolates, tobacco, and other dainties hard to obtain in wartime London.

Performing at Star Sound Studios on the sixteenth, Crowley made a record of the "Hymn to Pan" for Roy and Karl. A small independent theater for Radio Luxembourg's live audience shows, Star Sound opened in 1937; discs were recorded onto wax. Three days later, Star Sound refused to make any records, denying him the "Hymn to Pan" disc. He couldn't send Roy Leffingwell a record, but he did send him secret documents for the IX° on the twenty-fourth, believing Roy had earned them.

A disappointed Crowley wrote to Wilkinson on the twenty-first that "Oxford was off." The thought of the "Buddhist hells" of a cold hotel got him back to his "secret electric fire."[47] Instead, he entered the Phoenix Theatre to see H. M. Tennent's production of Wilde's *The Importance of Being Earnest* with John Gielgud as John Worthing, Cyril Ritchard as Algernon, and Edith Evans as Lady Bracknell: "John and Algy A1. Edith's voice overdone, rest of cast might have been better; they didn't play enough when not speaking." Knowing Wilkinson's affection for Wilde, Crowley wrote on the twenty-sixth a structural critique of Wilde's play, as well as a distinction between what he called "slaves" and people who can shoulder responsibility: "Most average men, even men very high up, funk responsibility. In Whitehall, it's a system!"

"Peter Brook," he declared, "is a producer" and a "character"; as an actor "not at all good. He is in danger of a swelled head: doesn't answer letters promptly, has too many things in his mind at one time. Wilde's wit was very artificial for the most part." Accepting Wilkinson's contention that farce should not be analyzed: "Your dialogue is infinitely subtler. . . . You don't seem to take this as seriously as I do: but then my conscience has always been praeter-Nonconformist in all matters of art."[48]

Crowley was delighted to announce he'd found lodging at 93 Jermyn Street opposite St. James's church, Piccadilly (where William Blake was baptized in 1757). Not only was the house number significant, but the telephone number "Whitehall *9331*" encapsulated the gematria of Hebrew *aleph* + *lamed* = 31 = AL = God, a secret key of *The Book of the Law*. The room would be free on November 16.

On October 27, Crowley entered Levy's Sound Studios at 73 New Bond Street to record the first and second Enochian calls. His invocatory voice failed him twice: "Hell!" Jacques Levy began producing records in Regent Street in 1931, before adapting a former Mayfair art gallery in 1937. Chief engineers were Ted Sibbick and Bill Johnson; Crowley's recordings are extant.

Recording excited the Beast. He told Germer on October 28 he wanted popular singer and pianist Yvonne Arnaud (1890–1958) to record "La Gauloise" now that Roy had done the music. He also wanted more news about Sascha, admitting there'd been no word from Yorke since their Cambridge outing a year ago; perhaps Yorke had been posted abroad. Crowley asked after Astarte Lulu (his and Ninette Shumway's daughter, now twenty-one)—"if she's there." Ninette's sister Hélène Fraux had surreptitiously removed Lulu (or "Loulou") from her parents' care in France: "No news since '29. She may be in U.S.A.—quite likely."[49] If so, her father wished to make provision in his will. Lulu was indeed in the States, but her foster mother hated Crowley; there would be no contact. After a long, happy, and accomplished life, Lulu died in California in 2014. Soror Estai received a card sent in October authorizing her (Jane) to make her own decision about withholding the password from Frater 132, which would put Smith temporarily outside the Order. Crowley informed her he seemed "stuck in London for the winter," and "should be regarded as a fragile and exquisite piece of Ming porcelain (or, more accurately, as an old cracked piss-pot) which will smash at the slightest jar." Prospective accommodation was "close to everything so as to avoid the risks of the Black-out;" but he would have to be kept warm (both difficult and expensive), being fed principally on seafood and fresh fruit—also expensive—but what with digestive and dental trouble, there was no other way to secure him the chance— "rather meager at the best—of getting through the winter alive." He would appear to her now as a "quiet old buffer."[50]

*Eheu fugaces*—"Alas, the fleeting years slip by," was Crowley's comment when he heard Dr. John Norman Collie (1859–1942) had died at Sligachan, Isle of Skye, on November 1. Crowley had admired chemist, explorer, and mountaineer Collie since climbing together in the 1890s. Collie conveyed his chemical and alchemical interests to young Crowley, proposing him—seconded by Sir Martin Conway—for membership

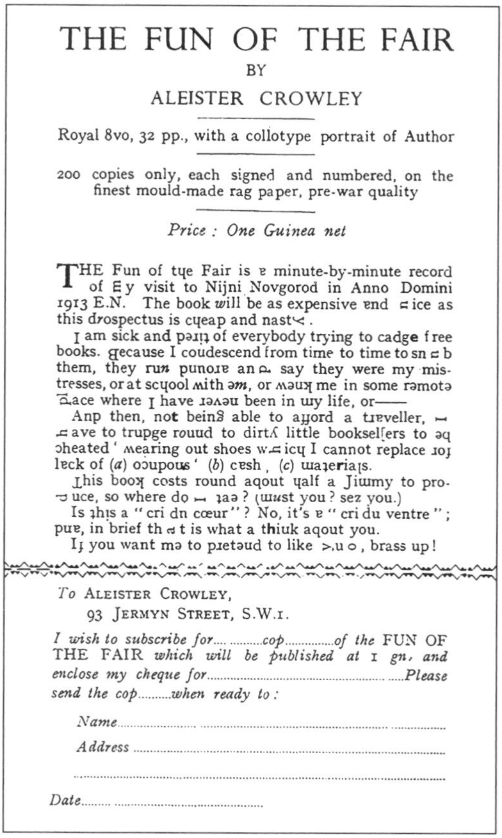

## THE FUN OF THE FAIR

BY

### ALEISTER CROWLEY

Royal 8vo, 32 pp., with a collotype portrait of Author

200 copies only, each signed and numbered, on the finest mould-made rag paper, pre-war quality

*Price : One Guinea net*

THE Fun of the Fair is a minute-by-minute record of my visit to Nijni Novgorod in Anno Domini 1913 E.N. The book will be as expensive and nice as this prospectus is cheap and nasty.

I am sick and pained of everybody trying to cadge free books. Because I condescend from time to time to send them, they run pumore and say they were my mistresses, or at school with me, or knew me in some remote place where I have never been in my life, or—

And then, not being able to afford a traveller, I have to trudge round to dirty little booksellers to be cheated ' wearing out shoes which I cannot replace for lack of (a) coupons ' (b) cash , (c) materials.

This book costs round about half a Jimmy to produce, so where do I come ? (must you ? sez you.)

Is this a " cri du cœur " ? No, it's a " cri du ventre " ; pure, in brief that is what I think about you.

If you want me to pretend to like you , brass up !

To ALEISTER CROWLEY,
    93 JERMYN STREET, S.W.I.

*I wish to subscribe for.......... cop...........of the* FUN OF THE FAIR *which will be published at* 1 *gn, and enclose my cheque for.................................Please send the cop..........when ready to :*

Name.......................................

Address ...................................

........................................

Date.......................................

*Fig. 12.9.* The Fun of the Fair *prospectus. (Courtesy of Ordo Templi Orientis and the 100th Monkey Press)*

of the Alpine Club. Crowley was blackballed, and the brilliant young climber Collie recognized in Crowley neither forgot his elder's generosity, nor the Club's slight.

Wanting a new publication for the winter solstice (December 22, 11:22 a.m.) Crowley chose his fine poem *The Fun of the Fair*. The fair was Nizhni Novgorod's in 1913; the fun was Crowley's. A famous annual event, it was held from the mid-sixteenth century to about 1929, attracting merchants from India, Iran, and Central Asia. Publication nearly thirty years later asked people to see that Russia was not something to inspire fear; the new Russian allies were not going to eat them; or was it published to persuade certain people—the Soviet Embassy, communists and fellow travelers, the Ministry of Information—he was sympathetic toward Russia? As a gesture toward new allies, it assured readers the Russian spirit was essentially unchanged since pre-Revolutionary times, soothing fears of the Communist International. On the other hand, since early purchasers included Soviet ambassador Ivan Maisky (1884–1975), Crowley may have been cozying up to fifth columnists for information (Maxwell Knight was cannily "on to" communist infiltration of Britain's security services).

"The merit of the poem," Crowley wrote to Wilkinson, "is that it gives every angle of A.C. mystic, cynic, winebibber, satyr, traveller, heliolater k.t.l. [et cetera] in swift kaleidoscope." He "would be grateful for a few words of introduction," . . . "I wish God loved me and would drop you here this very week. I'm all nerves about this solstitial outburst! . . . This time I want you real bad!" Wilkinson's assurance of an introduction earned "Thanks 1000 times in advance."[51] It arrived "though brief" on the ninth. When printed by the Chiswick Press and published by the O.T.O. at the solstice, *The Fun of the Fair* carried an extra sting in its tail, one any class warrior could enjoy: The "'Landed' Gentry" was added to some copies in mimeograph with acronym "F.O." footnoted as "Footlinski Okhrana"—*Okhrana* being the old Russian secret service.

A printing estimate for the poem came on November 5, just in time for Frieda's announcement on the eleventh that she wanted to stop Crowley's stipend as she'd only seventeen pounds a month to live on.

Baritone Laurence Holmes phoned on November 2. Meeting him that week, Crowley liked him, praising his interpretation of "La Gauloise." Next day, Crowley received a defense of Smith from Jack Parsons; brethren and sisters at S. Orange Grove would sort everything out—and

*Fig. 12.10. Eastern holy man (?)
by Cambyses Daguerre Churchill.
(Courtesy of the Warburg Institute, London,
and Ordo Templi Orientis)*

Cathrine came to tea, impressing Crowley with her sympathetic mental acuity: a joy to his heart. Tub, by comparison, he found dim, describing *The Fun of the Fair* as "interesting," wondering who "Ichabod" was.*

On Friday the thirteenth Holmes rehearsed "La Gauloise" with Miss Colleen Clifford on piano, generating four "demo" records. Bookseller Harold Mortlake received five pounds for the discs, Holmes five guineas, and Miss Clifford one guinea. Mortlake played the disc to Kenneth McAlpine at the B.B.C. on November 24, and Crowley followed up with a letter on the seventeenth about getting it broadcast. On November 30 Crowley looked at photographer Churchill's photo proofs. Three were excellent, one "just right" for *The Fun of the Fair;* one superb "Arab despot," and one Eastern holy man who looked like ecclesiastic Lord Irving.

---

*"Inglorious name of malicious priest in the book of Samuel," rhymed with "Novgorod" in the poem!

*Fig. 12.11.* The Fun of the Fair *frontispiece (Cambyses Daguerre Churchill). (Courtesy of Ordo Templi Orientis, and the 100th Monkey Press)*

The Temple Bar–based photographer was rechristened "Cambyses Daguerre Churchill" by Crowley on December 15, and the image chosen showed Crowley looking cheerful and "literary," with a huge meerschaum and equally huge floppy bow tie.

After looking at reshaded images on the seventh, Crowley decided to shave his head!

Holmes returned from a gig in Lancaster on December 1 to say he'd write to the French service of the B.B.C. about "L'Étincelle" ("La Gauloise" retitled = "The Spark"). Crowley wrote to Germer on the tenth that Holmes had that morning collected the last of the four records to play to a "very high man" in the BBC (Holmes had sung on the B.B.C. Home Service). This meant paying Holmes, the pianist, and "maybe an orchestra."[52] Holmes phoned Crowley on December 29 to say, "B.B.C. man hanging fire." Crowley cabled Roy on New Year's Eve, asking him for an orchestral variation on the "admirable" tune for "so many verses," of the July 4 hymn, pipping Holmes to sing it.

On December 2, Crowley wrote a long "rejoicing" letter to poet Trevor Blakemore (ca. 1880–1953), whom he'd met with Lady Harris at the Sesame Club, Grosvenor Street (Edith Sitwell was a member),

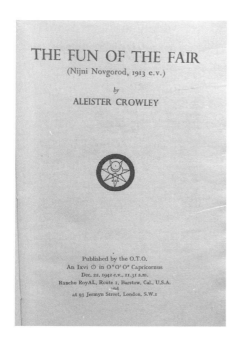

*Fig. 12.12.* The Fun of the Fair *title page.*
*(Courtesy of Ordo Templi Orientis, and the 100th Monkey Press)*

*Fig. 12.13.* The Fun of the Fair *dedication.*
*(Courtesy of Ordo Templi Orientis, and the 100th Monkey Press)*

> To the memory of
> Anny Ringler,
> Olya,
> and
> Marie Lavroff;
> and to a dear friend
> as yet unknown
> Sascha Ernestine André
> on the occasion of her marriage to
> my staunch
> Karl Johannes Germer.

for a fine lunch on November 16, where Frieda gave a lecture on the tarot. A Rudyard Kipling enthusiast, Blakemore was a member of the "Right Book Club," a conservative reaction to the influential "Left Book Club." Crowley wrote again on December 16, "correcting some of his [Blakemore's] idiot ideas about me" and a "crazily askew" horoscope Blakemore had done of 666.

At 11:31 a.m. December 22, Crowley ceremonially published *The Fun of the Fair*, tactfully dedicating it to Sascha Germer. The

Christmas (solstice) period found Crowley gifting numbered copies to friends, receiving fine wines and a few quid in return. He wrote sagely to Ben Stubbins on December 16: "I hope you'll get your friends to buy it [*The Fun of the Fair*]. This book is pure enjoyment, no nasty Magick, no boring Yoga: nothing but Enjoyment of Life!"

He noted Frieda was back and "penitent" so he hoped "that's over. . . . Please remember that I get most comfort from the solid support of my friends; see the prospectus!"[53]

Three days before the year's end, a book idea came to him: *Olla, A Book of Many Cities,* a gathering of sixty years of poetry. Each poem would put its author in a new place; that is, an old place: a memory not a memory when made. Was this around-the-world-in-sixty-three-poems Crowley's response to passport denial? In *Olla,* he traveled the world he knew so well in the poetry he'd lived. In his imagination, at least, he was free, and his past and poetry were one.*

---

*Olla*'s title came out of a debate with Wilkinson in March about the word's use in Catullus: *Ipsa olera* olla *legit* ("The pot finds its own herbs"), an epigram supposed to be foul. A German article suggested Catullus alluded to a Greek punishment where adulterers were sodomized with a radish; *olla* could also refer to the female genitals: usually passive, the "pot" here is active.

# THIRTEEN

# I Dreamed Time

*I DREAMED Time broke his Trappist vow to-day;*
*For some chance word you quaintly would employ*
*Evoked first paradise in my dulled sense*
*But could not give back primal innocence.*

ROBERT CECIL,
*LEVANT AND OTHER POEMS IX,* 1941

Denial of passport and California sunshine to "unsecured bankrupt" Crowley in 1942 probably shortened his life, making his last years an intermittent frustration of asthma and heroin. Bureaucracy can kill. Baphomet's absence from Pasadena not only exacerbated tremors among Stateside Thelemites, but arguably allowed space for Jack Parsons to pursue a path that embroiled him, along with L. Ron Hubbard, Sara Northrup, and Marjorie Cameron in a crazily distorted maelstrom that would ruin Jack's career and gift the world with Scientology. *And all for the want of a passport*—and by the end of '42, Crowley had lost another passport: his physical link to the IX°; the magnificent Beast would not "ride again."

Impotence had pros and cons, as Crowley noted on January 25, 1943:

Noticed that after sexual abstinence certain ideas become "obscene" disgusting and so on: includes contemplation of *yoni* (not *lingam* so much), disease, accident, spectacle of meat, ideas of war, pain

225

of the physical order and so on. . . . I conclude that humanitarian-
ism, pacifism—all such feelings—are functions of sexual weakness,
atrophy, or the like. This thesis can be developed very far.

"Retiring hurt" from translating five of Baudelaire's *Fleurs du Mal,*
Crowley had the additional irritant of Hamilton's teasing that the
*Evening News*'s editor had confided the "real reason for the boycott
[of Crowley's work]." Two days later, amid a "torrent of goose-babble,"
Hamilton said the "M.D.I." held the Beast's activities in America
1914–1918 against him.*
    Germer cabled January 14; Jane Wolfe had done the deed:

Beloved Frater 132 [Smith]

93

Pursuant to instructions from Baphomet, it is my duty to inform you
that for the time being you will be relieved of your function in the
Lodge, and that you will retire from the Community House at 1003
S Orange Grove Avenue Pasadena. Your full reinstatement will follow
the achievement of some definite personal action, conceived and executed by yourself alone, to the advancement of the work of the Order.
                            93   93/93 Fraternally in the
                            Bonds of the Order.
                            Estai [Jane Wolfe]. 516[1]

    An instruction swiftly followed by encouragement; they would tra-
verse the ordeal together: "You on the outside, I on the inside. . . . You
need to expand yourself, I need to take hold of things. I have always
shunned action, hence a certain ineffectualness, and I must be primed
for action. You must be primed for more wisdom. . . . I will ask for your
final decision this afternoon, please. Fraternally, Jane."[2]
    While Jane coaxed, Frieda phoned on the fifteenth: would 666
meet her friend, occult-enthusiast Edward Bryant (1920–1988) of

*"M.D.I." is most probably a transcription error for D.M.I. (Directorate of Military
Intelligence), or else N.I.D. or M.O.I.: Ministry of Information (propaganda)—the latter
acronym familiar to journalists.

"Holywood," Marville Road, Hemel Hempstead? Reportedly a Crowley reader, suburban "Ted" Bryant made little impression: "He seems an acquired taste, but has read a lot."

Crowley resumed translating Baudelaire and assembling *Olla* through a month pocked with air raids. Relief came with "parcels of food" from Germer, and "not-so-food" from 1705 Marshall Street in Regina's warm lawned leafy suburb of Houston, Texas.

—and Jane cabled Baphomet:

SMITH STILL HERE DEBATING OWN DECISION STOP RESENTS ORDER THROUGH ANYONE BUT YOU JACK UNSTABLE LETTER FOLLOWS[3]

Crowley addressed Jack's "instability": "My dear Jack, . . . The A∴A∴ system is quiet and controlled. . . . You do write rather hysterically about this 'dark and shining brother [Smith].' His writing to me is sufficient condemnation. . . . I do not like the look of any of this. I should say that you were in danger of obsession. What you most need is the Banishing Ritual of the Pentagram. And be damned careful that you do it right! Asana and Pranayama might also be helpful. . . . You should also practice *Liber Jugorum* and get more control. This is very important.

"Now, Wilfrid. Of course Regina was 'never more than a coarse, bouncing, blatant, bellowing cow, and he's very very well rid of her.' (This a verbatim report from *one* source!)

"He is an $8° = 3^{\square}$ only by the rule that makes you one if you choose to claim to be one. In his case, it was only a drunken freak; but so is jumping off the Brooklyn Bridge for a bet.

"He has not gone through any of the grades that lead up to it; I think he was passed to Neophyte, but he certainly never went further. Where are his records? What has he accomplished? His position in the Order is accordingly that of a Busted Flush. . . . It was his trying to hamper you that drove me to writing to you about it. . . . Now I do wish you would tell me <u>what</u> you owe to him—your whole outlook is utterly wrong and futile."

By contrast, Crowley explained his influence on the minds of Aldous Huxley, James B. Cabell, H. L. Mencken, playwright Lord Dunsany,

Somerset Maugham, H. G. Wells, and Arthur Machen (allegedly scared of Crowley). "What you don't know—as far as I can see—is History. I know of no precedent for a man with your ideas getting anywhere at all. You see, *you think the whole thing is a swindle.* You don't *believe* in the Masters. You don't trust *The Book of the Law* to look after itself." Jack imagined achieving *when* rich and powerful, et cetera. But Crowley insisted anyone intending to "upset the apple-cart" started *knowing* they could do it *from the point where they started.* "For it is the living faith, and not the blind belief, in your Truth that gives the genius to over-throw great cities. When you have got that, you won't have to ask me for a plan of campaign, or a way out of this or that, or anything else."[4]

With Jack hopefully stabilized, Crowley cabled Jane on January 23:

SMITHS RECALCITRANCE MAY PRECIPITATE IRREVOCABLE THUNDERBOLT STOP AIRMAILED JACK YESTERDAY STABILIZING ENCOURAGING STOP WRITING FULLY HOPEFUL YOUR [tarot] TRUMPS READY SHORTLY STOP LOVE FULL CONFIDENCE ALEXANDER CROWLEY[5]

And cabled Smith on the twenty-sixth:

CONGRATULATIONS PUBLICATION [Smith revived O.T.O. magazine, *Oriflamme*] STOP DO DEFLATE HEAD ANSWER LETTERS BEHAVE SENSIBLY MODESTLY GERMERS WORD GOES ALEXANDER CROWLEY[6]

Anticipating a "thunderbolt," Jack and Helen Parsons pleaded Crowley hold fire, with a swipe at Germer's representing and exacerbat-ing a "division of authority":

REMEMBER WE HAVE HARD JOB CANNOT LONG AFFORD TO LOSE WILFRID THINGS HAVE DEVELOPED WELL DIVISION OF AUTHORITY IS UPSETTING TO ORGANIZATION DON'T BELIEVE EVERYTHING YOU HEAR LOVE AND TRUST, JACK AND HELEN[7]

The Piccadilly Brasserie must have seemed a temporary oasis when Crowley met Louis Wilkinson there on the twenty-ninth for an

"Admirable Richebourg '29"—the "best wine either of us had tasted since many years." Fortified, Crowley visited Jewish refugee artist Jack Bilbo's "ghastly daubs; not even originally crude or infantile. Why does Frieda send me to such people?" Real name Hugo Bausch (1907–1967), Bilbo was a significant "outsider" artist, author, anarchist, activist, and founder of the Modern Art Gallery, Baker Street. Since gallery impresario Karl Nierendorf praised Crowley's art in 1931 as that of an outsider, 666 might have been more empathetic; perhaps the Richebourg interfered, for Crowley later met and liked Bilbo.

The Beast drew no comfort from poor Smith's letter of February 3: a plea of self-justification asserting that what Crowley considered "wrong" with him was that he was no substitute for the O.H.O.; but *how could he be?* Besides, Crowley probably didn't know that on January 16 the F.B.I. had descended on Agape Lodge, tipped off by Pasadena police (themselves alerted anonymously by a "Real Soldier" complaining of subversion and "Sex Perversion").* G-men who grilled Smith and Parsons concluded the "Church of Thelma" (*sic*) was a religious organization—maybe a "love-cult"—but not a cell of alien subversion.[8] Tensions remained high at 1003 S. Orange Grove, and Crowley's strictures didn't help:

My dear Aleister,

Thank you for the wire. I certainly owe you a letter. . . . In 1936 [according to "you"; i.e., Crowley] I was a whoremonger, dishonest, a black magician. My memory serves me well and besides I have looked up the files on that case. Now I am a clown, vile and have a swelled head. Personally I cannot take these criticisms too seriously, because I do not take myself too seriously, besides the accusations are so positively stupid and false. . . . I love simple things, animals, nature, enjoy the ingenuity of my hands, good literature and intelligent conversation. . . . The 835 dollars [sent] in a year is a very little we know, but still we could have used it to great advantage here. We

---

*According to Martin Starr, the malicious informer was probably a jealous boyfriend or husband, ex or spurned, of one of the women frequenting the lodge (Starr, *The Unknown God*, 284-85).

did our best. . . . It is my humble opinion that you are the greatest
being on the planet. But, I do not get cocky because you have written to me personally, or give myself airs because I am in direct touch
with the Master.

Us more particularly! We have been harried by the FBI thrice
lately, and other things are a continual source of annoyance. Can't
the internal unrest be stopped? You seem so often to be responsible
for the continual disturbances. . . . Best of love always,[9]

Different viewpoints crossed continent and ocean in long letters from Roy and Regina. Feeling "utterly worn out" (February 13),
Crowley addressed Jane:

You people are absolutely beyond my comprehension!

At the same time I want to say a few things which will clear up
any possible difficulties between us. I want to point out that it is
quite a long while since we met face to face. In all these years I have
turned into a very different man from the one you knew. But even
him you only knew very slightly, because of my invariable custom
of wearing a mask. I always behave to people as much as possible as
they expect me to behave, and it is a fatal error to base any conclu-
sions upon such observations.

Now this is my general complaint. Every member of the Order
has no *raison d'être* unless he is doing practices and recording them
and sending them in regularly for criticism and advice, but nobody
takes the trouble to do that. . . . They are not devoted to the work
of initiation, and consequently they do not make any progress.
[As for Smith] I gather from various reports that he is thinking of
running a Church of Thelema of his own personal manufacture.
But he cannot do anything with it, because he has no material. It
always comes back to me . . . it is really heart-breaking that in a
quarter of a century or so I can get absolutely nothing that I can
take hold of.[10]

Replying to Regina Kahl on the seventeenth, he referred to "the
witch's cauldron they have made of the Abbey."[11] Still, Green & Stone,
Chelsea's arts, crafts, and picture-framing shop, notified him of some

"17 lost lamb pictures," last seen twenty-three months previously: "some very much beloved. Stuck them up all round as best I could." Then Edward Bryant rang: "bored me for half an hour with disconnected drivel." Next day, Green the printers told him *Olla* wasn't possible by the spring equinox, so he decided on *The City of God* instead (first published in the *English Review* in January 1914).

A sign of the times: on February 19 Zatelli showed Crowley a Board of Trade letter refusing permission to import cigars for Winston Churchill! Bureaucracy again, and no one immune!

On February 22, a newly shaven-headed Crowley received his first blast from Lt. Grady Louis McMurtry 1574983, 1803rd Ordnance Medium Maintenance Company (Aviation Support), Sixty-Eighth Service Group, Pendleton Field, Oregon. McMurtry (1918–1985) would play a critical role in O.T.O. history after Crowley's death.[12]

Before being drafted in February '41, McMurtry encountered Jack Parsons at Clifton's Cafeteria, where a young Ray Bradbury and others met as the Los Angeles Science Fiction League. A sci-fi mentality would soon form an enduring, potent amalgam with magick.

So wowed was poet McMurtry by a Gnostic Mass in December 1940 he brought Claire Palmer and Marjorie Fox to Winona Boulevard for another on January 5, 1941. Initiated on June 13 with fiancée Claire Palmer and Sara Northrup, McMurtry, despite army service, remained

*Fig. 13.1.*
*Grady Louis McMurtry (1918–1985).*
*(Courtesy of Ordo Templi Orientis)*

close to—and quick to judge—Agape Lodge. He informed Crowley that Smith and Jack were so hostile to pregnancy that a girl with two children "became a veritable outcast" when found to be pregnant. Did people who preferred abortion to birth dominate the Order? Horrified, Crowley wrote to Germer. The Order needed "strong men . . . willing to accept responsibility." Abortion denied the child's True Will to be born. Indeed, 666 regarded all members' children as children of the whole Order. Believing someone had insisted on abortion, Crowley hastily sided with McMurtry: "What you tell me is truly abominable." Despite the inaccuracy of McMurtry's insinuations, Crowley now saw Smith's name since Vancouver ever tied to "sordid sexual squabbles." "Strong measures" were coming. Indifferent to the Parsons's request for "love and trust," he insisted to Jane on March 3 that Smith was a "nonentity," "an empty sack" who hadn't contributed to the work of the Order. As for "dividing authority," "Germer can be trusted absolutely to guide you all with wisdom through this time of crisis." "Victory is cumulative." Agape Lodge was vital for all publishing costs and work in general.[13]

Crowley's depression muddied waters. On February 25 he described himself as "still coasting along the shores of grim insanity in monsoon and fog—very like the Calcutta-Rangoon journey!" (1902; see Churton, *Aleister Crowley in India*). There was always chess. On March 1 he mentioned *1234 Modern End-Game Studies* by H. M. Lommer (1938), edited by Maurice Sutherland, but chess did little for his health. By Sunday, March 7, life seemed just black and white squares—one precipitating another:

> I sit and smoke
> Until I choke,
> Take heroin
> To breathe again,
> And then cocaine
> To clear my brain.
> To top with hashish
> Much too rash is;
> So let me clear
> My mind with beer,
> And call upon the loftiest genii
> With Anhalonium lewinii!

Fortunately, he never lost his sense of humor: keynote of a new project that would emerge after Bryant introduced Crowley to Mrs. Anne Macky over lunch at Hatchett's on March 12. Australian pianist and composer Anne Macky (1887–1964), founder of Melbourne's People's Conservatorium (later New Conservatorium) music school—which she ran successfully from 1917 to 1932—was living in tranquil suburbia at 15 Coniston Road, King's Langley, close to Bryant's home in Hemel Hempstead, Hertfordshire.*

Crowley's first meetings with Anne Macky went badly. A long afternoon talk on March 18 was recorded thus: "she *nearly* got thrown out." It may have been Macky's skeptical approach. Resistance ended with two guineas for Crowley's *Magick*.

Crowley's creative frustration is evident in his suggesting to Bryant on March 27 a collaborative book about Allan Bennett "*as he was,* not [Clifford] Bax's wishy-washy pastel chocolate-box 'Gentle Allan, meek and mild.'" Crowley started his portion on April 27, but Bryant proved disappointing: "Started my share of Allan's biography. E. B. flabbier than ever: I hardly expected him to turn up at all: at end made silly excuses for not coming again—wretched worm! He will never get anywhere, unless to make a linseed poultice."[15] Nevertheless, Crowley wrote, suggesting a secretary (Mrs. Burger of Temple Bar) might

---

*Born in Fitzroy, Victoria, third daughter of Englishman George Drew and Sarah Matilda Hawkins, Anne Maria Hawkins was influenced by her mother's cousin, music critic and poet Walter James Turner, who believed music was a revelation that helped people transcend material reality and open spiritual natures. Anne's surname came from a second marriage to New Zealander Dr. Stewart Macky in 1916. In Melbourne she pursued the latest artistic pedagogical aids such as Dalcroze Eurhythmics and the Tobias Matthay method, to much acclaim—her students' concerts in the city center were well reviewed in the Australian music press. Coming to England in 1932, she learned composition. The Australian Broadcasting Corporation would in time broadcast her compositions. At least before the war, she was a strong believer in peaceful socialist revolution, with everyone enjoying spiritual benefits from the raising powers of music.[14] She was also inspired by Steiner's Anthroposophy movement, believing the spiritual world accessible and applicable therapeutically and scientifically. She had an open mind, with ideologies constantly in flux. Her relationship with Aleister Crowley is practically unknown to musical scholarship. Betty O'Brien's important "Anne Macky: A Radical in her Time," (*Context 27 & 28* [2004], 71–82), does not mention it, though she does refer to Rudolf Steiner and Macky's enthusiasm for Manicheism in the 1950s.

stimulate new memories of Bennett (he needed a secretary, and here was an opportunity perhaps for Bryant to pay). He assured Bryant that "hundreds of interesting incidents" remained untold. Bryant should consider contacting George Cecil Jones, A∴A∴ cofounder, now of 41D London Road, Forest Hill: "He knew Allan a year before I did and he was always more intimate with him on the strictly scientific side than I was, although he was also of course a prominent member of the G∴D∴ . . . He saw something of Allan, moreover, when I was away, for instance during Allan's visit to England during the 1914–1918 period and must have plenty of interesting and amusing stories. I remember in particular that Allan had a device for detecting submarines; Jones, with infinite trouble, got hold of a man from the Admiralty to look into it. An appointment was made, and everyone was there but Allan. I don't know if you read *Inland Far* [1925] by Clifford Bax. . . . Allan had more chiaroscuro than almost any man I ever knew and Bax's whitewashing had the effect of concealing the supremely important thing about Allan," a man of "superhuman stature. His achievement in spite of his extreme poverty [was] absolutely stupefying." Bryant proved difficult. After a meeting on April 18, Crowley commented: "He does vampirize one."

Back on Smith's case on April Fool's Day, Crowley complained of lack of accounts, letters unanswered, and a total figure of £150 gathered until Germer supervised. "As to swelled head—I am told by several people, some of them entirely friendly that you have been laying claim to all sorts of degrees to which you have no shadow of right." Yes, Smith had an *honorary* tenth degree, but only "as my deputy in California. . . . The Grades in themselves are nothing except insofar as they are evidence of certain facts, and there have been plenty of people with all sorts of high degrees, perfectly genuinely acquired, who had really nothing in them at all. . . . You may remember that John Yarker was nobbled by the Toshosophist crowd. They tried to stampede the Order on his death [Memphis and Misraim Rites]. There is some small account of this in Eq[uinox] 1.10." Crowley was scathing regarding Smith's response to the F.B.I.: "You should have welcomed the investigators in the warmest way, assumed the offensive, taken the line that you thanked God that they had come to you at last, that the only thing you needed to establish your Work was to get the ear of people of sufficient importance, place, and intelligence to understand that the only hope of pulling the country—indeed all countries—through the present assault of bureaucracy and totalitarianism in one form or another is to adopt the Law of Thelema officially. . . . Instead of that, you act like a person found loitering suspiciously. . . . At the moment the Tarot, the Hymn for Independence Day and *l'Étincelle* are of supreme importance because they will reach a public of more or less normal people. We do not want any more drifting 'occultists.' We want the great political leaders, great industrials and people of that sort, the kind of person who does not subscribe 835 in a year but half a million dollars in a day, and every distraction or diversion of funds from the business of getting at such people is hardly better than throwing the money into the sea. . . . The trouble with you is that you are hopelessly parochial—and I am sorry to say that the parish appears to be Bow."[16]

On April 4 he went to see René Clair's *I Married a Witch,* starring Veronica Lake and Fredric March. Crowley's verdict: "excellent." The next day he purchased "ceremonial vodka" to dedicate *City of God.* Its new introduction began promisingly: "Poetry is the geyser of the Unconscious." Then he laid into T. S. Eliot, Ezra Pound, and W. H. Auden, who to Crowley had all abandoned the time-honored dignity of poetry for dubious effects: "Pedantry and preciosity, push and peacockry, are not the stuff of song." While Crowley had produced little *really good* poetry since splitting with Jeanne Robert Foster in 1915, he still knew what made poetry great. The first verse of *City of God,* written in 1913, describing a train journey to Moscow, is, to my eyes, magnificent:

Day after day we crawled
Beneath the leaden, flat,
Featureless heaven, across dull emerald
Field after field, whereon no aureate
Sunrise awakened earth's Magnificat,
Save at the marge where, rimmed with duller pines,
Dun earth mixed with black heaven, there unsealed
A red eye glowing through that furtive field,
As if the bloodhound of Eternity
Tracked the thief Time. Remorseless rain
Beat down, pale piteous monotony,
Upon the inexorable plain.

*Fig. 13.2.*
The City of God *frontispiece*
*(photograph by Cambyses Daguerre*
*Churchill).*
*(Courtesy of Ordo Templi Orientis*
*and the 100th Monkey Press)*

Printed late* by the Chiswick Press for April 20, the frontispiece depicted a magical Crowley in Arab garb with goatee beard and meerschaum, most effectively captured by Cambyses Daguerre Churchill's lens (an image sometimes called "the Arabian Alchemist").

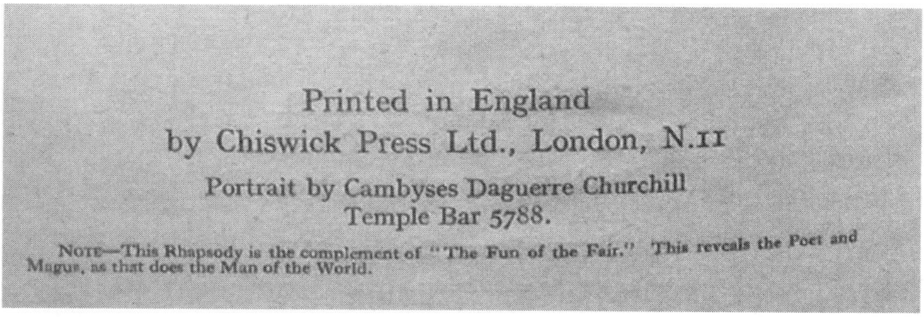

Printed in England
by Chiswick Press Ltd., London, N.11
Portrait by Cambyses Daguerre Churchill
Temple Bar 5788.
NOTE—This Rhapsody is the complement of "The Fun of the Fair." This reveals the Poet and Magus, as that does the Man of the World.

*Fig. 13.3.* The City of God *printing and photography credit.*
*(Courtesy of Ordo Templi Orientis and the 100th Monkey Press)*

---

*Diary entry April 15, 1943: "Chiswick Press calmly announces *City* not ready till Wed[nesday]. Next!!! What bastards of bastards! Real bad faith."

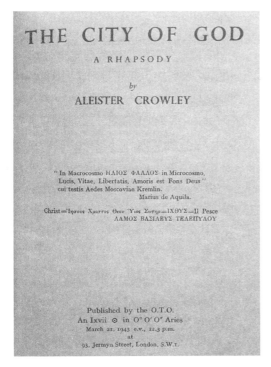

THE CITY OF GOD

A RHAPSODY

*by*

ALEISTER CROWLEY

" In Macrocosmo ΗΛΙΟΣ ΦΑΛΛΟΣ in Microcosmo,
Lucis, Vitae, Libertatis, Amoris est Fons Deus "
cui testis Aedes Moscoviae Kremlin.
Marius de Aquila.

Christ = Ίησους Χριστος Θεου Ύιος Σωτηρ = ΙΧΘΥΣ = Il Pesce
ΛΑΜΟΣ ΒΑΣΙΛΕΥΣ ΤΕΛΕΠΥΛΟΥ

Published by the O.T.O.
An lxvii ☉ in 0° 0′ 0″ Aries
March 21. 1943 e.v., 12.3 p.m.
at
93. Jermyn Street, London, S.W.1.

*Fig. 13.4.* The City of God *title page. (Courtesy of Ordo Templi Orientis and the 100th Monkey Press)*

⊛

On April 12 Crowley saw Katharine Hepburn and Spencer Tracy in George Cukor's *Keeper of the Flame:* "One of the best of its kind—the Happy American Family kind!" Two days later he entered the Garrick Theatre to see a play inspired by Graham Greene's novel *Brighton Rock:* "Not too bad: could have had her want to 'hear his loving voice as she dies,' and put on the record before the firing. He [Pinkie, played by Richard Attenborough] returns, and the cops get him. The end is much too good for him. I think Dulcie Grey stole the show from Hermione [Baddeley]; but there is nothing much in H's part. D.G. was *perfect.*" So impressed by Dulcie was Crowley that on May 2 he sent her *Fun of the Fair,* and some verses ending, "A young thing stole the show away / Her dulcet name is Dulcie Grey." Dulcie replied, and showbiz legend has it "regretted" doing so after he wrote asking, tongue in cheek, if he could sacrifice her at dawn at Stonehenge! Dulcie declined in equally playful spirit, saying early rising was not for her! Dulcie died aged ninety-five in 2011.

On the fifteenth he saw *Derrière la Façade* again (1939, George Lacombe): "It improves every time: one picks up fine points previously missed. Superb—beyond all praise: not a dull second."

Gerald Yorke made a reappearance on April 21. They had lunch, and Yorke bought *Fun of the Fair* and three copies of *The City of God* and said he'd send one hundred pounds to Chiswick Press for the tarot book. Seldom was 666 short of cussed phrases for Yorke, but Yorke's action beat all Smith's good intentions. When Crowley considered what Smith had spent on attempting an O.T.O. *Oriflamme* magazine, he was enraged, communicating to Germer that Jack Parsons's "poetry" would "revive ancient lies about drugs," while Jack's "political rant" was "contemptible," as was the magazine's appeal for funds. They had no right to reprint his material without permission. Prescient of things to come, Crowley fulminated: "Jack is surely an insane 'Black Brother'; his ravings and visions are outrageous. It all stinks of [C. F.] Russell. Didn't J[ack]. come from that gang? . . . Smith seems to have used the Order as a mere 'preserve' for hunting women." Baphomet reckoned he be expelled and done for embezzlement. Crowley's main concern was the tarot book. It had to be printed without delay because at any moment the government's metal requirements could expose the printer's type to sequestration. Crowley expected to be penniless about May 7.[17] He wrote similarly to Jane Wolfe on May 3: "Don't bother with *Oriflamme*—it's rubbish and will revive old stories of drug trafficking." The tarot book was nearly ready, but the government could demand the metal type before it was printed. "This leaves us on the brink of actual ruin and starvation, and you play the fool in Pasadena issuing ridiculous magazines and squabbling. It looks to me as if you were wasted out there—the whole crowd of you. You ought to join the Fighting French!"[18] Meanwhile the Bank of England was on to Crowley about money coming into the country from America, suspecting it was money owed for illegal business and presuming Crowley was sending money out of the country to pay U.S. debts.

On May 4 relaxation came in the attractive form of Loretta Young and Brian Aherne in Richard Wallace's thriller-comedy *A Night to Remember*—a film to remember, too. He saw it for the third time on May 8; the fourth on the twenty-fifth; and with Tub at the King's Cross Cinema on the twenty-eighth! Verdict: "Best I've seen of its kind." Having seen it myself a few times, I expect what Crowley particularly warmed to, apart from pace, dark wit, and romance, was the Greenwich

*Fig. 13.5.* A Night to Remember *poster (1942).*

Village setting, where Crowley spent happy, fulfilling days and nights in 1918–1919. He seized this visual passport again with Frieda at King's Cross, and at the Elephant & Castle cinema when he took Cath—the seventh time!

While Crowley fretted about his heroin supply, Wilfrid Smith sat alone pondering alleged misdeeds at Louis Culling's shack in Rainbow Valley, California, whence he addressed "Care Frater 666" on May 9 with quotations from *Liber LXV* to suggest he'd "got the message": "Go thou into the outermost places and subdue all things. Subdue thy fear and thy disgust. Then—yield!"[19]

Reflecting on his somewhat aggressive-sounding last letter to Jane Wolfe, Crowley sent a semblance of apology to his old acolyte: "This, as feeling a bit ashamed of myself for the truly Cephaloedian frankness of my last letter. And I was dictating against—which beat me, for I was unable to finish the Epistle to Helen [Parsons—she'd sent a long unsigned letter]. So I cut short: I had meant lots of love and praise! What bug is biting me? You'll wonder. This, my child. Not one of you seems to grasp the central Business Policy. Let me explain *very* clearly. My function is solely *to create Wealth.*" Creating wealth did not mean making a bit of money, but "I mean endowing the Order with a property which will constantly increase in value as time goes on." Castigations followed: "Smith himself might have been drilled and dressed and taught; he might have been a famous leader, High Priest in a Gnostic Cathedral! But owls and bats are born so. [owls wise, bats born blind, it was thought]." When Crowley saw the photos Smith sent of 1003's inhabitants: "They looked to me like hoboes! Sluttish, slattern, no trace of birth or breeding: I was aghast. . . . Ever yours TO MEGA THERION 666 and Aleister"[20]

*No trace of birth or breeding. . . .* What a snob Crowley could be! On May 12, one of the plebeians—Regina Kahl—had the audacity to gift him ginger and cookies. Another parcel came from Regina—still in Houston but moved to 1826 Colquitt Street—the next day. Lady Harris earned marks for sending the tarot pictures to Chiswick Press— now the "balance" of landed gent Yorke's one hundred pounds was in the general O.T.O. account. That May 13 saw another stricture head in Jane's direction: "I can't help wishing that you had been in charge of 80 Bronx hooligans for some years, like poor old Leah! (I wonder what happened to her [Leah Hirsig]; my last from her was in '31; she had somehow got to the Escurial!!)"[21]

On May 17, Crowley attended a lunch given by "R.H." at the Waldorf Grill for Tamil poet and editor James Meary Thurairajah Tambimuttu (1915–1983), cofounder of the literary journal *Poetry London* with Dylan Thomas.

Like Cecil, "Tambi" had poetry published by Caton (*Out of this War,* 1941). Crowley was astonished to find Tambimuttu was "grand-nephew of Ramanathan!"—Ceylon's solicitor general, who taught Allan Bennett raj yoga in Colombo in 1900–1901. Crowley found publisher Ivor Nicholson there and the guests "all clean, all bright, all likeable." Encouraged by T. S. Eliot, Tambimuttu published Stephen Spender, Anaïs Nin, Lawrence Durrell, Allen Ginsberg, Jack Kerouac, and Kathleen Raine.

Thinking of another bright and likeable thing, Crowley expressed further misgivings about Jack to Germer on May 17. Presuming him now in charge, "The real danger with that young man is his tendency to give way to unbridled impulses and his liability to obsession."[22]

Crowley considered Parsons again a fortnight later: "He is much too prone to assume that any communicating intelligence is what it claims to be. . . . I think it is much better to keep Jack on probation under your direct management." On a lighter note: "I have been asked to stay for a few days in the country with a millionaire in about a fortnight's time, and this may lead to something really big."[23] Receiving Evan Morgan's invitation to Tredegar Park, Monmouthshire, Crowley noted: "Well, I hope so." Doubt perhaps came from raid alerts and heavy gunfire; Gerald Hamilton was quitting London, eliciting Crowley's comment: "What a pitiful invertebrate! But he was shaken by my 'I told you so' re Hun collapse." German and Italian resistance in North Africa had ended on May 12 after the Allies entered Tunis, Crowley's old haunt of 1923 to 1925.

Crowley still hadn't given up on Wilfrid Smith, writing on May 18: "Well, can I help being glad that this affair is settled at last, although in so tragic a manner?" Crowley focused on Smith's sex appetite allegedly influencing relations with Order members. "Now don't regard yourself as 'out.' Shew your manhood and your devotion to 93 by putting over the Order on a big scale. . . . There was another Smith, Joseph his other name [founder of Mormonism], martyred and living, with a whole state of the Union tagged on to his tail [Utah]. No other American ever did a job that size! . . . And you have all his assets—the Book of the Angel and all the rest of the apparatus."[24]

Crowley wrote again ten days later announcing *Liber CXXXII,* specially tailored for Smith: a detailed itinerary of what Smith need accomplish following analysis of his horary chart, whose substance could be expressed in the word *Apotheosis,* and its conclusion: "*Wilfred T. Smith is not a man at all: he is the Incarnation of some God.*"[25] Smith's task was to locate the God's identity. Assembling *Liber CXXXII* in early June, Crowley listed portentous sections reminiscent of his own liturgical instruction to crucify a frog representing Jesus of Nazareth on *his* Greater Magical Retirement in New Hampshire in 1916 (*Stauros Batrachou*):*

---

*See Churton, *Aleister Crowley in America.*

The praxis: How Frater 132 should prepare himself. B The conditions of his dwelling among us. C To prepare his mode of life. D How *Deus quidam* [a certain God] should comport himself (1) to identify himself (2) to find purpose of this Incarnation (3) how thereby to exercise his peculiar function for the good of Mankind.

This practically involved Smith's living outside the house proper, entering only to perform priestly or "prophesying" functions, during which none should engage his loftiness in communication. Of course, the instruction embodies Crowley's old, vicious humor and poignant logic. Unmoved by mere human entreaty, Smith was convinced of himself, oblivious to criticism—so he must fathom what amazing God lurked behind this rare manifestation of omniscience. Crowley had taken a similarly perverse tack with Theosophist Henri Birven in Berlin in 1930, likening Birven to one whose conceit resembled a frog smoking; eventually so puffed up he'd burst. Crowley was trying to induce a *crisis* in Smith to break whatever scotoma prevented free flow of energy and access to his true Angel. Crowley later confided to Germer that the idea followed "our English plan of dealing with inconvenient M.P.s: they are raised to the Peerage!"*

While Crowley objectified Smith as a phenomenon of psychology, the real Smith wrote from "retirement" at the "Culling Hermitage, Rainbow Valley" on June 10, recounting contradictions in Crowley's correspondence since 1928, bewailing Crowley's repetition of *I am told, I am told:* "That is just it. You accept what they tell you. Look how you exploded over Grady's letter [insinuating abortion]. *Grady* for the love of Mikhl. No word of truth in what he conveys. The yarns about declaring 8°=3 and 9°=2 are just pure fabrication. Besides Grades and Titles never meant a damned thing to me personally." Concerning the F.B.I. men: "If you only knew the type they were! . . . in response to yours of May 18th, I have not yet become aware of the 'tragic' part of the settlement of this affair. . . . I am as near happy as I have ever been in my life. And I am away from people and can see the stars at night. What a sky! If I don't get some inspiration here I will just go out with a begging bowl."[26]

---

*O.T.O. Archive, Germer–A.C. Letters, August 30, 1943, 655.

*Fig. 13.6. Tredegar Park, 1940s.*

Crowley left Paddington Station on June 17 for eight days with Evan Tredegar: "Hellish crowd. Good porter got me a corner. Fool-swine opposite gave his seat to low cow with two loathsome brats. Hell!" When he arrived at Newport, Monmouthshire, a taxi took 666 to Tredegar Park, a rather austere brick mansion. Tredegar put Crowley in the Oak Room, the best in the house. Crowley's "old patron," the Marquis of Salisbury, slept there, as did General Lord Allenby, who entered Jerusalem on foot after ejecting the Turks during the Arab Revolt in 1917.

Next day was wild and wet. At night, Crowley played the vocabulary game "Analogies" and studied Tredegar's tarot book: "Very curious and interesting." Tredegar said he'd played chess for Oxford and England, so they played next day; Tredegar's skill impressed Crowley. Frieda joined the house party. On the twentieth Crowley was shown Evan Morgan's famous "Magick room"—"far greater" than Crowley had imagined. Crowley's comment is fascinating: "My one idea was to get out before any harm was done!" Presumably, Evan fancied "comparing notes" with Crowley on magick and, perhaps, some ritual work. On the twenty-third Crowley's diary states he had told Tredegar about the "Eye of Horus," an interesting admission, for Crowley usually employed the term as a euphemism for the anus and its place in XI° sex magick. Twice married, Evan was homosexual, so one may speculate.

It has been said, without authority, that having been removed from secret MI8 carrier pigeon service after disclosing his doings to two girl guides, Tredegar engaged Crowley to assist with a curse to eliminate the officer who'd dismissed his services. Crowley would never have been drawn to such an infringement of his Law, but perhaps Crowley feared something of the kind, which could explain his reaction to the room.

They had much in common, Crowley and Morgan, including friends, such as Nancy Cunard, who described Tredegar as a "fantasy" who could be a bitch. High up in Vatican circles, despite his occultism (or because of it), Tredegar had converted with relish. He'd also met Rudolf Hess before 1933—another possible conversation topic. Hess had been held under loose confinement in the county and permitted drives about.

Two days after returning to London on June 25, Mrs. Macky gave him a guinea, presumably to enter the O.T.O., expecting some kind of ceremonial rite: "She still wants formal nonsense—shows no curiosity about the value of the rite."

On the twenty-ninth Peter Brook invited an already socially over-whelmed Crowley as guest of honor to a Magdalen College party. Attendance on the Thursday meant canceling Tub and Maisie. A letter arrived from "C. Falconer, P.O. Box 44, Roseneath, Dumbartonshire." Cath was now a Wren—the Women's Royal Naval Service.*

Crowley entered Oxford's Randolph Hotel at 4 p.m. on July 1 to clean up for the party at Magdalen. Stanley "Nosey" Parker of the *Oxford Mail* interviewed him at 8:00. He was back at Paddington next day at 8:30.†

Back in Jermyn Street, Crowley found a packet of poems by Grady McMurtry and pondered how to get Yvonne Arnaud behind *l'Étincelle* ("The Spark"). The I Ching advised appealing to her ambition; he wrote on the seventh.

---

*Roseneath, Scotland, had been loaned to the United States as an amphibious training center, but after the North Africa landings, it became HMS *Roseneath* once more, with the U.S. Navy retaining sections of the base for "Seabee" maintenance services.

†When I corresponded with Peter Brook concerning memories of Crowley, Brook told me he found dwelling on the past unprofitable; one should be in the present. Brook eventually took Gurdjieff as master, as did Robert Cecil (email to author November 16, 2011).

On July 8 he noticed "some old pals from *A Night to Remember*" assembled to entertain in the Bob Hope and Dorothy Lamour vehicle *They Got Me Covered*. "This," opined Crowley, "is good, but not nearly so good. Worth a second visit—but not at 6/- [shillings]!" He *did* go a second time on the twelfth, and a third time on the twenty-third, finding it "still very fresh and good." On the ninth he saw *Five Graves to Cairo:* "Von Stroheim as Rommel quite excellent. . . . Air raid episode first class."

Attending the theater on July 21, he saw Freemason Donald Wolfit in *The Master Builder:* "Everybody barnstormed beyond belief. . . . One forgot their ranting, and lost oneself in the splendor of it all."

After a trip to the zoo on the twenty-sixth, Frieda introduced him personally to outsider-artist Jack Bilbo at an exhibition at 24 Charles Street at 9:30 p.m., outside, which was a "vast mob of slaves, in a queue a mile long! One dared to object to my passing alone. One bark and glare: he slunk back to his native dirt. Great fun!"

He saw *The Man Who Came to Dinner* again on the thirtieth: "Improves on second shot. Certainly as funny a farce I ever saw." Third time, August 7: "Oh very, very good!"

On August 4 he saw Robert and wife Ann Cecil: "She wept all over me! Bad weather—hustled by business and friends."

Edward Bryant came on August 8 accompanied by "Antique Antipodean Anthropophagist Aborted Arahatina, the Marchioness Macky of the Murrumbidgee, the Wailing Wombat of Wagga-Wagga, the Screeching Scribbler of Sonatas à la Scriabin. Educated them."

Judging by Smith's letter to Crowley from "Cullings Hermitage" of August 10, Crowley's method was having the curious effect of delighting its intended penitent. Meditating on *Liber CXXXII* Smith's "first reaction was surprise." He swiftly passed to other reflections: "This is a grand spot. I have reveled in nature like never before in my life—tanned from head to foot. And there are no people. You would love it, and I wish you were here."[27] Jane was caring for him well, and he would continue trying to turn a pot of peas into a sack of rubies.

Crowley felt "damned ill" again in mid-August, but still remembered the fortieth anniversary of his first marriage to Rose Kelly on the twelfth, noting the seventeenth would have been his father's 109th birthday.

However much he "advanced" at one level, the real "little Aleister" or "A.C." was always there, not self-pitying, though prone to nostalgia. On the sixteenth he received letters from Grady and remembered his *second* marriage's fourteenth anniversary. Meanwhile, Mrs. Macky informed him of her "True Will": "I would be one with the creative force of the Universe," so Crowley sent her Order motto: "FIAT YOD," where the Hebrew *Yod* (literally "hand") stands for divine creation, and the Latin-Hebrew could be translated "Let divine creation be complete."

On August 23, Anne Macky agreed to participate in a book idea, jokingly nicknamed "Magick for Morons." The idea was that Crowley's writings on magick sometimes proved inaccessible due to polyvalent allusions to literary and other sources and systems unfamiliar to non-specialists. So neophyte Macky would put natural, pressing questions, and Crowley would reply straightforwardly until understood. In other words, what Crowley found irritating about Macky would be transformed through alchemy of Q&A into pedagogic gold. Bryant helped with editing. Mrs. Macky accepted a contract for fifty letters, sent fortnightly. Work commenced, and by September 5 Crowley had sent Macky letter no. VI.*

On September 3, Italian prime minister Badoglio signed a secret armistice with the Allies. Crowley checked the I Ching: "*Po*-23!!!! Falling, or causing to fall," and remarked, "Now we shall see whether the Christians can turn it into defeat for us!"

In California, Smith returned to Pasadena and on September 14 wrote a plaintive missive beginning: "My very dear Aleister." He was sorry to leave the hermitage, and his "distaste" for 1003 had been "no wit alleviated. . . . I am sad." Smith was sick of being castigated for his spelling, his own letters used against him with Germer: "Would to God you knew your own people better"—and signed it: "With love, Wilfred."[28]

It is perhaps ironic that Crowley's former secretary Regardie came

---

*Unpublished until Israel Regardie's redaction of 1973, some think Crowley was "winding down." I disagree. Influenced by war experience and atmosphere, the letters are sharp, accessibly down-to-earth, prescient, modest, and entertaining. Some might think 666 tries too hard to be "chatty" and colloquial, but what became *Magick without Tears* succeeds in its aim for the most part, and its lightheartedness refreshes. Happily, a complete version with assistive tools is in the pipeline from Australian O.T.O. Head Stephen King, who I here thank for informing me about the real Anne Macky.

to edit *Magick without Tears,* as Crowley's reply of September 19 to Edward Bryant's comments about the "Tree of Life" shows Crowley's somewhat biased, spiteful estimation of Regardie's scholarship:

C[are]∴F[rater]∴ (Regardie-Regutny knows only what he has stolen & then messed up: please quote him no more!) . . . But Yesod [sefira: Foundation] is a member of Ruach [middle soul, including "reason"]; it is in Yetzirah [world of formation], not in Assiah [world of action]. Assiah is the perceptible illusion formed by Yetzirah, created by Briah [world of creation], and ordered by Atziluth [world of emanation]. Now do let me warn you against the pedant and the prig, especially when they appear in your own sphere. You seem fatally drawn to theology in its most arid form. Well, I hope I may shake off the sand now; the Governor of North Carolina [Joseph Melville Broughton Jr., 1888–1949] has just rung me up. Never more timely![29]

No surprise that things had turned sour at 1003. On October 1, Crowley received a letter of resignation from "puppy Jack [Parsons]: his snout glued to the rump of an alley-cat [Sara Northrup]." Crowley wasn't having any of it, addressing "My dear Jack" on October 19 as "elder brother and true friend." Jack was not to be offended by words that on the surface seemed antagonistic. There had been a "very great deal of misunderstanding in the past. . . . Personal affairs and prejudices

*Fig. 13.7. Sara Northrup.*

should never have been allowed to interfere with the Work. . . . I repeat—the responsibility is yours. . . . I very strongly disapprove of your description of Phyllis Seckler as an indigent cook. . . . You should not write insultingly of other members of the Order. You should try and get the best out of people." Jack replaced Smith "for malfeasance in office and larceny." Jack didn't grasp the peculiar greatness of Karl Germer: "I think you should try to put yourself more than you do in the position of other people before you judge them." Karl's weaknesses were clearly accounted for, "but you never know." Crowley chose him because "there was no one else." Karl had first-class integrity.

Turning to Smith: "You [Jack] are not an Englishman and you don't know the class from which Smith comes. Of that class he is a very unfortunate specimen. . . . With regard to bungling; you are not in a position to judge; for one thing anything I do is done with an eye on centuries to come. The immediate results of any action are no test of it from my point of view. One has to consider principles in long perspective. Another point is that as often as not I have no choice of action." Crowley made a good self-defense against a charge of pomposity (specifically addressed in a letter to Anne Macky in *Magick without Tears*). Jack should look for the twinkle but respect the experience; Crowley's universe was bigger than Jack's. "Some time ago I thought of writing a book on internationally famous people with whom I had been intimate. The number ran to over eighty. Am I wrong to suppose that you never met such people? . . . Like all young people, you are just a bit cocksure. You should learn humility in the same sense that I have learned it; or rather it has been kicked into me. Roughly speaking, the greater admiration you have for people, the greater your own nature. It shows you have the power for picking out the best. I don't like it at all what you say about witchcraft. All this black magic stuff is 75% nonsense and the rest plain dirt. There is not even any point to it. . . . I quite understand what you say about playing a game with Sara; it is a little risky to play in the power-house." Crowley's advice (and there was more) could have saved Jack from himself. Concluding, he hoped Jack would think over carefully his responsibility to "deserve the great honor which is yours."[30]

Crowley's universe was clearly bigger than the average, and no one could call him a bigot, despite cavalier lapses of temper and invective. He always saw the other side, noting on October 3:

> "To Hell with Huns and Jews!" you sing?
> Come, come now, think it over!
> All honour to our noble King,
> And General Eisenhower!

Perhaps getting down to brass tacks with Anne Macky and Jack Parsons encouraged some modest introspection. Like Winnie the Pooh, Crowley took time on October 24 to ponder:

> I often wish I could divine
> What's in this funny head of mine,
> This complicated tangled brain
> That is? is not? or is it? sane.
> No one has ever understood
> Why I was never any good,
> Or why my diamond brilliance
> Was dulled by causal circumstance.
> To further the dear cause of Knowledge
> I leave my cranium to the College
> Of Surgeons: they—unless too lazy—
> Will find out why I was three parts crazy
> And on the whole a perfect daisy,
> But far from our Exemplar J.C.
> Blast! That solution won't get past
> It's "sicklied o'er with the pale cast
> Of doubt"—Being dead, I may not know
> What engine made the damn thing go.

*And just as he'd found a moment's peace . . .* "Oh Gawd! McMurtry blew in!!! News from the Front indeed!" Lt. McMurtry exploded with a heap of questions on October 30, returning next day to chatter as German gunfire strafed the West End: "He argued high, he argued low, / He also argued round about him."*

On November 8, he wrote to Jane Wolfe, happy with his philosophical work on the tarot book: "I've got the Spiral Universe aligned with

---

*A quote from W. S. Gilbert on "Sir Macklin" in *The Bab Ballads*.

modern science, and the Qabalah dovetailed not only with the Yi King but with Geomancy, and so on. For the first time in my life I'm fully satisfied with the scholarship of it. Everything fits like a glove. Behold me happy!"

And Smith . . . "I *do* blame you for not having refused to receive Smith when he sneaked back, and made Jack break the pledge [to not talk to Smith] he had signed only a month or so before."

"Jack is a bit of a marshmallow Sundae, I fear. He does what the last person to talk to him tells him. I looked especially to you, on account of your Month on the Beach!* He is, moreover, too ready to emphasize the sexual side of life. This weakness enabled Smith to get his sympathies." The source of the "alley-cat" words for Sara was "a man in Washington who knows Jack." According to Crowley, Smith's antics "have discredited us in the eyes of all sensible people. . . . Do get Jack to see this: science, art, philosophy and the like are our prime care. The sex-ideas come a *very* long way behind. . . . All this frivolous promiscuity is the very reverse of the aim. . . . Love to all the loyal!"[31]

On the thirteenth: "McMurtry up till 11! Gawd! 7 hours talk!" Six days later, "Churchill" took themed photographs: "Eagerness" "Amusement" "very good indeed. The Shadow-Show experiment a success, as showing that it can be done. But as a picture we can do much better." The "shadow" shows an unpleasant profile with Crowley using his fingers to create a shadow of a goat on the wall. Looking at Churchill's efforts on December 8, Crowley remarked: "One A1, rest all dubious."

It appears from a letter of Crowley to Anne Macky on November 19 that a friend of hers had passed away. Crowley was sympathetic but philosophical:

It is difficult to write "cheering words" on occasions of this kind; it always sounds like, and usually is, humbug. And yet, as the immediate poignancy is past, and one can face the event with a calm mind, it is honestly helpful to remind oneself of certain fundamental ideas of philosophy. 1. It is a play of Nuit (*Liber Aleph*). 2. Every experience, however painful, is a gain; for it expands the universe of the mind, and enriches it. 3. Every experience is a *necessary* step, and in

*Referring to Jane's time in yogic "retirement" in a tent at Cefalù in 1922 (see page 202).

accord with one's True Will, for it is oneself and not another that originally determined the conditions of this life. 4. Enriched and ennobled by the friendship which is past, one is fit to grasp at new friendships of even greater significance and value.[32]

Jack Parsons replied with a cable on November 26. Crowley didn't find it "disloyal," only "confused." Sara Northrup sent fifty dollars with love. Grady McMurtry called in at Jermyn Street the following day for a marathon talk session, and Crowley spent the twenty-eighth "sleeping it off!" There were compensations; Grady lent him thirty pounds, a large sum in 1943. Crowley was immensely grateful, telling Germer it seemed he'd found his "impresario" at last.

On December 2 he finished Fiat Yod's letter No. X: "Nearly killed me." Eleven days later came a cable from Roy Leffingwell—"Rancho RoyAL, Route 1, Barstow California"—and Tredegar's housekeeper and secretary Cordelia Sutherland (1894–1980) told him Tredegar Park was being shut, and she was quitting Evan's service. Interested in Crowley's "Work," Cordelia proved an excellent occasional secretary.

He finished Fiat Yod's letter XIII on the sixteenth: "T'would be easier if she wrote: 'What do you think of (a) everything (b) nothing?' I could answer (a) nothing (b) everything."

McMurtry took up the whole of December 19, permitting an hour's "pleasant talk "with Robert Cecil in the early afternoon.

The next day he was at the cinema: *Sahara* proved a "pretty good film—and oh! The delight of seeing Home again!"—home being North Africa, scene of many deserted walks of magick and mysticism. Zoltan Korda's movie, set after Tobruk's fall in 1942, starred Humphrey Bogart with a stirring score by Miklos Rozsa. Crowley went again with Louis Wilkinson on New Year's Eve: "Honestly A1!"

Now well into London's Christmas season, Crowley met Frieda at 83 Duke Street (Fortnum & Mason) on the twenty-third to lunch at the Berkeley Grill: "*Not* very good: in fact, pretty bad. Coffee and Brandy at home A1."

On Christmas Eve he splashed out on a Cockburn '35 as an "Act of Truth [care to the wind, act of faith]. All shopping went easily." He then had a long sitting with Cambyses Churchill, who photographed his hands in symbolic "mudras" and some "ju ju poses."

On Christmas Day he wrote to Mrs. Macky, thanking her for the "seasonal wine," pleading: "please don't encourage my besetting sin of laziness. Curse me, kick me, worry me like a terrier with a rat, and I shall love you for it. And this is NOT masochism, either!"[33] Going out, he met British film and theater actress Lydia Sherwood (1906–1989), possibly at one of St. James's excellent pubs, and kissed her: "a perfect peach—under the mistletoe."*

Cecil rang him on the twenty-seventh and came for another afternoon's "very pleasant talk; but how futile the creature is! Simply scared lest he should get somewhere."

Another pupil whose progress troubled 666 was of course Jack Parsons. He wrote to Jane Wolfe about him on December 29:

> He must learn that the sparkle of champagne is based on sound wine; pumping carbonic acid into wine is not the same thing. . . . I wish to God I had him for six months—even three, with a hustle—to train in Will, in discipline. He must understand that fine and fiery flashes of Spirit come from the organization of Matter, from the drilling of every function of every bodily organ until it has become so regular as to be automatic, and carry on by itself deep down in the Unconscious. It is the steadiness of one's heart that enables one to endure the rapture of great passion; one doesn't want the vital functions to be excitable. . . .
>
> The great [*illegible*] light has been the arrival of McMurtry. I hope he will have knocked some of Jack's illusions out of him. He actually thought that I was "pompous"!!!!! How *you* could have let him harbor any such idea beats me! God forgive you! Well, dear girl, here's all the Blessings in my bag for the Happiest New Year that ever was or will be![34]

The next day he wrote a last letter of the year to Anne Macky, annoyed at her jibe that the O.T.O. was in decline:

> The O.T.O. is not dying; if "The Majority of the members are dead," that is true also of the human species! Why do you hate the

---

*Lydia starred in two films in 1942: *When We Are Married* and *Theatre Royal.* Kissing "under the mistletoe" is an English Christmas custom.

O.T.O. so much? I regret (in that sense) to inform you that a new Lodge was founded last month, and another is in contemplation. . . . May I remind you that we are now well into the second quarter [of the new book]—bar delay in delivery. A letter costs from 10/- to 15/- or more to type; so one has to be prepared. I must take the new letters down to the office on Monday, if I can; so I hope to have heard from you by then.[35]

On New Year's Eve, Crowley enjoyed a lunch party at the Ritz on Piccadilly. One imagines it was a joy: "Moules Marinières. Blanc de Volaille au Riz jelly. All tasted of pre-war! Coffee and '42 brandy at home." Frieda joined the party for tea. Piccadilly didn't know what Hitler had in store for 1944.

# FOURTEEN

# Monstrous Worlds

*How can nature create this setting*
*And pay no heed*
*To the drama the nations are plotting,*
*Which only plan effective range, not colour;*
*To fill the women's cheeks with palour*
*And daub the green fields with men's blood.*

ROBERT CECIL, "SPRING 1939,"
FROM *LEVANT AND OTHER POEMS,* 1941

January 4, 1944: Hitler orders mobilization of all children over ten years old. Within weeks, Russia breaks the siege of Leningrad; U.S. forces land at Anzio, thirty miles south of Rome; and French resistance unites as Les Forces Françaises de l'Intérieure. The war's tide turns, and Crowley explains the Secret Chiefs and angels to Fiat Yod, while Frieda admits a dhyana experience in a gorse field aged ten or eleven. Also on the fourth, Crowley saw Orson Welles as Rochester in William Wyler's *Jane Eyre.* Verdict: "very good but some *longueurs.*"

He wrote to Mrs. Macky: "I would like to see you this week, mostly to get you well started on the Astral."[1] Four days later, McMurtry met Mrs. Cordelia Sutherland, who was helping Crowley with the "50 Answers to Questions—First-Steps" book. McMurtry liked her "a lot." Shocking as Crowley found McMurtry's fragmentary culture, the lieutenant knew how to please: cigars and two pounds of Perique without import duty!—in contrast to Robert Cecil, who arrived on

*Fig. 14.1. Aleister Crowley at Jermyn Street, 1943. (Courtesy of the Warburg Institute, London, and Ordo Templi Orientis)*

the sixteenth wanting "Astral visions"; 666 "smote him, demanding the [Probationer's] Oath."

The next day, Crowley considered a new operation: "Objective Aleister," referring to Ataturk and his mother. "No news since September '42. There must be someone who knows what has (or hasn't) happened."[2] The plan was passed to Louis Wilkinson, living near Penzance, where Deirdre's mother, Mrs. Phyllis Bodilly, "late Marquise d-? [de Verdières]" came from.

Seeking a French singer for "l'Étincelle," Crowley met "Delysia" at Simpson's in the Strand on January 30. Familiar to English musical theater by that name, Alice Henriette Lapize had joined the Entertainments National Service Association in 1941 to entertain troops posted abroad. Patriotic supporter of Free French forces, she'd just married Commander René Kolb-Bernard of the Free French navy. Crowley met Delysia again next day before taking lunch with Cordelia.

Liberal Catholic Church priest Dr. E. B. Crow entered Crowley's life on February 6: 666 gave him a copy of *Yoga,* finding him "very charming and intelligent." Crow was trying to ascertain the relation of Christ to Bacchus and Osiris, noted Crowley, who "pressed [the] New Aeon on him," "conjuring" Crow to write a Horus ritual.

Delysia joined Crowley again at Simpson's on the seventh before he visited Charles II Street for the "most interesting show in town for years!"—Jack Bilbo's pamphlets now earned Crowley's praise as "absolutely priceless good sense."

## THE DUKE STREET–KING STREET BOMB

February 23: "Alert 10:04:31. Blast smashed at 10:36. High explosive in Duke St." A 2000 kg bomb hit the corner of Duke Street and King Street, St James's, 250 yards from Crowley's ground floor rooms at 93 Jermyn Street. Crowley heard it. It blew the front door's inside bolt clean off; the house shook, and every window was shattered. Finding his bed a deadly mess of glass he joined other residents in the basement kitchen. Trying to make cheerful talk, they held hands for fear of being alone—Crowley found it depressing. A "Mrs. De S." was near tears, but she'd "had a whack" from something—not in the house but in the Liaison coffee house lavatory in Prince's Arcade opposite.

The bomb "wiped out King Street and Duke Street," obliterating Willis's auction rooms. Had he been abed, he'd have been "cut to ribbons," he informed Louis on March 7. Electric light returned after an hour, however, and a "delightful night" was spent in an armchair by the fire.[3]

Crowley told Germer on the nineteenth that he found sporadic raids more unnerving than the long 1940–1941 raids. People's "capital of resistance is to some extent depleted," with everyone "weary of waiting for the invasion," as if the moment "our boys" were across the Channel all troubles would be over. "*Silly?* Oh very! But we're born like that." Some got frantic about evasive action—as he might himself but for having no money and nowhere to go, while the "tarot &c" had to be done. There were eight sets of color blocks to send to Germer for *The Book of Thoth* U.S. edition. Crowley reminded Stateside Germer how rooms he'd stayed in in Duke Street were gone: "That corner of Duke St. and King St. is now a commodious site for a 'fashionable West End square.' Everything flat. I stepped out the distance next A.M. [morning] roughly 200 yards from this house to the S[outh].W[est]. (We are facing the ruins of St James's parish Church.)"[4]

On the fourteenth he noted: "My morale is not all it should be, my nerves already much shaken by worry." On March 22 he wrote a "Note for the Bomb Shy" at a time when he was waking up five minutes *before* an alert:

Analysis of Blue Funk. I feel none at all in respect of fire, a great deal about being hit directly by 2000 kg. H[igh] E[xplosive]. Why?

Obvious. Similar to one's experiences of avalanches and stone-swept gullies. When one can do something, though actually hardly more than in theory, one is all right. But the waiting for an utterly unanswerable blow is unmanning. With disease, one has a similar feeling about paralysis or coronary thrombosis; but this is not pointed by an alert. The ignorant belief in the efficacy of prayer etc. is obviously a great help. Psychologically, varying with the depth of ignorance, lack of logic, and faith in faith. P.S. NOTE. "Panic" notably subsides when the [defensive] guns go off!

On March 1 he enjoyed an evening with Evan, Cordelia, "S.R.," and "Hitchcock"—possibly Alfred Hitchcock, who left Hollywood in 1944 after producer Michael Balcon commented on overweight British directors who'd left behind a shorthanded film industry trying to make films for the national effort. Feeling the call, Hitchcock was in London shooting a short film in French at the Welwyn Studios from January 20 to February 25 for the M.O.I. (Ministry of Information). A thriller about Gestapo penetration of Free French forces, *Bon Voyage* starred John Blythe, Janique Joelle, and the Molière Players, whose names were omitted to protect families in France.

By March 19, Crowley could inform Germer that two hundred sets of *The Book of Thoth* awaited the binder, so long as the Chiswick Press

*Fig. 14.2. Aleister Crowley at Jermyn Street, 1943. (Courtesy of the Warburg Institute, London, and Ordo Templi Orientis)*

was paid. A recent, crooked takeover had absorbed prepayments—"But the result is really splendid. You will be amazed when you see it." Right about that, he then made an arresting admission: "Please tell Sascha not to waste any water [tears] on me! My life has been a glorious joke, plus a success beyond my most extravagant dreams. But it's very sweet of her to be so nice about it all. Do assure her that merely to have been picked to do the Work that I have done, albeit so feebly and foolishly, is over-payment 10,000 times for any possible effort of mine."[5]

Still, Jermyn Street was a pain after closure of adjacent streets transformed it into a narrow, noisy thoroughfare. Lamenting the "racket" from newly arrived drunken U.S. and Canadian servicemen to Wilkinson and Fitzgerald, he escaped for a couple of days to the Cambridge Garden House Hotel. As he was trying to find somewhere to finish the Macky book project, Gerald Yorke welcomed him warmly in Cambridge, though he complained to Fitzgerald of being "generally bitched, buggered, and bewildered,"[6] a skit on "Bewitched, bothered, and bewildered" from Richard Rodgers' musical *Pal Joey* (1940).

Back in Jermyn Street for April 2: "McM[urtry] blew in at 5:30! He turned in his diary to me—they are tabu for the duration [military duties first]," adding poignantly: "That second front does seem nearer!"

At 5 p.m. on Tuesday, April 4, Crowley took a call from Cordelia: "The Angel has found me a room at the 'Bell' Aston Clinton near Aylesbury."

## THE BELL

The night before leaving Jermyn Street for the Bell Inn, Aston Clinton, Buckinghamshire, he went to see *They Got Me Covered* "for the eighth or ninth time." Apart from its fast humor and Bob Hope's style, the attraction is obvious. The story featured a cowardly newsman who foils a plot involving Axis spies determined to blow up Washington. It reminded Crowley of German sabotage directed at Washington during World War I, which he attempted to subvert, posing as a disaffected pro-Fenian journalist (see Churton, *Aleister Crowley in America*)—and for which effort he received naught but persistent opprobrium.

At 3:30 p.m. on April 8 his train steamed out of Marylebone Station, arriving an hour later at Aylesbury—then a charming country town. Five kilometers southeast of Aylesbury he found the Bell: "most delightful, really old" with a big open fire and "incredibly good food." There was, however, *nothing* to do, and no one to talk to: "I shall be forced to work—and at once. Tired with excitement and travel." He put it bluntly to Louis a fortnight later: "Having no one to talk to is boring."[7] Boredom would haunt his remaining years: "Never dull where Crowley is," but if no one was *there,* how would anyone know?

*Fig. 14.3. The Bell Inn, Aston Clinton, pre-war (from a postcard).*

*Fig. 14.4. The Bell Inn today. (Author's Collection)*

On April 24, as the Japanese evacuated New Guinea, Crowley received a first inquiry from 32nd-degree Freemason W. Dawson Sadler of The Larches, Four Oaks Road, Four Oaks, Sutton Coldfield. A fine characterful brick-built mansion in 1811 and still standing, The Larches is close to where I spent much of my childhood and school years. In 1944 Sutton Coldfield was a distinctly independent Warwickshire borough. Prominent Suttonian Sadler corresponded with Crowley for several years, and in depth. His first request was for two copies of *The Book of Thoth*, for which he paid twenty-one pounds on April 29.

Grady McMurtry "blew in" on the twenty-seventh, about to leave England with some 73,000 U.S. troops for the anticipated "second front." Whether this made Crowley start a beard "like a hadji" (after "Haj" to Mecca) next day is open to conjecture. A few days later, Crowley confessed to Wilkinson he was "fagged" and "beginning to feel impulse to walk in Spring woods."[8]

On May 6 he wrote to Gerald Hamilton, saying he was working on the "Yi King" and hoping "Ham" had "a quid to spare to square." Larger amounts occupied his imagination when writing to Germer on May 8 to reassure him Lady Aberconway's husband was the munitions magnate behind John Brown & Co., while Lord Tredegar owned 121,000 acres and many coal mines. It was not a question of small amounts such as £10 or £30 or £100 but of great sums to be expended after Crowley's death; this was Crowley's investment. The Order could moot the need for a memorial, for example. Some might say this meant no one should expect Crowley to pay out until he was dead!

Anyhow, he was now faced with the necessity of subletting 93 Jermyn Street, which he hoped to manage in the next fortnight.[9]

June 6, 1944. D-Day. "True time—4–8:00 A.M. Invasion started. This described in detail by 53!" The "53" was apposite I-Ching hexagram *Ji'an:* continual advance; steady progress; tree on a mountain. Spot on! Having time to think, Crowley curiously chose D-Day to write an important, deep letter to Gerald Yorke, explaining fundamentally what had gone wrong between them.

I have long wanted a real show-down; but when I was with you everything was so smooth that there seemed no opening. Also,

until recently I did not see the whole business clearly myself. . . .
I have always taken myself and my mission with absolute serious-
ness. I believed in the Chiefs, and in my authority, also that those
who opposed me were asking for trouble. I was, if you like, 80 percent crazy in the same sense that Mohammed was; and I have often
regretted that my common sense and my sense of humour prevented
me from going over the line. But I was never one tenth of one percent dishonest. Use your imagination! Suppose I had been a Spencer
Lewis, what a Garden Path I could have led you down, and nothing
would ever have persuaded you that it wasn't the Path of the Wise.[10]

When Yorke chose his motto *Volo Intelligere,* "I will to understand,"
Crowley took it as meaning he willed to be Master of the Temple in
the same sense he had himself. The Crux of M.T. initiation entailed the
annihilation of "all that I have, and all that I am." So what Yorke took
for abuse was rather "an Archbishop's rebuke." Furthermore, Crowley
suspected Yorke had transferred his "Oedipus" from his father, whom
he was afraid of, to Crowley, with whom Yorke knew he could "get away
with it."

On the eleventh, lack of heroin predominated: "Bloody Hell!"

Sunday, June 18: "Need of stimulation despite [heroin] privation.
Walked to Buckland to church [Methodist chapel] 9 [o'clock?] creeping
things Wesleyans. . . . The 'minister' a doddering creature, in tweeds,
most untidy. I couldn't make out a word he said. In church they were
singing a dreadful lugubrious hymn."

London was hit on June 13 by the first of Hitler's "revenge weapons,"
the V-1, called "flying bombs" and commonly "doodlebugs," which flew
with a churning growl from mobile launch sites on the French coast to
precalibrated distances, before cutting out and descending with exceptional force. Comparing them to the Egyptian *scarabaeus* or "dung
beetle" that carried its shit across the skies, Crowley answered Germer's
query sent from bomb-free New York on June 26; he needn't fret: the
Bell was thirty-six miles northwest of London, so "out of range" of the
V-1. "But while it lasted it was hellish for folk in London . . . these
kept coming all the time; no rest for anybody day or night." Sascha,
meanwhile, was performing music, and Crowley wished himself there

to publicize her, as he had for "Ratan Devi" in 1916. Assuring Germer two copies of *The Book of Thoth* were on the way, he wished Karl and Sascha good luck for their Catskills vacation, adding that cooking for themselves and sleeping in a tent were "part of contract."[11]

He wrote to Germer again next day: "Here at last are the cards!"[12] He meant the color blocks for the eight cards gloriously reproduced in *The Book of Thoth*. They'd be sent by sea for the U.S. edition. Lady Harris gave permission for four of the blocks, which would have to be returned.

Fitzgerald was also concerned about Crowley's risk from doodle-bugs. Contrary to what he'd told Germer, Fitzgerald was informed: "We are within range here, but it would be a fluke if we got it." Crowley commiserated with Fitzgerald's "lousy" feeling. It was "shared by all; it's the boredom of the war." Even in the firing line "*ennui* replaces fear."[13]

On June 28 at 1:48 a.m., Crowley was disturbed by an apparition of Frater Hieronymus Alpha (McMurtry) within an "oval of dim light. Dark blue clothes, standing at attention. Greeting returned, before I finished mine." He must have wondered if his heir was lost in battle—or was it an astral salute to his friend?

## A NEW GNOSTIC CHURCH—ALMOST

Someone at the Bell Inn must have had a gramophone, for on July 1 Crowley played "La Gitana," his sinuous, magical poem written while touring Spain in summer 1907. You can hear it today on YouTube and wonder at Crowley's interesting intonation. He then turned to the third O.T.O. alliance proposal from Dr. William Bernard Crow, or Mar Basilius Abdullah III (1895–1976), Patriarch of Antioch, Ancient Orthodox Catholic Church. To Crowley's amusement, he would also hear from "Cardinal Newman," not the recently canonized saint, but Hugh de Willmott Newman, consecrated by friend Crow in April 1944 as Catholicos of the West, Mar Georgius, Western Orthodox Catholic Church.

Crowley and Crow had much in common. Student of Jung, grandson of a freethinking Baptist minister, Crow was a distinguished biologist, expert on algae, with numerous degrees to his name. In 1931 he founded *Proteus: A Journal of the Science, Philosophy and Therapy of Nature,* demonstrating interest in Goethe, Steiner, and spiritual science. Concern with authentic magic and illuminism encouraged Liberal Catholic Church ordination in 1935 (a haven for Christian Theosophists). Crow shared Christian Theosophist concern for ancient lines of apostolic descent (laying on of hands) free of Eastern or Western (Roman) Orthodox control. Two episcopal lines predominated: the Old Catholic Orthodox Church (from which the Liberal Catholic Church sprang); and the Syrian Patriarchate of Antioch, a bishop of which had consecrated "wandering bishops" in Europe and America. Crow would also have heard of the supernatural or spiritual revival of a Cathar episcopacy and Gnostic Church in Paris in the 1890s (see Churton, *Occult Paris*).*

Aware the O.T.O. had inherited through Reuss and Papus a right to function as an *Ecclesia Gnostica Catholica,* Crow was interested in Crowley's Gnostic Catholic Mass and possible affiliation. Crow intuited an appetite for a British-based gnostic church in the postwar world. Crowley, of course, insisted on formal acceptance of the Law of Thelema for any serious bond; he was also scathing about the (to him) ridiculous titles Crow's friends gave one another. For Dr. Crow to call himself "Abdullah" was to Crowley a ludicrous obstruction to influence in the outside world; "lines of descent" also invited skepticism.

Crowley's *The Book of Thoth* prospectus stimulated other lines of correspondence, such as "Dion Fortune" (from her motto *Deo non Fortuna* = "From God, not Luck") to whom he replied on July 6.

On July 7 Crowley walked for nearly two hours. When the sun

---

*Mar Jacobus II (Herbert James Monzani-Heard, 1866–1947), Patriarch of the Ancient British Church, consecrated Dr. Crow as Mar Bernard, Bishop of Santa Sophia, on June 13, 1943; subsequently retitled Mar Basilius Abdullah III, Patriarch of Antioch in the Ancient Orthodox Catholic Church. Later that year, Mar John Emmanuel (Arthur Wolfort Brooks, 1889–1948), Bishop of the Apostolic Episcopal Church and the Old Catholic Orthodox Church suggested Abbot de Willmott Newman be elected Archbishop and Metropolitan of Glastonbury. Newman's friend Crow performed the consecration. On March 23, 1944, Mar Jacobus II formally united the Ancient British Church, the Old Catholic Orthodox Church, the British Orthodox Catholic Church, and the Independent Catholic Church into the Western Orthodox Catholic Church, or Catholicate of the West, with few clergy and virtually no lay membership. Five days later, de Willmott Newman was elected Catholicos of the West, Mar Georgius; consecrated by Mar Basilius Abdullah III (Dr. Crow) on April 10, 1944, in the Cathedral Church of St. Andrew, Stonebridge Road, Tottenham.

broke through the rain he saw the woods "crowded with sylphs etc."—
air spirits—"half seeing" them on four occasions, "but never long
enough to say what they looked like: about 5 f[ee]t tall and light brown.
All moving like crowds on a promenade."

Glad to be out of London, Robert Cecil visited between the eighth
and tenth, after which Crowley wrote to Wilkinson in Montacute,
Somerset, that doodlebugs had hit London badly: Cecil "saw the
Guard's Chapel [St. James's Park] go."[14]

With Cecil gone on the tenth, Crowley opened a surprising letter
from Gerald Yorke. It contained twenty-five pounds ("!!!!")—whether
gift or book order isn't clear. Yorke began "Dear Crowley"—which
rather hurt his feelings—for Crowley swiftly replied:

> Please, kind sir, I do dislike with my poet's ear the sound Crowley.
> Couldn't you make it Aleister? More warmly still, I should appreci-
> ate A.C., which takes me back to climbing days, when friends were
> friends.[15]

Then 666 moved on to doodlebugs:

> The doodlebugs . . . have rather upset things. Personal accounts make
> them out worse than the official story. W[inston].C[hurchill]. went
> to S[outh]. London with the V-sign and the grin, got catcalls; and a
> man chucked a chunk of rubble at them, with "Laugh that one off!"
> Bad show. This from my friend Robert Cecil (of F[oreign].O[ffice].)
> who spent the weekend here. He can't sleep at all in London, except
> in snatches from exhaustion. He actually saw the Guards Chapel
> smash. Now then, I think it is going to be much worse; I believe
> in their No. 2 weapon.* So I must give up Jermyn Street—unless it
> gives me up first! So I must hunt for a new place.[16]

Crowley was particularly interested in Yorke's question concerning *The Book of the Law*: "Why accept so revolting a book?" Yorke
had a point; it *was* Crowley's commitment to Thelema (particularly
*AL*'s third chapter) that parted ways with persons who might other-

---

*Prescient of Crowley: the V-2 ballistic missile hit London in September.

wise have helped. Crowley considered Yorke's question the basis for "Letter No. XL" for what was now called *Aleister Explains Everything*. Writing to Yorke next day, Crowley addressed it head-on:

"Mercy let be off!"* and so on. Well if you want to plant a piece of land with a new seed, you must destroy weeds, vermin and parasites. . . . In this case these weeds etc. may be things and people we love and reverence most dearly—it may be ourselves! Who cares? Certainly not the farmer. . . .

So I take what I can from the Book—and that scrap was enough to revolutionize and to illuminate my life, to solve all my problems, and to guide infallibly my course. For the rest, I merely strive to understand; also, to acquire that new, that infinitely lofty and remote, point of view. In this I have been sufficiently successful to convince me that such divergence as remains is due to my own imperfection of initiation.

There! You have dug out of me a clear and simple statement, helping my own mind immensely in the process. I hope you will keep this letter; one day it may be a valuable witness.

I add only that I think this. If you had had my experience or its equivalent, as you might very well have done, and may yet do, your point of view would differ from mine only in insignificant, personality-engendered details.

Yours A.C. 666,
old uncle Tom Cobley and all![17]

Crowley's argument here boils down to: "well, if you were me, you'd take it seriously too." *His* commitment needn't be doubted; Yorke should strive to understand as best he might. Had we experienced what Crowley claims he did, we could share his conviction. What constituted "proof" to Crowley would seldom convince without personal experience, and Crowley was the last person to have urged anyone to accept *The Book of the Law* on faith: "Success is thy proof: argue not; convert not; talk not over much!" (*AL* III:42)

---

*"Mercy let be off; damn them who pity! Kill and torture; spare not; be upon them!" (*AL* III:18)

Moving to Buckinghamshire (Summerlea, Lucas Rd., High Wycombe) made it easier for Mrs. Macky to lunch with 666 on the twelfth, at which Crowley doubtless enthused over new-bound first copies of *The Book of Thoth*. He wrote to New York a week later telling Germer *his* inscribed copy had just been mailed; other subscribers would receive theirs soon.

## THE BOOK OF THOTH

Chiswick Press's gilt-edged first edition *The Book of Thoth*, bound by Sangorski and Sutcliffe, is a treasure. Its (false) spring equinox publication date followed discussion with a Mr. Adamson of the Ministry of Paper Control (!) whereby only a "periodical" might use paper—hence the "Equinox" tag. The book presents the sole reproduction of eight of Lady Harris's "cards" with color veracity. Current editions of book and cards fall short of verisimilitude. Having seen the lucid full-size watercolors, I can vouch for their startling vividness and make a call for a perfected edition.

Crowley's text is important for card users as well as scholars of

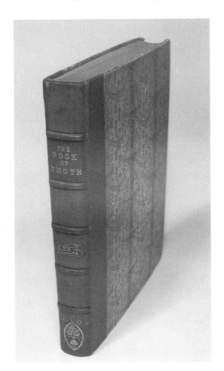

*Fig. 14.5. The Book of Thoth. (Courtesy of 100th Monkey Press)*

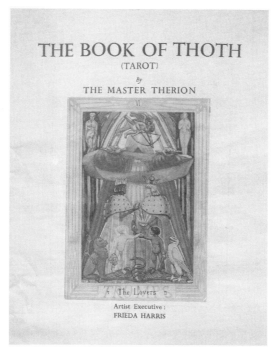

*Fig. 14.6. Prospectus for* The Book of Thoth.
*(Courtesy Ordo Templi Orientis, and 100th Monkey Press)*

*Fig. 14.7.* The Book of Thoth,
*Lust.*
*(Courtesy of Ordo Templi Orientis*
*and 100th Monkey Press)*

*Fig. 14.8.* The Book of Thoth,
*Ace of Swords.*
*(Courtesy Ordo Templi Orientis,
and 100th Monkey Press)*

Hermetism and Kabbalah. Following Lévi and Oswald Wirth, and adding significantly to them, Crowley presents the tarot as a dynamic philosophy of existence, embodying a symbolic system of conditional action within a spiritual universe informing natural forces. As such, Crowley created a gnostic text, albeit one reconstituted from the past with "Thelemic" insights incorporated.

The title derives from the tradition that Hermes Trismegistus, Greco-Egyptian embodiment of Thoth, god of wisdom, magic, and writing, inscribed universal wisdom in books whose preservation would preserve the world from destruction. Crowley's conception of the "Taro" (the universe as "wheel") encapsulates that wisdom as divinatory aid, incorporating the kabbalist Tree of Life of the *Sefer Bahir*. Crowley sees Thelema restoring and synthesizing an ancient system to shape future civilization.

Crowley expressed his problems and hopes for his *next* book in a letter to Germer of July 19: "Unless the foe [Germany] collapses suddenly within a month or two, I must give up 93 [Jermyn Street]. It is at present sublet, thank God, to a pal [Nancy Cunard]. But there is no sense in hanging on." He was now concentrating on the "now rather amusingly and accurately entitled 'Aleister Explains Everything.' I have a hunch about this book. It will sell in thousands and really put us on the map." It was aimed at those "repelled by the blah-mongers like Ouspensky, Waite. Yogi-this-that-& the other swami." He felt better; thanks to a good hour's walk every day.[18]

## NANCY CUNARD

Old acquaintance Nancy Cunard—after a life of independent publishing and political activism—was toiling as secretary for Free French forces and S.H.A.E.F. (Supreme Headquarters Allied Expeditionary Force). Desperate for rare West End accommodation, Nancy initiated correspondence, telling Crowley she "liked very much" Louis Wilkinson, whom she'd met that spring with the Powys sisters in Dorset and Montacute.[19] Louis probably tipped off Nancy about Crowley's flat. Crowley replied on July 22:

My dear Nancy,

Do what thou wilt shall be the whole of the law

How delightful to get a letter—and such a letter! from you, who have always played so great a part in the life of my imagination!

Many thanks for the war-poem; so fine in rhythm and expression, with such powers to make one visualize as well as experience your reaction.[20]

*Fig. 14.9. Nancy Cunard (1896–1965).*

Inviting her to the Bell, Crowley explained it was only two short bus rides from Oxford; a drink awaited her. Louis had enjoyed the Bell for a week, having an "A1 time" with "lots of fun" playing Fore & Aft and hosting a spelling bee. He asked her to pass his love on to their mutual friend, writer Norman Douglas (1868–1952), who'd also lived "a great and glorious life. How few of us there are, true Adventurers of the Spirit!" Crowley made fascinating observations of Paris, which they'd both known so well and so long. He thought the French in 1940 should have fought for it, making it a "Stalingrad" "and cutting the war short by two years."[21] He also sent Nancy a *Liber OZ* postcard. Remarking on life in London, he opined, "Queues are all right, so long as you remember to join it at the right end. I always do: the slaves never challenge one."[22] (*This* explains what Crowley understood by "slaves.")

On July 30 Crowley was delighted to hear from a still-living Lt. Grady McMurtry, "wrote from Normandy!"—and Crowley interrupted work on Letter XLIV of "A.E.E." to send a card to Jane Wolfe, now out of 1003 and living at 5169 ¼ Fountain Ave., L.A. A note from Christabel (Aberconway) received next day expressed her love for *The Book of Thoth* and gave 666 a good idea for Letter XLV: on Selfishness—"Wrote it straight off!"

He heard from Nancy again at the beginning of August, and replied:

> Beloved Dream Woman that you are!
> Do what thou wilt shall be the whole of the law
> It was so sweet of you to say you would come over.[23]

Could she pick up a suit for him from "Buchmansville"?—neonym for "Oxford," where U.S. missionary Frank Buchman founded the Oxford Group for Moral Rearmament (1938). Alcoholics Anonymous founders met through that group—*not* Crowley's scene.

He expected Nancy for lunch on August 5, but she couldn't make it, preoccupied as she was with meeting novelist, amateur linguist, geologist, botanist, gourmet, and zoologist Norman Douglas. Nancy's *Grand Man: Memories of Norman Douglas* recounts their relationship with Crowley. Douglas wrote to Nancy from the Blossom Hotel, Chester, on August 15, 1944:

*Fig. 14.10. Norman Douglas (1868–1952).*

I hang on here, hoping I may soon find an asylum somewhere. Nothing up to the present! I could go to Southwell Gardens, but I should be quite alone there. . . . Mrs. King has just written that they had "119 bombs" (official) in one night and that never a night passes without her house shaking. I wish we could both go to Crowley's village and stay there. Could I? I might be able to help you with some work. I would write them direct, but don't know whether "Aston Clinton" would find you. Yes, I'll risk it. Have written you with this post also to 162 Walton St, Oxford. Love to Aleister.[24]

Nancy arrived at the Bell on August 17—a memorable Thursday. Crowley's diary: "Nancy here. Delightful! Every minute a rapture!" Such a meeting of two remarkable poets reminds me of William Blake and Samuel Taylor Coleridge's encounter, described by critic Crabb Robinson as one of "congenial beings from another sphere." Nancy recalled the day in a letter to Gerald Yorke of October 24, 1954, sent from her little cottage at Lamothe Fénelon, Dordogne. She was sorry the world would never see his like again, uniquely wise:

what a galaxy he did offer himself to! This particular point seems practically the pivot of the man—man or magus—does it not?

I should have hated all the "hoolie-goolie" stuff, but that seems to have been long before. I can well imagine him absolutely terrifying many people—serpent's kiss and all (I have had the honour; no trouble whatsoever; it lasted about 10 days, very pretty, on my right wrist!)

La! . . . What a picture it evokes [the letters] even this short

sequence: there he was, in an excellent inn, see how well fed, with
plenty of [ration] coupons &c. . . .

It has been a pleasure to copy them for you, but alas that none of
us will see him again.

Very sincerely, Nancy Cunard[25]

The day after Nancy left, Crowley felt the loss: "Nancy fled—woe's
me!" Then he wrote:

> My own adorable Nancy,
> Do what thou wilt shall be the whole of the law.
> How too angelic a visit! But let it not be so "far
> between" next time! I cannot remember so
> few hours packed with so much rapture.[26]

Nancy posted a reply on August 23, aiming to clinch 93 Jermyn Street:

> I loved your poems. And keep on thinking of inspiring "La Gauloise."
> I went to take the room you told me of, by the week (£2 10/- I think
> you said) . . . I am told my petition to go to France has a good chance.
> So—I will, in any case, be ready to take it [93 Jermyn Street] this
> Wednesday (after tomorrow, August 23) by the week, if agreeable
> to you.
> I need nothing—a couch of sorts, a table if possible—a hook or
> two. . . .
> Love Nancy[27]

Contact with Norman Douglas was made by 666 with the familiar
greeting, *Do what thou wilt . . .* to which Douglas riposted on August 22:
"To hell with all Laws. It was delightful to see your elegant handwriting
again after all the years. . . . Let's meet up sooner the better."[28]

In *Grand Man*—written as though addressing Douglas—Nancy
recalled the Bell:

> "Crowley's village in Bucks"! It seemed a sort of happy backwater
> off the rushing stream of difficulties and events and he had betaken
> himself to it after being severely shaken by bombs in London. Now,

on the one occasion I was there to see him, he told me he was "working against Hitler on the astral plane." Far away and long ago was all that hoolie-goolie period of his (although these words, I admit, made me start), and he was a most interesting person to talk to. We had got on well when I met him first in London in 1933—no ectoplasmic or occult ties between us for an instant!

It would be delightful to have spent some time with you and him, and he welcomed the idea of your [Douglas's] arrival. I could almost visualise the general tone of the conversation you would have, if not the exact matter.

But alas, again: "So don't let Aleister fix up anything definite." [Douglas went to Wales and Cornwall][29]

When Nancy sent her Crowley letters to Gerald Yorke in October 1954, she noted in a charming covering letter: "Norman never got to Aston Clinton; it was one more of those misfires; for I would have dearly loved to see them together!"[30]

Douglas was at Peace Close, Somerset, when he contacted Nancy on August 28, 1944: "Had one or two nice letters from Crowley who seems to be as wizardish as ever."[31] Nancy reflected in *Grand Man* on Douglas's view of Crowley, and her own:

Now, thanks to AC, I found myself living in Jermyn St, in the house where the spiritualist proprietress had actually named a room after him (for séances) and where, although she threatened me with her "I shall need your room soon," I managed to stay for months. In this light he was indeed my benefactor, for lodgings were impossible to find. How much we talked of him on one occasion! Did you think, for instance, that he really used those little phrases with which he said he began and ended positively all of his letters? Did he carry it as far as this:

Messrs Buntleys Bank.

Dear Sirs,

"Do what thou wilt shall be the whole of the law
    Concerning the matter in hand . . ."

Ending with:
"Love is the Law, love under will.

> Yours truly . . ."
> A very fantastic figure,
> Crowley!

"Nothing in comparison to what he was," you [Norman Douglas] assured me and all those scarlet and sable events, were they not connected only with people who flung themselves blindly into whatever mysteries he seemed to represent? You were inclined to argue, although even to me, what I had just said sounded a bit too easily "dismissive." Such a mixture of good and horrible taste in that man . . .

He was hot stuff, and no mistake, my dear. They can stand a good deal in Italy, but in the end he was too much for them, and he had to go![32]

After Nancy, back to work . . . Crowley wrote to Germer on August 23: "Knocked sideways by the numbers of people who want *Thoth*." He felt it was the first time he'd been taken seriously by people in the occult world. Dion Fortune, for example: "a quite distinguished novelist," a woman of unique honesty, unusually rare in acknowledging the sources of her teaching, who had quite a following with a "publishing show on the side," the Fraternity of the Inner Light—then there were wandering bishops and cardinals, all suddenly interested. As to the latter, the "brains of this outfit is a Dr. W. B. Crow who is most enthusiastic and active. . . . I hope I have already cured him of playing Red Indians with all this nonsense of legitimate succession of the Dark Ages. . . . He is actively trying to put on the Gnostic Mass. . . . Other people could be roped in if only we had a proper plan."[33]

*A proper plan . . .*

He wrote to Grady McMurtry, beginning "Dear Louis":

You are the only man from the U.S.A. of the younger generation who has been properly blooded [a foxhunting term for initiation in the kill] and you know me personally with a remarkable degree of intimacy considering the shortness of our association. You are also, quite the most serious and intelligent of the younger lot. This singles you out as the proper man to take charge of affairs when the time is ripe. It is supremely important that you should understand fully the 9th degree if only because you are at an age and have the ability to make full use of the powers which it confers. It is therefore important to regularize your position.[34]

And he remembered Jane Wolfe:

J.W.P. [Jack Parsons] has not written for months; till he does, I can do nothing. . . . G.L. McMurtry sent him $80 to send on to me. That was about July 2nd. No news of it so far. . . . When the *Book of Thoth* arrives on the Coast, perhaps these idiots will realize who has the goods, and who has not. . . . The new book [A.E.E.] positively frightens me; the responsibility is bloody awful. I have to make up my mind about all sorts of questions that I have been inclined to dodge, *and* to put it in black & white. Hellish![35]

On September 2, he received first contact from Michael Houghton's friend David Curwen of 136 Marylebone Road. Curwen and Crowley began a long correspondence (see Churton, *Aleister Crowley in India*).

In September a V-2 ballistic missile (*Aggregat 4*) exploded in Chiswick. The V-2s' devastating speed and suddenness of explosion were terrifying.

Revising "A.E.E.," perhaps reflecting on Pasadena, or the off-duty behavior of some U.S. soldiers, Crowley joked to Louis Wilkinson on September 2: "I'm drawing up a 50,000-year plan to civilize the USA."[36]—which contrasts nicely with his diary entry eight days later: "Discovered why I like Americans. They are *friendly*."

Some time in the next fortnight he pulled himself out of a depression sufficiently to write an interesting letter to Yorke about a possible future:

I agree with you that the book [*of Thoth*] puts the coping stone on my Qabalah; it seems quite complete, and I certainly don't feel like doing any more. It may well be that my work in the future will be political in the main; I have a letter drafted to Vansittart [senior

British diplomat Robert Gilbert Vansittart, 1st Baron Vansittart, 1881–1957]. How well I remember your advice to "join the Nazis and come up with Hitler"! But I fear that I should hardly have got through all those purges. No, I was glad to leave his career in the hands of Soror I.W.E [Küntzel]. Shows you, doesn't it, the dangers of getting initiated halfway? At the same time, even if he had understood Thelema properly, the only weapon to his hand was Versailles. The world was not quite ripe for an international movement towards the revival of true Aristocracy. That, by the way, has been my deepest idea all my life. I began about fourteen with a "poem" to Rosebery [Liberal politician, Archibald Primrose, 5th Earl of Rosebery]. Verse 1 ends "And now my lord, in medias res [cut to the chase]: /Get rid of all your red Rad. Fleas!" . . . Most seriously I see no hope for the world at all unless we can get the reins in the hands of the cavaliers. The Old School Tie has such very swearing colours; the snobbery, stupidity, prejudice—etc. I could go on for a page—put all the best people off it as a system. This throws many of the best men on to the left wing. One thinks of Mirabeau and Lafayette. It's all appallingly difficult. One can't start offhand what must be the growth of decades, even centuries. But a return to a modified patriarchal-feudal system is the obvious gambit. We must first of all have a sound physical stock to pick out rulers from.[37]

On September 18 Crowley wrote to Wilkinson. He'd planned to return to London on October 16, but "London is getting it again—rockets—bad—Government letting out nothing so far. But sounds *very* bad." Crowley referred to one of the gliders sent to the battle raging at Arnhem that, "having failed to reach Holland, came down here! Just beyond Tring. Perfect landing; nobody hurt."[38] He also wrote to Germer that day: "age and asthma cooperate to do me down. It is really impossible for me to look after myself in petty boring ways." He mentioned a Miss Taylor whose sex life was "knocked out long ago" as just the person he needed. "Violent excitement and exercise start my heart playing the goat—which is annoying." Miss Taylor could give half her time for two pounds, ten shillings a week. After a wonderful summer, "I dread the dark days to come." He wanted to train McMurtry so "he might take our places when the time comes. He seems to have all the

INNER TRADITIONS
BEAR & COMPANY

**Inner Traditions • Bear&Company**
P.O. Box 388
Rochester, VT 05767-0388
U.S.A.

**PLEASE SEND US THIS CARD TO RECEIVE OUR LATEST CATALOG FREE OF CHARGE.**

Book in which this card was found _____

☐ Check here to receive our catalog via e-mail.

| Company _____ |
| ☐ Send me wholesale information |

Name _____ Phone _____

Address _____

City _____ State _____ Zip _____ Country _____

E-mail address _____

**Please check area(s) of interest to receive related announcements via e-mail:**

☐ Health           ☐ Self-help              ☐ Science/Nature      ☐ Shamanism
☐ Ancient Mysteries ☐ New Age/Spirituality  ☐ Visionary Plants    ☐ Martial Arts
☐ Spanish Language ☐ Sexuality/Tantra       ☐ Family and Youth    ☐ Religion/Philosophy

**Please send a catalog to my friend:**

Name _____ Company _____

Address _____ Phone _____

City _____ State _____ Zip _____ Country _____

Order at 1-800-246-8648 • Fax (802) 767-3726

E-mail: customerservice@InnerTraditions.com • Web site: www.InnerTraditions.com

requisite qualities, save the social. And the war, with my hints, will help that."[39]

Dawson Sadler came south from Sutton Coldfield, bringing Staffordshire-born Harold D. Podmore for lunch on September 30. Like Sadler, Podmore lived in leafy Four Oaks, at Hartopp Court. Crowley's reflection: "A most delightful day: charming men."[40]

He wrote again to Wilkinson on the twenty-seventh, opining that the V-2 rockets that had hit London were probably site finding; after that, they'd come down "like hailstones. Another personal theory is that the Hun is only just starting to fight seriously, now that the holy soil of the Fatherland has been invaded. Sorry to be gloomy. . . . Oh Christ. I do hope to see you soon, elusive one! Like a fucking leprechaun, hang it. Ever yours, Aleister."[41]

Receiving a "chit" (letter) on October 5 from favorite Wren, "Cath 52275 Naval Party c/o Base Fleet Mail Office Reading," he wrote to her, Curwen, Podmore (with a copy of "La Gauloise"), and to Anne Macky, hoping she wasn't ill (there'd been a long delay): "Now, please, it isn't fair to me to be slack. If you don't say 'I got further in six months with him than in six years with anyone else' it's a terrible blot on my 'scutcheon. I want definite achievement from you, progress actual and measurable; I wouldn't be put off by increase of self-satisfaction. I use the same criteria as are valid in profane science."[42]

Hearing on October 8 that 1940 Republican presidential nominee, lawyer, and liberal-conservative Wendell Lewis Wilkie had died, Crowley considered it a "bad blow for the U.S.A."

There was more news from America, reassuring this time. He informed Germer on October 26 that "Sister Grimaud" had told him Smith had finally started a "proper retirement."* He also told Germer he'd like to return to Jermyn Street, if money were easier and conditions right.

The end of the month saw an aggravating "interrogation over lunch" from a Ministry of Supply bureaucrat after someone complained about paper for *Thoth*. He told Fitzgerald on November 2 that though *Thoth* had already sold over fifty copies, with influence well beyond

---

*Helen Parsons's Order name "Grimaud" was from Athos's servant in *The Three Musketeers,* whom Athos trained to serve without speaking!

its circulation, and while "somehow it seems to have impressed people with the solidity of my scholarship," his nerves were "all in rags. . . . I am being worried by the Ministry of Supply because I made no charge for those prospectuses, and, knowing as I do how intensely they have struggled for the last forty years to catch me breaking the law, I am naturally scared stiff." He said Britain was following Germany's Gestapo, and the interference was not even run by police, but by "tupenny ha'penny ribbon clerks." He'd also heard from Pearl Brooksmith about a "ghastly adventure on her way up to London for shopping." She ended up being dug out from under a house.[43] Crowley wrote her an affectionate letter of commiseration. "The V-2 is no joke," he told Fitzgerald.

Where England was going was much on Crowley's mind. His concerns about State control entered "A.E.E.," and prescient fears for the national mentality seeped into this revealing letter to Gerald Yorke on November 2:

> I think that what is really lacking is the romantic view of life. I have always felt at home spiritually with Dumas *père* and Walter Scott. I have always considered my own life in exactly these terms. I have in fact, in my 70th year, preserved all the illusions of my 19th, and it really does seem to me that if a sufficient proportion of the people of this country had the same idea things would go a great deal more smoothly.[44]

On November 7 Crowley found himself depressed by Crow's letters. Crow claimed he'd chartered "several universities" yet "admitted that Newman's DD and DCL were bogus." Crowley loathed academic pretensions: "Show me the *man*," he'd say. He had more pleasure in corresponding with writer of detective novels Gladys Mitchell (born 1901) who wrote on November 9 (he replied on the thirtieth), but Dr. Crow wouldn't let up. On November 11 Crowley enlightened him about the Age of Aquarius, belief in whose peculiar properties would dominate popular magic in the sixties.

> To talk of the Ages of Pisces and Aquarius is incomplete. The Age has also the opposite sign as one of its characteristics, and this may at times be even stronger than the original sign. To call this the

Aquarian Age is really a joke. The characteristic so far has been much more that of Leo.[45]

The day he wrote on Aquarius, he recorded a Cypriot waiter's arrival: "I hear he is a 'conchie' [conscientious objector]. I, too, have a 'conscientious objection'—to giving my hand to one."

Frustration manifested itself in his discourse with Louis Wilkinson. Crowley wanted a heart-to-heart about moving to the Queen's Hotel, Hastings, if close both to the sea and a chess club. He really needed a two-roomed flat and a woman aged forty to fifty-five who could cook and take a motherly interest in him.[46]

On November 21, he had an idea: "Split A.E.E. into sections (1) Theory of Universe (2) Mag[ica]) technique (3) *AL* (4) Ethics (5) Man and his powers etc." This was never done, and the work—dubbed *Magick without Tears*—disappeared until Karl Germer made a typescript of over eighty letters in 1954 principally for O.T.O. members. It remained unpublished until 1973.

*Magick without Tears* reflects a sharp mind, terse, colorful, tempered by hard experience and profound thought. Occasionally it is prophetically direct, as in this glorious quotation from a "letter" or chapter on *Noise:*

> What I am about to complain of is what I seriously believe to be an organized conspiracy of the Black Lodges to prevent people from thinking.
>
> Naked and unashamed! In some countries there has already been compulsory listening-in to Government programmes; and who knows how long it will be before we are all subjected by law to the bleatings, bellowings, belchings of the boring balderdash of the BBC-issies?
>
> So nobody must be allowed to think at all. Down with the public schools! Children must be drilled mentally by quarter-educated herdsmen, whose wages would stop at the first sign of disagreement with the bosses. For the rest, deafen the whole world with senseless clamour. Mechanize everything! Give nobody a chance to think. Standardize "amusement." The louder and more cacophonous, the better! Brief intervals between one din and the next can be filled

with appeals, repeated 'till hypnotic power gives them the force of orders, to buy this or that product of the "Business men" who are the real power in the State. Men who betray their country as obvious routine.

The history of the past thirty years is eloquent enough, one would think. What these sodden imbeciles never realise is that a living organism must adapt itself intelligently to its environment, or go under at the first serious change in circumstance.

Where would England be today if there had not been one man, deliberately kept "in the wilderness" for decades as "unsound," "eccentric," "dangerous," "not to be trusted," "impossible to work with," to take over the country from the bewildered "safe" men?

And what could he have done unless the people had responded? Nothing. So then there is still a remnant whose independence, sense of reality; and manhood begin to count when the dear, good, woolly flock scatter in terror at the wolf's first howl.

Yes, they are there, and they can get us back our freedom—if only we can make them see that the enemy in Whitehall* is more insidiously fatal than the foe in Brownshirt House.

On this note I will back to my silence.

Young Kenneth Grant first wrote to Crowley inquiring after books he couldn't obtain at the Atlantis. Crowley replied on November 23. By the new year 1945, Grant was assisting Crowley's move from Buckinghamshire to Hastings, Sussex.

From Hollywood, an olive branch: Crowley wrote to Germer about it on November 29. "Jean Phillips† appears to be in close touch with Orson Welles and is anxious to interest him in my work." Crowley sent her "various things which might take his fancy. (You realize of course that his acceptation of one story of mine would make us for good and all.) It has occurred to me that 'The Three Wishes' might suit Orson Welles very well." Crowley paid three pounds, thirteen shillings, nine

---

*Whitehall, London, is the hub of government; "Brownshirt" refers to Nazis.
†Max Schneider's third wife Jean Stoddard Phillips (1909–1982) worked for Orson Welles's Mercury Productions from 1944 to 1945.

pence to have it typed and received a cable from Jean on December 5. She had "Equinox 7" but not Crowley's play *The Saviour,* a satire on American politics. She'd given *Mortadello* to Welles personally.[47]

Meanwhile, Sir Percy Harris was delivering parliamentary speeches about the terrible situation in Greece, where resistance to German invaders turned into civil war between communists and a British- and U.S.-backed government army. Crowley was caustic, writing on December 7:

> For hardships Greeks have undergone
> We British make amends,
> Drop bombs and parachutes upon
> Our liberated friends.

December 10, 1944: "Grant arrived; managed to get a taxi after all [it was Sunday]. Got his rising sun right. Aged 20 *Eheu fugaces* [*eheu fugaces labuntur anni* = "Alas, the fleeting years slip by" (Horace)]. Would I were at Nefta, and 25!" Hexagram 19, *Lin,* seemed appropriate: "Approach"—and then "H.A. [McMurtry] dashed in!! Oh so blasted tired! But *very* happy."

Crowley wrote to Dawson Sadler on December 14: "What a deplorable fool I am to have employed an even more deplorable ditto as secretary!" Lacking a copy of *Book 4,* part II, he'd borrowed Sadler's and got his secretary to type passages pertinent to A.E.E. Having returned it to Sadler, he found the typed section "I wanted most, and wanted instantly was missing." Crowley informed Sadler where it was: "Soror Virakam's story of how I disappeared and got levitated, chair and all, and I don't know what else" and asked Sadler to copy and send it. He closed it with his good wishes for the solstice.

Forty-six years after his own initiation, with McMurtry and Wilkinson at the inn, Crowley devised Grant's magical name, *OShIK,* with the value 400, from Grant's vision of his "angel," also spelt "A'Ossik" or "Aussic." Next day Wilkinson and Crowley drove up to Oxford for a "fairish lunch" at the Mitre on High Street—without McMurtry: the car was full. They discussed *U.S.S.R. The Story of Soviet Russia* (1944) "by old lover W[alter] D[uranty]," former *New York Times* Moscow correspondent. Back at the inn on the twenty-second, Crowley found a parcel of needles from Heppels missing, while McMurtry "blew in" to

two o'clock tiffin. After chess, McMurtry received "more solid instruction in IX° than I ever gave before to anyone! He is now quite OK for
the dues." McMurtry's account of his comrades' ignorance suggested to
Crowley adding a P.S. to his "letter" on "Education." McMurtry was
back again on Christmas Day (fog having "prevented McMurtry from
getting back at Germans") when they shared—Wilkinson was informed
in a letter of December 30—a "great glorious time."[48] Someone called
"Shinwell" said grace (perhaps chairman of the Labor Party "Manny"
Shinwell, heard on the B.B.C.), whereupon McMurtry and 666 immediately "said Will," the Thelemic equivalent:

A.C.: (*knocks 3-5-3*)

ALL: Do what thou wilt shall be the whole of the Law.

A.C.: What is thy will?

H.A.: It is my will to eat and to drink.

A.C.: To what end?

H.A.: That I may fortify my body thereby.

A.C.: To what end?

H.A.: That I may accomplish the Great Work.

ALL.: Love is the law, love under will.

A.C.: (*knocks once*) Fall to!

PART THREE

# RETIREMENT

# FIFTEEN

# Death Is King

*The serpent dips his head beneath the sea*
*His mother, source of all his energy*
*Eternal, thence to draw the strength he needs*
*On earth to do indomitable deeds*
*Once more; and they, who saw but understood*
*Naught of his nature of beatitude*
*Were awed: they murmured with abated breath;*
*Alas the Master; so he sinks in death.*
*But whoso knows the mystery of man*
*Sees life and death as curves of one same plan.*

ALEISTER CROWLEY, "THANATOS BASILEOS,"
"KING DEATH" OR "DEATH IS KING" FROM *OLLA*

January 3, 1945. While Lt. McMurtry fought in northeastern France as the struggle for Bure intensified the bitter Battle of the Bulge, British barges landed at Akyab, Burma, pursuing the Japanese.

*Akyab* . . . forty-four years had passed since Crowley steamed into Akyab searching for Allan Bennett. The world had changed, and Heppell's of Piccadilly, closed for the holiday, denied 666 his needles. Doing "quite well" on three grains a day until the dearth: "Thank the Most High Gods!" he cried when the sixth replenished supplies. Grant came two days before when "an exceedingly pleasant and fruitful talk" yielded Grant's "most unusual" horoscope.

Letters recommended Hastings for a move—*and the I Ching?* "You bet!" concluded Crowley as he determined on "Netherwood," a residential hotel above Hastings, found by Louis Wilkinson's twenty-nine-year-old son Oliver, recently retired from naval service in Iceland. Meantime, vacant hours passed with Walter Duranty's *U.S.S.R.*: "He quotes me now and again. Must ask him if he knows Ivan Narodny."

A "lovely time" was enjoyed on the ninth and tenth with Wren Cathrine—"more delightful than ever"—before illness put Crowley back to bed on the twelfth, whence he wrote to Germer that "down with pleurisy," regular help was vital: "There is a young man named George Kenneth Grant, not quite 21 years old. His intelligence is of the first order . . . has studied my work for three years." He was "as advanced at his age as I was at 25." Working in a bookshop, Grant paid one pound a week for board with family in Ilford, Essex. Could Germer foot some of his bill if Grant helped out? He might come *gratis* at first because training "for a career." "I am afraid this letter sounds like the howl of a trapped coyote."[1] Nevertheless, his diary for the sixteenth records "enjoying life almost unendurably"—with Charles Baudelaire: "oh, how he is I!" In his imagination, he was free.

*Fig. 15.1. Kenneth Grant, "taken [Michael Staley informed the author] by Kenneth's sister Kath, winter 1952, at Fawley Road, West Hampstead, where they lived at the time." (Courtesy of the Warburg Institute, London, and Michael Staley)*

By January 20, his temperature nearly normal (100°F), Crowley planned a "dash" to Hastings while, foreseeing his death, he appointed Wilkinson as the "natural man" to be literary executor.[2] Reminiscing to Wilkinson two days later about his fame for bons mots, especially in Paris, he remarked: "I had a real reputation there. Seymour de Ricci might remember a few," before recalling a party at Paterson's in 1927: "they appealed to me for the most foul, horrible, obscene disgusting word in the English language. I said 'Baldwin.'* A pity nobody was listening."[3]

Death was still on his mind when he wrote to Wilkinson on the twenty-seventh: "I have been borrowing life for the last six years or so, by means of injections. . . . This morning I found myself with 2½ grains to last till Monday if the postman failed me." He feared a heart attack from coughing and named Grant—though not yet twenty-one with no typing or shorthand—as "an ideal person to do all the hard work under your direction . . . so *hasta la vista*!"[4]

## NETHERWOOD

Next time Wilkinson would see the Beast was at Netherwood, East Sussex, whither he was driven on February 1. Far from the "eerie" establishment of myth, Netherwood was a cheerful, characterful house set in four acres. Built circa 1860–1870 and formerly a school, it was bought in 1935 after thirty-one-year-old schoolteacher Ellen Kathleen Johnson ("Johnnie") married left-wing, self-taught actor, playwright, and sometime journalist from southeast London, Edmund Charles Vernon Symonds (born 1899).

They renovated Netherwood into a residential hotel and guest house: a happy, Bohemian oasis for healthy living of body and mind with cultural talks by notable or interesting speakers, "Brains Trust" events for open-minded, freethinking persons, lively games, and first-rate cooking.†

---

*English-born, raised in France, historian Seymour de Ricci (1881–1942) became a French citizen. Conservative Stanley Baldwin: prime minister 1924–1929.

†I recommend Antony Clayton's *Netherwood: Last Resort of Aleister Crowley* (2012), for an engrossing illustrated account.

*Fig. 15.2. Netherwood, when a school.*

Inevitably, the war affected mood and pockets, but Vernon and Johnnie soldiered on, and it says much about them that they enjoyed Crowley's sharing his last three years with them.

Crowley took to the place, settling into his tiny room on the first floor while establishing his heroin prescription with local surgeon Dr. Charles Charnock-Smith. Grant sent from London a gold "Mohur Awadh Ghazi-ud-Din Haidar" (a Muslim mohur coin of AH 1236), which on the sixth Crowley put in someone's mouth for divination purposes "while I asked and twiddled." On February 27, Johnnie and Vernon agreed to employ Grant for a month, offering a cottage on the grounds.

Correspondence began, to Crowley's astonishment, with a query from Dion Fortune plus five guineas for the answer and three *Magick without Tears* letters.

Jack Parsons's cable on the thirteenth reassured:

SMITH LEAVING RAINBOW VALLEY NO FUNDS OR LODGING GEORGIA [Haitz] WILL ACCOMMODATE AS ALTERNATIVE TO HERE RANCHO ROYAL AVAILABLE ONLY IF LIBER 132 FOLLOWED LITERALLY ALL LOYAL TO YOU I WILL DO NOTHING WITHOUT INSTRUCTIONS PLEASE WIRE JOHN W PARSONS.

Crowley replied:

IDEAL FILM HERO EMERGES RETIREMENT DIVINELY SELF
CONFIDENT INDEPENDENT POWERFUL PREPARED CHARGED
VAGRANCY LUNACY LIKE HISTORICAL EXAMPLES STOP
FOLLOW SCRIPT 132 SCRUPULOUSLY AVOIDING OLD CONTACTS
STOP WROTE HELEN NINTH AC

On the nineteenth Crowley enthused to Wilkinson: Netherwood's cooking was just what he liked; Vernon was a "trump," and he and Johnnie were joining him at Oliver's "tomorrow night" for a "supper party of the Gods, I hope"—*and* he beat the famous E. M. Jackson at chess at Hastings's superb chess club, while making a "nice joke against a vegetarian faddist."[5]

In March, problems mounted in California. Regina Kahl had died. Crowley offered ten pounds for an annual lecture in memoriam. "There is no question of reinstating 132," insisted Crowley, having realized Germer, Mellinger, and Parsons constituted a triumvirate until McMurtry's return. "He is a God or out of it altogether. Why the devil nobody can understand so simple a position beats me." There would, he insisted, be trouble if Smith contacted members.

Crowley wondered what Germer meant by referring to his "worst style" in the latest "Letters": "I suspect it is when I take you up to 31,999 feet and drop you by parachute and it fails to open! Is that right?" There *is* a tendency in Crowley's writing to make you feel you're about to smash through a eureka moment, then suddenly it tails off or blurs. Crowley told Germer he wasn't a conventional philosopher, certainly no Platonist: "You retort that I am a lowbrow; and the answer is: yes, I am." He liked thoughts with structural definition. Moving on to politics and temptations of socialism: "All the totalitarian schemes add up to the same thing in the end, And the approach is so insidious the arguments so subtle and irrefutable, the advantages so obvious, that the danger is very real, very imminent, very difficult to bring home to the average citizen, who sees only the immediate gain, and is hoodwinked as to the price that must be paid for it." If you want absolute security, social and otherwise: welcome to Sing Sing![6]

On March 9 he addressed the Smith issue with Helen Parsons: "I am sure I don't know how you manage to dodge the absolute prohibition for any member of the O.T.O. to hold any communication soever with Mr. W.T. Smith (ex-Frater 132)."[7] He then addressed Mr. Smith: "you continue the old plan of parasitism; you cling desperately to just those people who risk their own existence by admitting yours. . . . Thereby you have blocked the plans of the Gods who would have welcomed you to their circle, and looked after you in every way."[8] Crowley wrote again to Germer: "He [Smith] must stand on his own feet, not on our toes." He said he'd send a total ban ("Interdict") on Smith's contacting members under separate cover.[9] On the sixteenth, a cable from Jack:

SMITH LEFT 1003 DUE TO MY FIRM STAND AS YOUR AGENT PROCEEDING INDEPENDENTLY OF ME UNDER CONTROL. JOHN PARSONS.[10]

Crowley was pleased.

OShIK took up residence on March 12, bringing from Jermyn Street Crowley's pen-and-ink drawing, *Totem*. Four days later, relief showed: "For days past I have been inordinately happy, so much so that it almost amounts to being 'fey.' I feel wretched in the knowledge that it cannot go on forever. Aiwaz! I invoke Thee!" Grant helped to group the A.E.E. letters, while Crowley wrote to Wilkinson on March 22: "Best Beloved Umfraville, . . . I enclose the Vernal greeting. . . . Your lively son's departure has left me lonely. . . . Luckily young Grant has been here for the last ten days. . . . P.S. You will find my epitaph for Bosie." "Bosie" (Lord Alfred Douglas), who embroiled Oscar Wilde in legal and social ruin, had just died in Lancing, aged seventy-four:

> Pull hard the plug, lass!
> Earth, ease thine itch!
> Now, at long last, exterminated the vilest vermin,
> Lord Alfred Douglas, The Atrabilious* Bitch.[11]

---

*A *Liber OZ* lettercard of May 24, 1946, to Wilkinson (OTOB3) corrected "atrabilious": "What an egregious ass I am! (You too might have thought of it). *Atrabilious* is merely the Latin for the Greek melancholy."

*Fig. 15.3.* Totem Pole on Pier, Woman with Bird Behind, *by Aleister Crowley. (Courtesy of Ordo Templi Orientis)*

Crowley tried to explain the "Interdict" to Jane Wolfe on March 23, starting with photos of the mass Smith sent years before:

Smith and the lanky lopsided person [Paul Seckler] who appeared in the photo with him was simply grotesque. They looked like scarecrows in nightgowns. They didn't know how to hold themselves or their weapons, and they didn't know how to wear robes. I was absolutely amazed that you should have allowed anything of the sort to pass. I was relying on your experience of stage and screen to produce the Mass properly, and why you did not do so is still a complete mystery to me. I have written to you before about this; I have told you that the Mass must be up to Hollywood standards as to their production. It is no wonder that it failed to attract people. Just consider how Aimee McPherson went to work. Compare the photographs of Spencer Lewis in robes which Clymer published in that enormous volume, with those taken after he had been in California for some years and got dolled up properly by some expert. He actually succeeded in making him a very fair imitation of an ancient Egyptian by cutting his beard in the right shape, and so on. Whoever you have for Priest he must be at least sixty percent as well as the average film-star. The same applies to the Priest: the others are not so difficult, as long as they do not actually jar with the principals. But why do I have to write all this to you when you know a billion times as much about the subject as I do? That's that! . . . Smith was nothing but a parasite. . . . He has spent his whole life attacking the problem of how to get money without working for it, and he has shrunk from no baseness, no dirtiness, in the pursuit of this ambition. . . . Have I got to explain to everybody all over again, that from the point of view of the Order and of every member [*illegible*] Smith is _dead_ [underlined four times].

If Helen persisted with Smith, she should be suspended until she desisted. Smith should be a "remittance man," supported to prevent starvation, but earning his own living, on condition of never entering California or communicating with members. Crowley didn't doubt he'd survive because due to population increase there were now "two and three suckers born every minute." If he were in East Oshkosh [Wisconsin] or Montana Butte or Titusville, "he would very soon find some fool of a woman to support him at the price of a little flattery and occasional jiggery-pokery." He signed the letter "Baphomet O.H.O."[12]

Meanwhile, Wilkinson was advised, when visiting Netherwood, to bring his own commentary, having agreed to edit a "popular" abridgment of Crowley's commentaries on *The Book of the Law* (which work lay unpublished until 1996).*

Crowley took part in a Netherwood brains trust on the thirty-first, imitating a popular radio program where experts responded to audience questions with all available wit. Regarding wit, Crowley felt Grant's in short supply, noting in his diary on April 4, "Young Grant runs up, blurts out: the V-2's have stopped over London. Can we go back to Jermyn Street?" Crowley wondered if Michael Juste was right about Grant—"mentally unstable," but then, "Mike" wanted Grant for his own Order!

As Berlin's collapse approached, Crowley wrote to Wilkinson about

---

*Some irony here, for before Wilkinson's and Breeze's *The Law Is for All* was published, Israel Regardie applied that title to *his* redaction of Crowley commentaries. On March 28, 1945, Crowley warned Jack Parsons against "Regudy."

punishing war criminals and an article about Hess, which discussion led him to whether he should have been fairer toward A. E. Waite, from whom he sought guidance in 1898. Without Waite "I doubt I should ever have got in touch with the Great Order." Unlike Waite, predecessors Kingsford and Maitland "gave us no idea of the weight of medieval literature." Blavatsky, "genius as she was," was far too "oriental" to produce the necessary effect. Waite, like Dr. Johnson, occupied a position "necessary at the time." "My flood of generosity is now staunched." Looking beyond the war's end, Crowley presumed the mood would be "awful"—prophetic.[13]

Having enjoyed Vernon as Pickering in a local production of Shaw's *Pygmalion* on April 25, he wrote to Germer about needing cash for Grant's services: "Grant has not made good in the housework; so if I am to keep him, I must dig out more cash, and I don't feel like doing so; in fact he is leaving at Whitsun, and he will have to find board and lodging somewhere handy, at £2 a week or near it." Crowley then moved to personal things, impressing on Germer how much their first walk together in Thuringia in 1925 had meant to him: "Of personal things—that first walk after you met me at Gera; something happened which is altogether of Eternity. I wonder how you feel! I am quite OK, sane and cheerful."[14]

Hitler was pronounced dead on May 2 (having committed suicide on April 30 in the Berlin "Bunker.")

Four days later, Crowley spent a "really delightful day with Cathrine. I wonder if I shall ever see her again—she's off to Australia." Next day: "War alleged 'over!' Morons surprised, excited, celebrating. It is hard to live in such a world." On the eighth he'd note: "Public Rejoicing = Private Annoyance!"

Germer wanted Crowley to join them in America: *difficult*. Principal objection was his health. He reminded Karl on May 6 of his old asthma machine for dispensing German product "Broncho Vydrin." It was very effective, but war had cut supplies. After the winter 1941 experience, walking across a room could stimulate an attack, allayed only by hypodermic and seven to eight grains a day. Could he get *that* in New York, if he carried letters from specialists? The U.S. tablets came as "Park Davis Nos. 144 and 197," a dose of which "unfetters my limbs."[15]

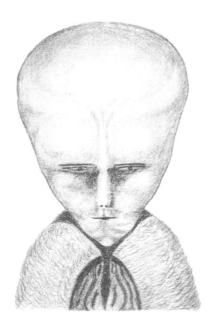

*Fig. 15.4.* The Lama
*by Aleister Crowley.*

On the eighth Aussik, having "helped a whole lot," received *The Lama:* an enigmatic drawing attracting curiosity today because of its otherworldly "alien" figure. *Lam* means "path," and some see Lam as an extraterrestrial or transdimensional figure.

Crowley had a "long talk with scolex ['worm'] Grant," bullied by his father, wondering: "What shall I do about him?" Writing to Jane Wolfe on May 10, he referred to ration coupons, chocolate, and Aimée Crocker (plutocratic U.S. celebrity and sometime lover) "when we could get anything we wanted." "If only there were more Aimées" (she died in 1941). "It is one continual agony for me. Worst of all, the despair into which I sink constantly deeper and deeper crushes my creative genius. I ask myself 'Why should I start to write so-and-so when there is not one chance in 50 of getting it even so far as the typescript stage?' I tell you it's intolerable—it's killing me by inches."[16]

He also wrote to Germer that day, in a dark mood troubled by "an unexpected source:" Grant. "He started A1; the G[reat]∴W[ork] was all; nothing else mattered. Now (bullied, I think, by his father, a bank clerk of the most vulgar type) all is reversed. The G.W. doesn't exist; he uses it only to put pressure on me."[17] The dénouement came on the fourteenth: "Grant's wiggles terminate in a sudden ultimatum; he must go on Wednesday, Cunt, of course!" He left after two days, leaving Crowley to describe Grant as "a Bore with no interest in the world in general." Kenneth married Steffi on February 26, 1946.

Germer's incessant questions kept his brain moving and help *us* grasp his subtleties: "You think I attach undue importance to birth," he barked at Germer. "No, I'm just like a breeder of racehorses; there must be something in that, while folk pay 500 guineas for the use of a stallion. But (a) magically the whole proposition is different, man being a microcosm, and horse a mere zodiacal species (b) biologically. Horses are bred for definite qualities. Men in any case are much more complex and misunderstood, are mated for all sorts of irrelevant reasons—social, financial, and the rest: to say nothing of whim." He realized this would make a good idea for a "Letter."

"What is a 'master?'" A master, Crowley wrote, is someone able to accept and discharge responsibility.[18] This could not be said of so-called master race believer Heinrich Himmler, regarding whom Crowley satisfactorily noted on May 24: "Himmler who put *Saturnus* in Concentration Camps—chiefly because he was my friend!—killed himself after capture."

Crowley spent June 1945 playing chess, worrying about heroin and domestic burdens, writing letters (to David Curwen, Mellinger, and Tub), all the while feeling ill. Cath visited, though her next letter (July 5) came from Sydney! He informed Germer on June 7 how McMurtry's last letter described a "joyride" to Pilsen (now in the Czech Republic), "enough to make you cry," and confessed he'd found McMurtry's visits "so helpful," and was now greatly looking forward to Frederic Mellinger's forthcoming visit—all the way from California.[19]

As if by magic on June 16: "H.A. [McMurtry] blew in! Brought a bottle of Sekt [sparkling wine] from Hochheim [in Hesse]." H. A. (Hieronymus Alpha) left on the eighteenth for London and Germany.

In July he concerned himself with Grant's report that he'd seen the original proofs for his unpublished short story collection *Golden Twigs* for sale at the Atlantis. He suggested Michael Juste let him have them; they were obviously stolen. Crowley wrote to Germer on July 9 that Juste sent the proofs, with a request for five pounds in return, writing

"DO WHO YOU WILL—THAT IS MY LAW"—thus incriminating himself. Crowley consulted a lawyer, and Juste consulted his.[20]

A "very passionate invocation of Aiwaz when I turned my light out" led to what 666 considered "the most astonishing dream" on August 3.

Hearing on August 7 of the atom bomb drop on Hiroshima, he saw in it possible fulfillment of the "war-engine" of *AL* III, writing to Wilkinson: "The 'Atomic Bomb' is interesting *AL* III:7.8. One of the men working on it was for some time at the Abbey in Cefalù."[21] Who this may have been I cannot say. He wrote more about this idea to Wilkinson on August 21: "We could explode a psychic Atomic Bomb with it, your literary skill, and my infamy as a Magus. Rather on the lines of the Elders of Zion, perhaps. Give the world a real scare. I have some *very* good ideas and know enough science to make it convincing."[22]

"Victory in Japan" (V. J. Day) was officially declared on August 15. World War II was over. An estimated 75 to 80 million people were killed between 1939 and 1945 in the biggest war ever fought; few believed it the last.

Survivor Crowley settled into Netherwood life, chatting at the chess club down in the town, finding opponents of real quality, winning many games but not all. On September 19 letters arrived from Madame Wellington Koo, wife of the Chinese ambassador; Wilkinson; and McMurtry. The twenty-fourth saw a theatrical brains trust with Netherwood aficionado C. E. M. Joad (from the radio program)

*Fig. 15.5. C. E. M. Joad.*

appearing with "Nell Gwynne," "Mephistopheles," "Queen Victoria," "Voltaire," and "Mother of 12." Crowley, who knew Joad from years back, found the spoof questions and answers amusing (he obviously wasn't "playing" Queen Victoria).

On September 24 he asked himself plaintively: "Shall I (a) struggle on alone? (b) find a chela? [disciple] (c) subside quietly and leave all to the Gods?" "People here are damned awkward," he moaned to Wilkinson that day. He could only get a secretary once a week and his one standby was "a Wren in Australia."[23]

The next day, he expressed keenness either for coming to the United States or Germer's coming to him. Conditions for travel had eased for "businessmen." Couldn't they transfer 1003 over to Crowley's name and justify "business" in Pasadena? It would be easier, Crowley suggested, if Germer could "pal up" with Robert Cecil at the British Embassy, Washington. Cecil could advise and probably assist.[24]

A gold pen from Agape Lodge cheered him on October 8, while Cathrine sent edible goodies from Down Under. On the nineteenth he reported: "W. B. Seabrook has killed himself at last, after months of agonized slavery to his final wife. Great stuff!" (see Churton, *Aleister Crowley in America;* writer Seabrook had deceived Crowley in 1918–1919). He died of a drug overdose in Rhinebeck, New York.

On the twenty-first Crowley extracted, without comment, a clipping wherein Victor de Laveleye, former Belgian minister of state, claimed to be the originator of the *V* sign, suggesting it to the Foreign Office in 1939.

On November 1, he was asked to "Vote for Vernon!" for the Town Council: "Rats! He had got in unopposed," noted Crowley, disdaining Vernon's leftist politics.

Crowley wrote to Louis Wilkinson on November 4, glad Wilkinson's close friend John Cowper Powys was better (died 1963) and was "delighted" Louis was coming from November 17 to November 19. The room was booked, and his friend should note: "November 18th is my 47th Magical Birthday!" He was "beating all the big noises at chess" and "feeling fit as an *Amati*"[25] (famous violin, better than a fiddle). He wrote again on November 7; could Louis bring his favorite whisky: Royal Vat—and wrote again on the tenth that Evan Morgan was coming to lunch on Tuesday with Mrs. Wellington Koo and the

Countess of Kenmare: "If you know either woman, phone me description, if useful."[26]

On November 12, before Mrs. Wellington Koo and Lady Enid Kenmare arrived at Netherwood, Crowley noted David Curwen's sending the book "*The Secrets of the Kaula Circle* by that snotty mongrel weasel Elizabeth Sharpe."* Crowley spotted criminal libel on pages 48–49, saved perhaps by Sharpe's disclaimer on the title page, suggesting the book might be fictional.

## THE CHINESE AMBASSADRESS

Crowley informed Germer on Wednesday, November 21, about "a terribly hectic week entertaining the Chinese Ambassadress and the Countess of Kenmare." Held on Tuesday the twentieth, the lunch, he believed, "was a very successful function indeed."[27]

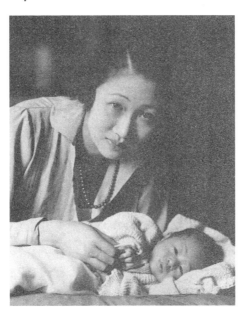

*Fig. 15.6. Madame Wellington Koo.*

---

*For the background to Curwen and Crowley and the question of tantric secrets, see *Brother Curwen, Brother Crowley* (ed. Henrik Bogdan). For the mystery of Curwen's sources solved, see Churton, *Aleister Crowley in India* (2019).

*Fig. 15.7. Lady Kenmare.*

The Chinese ambassador's third wife was fashionable social-ite Chinese-Indonesian Oei Hui-lan (1889–1992), First Lady of the Republic of China—in the late twenties when Wellington Koo acted as president. Her famous companion, strikingly photogenic Enid (née) Lindemann had wed fourth husband Valentine Browne, Viscount Castlerosse and Earl of Kenmare—Lord Beaverbrook's favorite gossip columnist—in 1943. He died within nine months. In Enid's daughter Patricia Cavendish's words: "Mummy's husbands tended to die rather prematurely." Lady Kenmare led an adventurous, eccentric life (she worked as a welder during the war), while bisexual son Rory Cameron (1913–1985) hosted aesthetically superior parties at La Fiorentina, Cap Ferrat, where Lady Kenmare would float about with a parrot on one shoulder and a hyrax on the other, surrounded by a host of poodles.

One would imagine, then, a fascinating occasion. However, despite Crowley's perception, and his note about Madame Koo's desire to impress upon Washington the need to unite China, and Crowley's assertion that China needed to restore ancient reverence for their own spiritual philosophies and ethical systems that had, after all, kept China at peace for over two thousand years, Madame Koo's reflection, years later, was one of disappointment, even disgust. According to Hui-Lan

Koo's second autobiography *No Feast Lasts Forever,* Lord Tredegar (who was absent on account of pleurisy) had led them to expect a seer able to will rain to fall precisely where wanted. Instead, "Whatever he had been in his prime, Enid and I found only a dirty old man, wallowing in drunkenness."[28] Lord Tredegar was not convinced. "He surpassed even the devil himself as a male witch when I knew him! I suggested it was just as well I hadn't known him then."

Lady Kenmare may have felt differently, as Crowley received a bottle of port from her on the twenty-seventh. Crowley sent Madame Wellington Koo a copy of *The Book of the Law*. She returned it, stating that while the book instructed its destruction after first reading lest dire consequences ensue, she was returning it in case he needed spare copies.

Crowley informed Germer on November 21 that McMurtry agreed to produce, with Jack Parsons, the new commentary on *AL;* Wilkinson agreed to edit on the eighteenth. Crowley then noted his view of Aldous Huxley's *The Perennial Philosophy* (1945): "I got the book by Huxley. I found it excessively stupid. If ever a man missed the way, it is he; and that in spite of our three days and three nights conference with hardly a break for sleep in Berlin, all those years ago."[29]

After Wilkinson left Hastings, Crowley wrote to Jane Wolfe in Hollywood, heading the letter "Private and Personal":

Dear Jane,

93

You are the only person whom I am continuing in this familiar style: 'cos I knows yer, pussonly! I hear too, that the Rituals were gabbled through. It will not do. An initiation should make a life-long impression; if it does not, it is not an initiation at all. Do impress this on Jack! . . . You remind me of "the bunch" in *Babbitt* [Sinclair Lewis's 1922 novel about middle-class vacuity]—also of Aimée Gouraud's "bunch" of which I was supposed to be an inner light. (I wasn't; but I let them play.) If I came out to the coast, I should join the Presbyterians after a week, to hang on to what fragments of sanity you-all leave me! . . . Jack's plan for the Lodge is not a bad one, if he will use the time of recess to get some idea of discipline, of dignity, of "reverence & godly fear" into the proceedings. . . . You do not need people of Jack's "own class & age," but serious, steady folk who will take the O.T.O. for what it is: an effort to reconstitute human society on a basis of Individual Freedom, Nobility, Generosity, and Wisdom. We don't want harum-scarum "good-times." *Why must my work be turned into a ribald jest and an excuse for scandal?*[30] [my italics]

On the twenty-third, 666 noted journalist, novelist, and publisher Miss Kay Dick's address as a place where he could find his short story "The Testament of Magdalen Blair" to send to "those women [Madame Koo and Lady Kenmare]." He also wrote that day to Louis Wilkinson about frustrations with Pasadena: "Yes, Parsons is my representative in California—always telling A.C. that so and so is living with so and so—and he doesn't know who any of 'em are!" Louis was requested to enter the O.T.O. so as to stand in as witness to David Curwen's initiation: "I may want you badly on Sunday as a witness re O.T.O. IX degree. Must fix you with Motto* &c."[31] More elucidation of Louis's role came on December 4: "I want you to be a IX° O.T.O. to witness the swearing in of a new [member] on Sunday. All you have to do is to stand by and *say not one word;* as soon as he has signed, depart and leave him with me. He goes back by the 5.5. (is it?) The point is: I don't want him pumping you about the Order. I'll explain further on Friday."[32]

Initiation at Netherwood at 12:12, December 16, didn't impress Bro. Curwen for, despite membership costs, no occult or institutional information came from tongue-tied Bro. Wilkinson!

On November 26, the name of Crowley biographer and literary executor-to-be John Symonds entered the frame. Crowley informed Louis of Symonds's desire to make his acquaintance. Lonesome Crowley wrote again to Louis on November 30. He'd sent Mrs. Koo *The Fun of the Fair* and Lady Kenmare *The City of God* but hadn't heard a word—

---

*Crowley to Wilkinson, December 6, 1945: "Re O.T.O. you ought to have a motto, one to express the deepest and truest will in you—to explain *why* you chose to come to this absurd planet, instead of staying comfortably home in your Star." December 15: "Gave L[ouis] U[mfraville] W[ilkinson the motto] 'Per Terram Ad Astra' [From Earth to the Stars] IX° whole theory of O.T.O."

"Frightened!" This was not polite. "The fact that no publisher or editor will look at anything of mine" belonged, he wrote, to the same problem, "that dates, mind you, from the start." Exceptions were William Collins, the Mandrake Press, Frank Harris, and Austin Harrison. "These were all due to personal contact. In the U.S.A. it was the same story. Ditto France and Germany." Was his work really all so bad or "so alien from the public taste?" Crowley explained: "This isn't wounded vanity, or pinched purse, or anything but plain bewilderment at the queerness of it all."[33] It is a most touching letter of the unjust rejection of a man's work, based on irrational fears.[34]

A week before Christmas, he heard from Professor Eliza Butler of Newnham College, Cambridge. Writing a book about magi, she wished to interview him. Crowley thought she would place him in the history of the great magi: a recognition whose absence he'd highlighted to Louis. A Christmas card from Robert Cecil in Washington, D.C., arrived on December 22.

At the end of the year, a memorandum attached to his diary noted that "if I should die I need someone to run the O.T.O. in England." Kenneth Grant was suggested as candidate.

# SIXTEEN

# Eddies of Obsidian

New Year's Day 1946 began on a high for Crowley: "If all days could be like this! Prof. Butler of Newnham came and talked (and made me talk) with such sympathy, consideration, and understanding that the day was a dream of joy!" Newnham College professor of German studies, Eliza Marian Butler (1885–1959) first heard of Crowley in 1937 when a guest of Baron Eduard von der Heydt (1882–1964), founder of the Monte Verità retreat, Ascona, Switzerland, haven for anarchists, nudists, Anthroposophists, Theosophists, lifestyle gurus, health and fitness therapists, Christian Scientists, Buddhists, magicians—and Theodor Reuss's O.T.O. supporters. Miss Butler herself was both fascinated by the

*Fig. 16.1. Professor Eliza M. Butler (1885–1959).*

occult and deeply suspicious of it. Studying in Bonn during the rise of
Nazism and related movements, she intuited kinship between German
magical traditions and mentalities enchanted by Nazism. According to
her autobiographical *Paper Boats* (1959), harsh winter weather on her
journey to Hastings depressed her spirits and increased a sense of fore-
boding. One senses the classic "demon Crowley" projection.

Arriving at the "nice, clean cheerful little place," she chatted with
Vernon until becoming aware of "a seedy figure in light tweed knicker-
bockers" who "materialized on the stairs." A grating voice uttered, "Do
what thou wilt shall be the whole of the law." "In that case, I'm for the
next train back," she thought to herself, but Crowley's traditional "And
a Happy New Year to you, Miss Butler" relieved anxiety.

Crowley's voice has been much remarked on. It was originally high-
pitched and mostly refined, but vocal nodules from years of wretching,
coughing, and asthmatic trauma had damaged it irreparably. *Reedy*
rhymes too easily with *seedy*. He was also painfully thin, skin texture
ravaged by climatic extremes, frustration, illness, and of course the poi-
son of heroin. Augustus John's startling portrait of him for *Olla* and
Frederik Mellinger's photographs show how the war and his illness had
whittled away his figure to skeletal features, though his eyes were alive.

Professor Butler observed that, while not too lined, he "seemed to
be disintegrating and to be surrounded by an aura of physical corrup-
tion. He had thick eye-glasses, a perpetual tear in the corner of one eye
and a flattish yellow face. Altogether he was more repulsive than I had
expected, and his voice was the ugliest thing about him: thin, fretful,
scratchy—a pedantic voice and a pretentious manner."

Crowley went upstairs to inject against asthma while Butler
lunched with Vernon Symonds. Crowley descended for coffee and
started "quoting grandiloquently from his own works," and what he
said in the "commonplace little dining-room" sounded to her "next door
to insane. Heads were turned and necks were craned all around us."
Vernon noticed nothing strange, but Butler couldn't understand how
"old Crow" ever got into Netherwood; she imagined the owners were
pressured into it, perhaps sinisterly!

Taking her life in her hands, she followed him to room number
thirteen where "the impress of his personality had combined with
the messiness of his habits" to generate "squalor, airlessness and [an]

indefinable atmosphere of pollution." The room contained a "battered writing table," half-empty bookshelves, a chaotic bed, cracked wash-basin, disturbing pictures of clashing colors, leering faces. 'All my own work,' said the magician, rather proudly, motioning me to a seat facing one of the worst of them. I surreptitiously crossed my fingers before I sat down, then I took my notebook and began to cross-examine the artist."

Feeling he might be tiring, she suggested freshening up at her billet in the town. Crowley, she felt, didn't like the idea of her going down to the sea, while she feared being stuck in Netherwood overnight and that he might stop the taxi from coming. The driver told her the roads were icy and The Ridge could get cut off; likely cause for Crowley's hesitancy. Buoyed by sea air, Professor Butler returned for tea and caviar in Crowley's room.

Butler wanted to compare Crowley with other magi in a kind of box-ticking exercise. Like others, distant travel in quest of knowledge followed formal initiation. He said he'd been recognized as a holy man in India and permitted to sacrifice a goat in sacred confines. Asked if he'd ever undergone a contest with another magician, he replied none in his era was up to it. Had he been tried by enemies? Agents of the "Black Lodge," Crowley confessed, had tried to thwart him, but were generally "dipsomaniacs or perverts." Crowley told her of the strange fires and things that happened during the Golden Dawn revolt in 1900 and in 1904 at Boleskine when Mathers magically attacked his ex-acolyte.

She was told by 666 that he'd taken up magick out of a "blue funk" about death and the vanity of ordinary achievement. He'd dabbled in black magic to find the elixir that would make life truly alive, but after initiation had kept rigorously to the white formula, attaining to its summit as prophet and priest of a new religion. Reading of his role's sublimity from *The Book of the Law,* he broke down in tears, whisper-ing to her, "It was a revelation of love." He told her magick was not *a* way of life, but *the* way of life.

She asked him about past lives, and Crowley revealed incidents recalled in meditations around the world. His memories of Cagliostro differed from accounts she had researched for her book. As he retired again to inject, she was left an account of what happened to his ene-mies (probably in *Thumbs Up!*). Returning next day to pay, Butler was annoyed he'd paid for her lunch and dinner already. As Antony

Clayton maintains, "Despite Crowley's gentlemanly behavior and full cooperation with the interview, Butler had little sympathy for him."[1] She would write of a "prolonged boredom mixed with repugnance and pity." While she'd initially intended a final chapter on Crowley for *The Myth of the Magus*—published in 1948—she decided against, writing to him in 1947: "You are too difficult for me to handle in that particular context." The only reference appeared in its conclusion: "Aleister Crowley claims to be the amanuensis of Aiwaz" and listed him with Cagliostro and Blavatsky, adding, "It may be objected that they do not speak so well nor so greatly as the magi of old, and the objection is just."[2]

A letter from Butler on January 4 was answered on the seventh, with Crowley insisting that while Blavatsky, Cagliostro, St. Germain, and others were important emissaries of truth, the quintessential magus communicated an epoch-defining Word—in his case *Thelema*—as the express will of the Masters for that aeon. In other words, a magus initiates an era. All else in his life was subsidiary to the great oath he'd taken to raise mankind. To her, doubtless, this was flaming ego—to him, an oath that cost him his ego; he was now something else.

Ever optimistic, he informed Germer on January 4 that Butler's intended study was the "most important thing that has come yet to the Great Work."[3]

He wrote warmly to Jane Wolfe at 51691 ¼ Fountain Ave. Los Angeles: "Dear Estai, . . . I always like to hear from you, if only for old sake's sake. I am very pleased with what you say about Jack. He does not keep me informed of his progress, but for that I am grateful to him. . . . Your method is the right one in every case. Drum Thelema into their skulls, and leave the rest to their Holy Guardian Angels."[4]

Troubled by printer problems delaying *Liber Aleph,* he complained of feeling "bloody lonely" to Louis Wilkinson on February 4, confessing *Liber Aleph* "began as a challenge to Freud, more or less."[5] Some relief came in a "chit" from Friedrich Lekve, thought lost to the Gestapo: "Hurrah!" cheered Crowley, learning that this O.T.O. survivor was safe with the British Military Government Detachment at Hildesheim.

On February 15 Crowley welcomed Frederic Mellinger, who gave him cigars "and a really gorgeous black leather locked portfolio—just what I've been hunting for for years." Mellinger captured the Beast at Netherwood in photographs.

"I had a glorious time last week with Mellinger," Crowley informed Saturnus. "It is hardly too much to say that he saved my life . . . the man I have been looking for for the last quarter of a century." Crowley "did astral" with Mellinger using a zechin of Pope Alexander VI. Mellinger envisioned people in the streets, dressed in the right period. He got his symbol wrong (guessing a lion), but the name came: "Alexander Borgia," though Crowley had that identity buried within him. Crowley regarded it an "excellent case" of attainment by way of vision.[6] Meanwhile, he lost his other divinatory coin, the gold mohur, and Mellinger crossed to Germany to find Lekve in Hildesheim, taking Crowley's *Liber AL* commentary with him.

Struggling with the commentary edit, Wilkinson asked Crowley to explain its theogony. Crowley tried: "Nuit is space, or all possible predicates. HADIT is any point of view. HERU-RA-HA (Ra-Hoor-Khuit plus Hoor-par-Kraat) is what I may call the dominant, the key in which all the music of life must be written for the next 2000 years or thereabouts." Ordinary intellectual logic does not apply "to the infinities." Discussion about level of understanding is based on the will to learn, he instructed. Louis reckoned it should be reduced to 25,000 words. Believing a small book lacked authority and value, Crowley proposed 80,000 words with an account of the book's appearance, adding: "I should like, if it were conceivable, to eliminate the idea of occultism," recognizing he was "shooting at a public who has probably never heard of me at all." His suggested title: *The Philosophy of Thelema*.[7] In another letter to Wilkinson of March 21, he emphasized the commentary was written twenty-five years ago "and in a peculiarly exalted state of mind which I can never regain; which is why I never dared touch it. Afraid even to read it."[8]

Fate smiled. On March 11, a "nice old man came to tend the garden—and found my gold Muhur!!!!" On March 15 Crowley told Wilkinson that C. E. M. Joad was expected the next day: "I wonder how he'll be after ten years since I last saw him."[9] He also remarked on Dion Fortune's recent death in Glastonbury: "There was a *very* secret understanding by which she acknowledged my authority; it is now a question of picking up her following . . . 50 to 100 people at a guess. Very difficult to know what to do." Concerning Wilkinson's new book

*Fig. 16.2. A.C. at Netherwood. (Courtesy of the Warburg Institute, London, and Ordo Templi Orientis).*

*Forth, Beast!:* "Joad says you never sent him proofs for approval. . . . So much to do—so little done, as [Cecil] Rhodes said."

Crowley wrote to Augustus John on the twenty-sixth, asking for "a sketch of me" for *Olla*. John obliged with enthusiasm. As if Wilkinson wasn't doing enough, 666 asked him on March 27 if he'd care "to glance through *OLLA*." Poems might be cut or replaced: "do what one will, one is always liable to forget something that sticks out seven miles." For example, he'd realized there were no poems on nature's beauty, which was at one time "my strong suit."[10]

*Fig. 16.3.* Olla *frontispiece by Augustus John. (Courtesy of Ordo Templi Orientis, and 100th Monkey Press)*

Well looked after, Vernon came up after supper on April 1 for a cigar, a drink of rum, and a consultation about *Olla*. The next day Frieda made four sketches (with *Olla*'s dust cover in mind): two Crowley considered nearly right, but not quite; two were "bloody awful." The next day he read his beautiful poem, "The Sevenfold Sacrament" (from *Equinox* III.I and the *English Review*, November 1911), which begins:

> In eddies of obsidian,
> At my feet the river ran
> Between me and the poppy-prankt
> Isle, with tangled roots embanked,
> Where seven sister poplars stood
> Like the seven Spirits of God.

It elicited tears.

*Fig. 16.4.* Olla *dust cover, by Frieda Harris.*
*(Courtesy of Ordo Templi Orientis, and 100th Monkey Press)*

He wrote to Jane Wolfe on April 3 about Jack:

In my judgment the only real trouble with him is his youth, and the flightiness which always goes with youth when they are made of good stuff, because their enthusiasms reach very deep and so are liable to carry them away for the moment. . . . [Louis Wilkinson] has been here for the weekend forcing me to discuss the infernal Commentary. [His inability to face it for so long was] due to my intense dissatisfaction with my work. You see I intended to put in a Qabalistic appendix; in fact the only reason for getting Mudd over to Sicily in the unluckiest hour of my life, was for this purpose, and of course he never did a stroke of work on it, so you can imagine that I am three parts dead.[11]

But Crowley *was* getting good notices. On April 4 he saw "Aleister Crowley Poet and Mystic" by F. H. Amphlett-Micklewright in the *Occult Review* and was astonished the article's author delineated a theme that unified his existence and work. Wilkinson's autobiographical novel *Forth, Beast!* (Faber & Faber) appeared next day, including a character based on Crowley and nearly twenty references to him, including several quotes.

Crowley asked Wilkinson on April 10 not to pull his punches in his essay on *AL,* as "Stephensen did, making a flop [P. R. Stephensen, *The Legend of Aleister Crowley*]. Trying to be judicial. And looked half-hearted. . . . We are in a position when the whole world may blow up like a Chinese cracker. The stablest institutions are the most likely to go first."[12]

Clinging to him like lichen, Wilkinson was the sole friend left for whom Crowley really felt intellectual union and respect. Picking up on characterizations in *Forth, Beast!* (a line from Chaucer, incidentally) on April 17, Crowley explained why he believed so many of his friends were ruined the moment they surrendered to marrying particular women:

What I dislike is the feeling that my friends by marrying have surrendered an essential portion of their personality. Before I met you my best friend was probably Fuller. He had not been married more than a year before the whole thing was broken up. When I came back from the States I found Eckenstein had married, and I never saw him again. I do not think there is any possible question of morbid attraction; I think I feel that the man is no longer worthy to be my friend, that he is not a complete man. Was Josepha [a character in *Forth, Beast!*] that red-headed woman I met you with on Coney Island? But you always kept these wives in the background; I do not think they really did vampirize you too seriously. Was the second one the girl I met when you had rooms over Regent's Park? . . . these women tend to bore me, and I have a strong feeling that they are equally bound to bore other people. Is this a personal idiosyncrasy, dependent on my own attitude to women? Somehow I don't think so. Anyhow Josepha puzzles me, because the first five minutes that I met her I realized that she was raving mad, and that you failed to see it baffled me. Don't you remember that she got a complex immediately about me, and started to put her foot down and all the rest of it, so it was perfectly clear to her at any rate that I saw through her. I think that you escaped my condemnation because you always treated your wives as mistresses; the idea of the ball and chain gets my goat buddy.[13]

His other respected friend was Lady Harris, who wrote to him on April 23 from the Castle Hotel, Brecon, South Wales, informing him of how a Mr. Edwards of the South Kensington Museum admired the tarot cards, and how *The Book of Thoth* could be supplied to the museum. She was moving out of Rolling Stone Orchard and asked him to send her a poem of his she liked.

## BABALON NOW!

Unsettling news from California concerning Jack Parsons caused initial hesitancy. He wrote to Germer on April 17: "I do not know much about Jack's illumination—when I say I expect it will 'blow over' I think that is sufficient criticism."[14]

It didn't blow over.

Jack thought his erotic fantasies represented more than natural sexual appetite. A favorite short story was Jack Williamson's science fantasy "Darker than You Think" (1940), containing themes of erotic domination, perhaps culturally rooted in Rider Haggard's *She,* but more subversive. Parsons linked his erotic "witchcraft" ideals to Crowley's figure of "Babalon." Babalon appears in *The Vision and the Voice* in his twelfth Aethyr reinterpretation of Revelation 17:4 as source of "abominations and filthiness" that fill a charioteer's ruddy cup. The cup's blood, however, rather than Revelation's "blood of the saints" is presented as wine of compassion. Revelation's drunken harlot, mother of whoredom, reflected "Babylon," Christian metaphor for Rome and the "god of this world." Crowley, however, following Anna Kingsford's *Clothed with the Sun* (1889), saw this as a visionary error, a misinterpretation of the dual nature of female deity. Thus was born "Babalon," female gnostic deity akin to "Barbelo," the late antique Sethian Gnostic "Divine Wisdom" figure (see my *Gnostic Mysteries of Sex*). All this was grist to Parsons's mill of latent and moving desires. As in postsixties feminism, words like *dyke* and *witch* were transgressively recast as proud escutcheons of womanhood, Parsons presciently grasping the subversive nature of the Thelemic revelation, but as an *overwhelming* apprehension.

Partly inspired by *Liber OZ,* Parsons in 1946 wrote *Freedom Is a Two-Edged Sword,* calling for women to seize the sword of spiritual, sexual, and political liberation, a "militantly empowered feminist witchcraft," as Erik Davis calls it.[15] Prescient and antipatriarchal, its militancy is striking: "Come back, woman, come back to us again! . . . Witch woman, out of the ashes of the stake, rise again! . . . Be cunning, oh woman; be wise, be subtle, be merciless." Envisioning a new woman, Parsons sees Babalon as counterpoise to the Aeon of Horus's explosive violence.

Parsons shared his convictions with sci-fi pulp author Lafayatte Ronald Hubbard (1911–1986), who likewise linked idealized spiritual and sci-fi fantasies in quest of a compelling postwar order.

On January 4, 1946, Parsons began what he'd call the "Babalon Working," initially operating with Hubbard as "scribe": invocations from Crowley's magical writings, combined with magical masturbation (VIII°) heavily inspired by Crowley's Algerian desert experiences that informed his *Vision and the Voice*—all aimed at attracting an "elemental" to assist in the earthly manifestation of Babalon herself. In other words, Parsons had taken on himself a role analogous to Crowley's in 1904 of inaugurating a revolution in the world.

On January 19 the remarkable Marjorie Cameron (1922–1995) arrived at 1003. Recently discharged from the U.S. Navy, she immediately "clicked" with Jack. Jack believed her the "elemental" result of rituals undertaken with Hubbard: sent by the Gods. Abed for a fortnight, convincing her he had a mission for the world, Parsons practiced what he knew of the IX° with Marjorie, hoping to incarnate the goddess on earth. Cameron left for New York on February 27 to see photographer boyfriend Napoleon. Next day, Parsons went alone into the Mojave Desert (possibly to a site of petroglyphs sacred to the Cojos Indians) and ritually invoked Babalon. He believed himself enveloped by the goddess's presence, commanding him to write "Liber 49," mooted as *Liber AL*'s fourth chapter, with content derived from O.T.O. material but outside its internal order, for *Liber AL* is emphatic that its three chapters suffer no addition. Parsons was convinced he must generate a magical "child" of indeterminate kind.

In March, with Hubbard's return, further invocations followed,

*Fig. 16.5. Marjorie Cameron.*
*(Courtesy of the Cameron Parsons Foundation,*
*Santa Monica, California)*

inspired by "Liber 49." Hubbard acted as seer, voicing the will of Babalon, as Parsons noted down instructions.

On March 6 Parsons wrote to an incredulous Crowley:

> I am under command of extreme secrecy. I have had the most impor-
> tant and devastating experience of my life between February 2nd and
> March 4th. I believe it was the result of the 9th working with the girl
> [Cameron] who answered my elemental summons. (She is now in
> New York.) I have been in direct touch with One, who is most Holy
> and Beautiful, mentioned in *The Book of the Law*. I cannot write
> the name at present. First instructions were received direct, further
> through Ron acting as seer. I have followed them to the letter. There
> was a desire for incarnation. I was the agency chosen to assist the
> birth, which is now accomplished. I do not yet know the vehicle,
> but it will come to me, bringing a secret sign I know. . . . Then it will
> be loosed on the world. . . . A manuscript is prepared, which will be
> released to the proper persons at the right time. . . .

Crowley responded carefully, urging Eliphas Lévi's advice that "the love of the Magus for such things [elementals; obsession with female "sirens'] is insensate and may destroy him." Parsons ignored Crowley's safeguards for testing "revelations," placing faith in Hubbard's and his own imaginations. On April 19, Crowley wrote to Parsons again: "You have got me completely puzzled by your remarks about the elemental—the danger of discussing or copying anything. I thought I had a most morbid imagination, as good as any man's, but it seems I have not. I cannot form the slightest idea of what you can possibly mean." He *did* have an idea: his own novel *Moonchild* (1929) suggested such possibilities—as fiction. He wrote as much to Germer, having received an "appalling letter from Louis [Culling] about Jack" on May 20: "Apparently he, or Hubbard, or some-body, is producing a Moonchild. I get fairly frantic when I contemplate the idiocy of these goats." Crowley suspected a swindle, a suspicion soon confirmed. Hubbard had already weaned Betty into amorous embrace, a liberty accepted by Parsons according to his metafeminist Babalonian principles, and one whose portents he failed to see. Perhaps Crowley's arch treatment of Smith as incarnate "God" of unknown origin had tipped Jack's rocket-propelled imagination too far. Some commentators today see beyond Parsons's magical ill-discipline to a powerful social vision with legitimate meaning. As Erik Davis puts it, "we might locate his 'Woman Girt with a Sword' at the halfway point between Crowley's Babalon and the independent goddess of later popular witchcraft. In Abrahamsson's words, 'Parsons reformulated what Crowley had already defined,' drawing the Babalon current away from Crowley's solar-phallic fixations and releasing it into a post-patriarchal or proto-feminist frame that amplified the martial element."[16]

Meanwhile "back on Planet Earth," as Woody Allen might say, Crowley attended a Netherwood lecture given by former atheist C. E. M. Joad. Crowley recognized its wit but was bored by the birth control theme. Had Joad "cashed in on God?" Crowley asked. "I have a right to change my mind," answered Joad. Crowley riposted: "But mild language for such a tremendous spiritual upheaval. *He*: 'Oh well, I can't issue a writ: he sent me the proofs.' Then we discussed other things."

Writing to Wilkinson on April 24, Crowley was sorry his friend lacked math as the "Author of this book [*AL*] is in possession of knowledge and power beyond anything with which we are familiar." He wanted Wilkinson's introduction to assert intelligences existed not directly accessible to the senses, as science proved there were energies inaccessible to ordinary sense. Crowley saw *AL* validated by repeated intelligent patterns, which he could neither have constructed nor attempted (in ordinary conditions). That in certain rare circumstances, "communication between human beings and such intelligences is possible" was the text's most significant claim. Whether such intelligence was incarnate or discarnate, was irrelevant. Wilkinson's task was to attract serious investigators to the book's claims, demonstrating absolute openness to "investigation of the facts alleged. But it must always be matter of fact, never of rhetoric."[17] Crowley himself had no doubt of the truthfulness of the claims and was confident unprejudiced science would support them. Crowley never "tested" Aiwass *at the time*. Such would have entailed testing *himself* at the time. While treating it initially with disdain, internal features, incrementally accrued, and found meaningful long after he took it down made its authority impossible for him to contradict, despite personal resistance to elements of its message and incomprehension of certain passages.

A wire from *Lilliput* magazine arrived on May Day requesting an interview for an article on magic. Mr. John Symonds duly arrived on Friday, May 3, with "Robert Cecil's pal" astrologer Rupert Gleadow. The meeting opened Symonds's biography *The Great Beast* (1951). Gleadow followed up with a letter on the seventh. Discussing prophesied apocalypses through history, Crowley asserted the world's "destruction by fire" in April 1904; "that is, according to the initiated doctrine." Crowley recounted meeting *Lilliput*'s assistant editor to Wilkinson on May 7: "we had a very pleasant day."[18] One thing that astonished the Beast was that while both young men were well educated, they did not understand Crowley's references to Browning's poem, "James Lee's Wife." Crowley was incredulous: *Was it possible, Browning was no longer taught?* He mentioned this because one thing he hoped Wilkinson would achieve as editor of *AL* was to overcome Crowley's reputation for "obscurity": difficult if young educated people didn't even know Browning's "famous poem"! He was also concerned at Wilkinson writing an introduction of only 2,000 words. Considering it inadequate and likely swamped by the commentary, he made a fascinating admission: "Of course there is perhaps a certain degree of misunderstanding on my part, due to the fact I have such an antagonism to the commentary itself. My feeling about the whole thing is that I wish none of it had ever happened. I know this sounds absurd; but I have an absolutely passionate feeling of wanting to suppress myself. I cannot imagine why it should be so deep-seated, but there it is." He wanted it clear that "the most important person" in the commentary was Louis, not himself, even if that meant putting his introduction in extra-large type! If Wilkinson didn't accomplish this he felt the book would "pass totally unnoticed as one of A.C.'s cranky notions."

Moving on to Jack: "I do not know what is happening to Jack Parsons, he seems in a peculiar state and it is about time I heard from him." A postscript urged Louis to get April's *Occult Review* from publishers William Rider at 68 Fleet Street—"best thing that's happened to us in 100 years."[19]

On May 11, he played seven chess games at the Argosy Café, Parkhurst Road, against Bexhill. He also had letters from Mildred and Roy Burlingame, who were supposed to be running Agape Lodge during Parsons's peculiar operations.

Replying to Germer about Canadian Theosophist and Crowley

admirer Alexander Watt, he said he'd "been in communication with him vaguely for some time, and asked him to get in touch with you as he is using the same symbols and other means of identification [in his Theosophical Lodge] as we do. I think he is quite a good man from the little I know, so I hope you will work him into our general system. . . . I do not understand all this business about Jack. I have not heard from him for quite a long while, but in his last letter he promised to send me a full account of his latest cavortings. . . . I do not understand at all about Jack; but it does not look too good. However, I think that your personal presence may make a great deal of difference. Get with McMurtry and descend on the Lodge!" Germer should work with Grady and Frederik Mellinger; they'd make a good team. "California does harm to our movement."

Germer was still going on about Crowley's attitude to Germans. Crowley insisted he didn't want to see a German sentry outside Trinity, Cambridge! As for World War I, "objectively, Britain might have been better governed by the Hohenzollerns, that is if I were neutral, but I was not a neutral, I was an Englishman, and I naturally wanted to run my own show."[20]

Having received "appalling" news of Jack from Louis Culling on the twentieth, he cabled Germer, who received the following on May 22:

SUSPECT RON PLAYING CONFIDENCE TRICK JACK EVIDENTLY WEAK FOOL OBVIOUS VICTIM PROWLING SWINDLERS OLLA PROCEEDING RAPIDLY. CROWLEY[21]

Betty and Hubbard fled with $10,000 of Parsons's money, with which they bought a yacht. Parsons tracked them to Florida. Hubbard would marry Sara Northrup, and Parsons would quit the O.T.O. and adopt the title "Belarion Armiluss Al Dajjal AntiChrist."

And Vernon Symonds could be contacted for two months from June, "c/o Court Players, South Parade Pier, Southsea": an altogether more modest proposal.

Crowley could only equate the disappointed promise of Jack with Charles Stansfeld Jones and Victor Neuburg, and did so in a letter to Germer of May 31: Stansfeld Jones rushed his "Master of the Temple" grade and got a "revelation" that produced nothing of worth. Neuburg fell "under the influence of an old vampire." "It seems to me on the information of our brethren in California that (if we may assume that to be accurate) Frater 210 has committed both these errors. He has got a miraculous illumination which rimes with nothing, and has apparently lost all personal independence."[22]

On June 6 the proofs of *Olla* arrived, and bad news about Vernon in Southsea: "the whole place is upset, Vernon having got into the clutches of a con man, and Johnnie and Sylvia have asked me to go to the rescue."[23] On the tenth David Curwen arrived with one Barbara Kindred: "lovely girl. Wish I were 70 again!" Consulting the I Ching: "is she for anything in his life?" he concluded, "Avoid marriage." He wrote to Miss Kindred on the twelfth after another visit.

Louis was informed on June 13 of the death of Mr. Kirk of the Chess Club: "I knew him but slightly, yet I feel that I have lost a dear friend. A man of infinite charm." Crowley had procured new glasses, but he still could hardly read. He needed Mr. Affleck Greeves, oculist of Wimpole Street.[24]

On June 18, John Symonds ingratiated himself, saying he "adored" *Magick without Tears,* while genuine aficionado Lady Harris came and "talked all day." Crowley wrote to W. B. Crow: "Before closing I ought to tell you that certain persons in London are proposing to form a Society for the study of my work; they are to deal rather with the poetic than with the

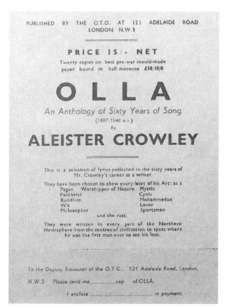

*Fig. 16.6. Prospectus for* Olla. *(Courtesy of Ordo Templi Orientis, and 100th Monkey Press)*

Magical side of it. In this way it will be possible to get a much greater number of people interested, and it may be that 'those who come to scoff remain to pray.'" Apparently, Curwen wanted to contact the more intelligent of Crow's followers in London. Yorke added to this a note about Curwen: "A furrier in London. He had been a member of the Bhairavi Branch of Hindu Tantrites who practiced an oriental variant of IX° OTO. He corresponded with A.C. on the subject and I met him. A strange character."[25] Crowley also wrote to Germer on June 18, with a copy for Capt. G. L. McMurtry, 1661 Sacramento Street, Apt. 3, San Francisco: "you fail to make my flesh creep with yours of June 12. It is inconceivable after all these years, but you seem to fail to understand how Magick works. The safeguards are *automatic*. . . . You seem to reproach me for having trusted Frater 210 as deeply as I did; but I did this on purpose in accordance with an ancient and well-known magical formula. . . . In our case the deeper I trust a man the deeper he is committed to the appropriate penalties should he betray that trust [e.g., schizophrenia; qliphoth of Kether].[26]

Local doctor McGowan called on the nineteenth to take Crowley's pulse: "slightly quicker than last September." Two days later, Barbara Kindred telephoned to arrange a visit on the twenty-third. She came at 12:25 and . . . "Yes: and I am left rather wondering."

Vernon was back, talking of starting a beauty parlor. Crowley's verdict: "Beauty Parlour—in this squalor! ¾ mad!" Meanwhile, John Symonds began questioning Crowley, who confessed: "The mainspring of my life is my Path in the Order of A∴A∴ to devote myself wholly to the uplifting of the human race."[27] Symonds asked if he was anti-Semitic. Crowley replied: "Semite." "I am far from 'anti'—ask the Anglo Palestinian Society (here last week) about our long friendly discussions. . . . Mellinger . . . my head man in Germany is a Jew. . . . When a minority is strong enough to make trouble, it always does so."[28] Crowley believed attitudes to Jews were transformed in his lifetime—the Russian Revolution changed everything. After that, Jews were everywhere regarded as communists.

On June 27, Crowley went to London for a 2 p.m. appointment with celebrated ophthalmic surgeon Reginald Affleck Greeves (1878–1966) at 23 Wimpole Street. The expert declared pipe smoking a culprit. Relieved it was curable, Crowley was sad because tobacco was a lifelong friend. He tried to go slowly, but problems on the thirtieth convinced him of strictness: "4 pipes and several puffs," and considered "ceremonial renunciation." The day before he'd written to Louis: "If in Copenhagen please call GRUNDDAL SJALLUNG [see page 104] (Magister) Our GM [Grand Master] there, Tell him of our great revival, and ask him to get in touch with me. He may have died, or moved . . . I'm all nerves without my pipe."[29]

Invited to Sunday lunch with artist Augustus John on July 14, he was driven by car early to 33 Tite Street, Chelsea. He examined John's horoscope: "The first time (I think) we have had all the bars down. I felt pure Love. He asked me to pose again, and will come here to do it. A glorious sketch; he will get Chiswick Press to collotype it himself." His problems with blindness eased and allowed a half pipe on the twenty-first with abstinence ending at noon on the thirty-first.

Surprisingly, Crowley informed Louis about Jack on July 27: "the Parsons mess is too complex for letters. But he is penitent, and will, I'm sure, make good."[30] On August 12, John Symonds offered his services as literary agent and secretary. On August 17 Crowley was disappointed to hear Barbara Kindred couldn't come and returned one pound, leaving him asking, "Why?"

A new lady appeared on September 2 by way of letter: Jacintha Laura M. Buddicom of Little Bogey, 8 Pond Place, SW3, childhood friend of George Orwell. Crowley also enjoyed a "pleasant visit" from artist Clement Cowles (1894–1981) and "Sylvia." John Symonds wrote about *Olla* proofs. Crowley mentioned Symonds's visiting in a letter to Louis of September 3, adding: "I have certainly been on the edge of insanity." He wrote of "a cosy corner to die in. . . . A visit to me here is like seven rest cures, so choose your own date. . . . How am I? Dunno. Have just sent for D[octo]r. But I have certainly been on the edge of insanity. Mixing up the morning with the evening. I am really worried about my future. . . . *Olla* is going on well, if only we can get some more paper. I don't know where I am. A day or so with you would do me worlds of good. Asking pardon for so stupid a letter. Yours Aleister"[31]

He spoke of McMurtry to Germer on September 9: "He is a fine youth and when the time comes he will be able to discharge his responsibilities with swinging success. . . . The question of Jack remains very difficult. Grady's report [on Agape Lodge] is almost entirely favourable and yours of the proceeding is apparently very different."[32]

Frederic Mellinger was in Netherwood again, but this time Crowley was finding his intensity a "strain," felt also by Frieda* when she arrived on the nineteenth.

October saw letters from Evan Morgan and Podmore and Sadler in Sutton Coldfield, the latter astounding Crowley by his "record-breaking for meanness and impudence!" (October 8). On the tenth he was writing via Jane Wolfe to Germer: "Everything here is in a complete muddle; I have lost my list of addresses, including yours, and all I can do is to ask Jane Wolfe to get this to you somehow. Forgive this, but I am really at the last gasp."[33] A little relief was afforded on the twenty-sixth when Miss Buddicom wrote to say she'd edit *Magick without Tears* and suggested a Letter on "Geomancy." Nevertheless, Crowley was feeling confused, writing to Wilkinson in November that "I do not seem to know what to do with myself," and that having booked rooms for Wilkinson's next visit on December 17: "I think that the planet is finished from what Einstein says."[34]

On December 11, Crowley suffered: "Worse night I can remember. Began with diarrhea then insomnia then one of the worst dozen nightmares of my life: mostly out of the Apocalypse. *And both* my watches stopped at 2:30 A.M.!!!"

Christmas cards from Robert and Kate Cecil arrived on Christmas Eve as Crowley suffered from constant fatigue.

---

*This is perhaps an appropriate moment to note that Frieda's death is often mistakenly recorded as May 11, 1962. Thanks to Sigurd Bune's efforts we may learn that some years after her husband's death, Frieda moved to a houseboat on the lake at Srinagar, Kashmir, where she died, aged 85, on November 5, 1962. She was buried at the Christian cemetery at the Sheikh Bagh on the banks of the Jhelum River, which Crowley had crossed sixty years before. Eileen Hewson FRGS's *Graveyards in Kashmir, India* (Kabristan Archives, 2008) mentions her grave as Grave 58, New Plot Central, Srinagar Cemetery, with the inscription:

MARGUERITE FRIEDA HARRIS died November 5th 1962.
Fear no more the heat
Of the sun
The winter's furious
Rages.
LADY FRIEDA HARRIS died aged 86 years.

In fact, she was 85, having been born on August 13, 1877 (Birth Registers). The verse seems inspired by Shakespeare's *Cymbeline,* Act IV, Scene II; Before the cave. Song: "Fear no more the heat o'the sun, Nor the furious winter's rages."

# SEVENTEEN

# The Universe

A new year visit from Frieda brought some ease, as did reading Cyril Connelly's *Unquiet Grave* (1944), a self-deprecating journey through life inspired by Palinurus's soul's journey through the underworld after falling from Aeneas's ship in the *Aeneid:* at least the Beast wasn't alone in the throes of half life.

Paranoia was Germer's almost constant companion, a state Crowley addressed on January 14, 1947:

> My mind is now quite at rest, or would be if only I could get you to cut out this infernal nonsense about Black Magicians and Evil currents, and all that.
>
> What on earth is the good of belonging to the Great Order if it does not automatically protect you from anything of the kind? So do please cut it out.
>
> I had much better stop here or I shall drop into such German as I remember from Hanni Jaeger's conversation: it was very useful German, but it was not polite![1]

He wrote a Valentine's Day letter to Sascha. While selling "admirably," there were no reviews yet of *Olla.* "You have no idea how dull and dismal the whole country is . . . the best chance of making things work is for this crew of imbecile swine [Labor government] to [*illegible;* resign?]; a new general election is possible, even probable; the news is indescribable. . . . If only Winston were 20 years younger. But he isn't! . . . Meanwhile I'll be in the lounge (which happens to be empty)."[2]

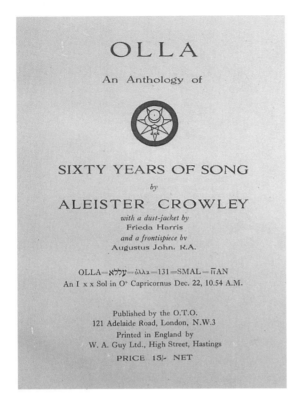

*Fig. 17.1.* Olla *title page.*
*(Courtesy of Ordo Templi*
*Orientis, and*
*100th Monkey Press)*

*Liber Aleph* was now ready for printers, whose work was "messed up" by electricity cuts.

On February 20 Frieda wrote on Sesame Club–headed notepaper, inquiring after his health and describing how son Jack admired *The Book of Thoth*'s artwork, but his wife criticized the text, which infuriated Frieda. Could Crowley "write them an erudite and sarcastic letter, shattering their criticisms?"

March weather was terrible, with trees crashing everywhere. Wilkinson was invited to come and "enjoy the rapture of WHITE!"[3] As heavy snows melted, half of England, Crowley informed Germer, was flooded; he nearly died. Waking up to find his syringe clogged he went back to bed and sent his Holy Guardian Angel to see about lunch, so frightening his hostess she dispatched a man in heavy snow to fetch his helper to put him in bed with a hot-water bottle. The helper cleaned the syringe and trudged over a mile in heavy snow to the doctor, who came to find Crowley's heart only just ticking. An injection brought him round in two minutes. Half an hour later, he'd have been dead. "Moral: trust your H.G.A."[4] "H.G.A." was explained to Germer in a letter of April 10: "The Holy Guardian Angel is an individual, just as you and I are. But he lives in four dimensions just as we do in three. (A very rough summary. He belongs to a different *order* of Nature.) Don't confuse with the 'Higher Self' as such, which are merely parts of one's own being. Deep love to you and Sascha."[5]

James Laver (1899–1975), Keeper of the Victoria & Albert Museum, came on March 27: "Most delightful interview, A.C. at his best. Sold him a Tarot 12 guineas." Laver left a record.[6] Being interested in whether there was a rationalistic explanation for magic, Laver asked if investigations of telepathy offered a rational road; Crowley said all his work was rationalistic. Laver suggested Blake's idea: to do the trick, take imagination to the point of vision. Laver obviously realized magick was something we "do to ourselves," commented Crowley, but it was wiser to think of particpants in the process as separate beings lest one's ego become inflamed, inviting obsession, imagining one was personally important in the deliberations of eternity (thinking of Parsons?). Laver compared mysticism to occultism. Crowley accepted mysticism was the faster road, but the path of occultism was "not so steep."

Laver also asked about Mathers and the Golden Dawn. Crowley confessed he was rather "bluffing" in his early encounter with the Order, but that he had respect for Mathers. He admired Dion Fortune, who had the courage to admit what she owed to Crowley. Asked about Hitler, Crowley explained Martha Küntzel's claim to have acquainted

*Fig. 17.2. James Laver (1899–1975).*

Hitler with *The Book of the Law,* but Hitler misunderstood it, bringing disaster onto himself and all he did. Crowley showed Laver his I Ching "rods," warning Laver not to touch them; they were full of his "emanations," and highly personal. Laver concluded Crowley a likely sometime blackmailer, and "fraud," but left open the question whether he was *only* a fraud. Crowley wrote to Wilkinson on March 28: "James Laver came yesterday. . . . One of the most delightful afternoons I've spent in years. I hope he felt the same. . . . Lovingly Yours, Aleister."[7]

The printer promised first proofs of *Aleph* before May's end. His own end was again on his mind when he wrote to Dr. Charnock-Smith on March 29: "I have reserves of 2 1/4 gr[ains]. To keep up the routine. I need 10 gr. From your kindness. . . ." He was short of sleeping tablets "(Veronal or Dial Ciba—either suits me) and the Tab. Apen [?] P.D. & Co. The constant failure of supplies to reach me on the due day is very much on my nerves; if it were not that I should hate to hurt Dr. Brown Thomson's feelings, I think I should try to make another arrangement. Yours sincerely, Aleister Crowley." Audrey E. Lagg replied: "Dr. Charnock Smith is ill, & Dr. Magowan will not be here until to night. I have sent the heroin & the Tab aper by bearer, and have neither Veronal or Dial."[8]

"Was ill yesterday," he informed Wilkinson on April 19: "God knows why. Better today. Three days ago I made a date with my lawyer [to make a will] for next Monday 3 P.M. Must back to bed."[9] On the twenty-fifth he wrote to Fitzgerald about his asthma: "I still have no trouble with it, but other matters rather bother me, and this frightful winter has decidedly done me down. . . . In fact on March 8th the doctor arrived just in time to save my life. Had he been twenty minutes later he would probably have found me dead." It was accidental: the heat was turned off when he was half-dressed and half-asleep. They forgot to turn it on and found him three parts frozen.[10]

He also sent encouraging news to Germer that day: "I am very much better now all round, especially this morning when John Symonds sent me a copy of the Spring *Occult Review,* which has a 3½ page review of *Olla* done with astonishingly deep insight and breadth of comprehension. . . . I fear it is quite out of the question for me to come to the U.S.A. I am so feeble that a ¼ mile walk is about my limit. . . . I am in fairly constant need of attention."[11] Germer was on again about

Germans; Crowley wrote on May 2: "P.S. Wherever did you get the crazy idea that I hated Germans? Germans have done more to shape my life than all of the rest of the nations put together! Eckenstein, Fraulein Sprengel, Theodor Reuss, Otto and Martha, and now you. You seem to be unaware how much I look up to you! I have always said that you were miles ahead of me spiritually. You don't express this in books, etc. because that job was given me by the Masters. But on purely personal grounds, you come first. My one aversion was the arrogance of the Prussian Officer class: e.g., Von Papen."

Crowley hoped Germer would come. Robert Cecil might help; England wouldn't turn away anyone with dollars to spend now![12]

May 13: "Deirdre phones!!!!!!!!! Ataturk all right. I praise the Gods." He wrote to Fitzgerald: "A miracle has just happened. The Girl Pat and Aleister Ataturk whom I had long since given up for dead are in London! She phoned me last night. I am delirious with joy. They come here Thursday."[13]

Son Aleister came to Netherwood with Pat on the fifteenth. He told Germer about it on May 23: "Been obliged to make a will." His old one was overturned because Pat before the war had the crazy notion of becoming a doctor and went to Basle, dodging the war in France, Italy, Germany, Italy, Yugoslavia, Cairo. She got to Jerusalem in '41 and came down from "last Thursday till Saturday." His "kid was of a very curious character which I have not had time to study properly."[14]

Gerald Gardner (1884–1964), founder of modern witchcraft, arrived on May 27, for the first time. As is well known, Gardner's early writings about Wicca were greatly enhanced by Crowleyan ideas and quotations from The Book of the Law, many of which Doreen Valiente expunged or turned into paraphrases, so the debt is not as obvious now as in earlier days. Crowley authorized Gardner to set up an O.T.O. camp, but Gardner never attempted to establish it.

On June 6, new publisher John Bunting visited: "I felt an immediate attraction for him. . . ." Bunting could've helped with distribution problems that had dogged Crowley's efforts for years. He informed Symonds of their "very extended business talks together" on June 10.[15]

Things seemed to be looking up. He told Germer on June 15: "Miss Buddicombe [sic]—to whom all praise!—has completed the rearrangement of the 'letters' of *Magick without Tears*. There are 75 in all. . . . It has been very nice having Louis Wilkinson all week with a friend but on other hand rather exhausting." Crowley defined magic's relation to mysticism: the former is for getting in touch with individuals on a higher plane than ours; the latter is raising ourselves to their level.[16] Impressive.

Now famous for his Pulitzer-winning biography of Oscar Wilde (1988), young Richard David Ellman arrived on June 25 for a long talk about "[the Golden Dawn] smash, Mathers, Yeats etc." Ellman's account of his overnight stay was not complimentary. Ellman wouldn't have found Crowley shared his great admiration for Yeats, nor would he have savored Crowley's story of Yeats's attempt to bewitch him through black magic and Althea Gyles. Had Ellman known of Yeats's covert attempts to scuttle Crowley's boat in New York in 1914 to 1915 he might have adjusted his prejudice (see Churton, *Aleister Crowley in America*), but one doubts it. James Laver came again that week for "delightful talks— and one hell of a storm!"

Crowley mentioned Ellman, ever optimistically, in a letter to Germer of June 30 he hoped would "catch him" before Germer left New York: "I notice that quite a number of the younger men are beginning to take notice of me. In particular, I had a two days visit from an American named Richard David Ellman on the 25th and 26th." He wanted to dig out of him details of the G∴D∴ affair, "though he could have got it from the *Equinox*." "Looks like a Minerval camp in the summer if plans go OK [a reference to Gerald Gardner]."[17]

Crowley wrote to John Bunting on July 2 about *Magick without Tears*.*

---

*It appears from a reminiscence that Bunting knew Crowley through his publisher father, with whom Crowley was apparently spotted in the mid-1940s by a friend of young John Bunting: "I remember seeing Aleister Crowley walking in Hampstead in the mid 1940s. He was pointed out to me by another boy called John Bunting. Crowley was staying with Bunting's father the writer and anthologist Daniel George Bunting [1890–1967, reader for Jonathan Cape, who published numerous works under the name Daniel George] in East Heath Road where it meets Whitestone Lane, an area now infested by oligarchs. As I recall he had a beard and was wearing a kilt and possibly carrying a sword stick with an entwined silver snake. I have heard of him wearing a kilt but seldom a beard and he is not known to have associated with Daniel George but I am certain it was him."[18]

Anxious to see Crowley before it was too late, Saturnus sailed to Antwerp on September 26. Three days later Crowley's "secretary" wrote: "Dear Mr. Germer, Mr. Crowley has asked me to let you know that he has been very ill but is now slowly recovering. He is deeply disappointed at the breakdown of your plans to visit him, but thinks it might be even an advantage from the point of view of the Great Work. Sincerely, D. Noalies. Sec."[19]

Roused for a brief period, Crowley wrote to Ted Bryant on October 2. Could he get *Little Essays* and *Heart of the Master* translated into German, and published in Zurich? "Please propose what fees you propose to pay."[20] A.C.'s signature was very shaky. An undated letter to Bryant from the same period asks its recipient to admire the new unicursal hexagram motif at its letterhead: "Dear Edward, how do you like the new paper?" Crowley reckoned Bryant's generation didn't see that stability comes when you "lose yourself dynamically in passionate toil," where all the doubts and hesitation would disappear. "Life is a gyroscope: the faster it spins, the steadier it is." Another point: to feel yourself one of the Chosen Ones, "you must believe in yourself, and in your Holy Guardian Angel; so then you *can't* go wrong. Thus you come to interpret every phenomenon as a particular dealing of God with your soul, and so you bake brioches from shingle [?], and make wine of Iacchus from the sourest grapes." But the only way to begin is to fling yourself into the fray, utterly regardless of the cost, utterly regardless of the goal: "For thou canst create nothing that is not God."[21]

Crowley wrote to Germer on October 14: "I have not been well enough to answer your letter till now. There seems nothing the matter with me but extreme exhaustion lasting over many years and now I've got to pay for my over work." What could Germer do? Crowley didn't think the ninth degree was "any good in such cases but no harm trying." There was "nothing to be done but trust to the Gods." Max Schneider was in trouble; could they raise a fund in the Order to help, mentioning all Max's years of service. Crowley offered ten pounds. Cables about funds transfers were not getting through.[22]

Crowley's last diary entry: "Sent *Olla* to Patrick Dickinson, BBC." Patrick Dickinson hosted a poetry program on the radio.

On November 5 Crowley tried to answer Germer's timely question on how to frame future policy for the O.T.O. Crowley replied that he didn't understand the question: "What you have got to do, I think, is to try to see the whole situation from the point of view of the Gods."[23]

Germer's last word from his friend was sent by cable on November 18, 1947:

PERDURABO BORN 49 YEARS AGO THERION SENDS DEEPEST LOVE HIGHEST BLESSING YOURSELVES AND THELEMITES THE UNIVERSE. ALEISTER[24]

Aleister Crowley died on December 1, 1947. He was seventy-two.

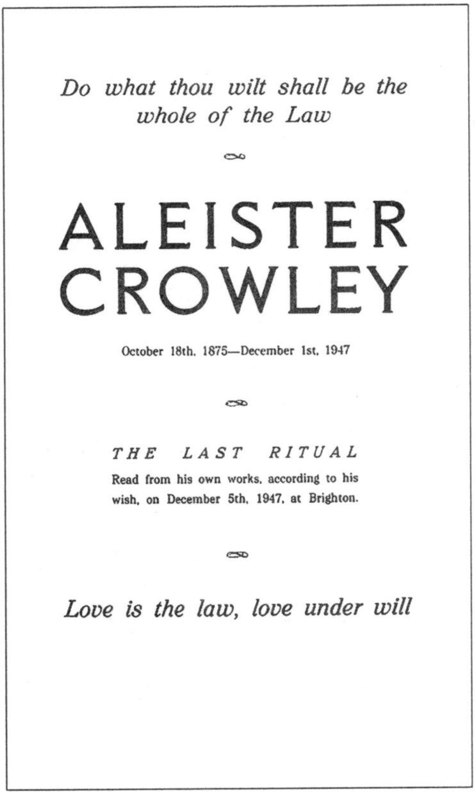

Do what thou wilt shall be the
whole of the Law

∞

# ALEISTER CROWLEY

October 18th, 1875—December 1st, 1947

∞

THE   LAST   RITUAL

Read from his own works, according to his
wish, on December 5th, 1947, at Brighton.

∞

Love is the law, love under will

*Fig. 17.3. "The Last Ritual," service booklet for Crowley's cremation at Brighton crematorium, December 5, 1947. (Courtesy of 100th Monkey Press)*

# Chronology 1875 to 1932

## Crowley's Life before He Returned to England

### 1875

Edward Alexander Crowley was born on October 12 at 30 Clarendon Square, Royal Leamington Spa, Warwickshire. His father, Edward Crowley (1829–1887), of notable Quaker lineage, had embraced the religion of the exclusive Plymouth Brethren, of which he was a leading evangelist. Living comfortably on investments partly derived from the family firm, "Crowley's Ales" of Alton and Croydon, he married Emily Bertha, née Bishop (1848–1917), in 1874. Emily's grandfather was James Cole, inventive genius of clocks, known to Wordsworth and Coleridge as "Conjuror" Cole, of Nether Stowey, Somerset. Cole died in an asylum ca. 1840. Emily's father, dairy farmer John Bishop, married James Cole's daughter Elizabeth. Emily Crowley embraced strict Plymouthism, with its literalist approach to the Bible and disdain for other churches.

*Fig. C.1. Trademark of Crowley's Ales, Alton, Hampshire.*

### 1883 to 1884
Living in Redhill, Surrey, Crowley attended Arthur Habershon's White Rock evangelical boarding school, Hastings St. Leonard's, Sussex.

### 1885 to 1888
A pupil at Ebor preparatory school, Cambridge, run by Plymouth Brethren convert Rev. Henry d'Arcy Champney (1854–1942), Crowley was abused with cruel punishments that damaged an already fragile health. Crowley's uncle, Jonathan Sparrow Crowley (1826–1888), had Champney's school investigated and closed.

### 1887
Edward Crowley died from cancer after Brethren eschewed the royal physician's advice in favor of a novel "electrical" remedy. Edward's widow and her brother—evangelical clerk Tom Bishop—assumed authority over eleven-year-old Crowley.

### 1891
TORQUAY: Crowley saw his freethinking tutor Archibald Charles Douglas dismissed for religious deviance after introducing Crowley to cards, girls, smoking, and thinking for himself. Sent to Malvern College, Crowley joined the Cadet Corps of the First Worcestershire Royal Artillery Volunteers, swearing loyalty to the crown. Unhappy with Malvern's bullying and homosexual subculture, Crowley sought release. His mother removed him to Skye, where sterile medicine pioneer Sir Joseph Lister introduced Crowley to rudimentary mountaineering. As Crowley's poor health—which attracted bullying—improved, he performed dangerous feats to prove to himself he'd overcome cowardice and passivity.

### 1892
TONBRIDGE SCHOOL: After he was strengthened by exercise, Crowley's schoolfellows respected him. He excelled in classics, religious studies, history, and science.

### 1892 to 1895
Lodging at East Dean, Sussex, he joined chemistry classes at Eastbourne College and took up chess. The *Eastbourne Gazette* dismissed Crowley's

remarkable climbs on Beachy Head as "foolish." After a fight with Brethren host Monsieur Lambert, Crowley returned briefly to his mother's house at Streatham. Outstanding mountaineering achievements in the French and Swiss Alps culminated in a solitary ascent of the Eiger in summer 1895.

## 1895

Recommended by Prime Minister Lord Salisbury and Croydon M.P. Charles Thomson Ritchie, Crowley entered Trinity College, Cambridge, to study chemistry and modern literature, intending to join the diplomatic service.

## 1896 to 1897

DECEMBER 31, 1896, STOCKHOLM: Scottish salesman James L. Dickson initiated Crowley into homosexual sex.

SUMMER 1897: After a trip to St. Petersburg to learn Russian, an existential crisis overwhelmed him. Since the inevitability of death nullified any lasting value to be gained from professional success, he sought a spiritual solution to the pain of the world and began to study magic. A £45,000 inheritance removed any need for a career or sitting for degree examinations, and he went his own way. In autumn 1897 he became romantically involved with Decadent entertainer and Cambridge "Footlights" luminary Herbert Charles Pollitt (1871–1942), who seduced Crowley in a Birmingham hotel exactly a year after his Stockholm experience.

## 1898

SUMMER: Having regretfully ended the affair with Pollitt, Crowley published undergraduate verses: *Aceldama, A Place to Bury Strangers In*. When A. E. Waite's *Book of Black Magic and Pacts* was published, Crowley contacted the author for guidance. Waite recommended Karl von Eckartshausen's *Cloud upon the Sanctuary* (1804). Crowley absorbed its message that adept masters secretly governed terrestrial changes, and he sent a "call" to serve them—answered, he believed, in Zermatt, Switzerland, where a meeting with chemist Julian Baker led to an introduction to alchemist-chemist George Cecil Jones, and through these two he entered the Hermetic Order of the Golden Dawn, supposed portal to "the Secret Chiefs."

NOVEMBER 18, 1898: Assuming the motto *Perdurabo,* "I will endure" ("to the end"), Crowley entered the Golden Dawn's Outer Order, soon attracting attention from impecunious Order leader Samuel Liddell "MacGregor" Mathers (1854–1918).

## 1899

PARIS: Mathers plotted "legitimist" risings in Europe and possibly England against "illegitimate" monarchs. Crowley embraced Legitimism, later claiming gun and tactical training for a "Carlist" uprising in Spain.

Crowley befriended Mathers protégé Allan Bennett. Bennett moved into Crowley's Chancery Lane apartment, insisting Crowley rid himself of "goetic" forces.

AUTUMN: Crowley purchased Boleskine, an estate by Loch Ness to practice Mathers's literary discovery, the "Sacred Magic of Abra-Melin the Mage." Through ritual purification and making of talismanic squares, it promised "knowledge and conversation of the Holy Guardian Angel."

## 1900

MARCH 24: Informed of Mathers's plotting, Inner Order members overthrew Mathers. Mathers retaliated, using Crowley. When Mathers revealed the G.D. founding documents were forgeries, the Order exploded.

JULY: Adept on a quest, Crowley sailed to New York, thence to Mexico City as Irishman Isidore Achille O'Rourke (acronym for Gnostic deity IAO), posing as an éminence grise of European politics. Freemason and journalist Don Jesùs de Medina Sidonia raised Crowley to the thirty-third degree of an "irregular" Scottish Rite Masonic order; Crowley's concern with Legitimism ceased.

DECEMBER: Mountaineer Oscar Eckenstein joined Crowley to scale Mexico's high peaks in record time.

## 1901

Crowley visited Allan Bennett in Colombo, Ceylon. In Kandy they practiced raj yoga.

OCTOBER 2: Crowley attained dhyana, obliterating structure of thought and accompanied by vision of a transcendent human form.

Having explored south Indian temples and appeared as a yogi, Crowley sailed to Calcutta to meet tea trader friend Harry Lambe and later, architect Edward Thornton, with whom he explored Burma. Crowley found Bennett—now a Buddhist monk—at Akyab.

## 1902

MARCH: He visited Varanasi, Agra, and Delhi, and worked on numerous poetic works and philosophical studies.

MARCH 23: Crowley joined Eckenstein's expedition to ascend K2 (Karakoram), reaching a record height of about 21,613 feet.

PARIS, NOVEMBER: A Buddhist, Crowley attracted favorable Parisian press attention when visiting Cambridge friend, Gerald Kelly, who was learning to paint in Montparnasse.

## 1903

AUGUST 12: He met Kelly's sister, widowed Rose Skerrett, in Scotland; they fell in love, married, and honeymooned in France and Egypt. Crowley invoked the "sylphs" in the Great Pyramid's King's Chamber.

They explored Ceylon.

## 1904

When they returned to Europe via Cairo as Prince and Princess Chioa ("Beast" in Hebrew) Khan, Rose told Crowley in March that "they" were waiting: it was "all about Osiris" and "the child." Rose pointed to a stele from the old Bulaq Museum collection on the Cairo Museum's top floor, declaring: "There he is!" It was "Stele 666."

APRIL: A tongue lesion contracted in Ceylon was affecting Crowley's sensorium. They rented a ground-floor apartment in the new Standard Life Insurance Building,* southwestern corner of Midan Soliman Pasha.[1]

Rose instructed Crowley to enter the apartment's "temple," for one hour at noon on Friday, April 8; Saturday, April 9; and Sunday, April 10. As though from a corner of the room, while seeming to

---

*The apartment was probably sublet from Col. George Mackworth Bullock, K.C.B. (1851–1926). Appointed Brigadier-General commanding Alexandria District, Bullock left Cairo in 1904.

*Fig. C.2. Standard Life Insurance Building (center),
Soliman Pasha Square, Cairo, seen from the Savoy Hotel, late 1900s.*
The Book of the Law *arrived here, in the ground floor room to
the left of the main entrance on the side street.*

sound in his heart, a voice of "pure" English dictated three chapters of
*The Book of the Law.* Rose named the messenger "Aiwass." Planetary
destiny was unveiled in a most peculiar fashion.

Crowley returned to Europe.

JULY 28: Daughter Lilith was born.

### *1905*

Crowley was convinced a new Order was impossible until he attained
samadhi or "union with God."

MAY: Crowley led an expedition to Kangchenjunga on the Nepal-
Sikkim border. It ended in tragic failure.

The Crowleys headed from Calcutta for southeastern China,
through Burma. Crowley intended to complete the Sacred Magic of
Abra-Melin on the road, imagining an inner temple, invoking by prayer
the "Augoeides" or "dawning light," that the divine beyond his crum-
bling reason might come.

*Fig. C.3. Aleister Crowley, ca. 1905. (Courtesy of Ordo Templi Orientis).*

## 1906

Crowley sailed alone from Hong Kong to Shanghai, then to Vancouver, east across Canada, and down to New York to encourage "Kangchenjunga II."

Invoking Augoeides, he returned to Liverpool, where he heard daughter Lilith had died of infection at Rangoon on May 1.

OCTOBER 9: Crowley experienced samadhi at the Ashdown Park Hotel, Surrey.

George Cecil Jones helped formulate the A∴A∴, *Astrum Argenteum*, or Order of the Silver Star (there are variant interpretations of the acronym).

WINTER: Daughter Lola Zaza was born.

## 1907 to 1908—Years of Fulfilment

January 1907, Bournemouth: Crowley experienced *atmadarshana,* a divine vision of the universe. He becomes a spiritual teacher.

On February 28, 1907, he met Trinity College poet Victor Neuburg (1883–1940). Appearances at Cambridge University's Magpie & Stump debating society roused the University Christian Union's hostility.

AUTUMN: Crowley began to receive the "Holy Books."

## 1909

Crowley published Golden Dawn rituals in his book-length periodical, the *Equinox*.

NOVEMBER: Crowley and Neuburg traversed the Algerian desert, where "Aethyrs" were invoked with "Calls" derived from the late sixteenth-century angelic séances of John Dee and Edward Kelley.

DECEMBER 6: Crowley evoked the "Demon of the Abyss," or essence of Dispersion and ego annihilation, "Choronzon."

An M.P. (probably *John Bull* publisher Horatio Bottomley) contacted Trinity Fellow Rev. Ernest Barnes, accusing Crowley of homosexual acts with students. Bottomley tried to blackmail Crowley. Trinity College Vice-Master, Reginald St John Parry, banned Crowley from Trinity, forbidding his addressing the Freethinking Association. Crowley wrote politely to Parry; Parry withdrew.

## 1910

JANUARY 10: Crowley divorced from Rose. Mathers issued an injunction against Crowley's publishing Golden Dawn rituals; Crowley won. Press coverage stimulated irregular Masonic organizations into awarding him diplomas.

Crowley took Australian violinist Leila Waddell to Venice. He penned the *Rites of Eleusis,* performed from October to November at Caxton Hall, Westminster. Blackmailer De Wend Fenton of the *Looking Glass* magazine published a smutty dismissal of the Rites to secure a payoff. Fenton named G. C. Jones an associate of "villain" Crowley.

## 1911 to 1912

George Cecil Jones sued the *Looking Glass* for libel. Cross-examination suggested Crowley was homosexual—Jones was damned by association.

LATE AUTUMN: Crowley met American Mary d'Este Sturges at London's Savoy Hotel. At Biarritz, Mary received "messages." Crowley and "Soror Virakam" (Mary) wrote the first part of what would become *Magick.*

SPRING 1912: German Freemason Theodor Reuss accused Crowley of revealing Ordo Templi Orientis's supreme secret. Crowley offered to

*Fig. C.4. Portrait of
Crowley by Augustus
John.* The Equinox,
*March 1912.
(Courtesy: Ordo Templi
Orientis)*

transform the O.T.O. into a ten-degree system, with its sexual secret as ninth Degree. Reuss made Crowley head of the British O.T.O. and Grand Inspector General for the O.T.O in America.

DECEMBER 2, 1912: Crowley made his first successful experiment with sex magick, for health.

## 1913

SUMMER: Crowley took the "Ragged Ragtime Girls" to Moscow, where he wrote a "Catholic Gnostic Mass."

## 1914

JANUARY 1914: Crowley practiced homosexual magick with Victor Neuburg in Paris, invoking Hermes and Jupiter.

SUMMER: Crowley climbed alone in the Alps. World War I began; he participated in a pro-Allied money-raising deal in New York.

The deal addled, Crowley contacted pro-Allied corporate lawyer John Quinn, collector and modern art promoter. Crowley was offered contacts and magazine articles.

## 1915

Crowley inveigled himself into Germany's New York *Propaganda Kabinett,* led by Franz von Papen, Captain Boy-Ed, and George Sylvester Viereck. They aimed to stop America from supporting the Allies. Posing as a pro-Irish Republican rebel and poet, Crowley wrote disinformation propaganda, keeping British intelligence officer Everard Feilding informed. As far as we know, Crowley failed to convince other intelligence officers of his usefulness.

LATE SUMMER: He fell in love with journalist, art critic, and poet Jeanne Robert Foster (1879–1970), and traveled west with Jeanne and her elderly husband, Matlack Foster.

## 1916

SUMMER: The Grade of Magus was attained during magical retirement at astrologer Evangeline Adams's cottage at Newfound Lake, New Hampshire. Having ghostwritten a comprehensive treatment on astrology for Adams, he wrote a treatise on Christianity, the *Gospel according to St. Bernard Shaw.*

## 1917

APRIL: Crowley's mother died. Enduring poverty in New Orleans, he wrote the novel *Moonchild.* He lived in sickness and poverty in New York with Dutch painter and fellow adept Leon Engers (1890–1970).

## 1918

Editing Viereck's cultural journal the *International,* he lived—and painted—in "Genius Row," Washington Square, Greenwich Village. Leah Hirsig entered his life. The Justice Department Bureau of Investigation investigated Crowley inconclusively. British military intelligence denied he was their agent. Crowley exhibited paintings at the Liberal Club, Greenwich Village, and promoted Leon Engers's "psychochromes."

## 1919

Followers C. S. Jones and ex-sailor C. F. Russell tried to establish the O.T.O. in Detroit, using Crowley's new "Blue" *Equinox.* Crowley's activities were derided as anti-Christian libertinism.

DECEMBER: Crowley returned to England; he was not arrested.

## 1920

PARIS: He met old friend the Hon. Everard Feilding, while *John Bull* in England called Crowley a "traitor." Leah Hirsig, son Hansi, friend Ninette Fraux, and son Howard arrived. Crowley decided on postwar retirement in Sicily. A rented villa became an "Abbey of Thelema" at Cefalù.

## 1921 to 1922

Crowley's cocaine and heroin intake (heroin was prescribed by the family doctor for bronchitis and asthma) became an addiction nightmare as the abbey attracted visitors: Hollywood actress Jane Wolfe, C. F. Russell, ex-pat Australian Frank Bennett, writer Mary Butts, and her lover, Cecil Maitland. Wolfe and Bennett experienced personal revelations.

In London seeking finance, Crowley proposed a novel about the "drug scare" to Collins editor J. D. Beresford. *The Diary of a Drug Fiend* was published in 1922: "A BOOK FOR BURNING" declared editor James Douglas of London's *Sunday Express*.

## 1923

Model "Betty May" and new husband, Oxford graduate Charles Frederick Loveday, visited Cefalù. Ignoring Crowley's advice to avoid stream water, Loveday died of enteric fever on February 14. Betty gave sensational accounts to English journalists after journalists got her drunk. The *Sunday Express* and *John Bull* pilloried Crowley as Satanist cannibal, traitor, sex pervert: "the wickedest Man in the World."

APRIL 23: Mussolini ordered Crowley's deportation. Persecuted, poor, addicted, Crowley floundered in Tunis.

## 1924

PARIS: He suffered a health breakdown, saying later, "I died." "Reborn," he attracted Dorothy Olsen from Chicago, who replaced Leah as Scarlet Woman. Dorothy paid for a North African trip. Crowley issued a declaration (against Krishnamurti's followers) addressed "TO MAN." The true "World Teacher" was, it declared, the "Master Therion."

## 1925

Leipzig bookseller-Theosophist and German O.T.O. Head Heinrich Tränker arranged a conference at Hohenleuben near Gera,

Germany. Crowley met Tränker's Berlin associates and Theosophists Martha Küntzel and Karl Johannes Germer; Crowley was accepted as O.T.O. Head, but not of Tränker's *Collegium Pansophicum*. When the latter requested German police eject Crowley, Tränker alienated Berliners Albin Grau and Eugen Grosche, who formed the *Fraternitas Saturni* in 1926; Germer and Küntzel became allied to Crowley.

## 1926 to 1928

FRANCE: Crowley tried to raise money and persuade officials to allow Ninette and daughter Lulu out of poverty in Sicily.

LATE 1927: Cambridge history graduate Gerald Yorke, heir to father Vincent Yorke's commercial fortune, flew to Paris as Crowley's student. Yorke organized publication of *Magick in Theory and Practice*, hiring ex-actor and publicist Carl de Vidal Hunt to reboot Crowley's literary career.

## 1929

Crowley exposed de Vidal Hunt's marriage scam involving Spanish royalty. When Yorke curtailed Hunt's "services," Hunt threatened to report Crowley to the Prefecture of Police; Crowley was subjected to a *refus de séjour* due to complaints from Crowley's opponents, including the sister of his new American secretary, Israel Regardie. Ninette Fraux's sister Hélène located Lulu (Ninette and Crowley's daughter) in France, taking her to the United States without his knowledge.

Crowley left Paris in a publicity blaze, with Nicaraguan "High Priestess of Voodoo" Maria Theresa de Miramar.

Yorke arranged a London meeting between Crowley and Lt. Col. John Fillis Carré Carter, head of Britain's Special Branch police interface with MI5. Carter gave Crowley the All-Clear but insisted Crowley marry de Miramar if he wanted her in England.

## 1930

Yorke's publishing syndicate Mandrake Press published much of Crowley's "autohagiography," *The Spirit of Solitude.*

Karl Germer promised £2000 of wife Cora's money for a German publishing program, plugged into Mandrake. Crowley traveled to Berlin.

A newspaper article stimulated modern art promoter Karl Nierendorf to propose a Crowley exhibition.

AUTUMN: Crowley was in love with young artist Hanni Jaeger of Santa Barbara, California, and they met poet Fernando Pessoa in Lisbon. Pessoa assisted a publicity ruse: a suicide note discovered by the Boca do Inferno, near Cascais on the Portuguese coast.

Hanni left Crowley in Lisbon. He rushed back to Germany.

## 1931 to 1932

Crowley made an artist's life in Berlin with Hanni: a frantic lifestyle funded by Germer.

He entertained Aldous Huxley, Christopher Isherwood, and various political figures, sending reports to Col. Carter.

Berlin's only exhibition devoted to an Englishman, held at the Porza Gallery, from October to November 1931, netted possibilities for artist Crowley. A manic Germer, meanwhile, detested Crowley's new Scarlet Woman, Bertha Busch.

MARCH 25, 1932: Carter warned Yorke that Crowley must cease reporting: "If I am not wrong the German Police will be looking at his letters and keeping him under surveillance and if they twig a letter from

*Fig. C.5. Nazi S.A. in Spandau, Berlin.*

me to him that there may be considerable trouble for him and perhaps for all."[2]

MAY 31, 1932: President Hindenburg invited Franz von Papen to form a government.

Crowley informed Yorke that he must hide Crowley's real politics when meeting communist spying-target Gerald Hamilton, or Crowley faced murder.

JUNE 1, 1932: Von Papen assembled a Cabinet against a rising Nazi tide, and Crowley appointed Californian O.T.O. member William Talbot Smith of 1746 Winona Boulevard, Hollywood, O.T.O. Acting Headship, should he die.

JUNE 18, 1932: Making last-minute efforts to raise cash, Crowley packed his bags to leave Berlin. Time had run out, and he with it.

# NOTES

## Endnote Abbreviations

**UNLAC:** Aleister Crowley.

**ACF:** O.T.O. Archive, Folder AC–Frieda Harris.

**BM:** O.T.O. Archive, Folder Bryant–Macky.

**HL:** O.T.O. Archive, Harris Letters, Warburg Institute.

**JWA:** O.T.O. Archive, Folder AC–Jane Wolfe, file A.

**JWB:** O.T.O. Archive, Folder AC–Jane Wolfe, file B.

**JWC:** O.T.O. Archive, Folder AC–Jane Wolfe, file C.

**JWD:** O.T.O. Archive, Folder AC–Jane Wolfe, file D.

**JWE:** O.T.O. Archive, Folder AC–Jane Wolfe, file E.

**NS15CS:** YC NS15, AC–W. T. Smith.

**NS15SC:** YC NS15, W. T. Smith–AC.

**NS115CY:** YC NS115, AC–Gerald Yorke.

**NS117F:** YC NS117, AC–E. N. Fitzgerald.

**NS117S:** YC NS117, AC–Ben Stubbins.

**OTOB1:** O.T.O. Archive, Folder AC–Wilkinson Letters HRC; Section I, copies of letters from AC to Louis Wilkinson.

**OTOB2:** O.T.O. Archive, Folder AC–Wilkinson Letters HRC; Section II, copies of letters from AC to Louis Wilkinson.

**OTOB3:** Section III, copies of letters from AC to Louis Wilkinson 1917–1947.

**OTOG:** O.T.O. Archive, Germer–AC Letters.

**YC:** Yorke Collection, Warburg Institute.

# CHAPTER ONE.
## NEVER DULL WHERE CROWLEY IS

1. OTOG, June 22, 1932, 313.
2. OTOB1, July 13, 1932, Albemarle Court.
3. OTOG, August 25, 1932, 316.
4. Crowley to Schneider, July 31, 1933, WTS Papers, cited in Starr, *The Unknown God,* 197.
5. Starr, *The Unknown God,* 197.
6. Starr, *The Unknown God,* 194.

# CHAPTER TWO.
## POTTED SEX APPEAL

1. OTOG, April 22, 1933, 320.
2. OTOG, May 1, 1933, 321.
3. OTOG, July 2, 1933, 323.
4. OTOG, July 11, 1933, 324.
5. OTOG, July 2, 1933, 323.
6. Kahl to AC, August 13, 1933, WTS Papers, cited in Starr, *The Unknown God,* 195.
7. AC to Smith, August 29, 1933, WTS Papers, cited in Starr, *The Unknown God,* 195.
8. OTOG, September 6, 1933, 325, 161.
9. OTOB1.
10. NS15SC, December 2, 1933, 83.
11. YC NS15, Germer–Smith, December 10, 1933, 84.
12. OTOG, November 2, 1933, 329.

# CHAPTER THREE. JUSTICE SWIFT

1. NS15CS, March 25, 1934, 86.
2. JWB, c/o Dennes [AC's trust lawyer], March 25, 1934.
3. NS117F, Barton Brow, Torquay, March 19, 1941. (Fitzgerald's first letter to Crowley is located at NS117F, 99.)
4. NS15SC, April 1934, 87.
5. YC NS15, Pearl Brooksmith–Smith, August 12, 1934, 88.

6. NS15CS, September 1934, 89.

7. NS15SC, October 21, 1934, 89.

## CHAPTER FOUR.
## UNBELIEVABLE TERROR

1. NS15CS, March 1934, 93.

2. NS15SC, May 6, 1935, 94.

3. NS15CS, Sol in Taurus [May] 1935, 95.

4. NS15SC, May 30, 1935, 96.

5. NS15CS, June 3, 1935, 97.

6. NS15SC, June 3, 1935, 98.

7. NS15SC, June 14, 1935, 100.

8. NS15CS, "3 June" 1935, 101.

9. NS15CS, 30 June 1935, 102.

10. NS15CS, August 15, 1935, 106.

11. NS15CS, August 22, 1935, 108.

12. NS15CS, "10 August" [error; the letter refers to 23rd September autumn equinox] 1935, 112.

13. NS15CS, October 18, 1935, 113.

14. NS15CS, October 30, 1935, 115.

15. O.T.O. Archive, Folder 1935 July–Aug, AC to Lewis, file 1.

16. O.T.O. Archive, Folder 1935-11-06, Lewis to AC, file 2.

17. O.T.O. Archive, Folder 1935-12-02, AC to Lewis, file 3.

18. O.T.O. Archive, Folder 1935-12-02, AC to Lewis, file 3.

19. OTOG, September 16, 1935, 331.

20. OTOG, September 16, 1935, 332.

21. OTOG, September 16, 1935, 333.

22. OTOG, September 16, 1935, 334.

23. OTOG, September 16, 1935, 335.

24. OTOG, September 16, 1935, 337.

25. NS15CS, December 13, 1935, 118.

## CHAPTER FIVE. BAR 666

1. NS15CS, January 3, 1936, 120.

2. Starr, *The Unknown God,* 235.

3. JWA, January 11, 1936.

4. NS15CS, June 9, 1936, 135.

5. YC NS117, AC to C. R. Cammell, 68 Warren Drive, Tolworth Surrey, November 1936, 88.

6. OTOB2, 56 Welbeck Street, September 22, 1936.

7. OTOG, December 22, 1936, 343.

8. OTOG, undated 1936, 345.


# CHAPTER SIX.
## LIVING IN A TURKISH BATH

1. OTOG, January 22, 1937, 346.

2. OTOG, February 26, 1937, 350.

3. OTOB2, March 15, 1937.

4. OTOG, May 13, 1937, 367.

5. OTOG, May 13, 1937, 370.

6. JWB, "date: 1934–1936."

7. NS15CS, September 6, 1937, 157.

8. OTOG, undated, 378.

9. OTOG, undated, 386.

10. OTOG, undated, 381.

11. OTOG, undated, 383.


# CHAPTER SEVEN.
## SERIOUSLY ON THE PATH

1. NS15CS, January 31, 1938, 162.

2. NS15SC, February 14, 1938, 161.

3. NS15CS, January 31, 1938, 162.

4. Cited in Lloyd, *Constant Lambert,* 236.

5. NS15SC, April 21, 1938, 164.

6. JWC, March 25, 1938.

7. OTOG, February 8, 1938, 405.

8. OTOG, February 10, March 13, March 16, 1938, 405–7.

9. O.T.O. Archive, Percy Harris Letters, October 13, 1938.

10. OTOG, 415.

11. OTOG, 417.

12. OTOG, 418.

13. OTOG, 420.

14. OTOG, "Friday," 421.

15. JWC, BCM/ANKH, May 11, 1938.

16. JWC, 24 Chester Terrace, SW1, undated, 1938.

17. HL, May 12, 1938.

18. HL, June 7, 1938.

19. HL, June 7, 1938.

20. HL, June 12, 1938.

21. HL, undated 1938.

22. HL, June 26, 1938.

23. OTOG, June 30, 1938, 437.

24. HL, undated 1938.

25. OTOB2, 6 Hasker Street, July 19, 1938.

26. OTOG, 6 Hasker Street, August 31, 1938, 443.

27. HL, undated 1938.

28. HL, October 14, 1938.

29. OTOG, October 15, 1938, 447.

30. OTOG, October 15, 1938, 451.


## CHAPTER EIGHT.
## KHING KANG KING

1. OTOG, 6 Hasker Street, January 10, 1939, 459.

2. OTOB2, February 21, 1939.

3. HL, undated 1939.

4. NS15SC, March 7, 1939, 173.

5. OTOG, March 16, 1939, 462.

6. Stout, *Universal Majesty, Verity & Love Infinite*.

7. OTOG, May 10, 1939, 465.

8. NS15SC, June 20, 1939, 174.

9. OTOB2, July 24, 1939.

10. OTOB1, August 2, 1939.

11. OTOB3, August 6, 1939.

12. NS15SC, August 18, 1939, 180.

13. OTOG, 57 Petersham Road, September 1, 1939, 471.

## CHAPTER NINE. HAPPY DUST

1. YC E22, Draft letter, 57 Petersham Road, Richmond, September 4, 1939.

2. OTOG, received September 24, 1939, 473.

3. NS15SC, September 1, 1939, 181.

4. YC EE2.

5. NS15SC, September 10, 1939.

6. Spence, *Secret Agent 666,* 248.

7. Spence, *Secret Agent 666,* 248.

8. OTOB2, 57 Petersham Road, September 15, 1939.

9. NS15CS, September 21, 1939, 184.

10. YC EE2, draft, ca. 1939.

11. YC EE2, draft, ca. 1939.

12. HL, October 16, 1939.

13. OTOB2, 57 Petersham Road, October 17, 1939.

14. OTOB2, 57 Petersham Road, October 22, 1939.

15. NS15CS, October 17, 1939, 186.

16. OTOG, November 7, 1939, 478.

17. Whitehouse, "Rolling Stone Orchard."

18. HL, November 7, 1939.

19. OTOG, December 31, 1939.

20. OTOG, December 19, 1939.

21. OTOG, Rolling Stone Orchard, December 22, 1939.

22. OTOG, Rolling Stone Orchard, December 22, 1939.

23. OTOB2, 57 Petersham Road, December 28, 1939.

24. HL, December 29, 1939.

25. ACF, January 5, 1940.

## CHAPTER TEN. WHAT CROWLEY DOES THIS YEAR, ENGLAND DOES NEXT

1. OTOB2, 57 Petersham Road, January 14, 1940.

2. OTOG, 502.

3. OTOG, February 23, 1940.

4. OTOG, February 23, 1940, 507.

5. OTOG, March 8, 1940, 509.

6. OTOG, May 2, 1940, 517.

7. NS15SC, August 29, 1940, 190.

8. Starr, *The Unknown God,* 262–63.

9. YC NS117, AC–Charles Cammell, September 29, 1940, 86.

10. NS15CS, The Gardens, Middle Warberry Rd., Torquay, Devon, October 9, 1940, 192.

11. OTOB1, Middle Warberry Rd., October 22, 1940.

12. OTOB2, Middle Warberry Rd., December 1, 1940.

13. OTOB2, Middle Warberry Rd., December 8, 1940.

14. NS15CS, c/o Dennes, December 16, 1940, 193.

## CHAPTER ELEVEN. ROBED AS A WARRIOR

1. Crowley, *Magick without Tears,* 93.

2. YC D9.

3. YC NS22, Royal Court Diaries, February 14, 1941.

4. YC NS117, Special notes on *V*-sign book by Yorke in black diary.

5. NS117F, August 11, 1941, 103.

6. NS117F, April 27, 1941, 104.

7. NS117F, March 10, 1941, 101.

8. JWC, c/o Dennes & Co., Clifford's Inn, London EC4, February 12, 1941.

9. YC NS117, AC–Charles Cammell, March 1941.

10. OTOB2, Middle Warberry Rd., March 16, 1941.

11. NS15SC, March 21, 1941, 194.

12. Starr, *The Unknown God,* 253.

13. Starr, *The Unknown God,* 257.

14. OTOB2, Barton Brow, Barton Cross, Torquay, April 5, 1941.

15. O.T.O. Archive 1941-04-11, Crowley–Harris, Barton Brow, April 11, 1941.

16. NS15CS, May 6, 1941, 199.

17. YC NS22, Memorandum, Royal Court Diaries, May 9, 1941.

18. Colville, *Footprints in Time,* 112.

19. YC NS117, AC–NID, Barton Brow, May 14, 1941.

20. YC EE2.

21. Quoted by Spence, *Secret Agent 666,* 242; orig: UKNA KV4/186, Liddell Diary, April 10, 1941.

22. NS117, Memorandum, AC to unknown, undated 1941–1942, 64–65.

23. NS117, Memorandum, AC to unknown, undated 1941–1942, 67.

24. NS117F, Batch 2, Barton Brow, May 12, 1941.

25. NS15CS, May 15, 1941, 196.

26. NS15SC, May 19, 1941, 197.

27. Colville, *The Fringes of Power,* 97.

28. OTOB2, 10 Hanover Square, July 17, 1941.

29. YC EE2.

30. OTOB2, 10 Hanover Square, August 4, 1941.

31. NS117F, 10 Hanover Square, August 11, 1941.

32. YC E21.

33. Smith, *The Books of the Beast,* 62.

34. OTOG, May 2, 1940, 237.

35. NS15CS, Sol in O° [September] 1941, 198.

36. NS15SC, September 22, 1941, 201.

37. YC EE2.

38. OTOB1, October 30, 1941.

39. NS117F, 10 Hanover Square, November 9, 1941, 99.

40. NS117F, 10 Hanover Square, November 30, 1941, 99.

41. OTOB1, December 15, 1941.

42. NS15SC, December 20, 1941, 201.

## CHAPTER TWELVE.
## IN THE HOUR OF BATTLE

1. OTOG, January 9, 1942, 562, 247.

2. NS117F, January 8, 1942.

3. OTOB2, 10 Hanover Square, January 8, 1942.

4. YC NS45, Typescript with notes by AC.

5. NS15CS, 10 Hanover Square, January 24, 1942, 202.

6. OTOG, January 24, 1942, 564.

7. OTOG, January 28, 1942, 566.

8. YC NS22, Royal Court Diaries, January 30, 1942.

9. OTOG, February 5, 1942, 565.

10. YC D9, AC–Wilkinson, February 6, 1942.

11. Pile, "Information and Policy 1939–40," in appendix 1 of *Churchill's Secret Enemy.*

12. OTOG, February 14, 1942, 569.

13. YC EE2, AC–NID, 10 Hanover Square, February 17, 1942.

14. NS15SC, 10 Hanover Square, February 27, 1942, 203.

15. NS15CS, 10 Hanover Square, undated, 205.

16. OTOG, March 4, 1942, 570.

17. OTOB2, 10 Hanover Square, March 5, 1942.

18. OTOG, March 9, 1942, 571.

19. Simpson, *In the Highest Degree Odious,* 333–34.

20. Champion, "Spies (Look) Like Us," 552.

21. Griffiths, *What Did You Do During the War?,* 108–9.

22. OTOG, AC–Schneider, March 19, 1942, 572.

23. JWC, 10 Hanover Square, March 20, 1942.

24. JWC, 10 Hanover Square, March 31, 1942.

25. JWC, 10 Hanover Square, April 1, 1942.

26. OTOG, April 4, 1942, 575.

27. NS117S, 10 Hanover Square, April 19, 1942, 91.

28. NS117S, 10 Hanover Square, April 22, 1942, 91; 140 Piccadilly, June 1942.

29. OTOG, May 1942, 581.

30. Lamburn, Wilkinson, and DeBruin, "Letters to Alyse Gregory 1941–43."

31. Lownie, *Stalin's Englishman,* chap. 18, n25.

32. JWC, 140 Piccadilly, June 8, 1942.

33. NS15CS, 140 Piccadilly, June 8, 1942.

34. Starr, *The Unknown God,* 271–73.

35. JWC, 140 Piccadilly, June 16, 1942.

36. NS117S, 140 Piccadilly, June 1942.

37. Lownie, *Stalin's Englishman.*

38. NS117S, 140 Piccadilly, August 6, 1942.

39. NS15SC, 1003 Orange Grove Ave., Pasadena, Calif., 210.

40. OTOG, August 1942, 593.

41. OTOB1, 140 Piccadilly, September 2, 1942.

42. YC E21.

43. OTOB1, 140 Piccadilly, October 2, 1942.

44. OTOG, October 5, 1942, 597.

45. NS15CS, 140 Piccadilly, October 4, 1942, 211.

46. OTOB1, 140 Piccadilly, October 7, 1942; October 13, 1942.

47. OTOB1, 140 Piccadilly, October 21, 1942.

48. OTOB1, 140 Piccadilly, October 26, 1942.

49. OTOG, October 28, 1942, 604.

50. JWC, October 1942.

51. OTOB2, November 6, 1942.

52. OTOG, December 10, 1942, 613.

53. NS117S, 93 Jermyn Street, December 16, 1942, 96.


## CHAPTER THIRTEEN. I DREAMED TIME

1. YC NS15, J. W.–Smith, January 1943, 212.

2. YC NS15, J. W.–Smith, January 15, 1943, 213.

3. OTOG, J. W.–AC, January 1943, 619.

4. OTOG, January 1943, 620.

5. JWC, Western Union Telegram to 1003 S. Orange Grove, Pasadena, Calif., AC–J. W., January 23, 1943.

6. OTOG, Cable, January 26, 1943, 619.

7. OTOG, Cable, January 27, 1943, Jack and Helen Parsons–AC, 619.

8. Starr, *The Unknown God,* 284–85.

9. NS15SC, February 3, 1943, 217.

10. JWD, 93 Jermyn Street, February 16, 1943.

11. JWD, AC–Regina Kahl, 93 Jermyn Street, February 17, 1943.

12. OTOG, AC–McMurtry, February 1943, 622.

13. JWD, 93 Jermyn Street, March 3, 1943.

14. O'Brien, "Anne Macky," 71–82.

15. BM, 93 Jermyn Street, undated, 1943.

16. NS15CS, 93 Jermyn Street, April 1, 1943, 219.

17. OTOG, April 24, 1943, 631.

18. JWE, 93 Jermyn Street, May 4, 1943.

19. NS15SC, Rainbow Valley, California, May 9, 1943, 220.

20. JWE, 93 Jermyn Street, May 9, 1943.

21. JWE, 93 Jermyn Street, May 13, 1943.

22. OTOG, May 17, 1943, 637.

23. OTOG, May 31, 1943, 641.

24. NS15CS, 93 Jermyn Street, May 18, 1943, 221.

25. NS15CS, 93 Jermyn Street, May 28, 1943, 222.

26. NS15SC, 93 Jermyn Street, June 22, 1943, 224.

27. NS15SC, "Cullings Hermitage," August 10, 1943, 225.

28. NS15SC, 1003 S. Orange Grove, September 14, 1943, 226.

29. BM, 93 Jermyn Street, September 19, 1943.

30. JWD, 93 Jermyn Street, October 19, 1943.

31. JWE, 93 Jermyn Street, November 8, 1943.

32. BM, 93 Jermyn Street, November 19, 1943.

33. BM, 93 Jermyn Street, December 25, 1943.

34. JWE, 93 Jermyn Street, December 29, 1943.

35. BM, 93 Jermyn Street, December 30, 1943.

## CHAPTER FOURTEEN. MONSTROUS WORLDS

1. BM, 93 Jermyn Street, January 4, 1944.

2. YC D9, AC–L. U. Wilkinson, January 17, 1944.

3. OTOB2, 93 Jermyn Street, March 7, 1944.

4. OTOG, March 19, 1944, 664.

5. OTOG, March 19, 1944, 664.

6. NS117F, March 28, 1944.

7. OTOB2, Bell Inn, April 23, 1944.

8. OTOB2, The Bell, May 1, 1944.

9. OTOG, May 8, 1944, 666.

10. NS115CY, Bell Inn, June 6, 1944.

11. OTOG, June 26, 1944, 669.

12. OTOG, June 27, 1944.

13. NS117F, Bell Inn, July 12, 1944, 113.

14. OTOB2, The Bell, July 10, 1944.

15. NS115CY, Bell Inn, July 10, 1944.

16. NS115CY, Bell Inn, July 10, 1944.

17. NS115CY, Bell Inn, July 11, 1944.

18. OTOG, June 27, 1944, 672.

19. YC NS117, seven letters from AC to Nancy Cunard, June–August 1944, 117.

20. YC EE2, AC–Cunard, Bell Inn, July 22, 1944.

21. YC NS117, seven letters from AC to Nancy Cunard, June–August 1944, 117.

22. YC NS117, seven letters from AC to Nancy Cunard, June–August 1944, 117.

23. YC EE2, AC–Cunard, Bell Inn, August 1944.

24. Cunard, *Grand Man,* 90–91, 197–200.

25. YC NS117, Letters from N.C. to G.J.Y., Lamothe Fénelon, Lot, France, October 24, 1954.

26. YC EE2, AC–Cunard, Bell Inn, August 18, 1944.

27. YC EE2, Cunard–AC, August 23, 1944.

28. YC E21, Norman Douglas–AC, August 22, 1944.

29. Cunard, *Grand Man,* 90–91, 197–200.

30. YC NS117, Letters from N.C. to G.J.Y., Lamothe Fénelon, Lot, France, October 24, 1954.

31. YC E21, Norman Douglas–Nancy Cunard, August 28, 1944.

32. Cunard, *Grand Man,* 90–91, 197–200.

33. OTOG, August 23, 1944, 676.

34. OTOG, August 24, 1944, 673.

35. JWE, Bell Inn, August 31, 1944.

36. OTOB1, September 2, 1944.

37. NS115CY, The Bell, September 1944.

38. OTOB1, September 18, 1944.

39. OTOG, September 18, 1944, 675.

40. Diary, October 9, 1946.

41. OTOB1, September 27, 1944.

42. BM, October 5, 1944.

43. NS117F, The Bell, November 2, 1944.

44. NS115CY, November 2, 1944.

45. O.T.O. Archive, AC–W. B. Crow, November 11, 1944.

46. OTOB2, Bell, November 19, 1944.

47. OTOG, November 29, 1944, 681.

48. OTOB1, December 30, 1944.

## CHAPTER FIFTEEN. DEATH IS KING

1. OTOG, January 18, 1945, 683.

2. OTOB1, January 20, 1945.

3. OTOB1, January 22, 1945.

4. OTOB1, January 27, 1945.

5. OTOB1, Netherwood, February 19, 1945.

6. OTOG, March 8, 1945, 687.

7. OTOG, AC–Helen Parsons, March 9, 1945, 688.

8. OTOG, AC–W. T. Smith, March 9, 1945, 688.

9. OTOG, March 1945, 669.

10. OTOG, Telegram, J. Parsons–AC, March 16, 1945, 670.

11. OTOB2, Netherwood, March 22, 1945.

12. JWE, Netherwood, March 23, 1945.

13. OTOB1, April 17, 1944.

14. OTOG, April 25, 1945, 673.

15. OTOG, May 6, 1945, 682.

16. JWE, May 10, 1945.

17. OTOG, May 10, 1945, 674.

18. OTOG, May 16, 1945, 676.

19. OTOG, June 7, 1945, 678.

20. OTOG, July 9, 1945.

21. OTOB2, August 7, 1945.

22. OTOB2, August 21, 1945.

23. OTOB2, September 24, 1945.

24. OTOG, September 25, 1945, 689.

25. OTOB2, November 4, 1945.

26. OTOB2, November 10, 1945.

27. OTOG, November 21, 1945, 690.

28. Koo, *No Feast Lasts Forever,* 254.

29. OTOG, November 21, 1945, 690.

30. JWD, November 22, 1945.

31. OTOB1, November 23, 1945.

32. OTOB3, December 4, 1945.

33. OTOB2, December 6, 1945.

34. OTOB1, November 30, 1945.

## CHAPTER SIXTEEN. EDDIES OF OBSIDIAN

1. Clayton, *Netherwood,* 133.

2. Butler, *The Myth of the Magus,* 266.

3. OTOG, January 4, 1946, 692.

4. JWD, January 29, 1946.

5. OTOB2, February 4, 1946.

6. OTOG, February 27, 1946, 695.

7. OTOB1, March 6, 1946.

8. OTOB1, March 21, 1946.

9. OTOB2, March 15, 1946.

10. OTOB2, March 27, 1946.

11. JWD, April 3, 1946.

12. OTOB1, April 10, 1946.

13. OTOB3, April 17, 1946.

14. OTOG, April 17, 1946.

15. Davis, "Babalon Rising," based on a 2015 talk at PantheaCon.

16. Davis, "Babalon Rising," 177.

17. OTOB1, April 24, 1946.

18. OTOB3, May 7, 1946.

19. OTOB3, May 7, 1946.

20. OTOG, May 14, 1946.

21. OTOG, received May 22, 1946, 702.

22. OTOG, May 31, 1946, 703.

23. OTOB1, June 6, 1946.

24. OTOB2, June 13, 1946.

25. YC NS117, AC–W. B. Crow, June 18, 1946.

26. OTOG, June 18, 1946, 747.

27. YC NS117, AC–J. Symonds, June 25, 1946.

28. YC NS117, AC–J. Symonds, 136.

29. OTOB1, June 29, 1946.

30. OTOB1, July 27, 1946.

31. OTOB1, September 3, 1946.

32. OTOG, September 9, 1946, 706.

33. JWD, October 10, 1946.

34. OTOB2, November 11, November 18, 1946.


## CHAPTER SEVENTEEN. THE UNIVERSE

1. OTOG, January 14, 1947, 717.

2. OTOG, February 14, 1947, 718.

3. OTOB2, March 5, 1947.

4. OTOG, March 5, 1947, 719.

5. OTOG, April 10, 1947, 722.

6. Clayton, *Netherwood,* 168–74.

7. OTOB2, March 28, 1947.

8. O.T.O. Archive, AC to Dr. Charnock-Smith, Netherwood, The Ridge, March 29, 1947.

9. OTOB2, April 19, 1947.

10. NS117F, April 25, 1947.

11. OTOG, April 25, 1947, 725.

12. OTOG, May 2, 1947, 727–28.

13. NS117F, May 13, 1947.

14. OTOG, May 23, 1947, 729.

15. NS117, AC–John Symonds, June 10, 1947.

16. OTOG, June 15, 1947, 731.

17. OTOG, June 30, 1947, 734.

18. "A Sighting of Aleister Crowley," attributed to a Jot associate, "now in his 80s. This entry was posted in Uncategorized on March 17, 2013." Jot101 (website).

19. OTOG, September 29, 1947, 733.

20. BM, October 2, 1947.

21. BM, undated 1947.

22. OTOG, October 14, 1947, 735.

23. OTOG, November 5, 1947, 738.

24. OTOG, November 18, 1947, 739.

## CHRONOLOGY 1875 TO 1932

1. www.forthethelemites.website. *A Study of the Cairo Working* by "Perdurabo ST." (Sigurd Bune).

2. Churton, *Aleister Crowley: The Biography,* 354.

# Bibliography

Anand, Mulk Raj. *The Hindu View of a Persian Painting*. London: Faber & Faber, 1930.

Butler, E. M. *The Myth of the Magus*. Cambridge: Cambridge University Press, 1948.

Champion, Brian. "Spies (Look) Like Us: The Early Use of Business and Civilian Covers in Covert Operations." *International Journal of Intelligence and CounterIntelligence* 21, no. 8 (May 19, 2008): 533–64.

Churton, Tobias. *Aleister Crowley in America: Art, Espionage, and Sex Magick in the New World*. Rochester, Vt.: Inner Traditions, 2017.

———. *Aleister Crowley in India: The Secret Influence of Eastern Mysticism on Magic and the Occult*. Rochester, Vt.: Inner Traditions, 2019.

———. *Aleister Crowley: The Beast in Berlin: Art, Sex, and Magick in the Weimar Republic*. Rochester, Vt.: Inner Traditions, 2014.

———. *Aleister Crowley: The Biography*. London: Watkins Publishing, 2011.

———. *Gnostic Mysteries of Sex: Sophia the Wild One and Erotic Christianity*. Rochester, Vt.: Inner Traditions, 2015.

———. *Occult Paris: The Lost Magic of the Belle Époque*. Rochester, Vt.: Inner Traditions, 2016.

Clayton, Antony. *Netherwood: Last Resort of Aleister Crowley*. London: Accumulator Press, 2012.

Colville, John. *Footprints in Time*. London: Collins, 1976.

———. *The Fringes of Power: Downing Street Diaries, 1939–1955*. London: Hodder & Stoughton, 1985.

Crowley, Aleister. *The Book of the Law*. Newburyport, Mass.: Weiser Books, 1987.

———. *The Diary of a Drug Fiend.* Eastford, Conn.: Martino Fine Books, 2013.

———. *The Equinox of the Gods.* Phoenix, Ariz.: Falcon Press, 1981.

———. *Magick without Tears.* Phoenix, Ariz.: Falcon Press, 1983.

———. *Moonchild.* London: Mandrake Press, 1929.

———. *White Stains.* N.p.: CreateSpace Independent Publishing Platform, 2015.

Cunard, Nancy. *Grand Man: Memories of Norman Douglas.* London: Secker & Warburg, 1954.

Davis, Erik. "Babalon Rising: Jack Parsons' Witchcraft Prophecy." In *A Rose Veiled in Black: Arcana and Art of Our Lady Babalon,* edited by Robert Fitzgerald and Daniel A. Schulke. Richmond Vista, Calif.: Three Hands Press, 2017.

Griffiths, Richard. *What Did You Do During the War? The Last Throes of the British Pro-Nazi Right, 1940–45.* New York: Routledge, 2016.

Hamilton, James Douglas. *The Truth about Rudolf Hess.* Edinburgh: Mainstream Publishing, 1993.

Hamnett, Nina. *Laughing Torso.* London: Constable & Co., 1932.

Huxley, Aldous. *After Many a Summer Dies the Swan.* London: Chatto & Windus, 1939.

Koo, Hui-Lan. *No Feast Lasts Forever.* With Isabella Taves. New York: Quadrangle/New York Times, 1975.

Lamburn, Joan, Chris Wilkinson, and Louise DeBruin. "Letters to Alyse Gregory 1941–1943." *Powys Journal* 26 (2016): 139–74.

Lévi, Eliphas. *Key of the Mysteries.* Translated by Aleister Crowley. London: Rider, 1977.

Lloyd, Stephen. *Constant Lambert: Beyond the Rio Grande.* Woodbridge, UK: Boydell & Brewer, 2014.

Lownie, Andrew. *Stalin's Englishman: The Lives of Guy Burgess.* London: Hodder & Stoughton, 2015.

Masters, Anthony. *The Man Who Was M.* Oxford: Blackwell Publishers, 1985.

McGinty, Stephen. *Churchill's Cigar: A Lifelong Love Affair through War and Peace.* New York: Pan Macmillan, 2010.

O'Brien, Betty. "Anne Macky: A Radical in her Time." *Context: Journal of Music Research,* no. 27/28 (January 2004): 71–82.

Osley, Anthony. *Persuading the People: Government Publicity in the Second World War.* London: Stationery Office Books, 1995.

Pile, Jonathan. *Churchill's Secret Enemy*. N.p.: Create Space Independent Publishing Platform, 2012.

Regardie, Israel. *The Eye in the Triangle*. Phoenix, Ariz.: Falcon Press, 1970.

Simpson, A. W. B. *In the Highest Degree Odious: Detention without Trial in Wartime Britain*. Oxford: Oxford University Press, 1992.

Smith, Timothy d'Arch. *The Books of the Beast*. London: Mandrake, 1991.

Spence, Richard. *Secret Agent 666*. Port Townsend, Wash.: Feral House, 2008.

Starr, Martin. *The Unknown God*. Bolingbrook, Ill.: Teitan Press, 2003.

Stephensen, P. R. *The Legend of Aleister Crowley*. London: Mandrake, 1930.

Stout, Adam. *Universal Majesty, Verity & Love Infinite, A Life of George Watson Macgregor Reid*. The Order of Bards, Ovates & Druids Mount Haemus Lecture for the Year, 2005.

Symonds, John. *The Confessions of Aleister Crowley*. Edited by Kenneth Grant. London: Penguin Books, 1989.

Whitehouse, Deja. "Rolling Stone Orchard—the Artist's Wartime Retreat." *Signpost, The Journal of Chipping Campden History Society* 7 (1937): 7–10.

# Index